Food Sovereignty the Navajo Way

FOOD SOVEREIGNTY THE NAVAJO WAY

COOKING WITH TALL WOMAN

Charlotte J. Frisbie

WITH RECIPES BY Tall Woman AND
ASSISTANCE FROM Augusta Sandoval

University of New Mexico Press | Albuquerque

Library of Congress Cataloging-in-Publication Data
Names: Frisbie, Charlotte Johnson, author. | Mitchell, Rose, approximately 1874–1977. |
    Sandoval, Augusta.
Title: Food Sovereignty the Navajo Way: Cooking with Tall Woman / Charlotte J. Frisbie;
    with recipes by Tall Woman and assistance from Augusta Sandoval.
Description: Albuquerque: University of New Mexico Press, 2018. |
    Includes bibliographical references and index. |
Identifiers: LCCN 2017003583 (print) | LCCN 2017025034 (e-book) |
    ISBN 9780826358882 (e-book) | ISBN 9780826358875 (pbk. : alk. paper)
Subjects: LCSH: Navajo Indians—Food. | Navajo Indians—Nutrition. | Navajo cooking.
Classification: LCC E99.N3 (e-book) | LCC E99.N3 F83 2017 (print) |
    DDC 641.59/29726—dc23
LC record available at https://lccn.loc.gov/2017003583

Cover photograph courtesy of the author
Cover designed by Lila Sanchez, interior designed by Felicia Cedillos
Composed in Minion 10.25/14.25

To Navajo people everywhere

In the hope that this work will contribute to the rebirth of interest in earlier ways of healthy living, the revival of earlier food knowledge and practices, and the establishment of food sovereignty

CONTENTS

ILLUSTRATIONS

ACKNOWLEDGMENTS

This project has been in the works since my days of working with Tall Woman, 1963–1977, so there is an unending list of people to be thanked for helping with various parts along the way. Given this reality, I fear I will fail to mention someone; if I do, please understand that it is totally unintentional. So many people provided consistent and continuing interest, numerous kinds of assistance, and regular encouragement that I know that this work could not have been completed without them. Occasionally the endnotes will demonstrate how specific individuals' help was crucial in accessing and then understanding data in different sections of the work.

Of course, the major thanks go to Tall Woman herself for her willingness to share her knowledge of foods with me and for patiently answering my unending questions. And since it was impossible to finish this work during her lifetime, I am also greatly indebted to her daughter, Augusta Sandoval, as well as other family members—Isabelle Deschine, the late Evonne Shirley, Lena Shirley, Cecilia Sandoval, Cynthia Sandoval, Regina Sandoval, and Tall Woman's now-deceased daughters, Mary Davis, Ruth Shirley Yazzie, and Agnes Sanchez—for help while finalizing the recipes. Without their assistance and support, living up to my promise to their mother and grandmother about getting her recipes published would have been impossible.

In addition, others deserve a public expression of gratitude for specific kinds of assistance.

For help with language issues: Timothy Begay, Richard Begay, Steven

Begay, Klara Kelley, Harris Francis, Tony Webster, Martha Austin-Garrison, Allen Manning, Ossy Werner, and Kathleen Manolescu.

For help with photographs: Dan Woodward, Ted Frisbie, Klara Kelley, Augusta Sandoval, the late Evonne Shirley, Isabelle Deschine, Oliver W. Johnson, Martha Blue, Steven Begay, Cecilia Sandoval, Ailema Benally, Nichole McCabe, John Byram, Jennifer Frisbie, Dan Goran, and Lindsay Highlander.

For help with government records: Melissa Conner and Suzanne Callor of the Summer Food Service Program; Victor Oliveira, Alex Majchrowicz, and Nancy Theodore of the Food Distribution Program, US Department of Agriculture; Mallory Black, a freelance reporter for and founding journalist of *Native Health News Alliance*; Jon Colvin; the late David Brugge; the late Bill Beaver; Sister Adelaide Link; Aline Davis; Irving Nelson; and Clarenda Begay.

For help with Navajo Nation Council policies: Amber Kanazbah Crotty, Sharon Sandman, Gloria Begay, and Klara Kelley.

For help with other references: Klara Kelley, Joanne McCloskey, Stephen Kunitz, Deidre Johnson, Dave Snow, Lyn Johnson, Jon Colvin, Sam Pearson, Augusta Sandoval, and Clarenda Begay.

For help with Chinle community history: Father Blane Grein, Jon Colvin, Augusta Sandoval, Klara Kelley, Sister Christa McGill, Sister Adelaide Link, Glenn Stoner, Shirley Stoner, Harris Francis, Arthur Newman Jr., Linda Kee-Rockbridge, the late Sybil Baldwin, the late Margaret Garcia Delaney, Mary Jones, Jasper Tso, Cindy Yurth, and Fleming Begaye Sr.

For help with plants: Wendy Wolfe, Klara Kelley, Barbara Lacy, Frank Morgan, and Steven Begay.

For discussions about history in general: the late Dave Brugge, Dave Snow, Jim Faris, Frank Morgan, Paul Zolbrod, Joanne McCloskey, Kathy M'Closkey, Ron Maldonado, Klara Kelley, Harris Francis, Miranda Haskie, Ossy and the late June Werner, Ted Frisbie, Wendy Wolfe, Stephen Jett, Kathleen Manolescu, Martha Blue, Jon Colvin, Father Blane Grein, Barbara Lacy, Bob McPherson, Jennifer Denetdale, Steven Begay, Zonnie Gorman, Scott Russell, Stephen Kunitz, Dana Eldridge, Timothy C. Begay, Tamara Billie, the late Bill Beaver, and Sister Adelaide Link.

For reading drafts of various sections over the years: the late Dave Brugge,

Klara Kelley, Steven Begay, Ted Frisbie, Kathleen Manolescu, Harris Francis, Augusta Sandoval, Jon Colvin, Father Blane Grein, Joanne McCloskey, Wendy Wolf, and Jasper Tso.

For discussions about the current publishing world: Elizabeth Hadas, Tony Webster, Kathy M'Closkey, Martha Blue, Jonathan Batkin, and John Byram.

For critical reading and evaluating the final manuscript: Steven Begay, Miranda Haskie, Joanne McCloskey, and Frank Morgan.

For helping to choose both the working title and the final title: Clarenda Begay, Steven Begay, Klara Kelley, John Byram, Elizabeth Hadas, Miranda Haskie, Lyn Johnson, Stephen Kunitz, and Joanne McCloskey.

For invaluable assistance with computer problems: Mary June-el Piper, Helena Frisbie-Firsching, Dan Goran, Ellen Koskoff, Elizabeth Frisbie, Sam Pearson, and John Byram.

For editorial guidance and expertise: John Byram, James Ayers, Marie Landau, and Judith Antonelli.

For artistic design: Felicia Cedillos.

For help with proofreading: Sara Albers, Helena Frisbie-Firsching, and Gwynn Frisbie-Firsching.

Finally, for daily everything: Ted, my husband of more than fifty years; our daughters, Elizabeth and Jennifer; and Elizabeth's two daughters, Helena and Gwynn. Also, though not local and thus not daily: my brother, Charles, and my sister, Ann. In various ways, all had to endure my single-minded focus on this project, especially while I was preparing different versions of the manuscript for submission. For daily matters, it meant patiently putting up with my ignoring of family issues that needed attention, of regular home maintenance, and of farmwork while I was totally immersed in finishing the manuscript before April 1, 2016, for the initial submission and then again during September 2016, when I was focused on completing all revisions by October 1. My family's consistent support, professional interest, assistance, and love have been paramount in my ability to bring this project to completion, and I remain forever grateful for all of it.

Any errors that have crept in along the way, despite all the help, certainly belong to me; I can only hope that they are minimal and that the result is pleasing to Tall Woman's family and others involved with this project.

Introduction

THIS BOOK WAS originally entitled *Defeating Hunger, Making Something from the Earth: Traditional Navajo Food, Cooking, and Food Sovereignty.* "Hunger" here refers to the Navajo Origin account of the Twins, the two sons of the deity Changing Woman who traveled the world, killing the monsters that were destroying it and making it uninhabitable. Although most of the monsters were eradicated, a few were spared so that humans would remain diligent about and actively involved in their own health and well-being. One of the monsters allowed to live on the Earth's Surface by Monster Slayer (one of the Twins) was Hunger. Thus, Hunger—like Poverty, Old Age, and some other monsters—is alive and real, and exists to remind Earth Surface People to work the land and know how to survive without any waste.

That original working title and the final one, *Food Sovereignty the Navajo Way: Cooking with Tall Woman* (decided on during multiple conversations with colleagues and the publisher) frame the many changes in Navajo food-ways that 'Asdzáán Nééz, or Tall Woman (a.k.a. Rose Mitchell), experienced during her long life (1874–1977). In her younger days, hunger (*dichin*) was essentially a lack of calories, always living close to starvation; this state was combatted by utilizing everything that Mother Earth, or nature, provided. By the time Tall Woman's life was over, and even continuing to today, almost forty years later, hunger had become a manufactured, engineered craving for junk food, full of calories but without nutritional value. Indigenous peoples the world over share this problem, and through the ever expanding food sovereignty movement they are finding ways to return to their traditional foods, fight big chemical and agribusiness corporations and the use of genetically modified organisms (GMOs), and defeat this new type of hunger.

Although years ago this work was envisioned as a collection of Tall Woman's recipes for traditional Navajo foods, once I started working on what she had told me, I realized a number of things. A major one, of course, was that her ways of feeding her family were perfect examples of food sovereignty, before there was a movement with this name. Another was that background information was needed for readers not familiar with either the US Southwest or the Navajos. Since the literature on that is plentiful and I intend to retain a focus on foods, I will address only a few contextual issues. But first let me summarize some of the details of my experiences.[1] Full explanations of fieldwork methodologies, procedures, negotiations, and decision making during the preparation of the resulting text are provided in the introduction to Tall Woman's life story (Mitchell 2001, xxii–xl). As noted there, her (maternal) clan was Kiyaa'áanii (Towering House People) and she was born for (i.e., her father's clan was) Tó dích'íi'nii (Bitter Water People).

I had the privilege of living with Tall Woman and her family in Chinle, Arizona, on and off during graduate school and other responsibilities, from June 1963 until her death in 1977. At the time I was focused on learning about hózhǫ́ (harmony, peace, balance, happiness, good health, and good fortune), a core value in Navajo philosophy that ideally guides your life. Traditionally, your thoughts, words, and actions should demonstrate that you have achieved an in-depth understanding of this philosophy and have learned to live according to it. If you have attained a real understanding of hózhǫ́, then your life and the lives of your family, your farm animals, and everything else associated with you will exemplify this ideal. My initial anthropological work was on the Kinaaldá (Girls' Puberty Ceremony) and some related ethnomusicological work on the Corn Grinding Songs and ceremonial music, especially from the Hózhǫ́ǫ́jí (Blessingway) (Frisbie [1967] 1993).[2] Tall Woman was still enjoying good health when I first met her and was actively involved in herding sheep, weaving, milking goats, cooking, growing crops, roofing the cook shack, helping with ceremonies, raising grandchildren, and more.

Until Tall Woman became bedridden, she was in charge of the ch'iyą (food) for the family, preparing meals during the day and frequently doing tasks associated with such preparations. Meals most often included mutton in a stew or some other form, occasionally other meat (such as beef, goat, or pork), one of many kinds of bread, and coffee. I quickly realized that some of the items she prepared had come from the trading posts we went to when necessary (Kelley and Francis 2006–2015, forthcoming; Russell 1991).[3] Tall Woman used powdered milk, flour, cornmeal, sugar, lard, and dried beans (especially pintos), and she loved certain canned fruits and vegetables such as tomatoes, apricots, peaches, peas, and applesauce. Some supplies came from the Commodity Food Program (see appendix A), including rice, peanut butter, various kinds of noodles, cereal, lard, and canned milk. Like many people, the members of her family readily shared their commodities with others, including some who were not eligible for the foods because of temporary employment or other assets.

Living with Tall Woman made it clear to me that it would be almost impossible to determine just how commodity foods affected meals in a Navajo household, because many factors had to be considered. Among these were who was cooking for whom, when these people would be eating, what time of day it was, what season it was, and who else might come by. Individuals also developed preferences for certain items and, both within and between households, sometimes traded foods after picking up their commodities. The food that nobody liked might be fed to hungry puppies or even given away to a food bank. Just as the Food Stamp Program cannot always control how the stamps are used, the Commodity Food Program could not ensure that all people ate the foods they received through the program.

While I was recording her life story, Tall Woman, who was well-known for her knowledge of the environment and the food and medicinal resources it contained, made many comments about how to treat various illnesses; she also frequently talked about foods she liked and how she fixed them for her family. At first these comments were not separate, focused discussions in response to specific questions from me; instead they were included as part of her life, her knowledge, and the things she was most interested in. She wanted her children, her grandchildren, her great-grandchildren, and others, both Navajos and not, to know about them in the future.

However, despite her wishes, two entities changed the plan. The Cultural Resources Compliance Section of the Navajo Nation Historic Preservation Department (NNHPD) felt strongly that all information about 'azee' (medicine), especially the medicinal uses of plants, should not be part of her published story because it was intellectual property, traditional cultural knowledge in need of protection and restriction. Although her children objected strongly, I understood the NNHPD's concerns and concurred. Then, after the NNHPD review of the manuscript, the publisher decided that given the length of her narrative, the recipes would have to be removed and saved for a later, separate publication. Given the realities of publishing costs, once again it was necessary for me to agree.

Since too many years had passed between Tall Woman's death in 1977 and the publication of her story in 2001, and my own availability to revisit our conversations about foods and recipes had been delayed, I asked for help from her daughters when I had questions. All of them were still alive when I was finalizing Tall Woman's story, but alas, between 2001 and 2014, six of her children passed away: four daughters (Mary Davis, Ruth Yazzie, Agnes Sanchez, and Garnett Bernally) and two sons (Seya Mitchell and Howard Mitchell). Thus, it fell to the two remaining children, Augusta Sandoval and Isabelle Deschine, to assist with the work involved in bringing her recipes and cooking knowledge into print, which they graciously did.[4]

Although a brief look at the pages that follow will make it clear that this is not the usual Anglo cookbook, with sections for appetizers, snacks, salads, meat, fish, dairy dishes, eggs, casseroles, pastries, and desserts, Tall Woman's recipes have been organized in a way that makes sense to many Navajos familiar with preparing traditional foods.[5] Before we turn to the recipes, however, some background information is necessary. This is particularly important now, given the international food sovereignty movement in which indigenous peoples around the globe are returning to earlier methods of subsistence and their own traditional foods, to combat contemporary diseases such as diabetes and obesity and to reestablish healthy lifestyles and control over their own food systems.

Historical Background with a Dietary Focus

To put Tall Woman's recipes in context, it is first necessary to provide an overview, albeit condensed, of Navajo history and food resources as they have been known. Tall Woman was born six years after many Navajos returned from incarceration at Fort Sumner in New Mexico, and her life included government ration programs; mandated education; the arrival of the railroad, trading posts, missionaries, boarding schools, and the automobile; a shift from a subsistence economy to a wage-labor economy; World Wars I and II; stock reduction; the Commodity Food Program; and so much more.

I have chosen to organize the overview that follows historically, moving by decades or groups. Chapter 1 provides a historical overview of the Navajo diet and Navajo dietary research in conjunction with what was known about this diet at different points in time. The researchers, mainly outsiders, responsible for recording this information are identified, and the results of their studies are documented. Chapter 2 provides an overview of subsistence practices—gathering, hunting, herding, and farming (or, in anthropological terms, foraging, pastoralism, and horticulture)—with all of the related equipment, techniques, and work involved at different times of year. This recaps some of the information available in Tall Woman's own story (Mitchell 2001), but in a way that focuses on food and diet. Tall Woman's recipes follow in chapter 3, organized into seven sections defined by her daughters. Finally, chapter 4 explores current information on the international food sovereignty movement and its connections with the Navajo Nation.

Two appendixes are included at the end of the book. Appendix A documents and explains the Commodity Food Program that was part of Tall Woman's later life. Appendix B reconstructs and records the history of fast food and other kinds of restaurants in the community of Chinle, Arizona. It is based on my own knowledge from having worked in that community from 1963 to the present, as well as on information from four others who have lived and worked in the community for long periods. Also included is a glossary of the Navajo words used in this book. Finally, the references list the available sources that proved most helpful.[6]

Perhaps the quickest way for the reader to get oriented, if Navajo history is not well-known, is to enjoy both Frank Mitchell's (Mitchell [1978] 2003) and Tall Woman's (Mitchell 2001) own stories in full.

1 | An Overview of the Navajo Diet and Navajo Dietary Research

ACCORDING TO NAVAJO oral tradition, Navajo ancestors emerged onto the present earth's surface along with deities at Hajíínáí, the Emergence Place, not far north of present Navajoland.[1] According to some accounts, specific Holy People ascended from the Lower Worlds, bringing certain implements and knowledge with them for the good of all. Although there are very few accounts of the origins of particular plants, corn is primordial, from time immemorial. It is divine, a gift of life, not a human creation. First Man and First Woman were transformed from two primordial ears of corn (Reichard 1963, 23, 433).

At least some of the foundational Emergence and Blessingway narratives credit Changing Woman with the creation of horses, sheep, and goats (Wyman 1970, 244–45). Goddard's (1933, 128) account of the activities in the Lower Worlds notes that when the Yellow World became crowded, its inhabitants made five chiefs: large snake, bear, wolf, panther, and otter; these held a council and established clans. First Man said, "There will be hermaphrodites who will know women's work and who will live like women. They will know the ways of both men and women."

Other accounts attribute the creation of various kinds of wild and domesticated animals to the Sun and a supernatural being known as the Sun's younger son, the invisible Moon Bearer, the "One who grabs breasts," or Begochidí.[2] The creations credited to these two include sheep, horses, swine, goats, mules, cows, fowl, deer, worms, and insects (Reichard 1963, 388–89;

Matthews 1897). Begochidí is described as fair-skinned, red-haired, and blue-eyed and is sometimes viewed as the forerunner of Americans or Mexicans.

Some narratives credit various beings with bringing seeds from the Lower Worlds during the Emergence, and these seeds became the source of planting for both Puebloans and Navajos. Turkey is frequently mentioned, and the seeds are usually for corn, beans, and squash, among other plants. For example, Goddard (1933, 128) says that First Man, First Woman, and Turquoise Boy planted white, yellow, and blue corn, respectively, and then Turkey planted "brown corn, then watermelon seeds, muskmelon seeds, and last spotted beans." Matthews (1897, 172–73) has Turkey shaking grains of white, blue, yellow, and variegated corn from its wings, followed by pumpkin (or maybe squash), watermelon, muskmelon, and bean seeds, four of each, each time. Wheelwright's (1946, 12) Feather Chant account has Turkey shaking corn, beans, tobacco, and squash seeds out from under his wings.

Newcomb (1967, 38–41) credits Turkey with remembering to bring the seeds stored in big sealed storage jars as all living things ascended into the next world because of oncoming floods: "With no storage of food supplies, there would have been hunger and starvation during the winter" (40). As Turkey flapped his wings, out fell white, red, blue, yellow, and variegated corn; beans and sunflower seeds; squash, melon, gourd, onion, and pumpkin seeds; and also the small seeds of wild millet, wild rice, barley grass, tobacco, cane grass, mustard, and sage. Turkey was decorated with all that he had saved from the flood and brought from the Lower Worlds: the colors of corn, the brown of tobacco seeds, melon seeds on his feet, a bean vine on his forehead, soft feathers with sunflower pollen, and a beak with wild barley; the scales on his legs were the seeds of squash and gourds.

Haile (1981, 33–34) credits the *nádleeh*, the so-called transvestite or hermaphrodite, with the first squash, watermelon, and gourd seeds as well as a number of seeds for psychoactive plants. Some accounts also credit the *nádleeh* with making certain cooking tools in the Lower Worlds (Goddard 1933, 128; Matthews 1897, 70–72; Haile 1981, 33–34; Reichard 1963, 140–41). These include gourd dippers, grinding stones, pottery, hairbrushes, stirring sticks, water jars, earthen bowls and spoons, and baking stones. For example, Matthews credits the descendants of First Man and First Woman with making a great farm and creating plows from cottonwood boards, hoes, and stone axes but getting seeds from the Pueblos. The *nádleeh*, guarding the farm's irrigation ditch, created pottery (a plate, bowl, and dipper) and a wicker water bottle.

Were I a Navajo trained in ceremonial knowledge and philosophy, and also of the conviction that such understanding should be shared in print so that today's youth could theoretically have ready access to everything they need in order to live good lives in the future, this book would have been written from that perspective. But obviously I am not. I did have the good fortune to start learning about Navajo culture in graduate school in 1962 and then to continue learning through firsthand experiences. However, I am in no position to claim any kind of expertise about traditional Navajo points of view, nor will I ever be. I remain an outsider, an academic versed in anthropological training and perspectives who believes that both points of view should be included whenever possible.

Thus, I will present anthropological interpretations, except in a few cases in which my own earlier learning allows me to understand other perspectives or when ceremonialists who assisted me with this project told me something that they said I can share. Whether it would even be possible for interested Navajos to assemble knowledge today about the old foods, cultivated and wild, and the narratives associated with their creation and development is a major question. The same is true for assessing just how much of the knowledge that remains is still being transmitted to younger generations through the training of future ceremonial practitioners or through various school programs designed to help perpetuate Navajo language and culture.

In contrast to the Navajo origin explanations, anthropologists claim that Navajos descended from two main groups of ancestors: Athabaskans, who spread from Canada into the Southwest, and Puebloans, who occupied the Southwest for millennia. The Athabaskans lived off the land and survived mainly by foraging, perhaps adding a little farming as they moved south. The Puebloans were farmers. By the time of early Spanish contact in the 1500s, the ancestral Navajos were living by gathering, hunting, and a little farming. They would have had extensive, fine-tuned, shared knowledge of the environment, of all the plants and animals to be found therein, and of farming. By the 1600s, those nearest the Spanish settlements, at least, had added flocks of sheep and goats to their livelihood (Bailey and Bailey 1986, 11–17). This mixture of gathering, hunting, farming, and herding was the Navajo means of acquiring food through the late 1800s.

At this time the Navajos moved with their animals as necessary but also farmed whenever possible. The farming was usually dry farming (not irrigated), since permanently flowing water sources on their lands were few and far between.[3] In time mutton became a primary part of their diet, and corn was also a major staple. Other crops the Navajos enjoyed and planted were melons and squash. In some areas, such as Canyon de Chelly, Arizona, it was possible to also grow fruit trees, such as peach, apple, and apricot trees. Elsewhere, beans could be grown.

Klara Kelley (personal communication, 2013), who has done extensive work with documents in the Navajo Land Claims Collection of the Navajo Nation Library, graciously contributed the following upon request:

> Navajo elders interviewed circa 1960 recalled that food sources of their parents and grandparents in the mid-late 1800s included hunting, gathering, farming, and herding. In the driest part of Navajoland, the far southwestern section, people depended on herding more than farming, but everywhere else, elders emphasized farming more than herding. Crops were mainly corn and squash, with some melons and beans. Farms of many families were clustered together in places with the best runoff water. Wild game consisted mainly of deer, antelope, rabbits, prairie dogs, groundhogs, and sometimes porcupines, with bighorn sheep also mentioned for people of northern Navajoland, and turkey for those in the southwestern part. Wild plants most commonly mentioned were pinyon [pine] nuts, juniper berries, yucca fruit, wild grass seeds, various berries (wolfberry, sumac), wild potatoes, wild onions, wild carrots, greens (probably beeweed), tansy mustard, and goosefoot or amaranth, with mescal for people along the southern edge of Navajoland and wild walnuts and grapes for those in the southwest.[4]

Colonial governments also recognized Canyon de Chelly as the garden spot of Navajoland.

Readers familiar with Southwestern history know that shortly after US involvement in the region and the end of the Civil War, emphasis was put on ending raiding and other problems allegedly caused by the Navajos. After several skirmishes and military campaigns to destroy the Navajos' crops, the US Army rounded up and marched many Navajos to Fort

Sumner, New Mexico, where they were incarcerated (1863–1868). As many researchers point out, including Kopp (1986) and those at the Diné Policy Institute (DPI) (2014), unlike earlier incidents leading to changes, these events brought forced dietary adaptations and dependence on external food sources, many of which were nutritionally inferior to the Navajos' traditional diet. Coolidge and Coolidge (1930, 272) list the following among the things the starving Navajos ate: "doves, rats, mice, prairie dogs, locusts, porcupine, badger, lynx, three kinds of greens, the inside of strawberry cactus, seeds, and roots."

Many of the Navajo stories recorded by Johnson (1973) mention the foods available at Fort Sumner and, in a few cases, at the time of surrender before the Long Walk (the march to Fort Sumner). The food at surrender included bacon, white flour (frequently infested with vermin), and coffee (113). The food during incarceration included "rations" (which often meant coffee, flour, and sugar); cows and some pigs butchered by white men (and Navajos detailed to do such work), but never enough meat (which was also sometimes rotten) to go around (146, 191, 202); bacon, flour, corn, coffee beans (often said to be green), and sugar (119). Some stories also mentioned salt, baking powder, and other items (202) and said that the Navajos were shown how to use these products. Others listed dry corn, beans, acorns, and one slice of bread (238, 242, 243, 249–50). At least one mentioned people making clothes from flour sacks (215). As the accounts illustrate, many people died from ingesting a mush they made from flour and water or from eating the green coffee beans (214, 224, 229).

According to Eldridge (2012), this is when the Navajos started becoming dependent on the US government for food, especially the flour, sugar, and coffee she sees as the cornerstones of government food distributions. Eldridge, Tapahonso (1998, 7–10) and Iverson (2002, 65) attribute the origins of frybread (also called fried bread) to this period.

Even when the Navajos adopted foods from others, they often developed different ways of preparing them or discovered that by changing the cooking conditions they could turn them into something else. One clear example of the latter is the tortilla. A tortilla was made from the same dough used for making frybread, but for everyday use it was cooked on a dry skillet, on a griddle, or even on a wire mesh grill over coals outside. Stew was easily made by just adding potatoes to boiled mutton, since it was common to have few, if any, other vegetables. Although mutton stew became a food for special occasions, whether it was actually served depended on many factors, such as transportation, income, the availability of ingredients, and the preferences of the individuals involved.

The so-called American period (in contrast to the earlier Spanish and Mexican periods), which many start with the Long Walk and the incarceration at Fort Sumner, brought drastic changes to dietary habits, the environment, the economy, and just about every other aspect of Navajo culture. Government rations included some food items; seeds, mainly of corn and wheat (Bailey and Bailey 1986, 45); farming tools; and a certain number of animals, mainly sheep and goats. The Treaty of 1868 allocated more money for seeds and farming equipment than for livestock, and from the spring of 1869 until 1879, when original payments ended and even later when they resumed with different funding, seeds and equipment were emphasized.

The seeds were for crops already familiar to some Navajos—such as beans, watermelons, muskmelons, squash, and pumpkins—as well as for new crops: turnips, beets, sugar beets, spinach, cauliflower, parsley, asparagus, rutabaga, and potatoes. Of the new crops, only potatoes took hold. The equipment available from the government consisted of hoes, sickles, spades, mattocks, and axes (Bailey and Bailey 1986, 46), with shovels and pickaxes being added in the 1870s and plows in the 1880s. The Navajos preferred to use their traditional farming methods and their digging sticks but eventually added hoes, shovels, plows, and rakes. Of course, the intensity of the farming varied from place to place, depending on climate and the floodwaters available for irrigation.

When the Navajos returned from Fort Sumner in 1868, Hispanic and Anglo settlers had taken control of the Navajos' best hunting and gathering lands, the uplands around the edges of Navajoland. With farming places in their remaining lands also limited, the Navajos had to be creative about food sources, especially in 1868–1878. Some increased their reliance on hunting, almost pushing antelope and elk herds into extinction. They solved their need for hides for making moccasins with requests for hides from ration beef cows. The Navajos also continued gathering roots, nuts, fruits, bulbs, seeds, and leaves of wild plants (Franciscan Fathers 1910; Matthews [1902] 1995; Elmore 1943).[5] Pinyons were important when plentiful; one report of diet in 1881 lists them along with acorns, grass seeds, sunflowers, wild potatoes, and the inner layers of the pine tree (Bailey and Bailey 1986, 49). Some Navajos depended more on herding, both as a food source and for something to exchange at trading posts for mass-produced foods (Kelley and Whiteley 1989). And before about 1872, they did resort to some raiding of their Hispanic, Anglo, and Pueblo neighbors for food (Bailey and Bailey 1986, 30, 38–39).

As many of the scholars cited here note, the Navajos were recovering their earlier self-sufficiency by 1880 because of the judicious management of their livestock, their willingness to try new ration items, and their recognition of other uses for the available items. For example, until 1878, pans, pails, plates, cups, kettles, and dippers were common government-issue items; the available blankets could be unraveled for yarn; wool and wool cards could be requested; and laborers could request pay in Mexican coins instead of food in order to obtain silver for silverwork.

In the latter part of the nineteenth century the economy changed significantly—first with the arrival of trading posts and traders, which actually started in the late 1860s, and then with the advent of the railroad in the 1880s (which took rangeland and water sources while bringing good and bad components of Anglo culture to the Navajos).[6] These stores could stock products unknown earlier to some of the Navajos, such as tea, salt, white flour, sugar, coffee, baking powder, rice, calico cloth, tools, and manufactured goods.[7] Traders became the source for many of the earlier ration items, and the Navajos, using their weavings, wool, jewelry, and livestock—through barter, pawn, credit, and cash—could acquire foodstuffs, tools, calico cloth, and other manufactured items. It was clear that some Navajos had also become proficient at blacksmithing, having learned ironwork from the Spanish. Trading post inventories varied with regional or local preferences and needs. Canned goods, fruit, smoked meat, and clothing for men were common (Russell 1991).

The Twentieth Century

People interested in the Navajo diet over time can be grateful that for the period beginning in the 1900s, we can turn to the work of Wendy Wolfe (1981, 1984).[8] In the sections that follow, I have, with her permission, depended mainly on her work, which extends to the early 1980s; where appropriate, it is augmented by data from others, including Carpenter and Steggerda (1939), Steggerda and Eckardt (1940), Bailey (1940), and my own experiences.

1900–1920

At the turn of the twentieth century, the Navajos were sustaining themselves through a combination of pastoralism, horticulture, the gathering of wild plants (such as wild spinach, pinyon nuts, yucca fruit, and berries), and the hunting of small animals (such as rabbits and prairie dogs). The traditional diet with which the Navajos began the new century has been praised by contemporary researchers, since as Wolfe, Weber, and Arviso (1985) and others have shown, the traditional diet included foods from each of the four basic groups, and unlike today's diet most traditional foods were nutritious. Bread and cereal provided fiber, iron, and vitamin B-complex (and, with culinary ash, minerals such as calcium). Fresh and dried wild plants, fruits, and berries were common and, in time, were joined by cultivated squash and melons. The fruits and vegetables provided vitamins A and C, fiber, and other necessary elements. Meat, both wild and domesticated (and including almost all parts of some animals) provided protein, iron, and other minerals. Pinyon nuts and seeds from squash and tumble mustard also provided protein. Milk and cheese from sheep and goats provided calcium, but an even more important source of that was culinary ash and clay.

Generally, there was much more gathering in the first two decades of the century than later. Wolfe (1984, 113) says that small flocks of goats and sheep were common in 1900–1920, with the Navajos still eating much wild meat, especially rabbit, as well as native plants such as wild celery, wild onion, wild spinach, yucca fruit, and pinyon nuts. Other popular items in the diet were native salt, cornmeal, goat's milk pancakes, cornbread, cornmeal mush, paperbread (a very thin cornmeal bread), blue bread (bread made from blue corn flour), sweetened baked cornbread, dumplings made from ground wild pigweed or goosefoot, *tł'ohdeeí* (grass whose seeds fall) seeds, and poured bread (also called hurry-up bread or quick bread). The rabbits caught during group hunts were roasted underground (i.e., in the ground), as was the meat of antelope, deer, and sheep. Dried apricots were boiled; they were grown along with melons and squash wherever possible. Wild teas, both Mormon and Navajo kinds, were harvested; so were wild seeds, which were ground and added to cornmeal or made into cakes by themselves. This was *not* a time of sugar or candy. The only two methods people reported using to sweeten their foods, especially cornmeal dishes, were the addition of *dleesh*, a light-colored clay that contains magnesium, and *biínídoot'aal*, sucking on the cornmeal until the enzymes in the saliva converted the starch to sugar; this sweetened meal was then added to the rest of the batter. Salt was actually harvested, reportedly being obtained by scraping off *łeeyáán*, the white crusty alkali surface of some soils, and using that for salt.

Over time the goat and sheep flocks increased, and new problems of drought, overgrazing, the drying up of the ground, erosion, and other issues affected the land. But even worse, during the 1918–1920 period, the Navajos, other Native Americans, and at least twenty million other people around the globe were decimated by the Spanish influenza pandemic (Mitchell 2001, 426–27n2; Brady and Bahr 2014). When those who survived started to recover, flocks had to be reduced given the changes in the landscape. This of course meant less meat and less milk per person and more reliance on foods purchased at the trading posts or obtained through government rations. Since the Navajos had no electricity, running water, or refrigeration, it was not possible to keep fruit and vegetables fresh for very long or to store dairy products and eggs. Thus, trading posts did not carry such items.

Many of the wild plants that had been plentiful in earlier times and on which the people had depended did not fare well in drier environments; they therefore became less dependable as sources of food and were used less often. Horticulture was difficult in many places unless the conditions made irrigation possible, even for short periods, using washes (seasonally dry stream-beds found in the western United States) and a series of hand-dug ditches.

THE 1920S AND 1930S

Many scholars report that climate changes became noticeable and that the land was already drier by the 1920s. Wolfe (1984, 113–18) reports several factors that affected dietary changes at this time. Overgrazing and climate change were both major factors; because of them, wild plants and animals that had been important food resources became increasingly scarce, harder to find and use in the diet. Related behaviors, such as making the ash necessary for specific corn dishes, also declined. At the same time, store and trading post food items became increasingly available, especially for those with access to cash or other resources to barter, trade, or pawn for food. This led to less use of wild plants as food, even though other vegetables did not replace them in the overall diet.

Concurrently, some researchers note, there was an increase in the preference for the tastes of sugar and salt, in the desire for less time-consuming ways of preparing foods, and in the encouragement by both peers and outsiders to adopt new foods and try new things to eat. Significantly, Wolfe (1984) found that Navajos who were poorer and thus less able to replace traditional foods with some of the new foods but who were still able to gather edible wild foods and hunt wild animals actually had *better* nutrition—more vitamins in their diets than those who ate increasing amounts of highly processed Anglo foods known to be low in nutritional value. Most research shows that the days of the traditional diet were over for the Navajos by the end of the 1920s.

Wolfe (1984) grouped 1925–1939 as a distinct period in her study of diet changes among the Navajos. Her research identified the popular foods in 1925–1935 as kneel-down bread (made during harvest season from freshly ground corn wrapped in corn husks and baked in the ground) in boiled goat's milk; cornmeal mush; goat's milk pancakes; a stew of boiled mutton, corn, and squash; fried mutton; and a stew of hominy and mutton. Meat included mutton and horsemeat that was either fried or boiled. Winter was the preferred time for butchering cows, horses, and donkeys for meat and other uses, since the meat kept better in cold temperatures.

Wheat was being grown by many Navajo farmers, so it was readily available in some places in the 1930s. Wheat tortillas, goat's milk pancakes made with both wheat and corn flour, blue bread, and corn dishes were also popular. Wheat flour was readily available from the stores by the 1930s and in time started to replace the use of corn flour and ground wild seeds. The growing, drying, and grinding of wheat sprouts also provided another sweetener.[9] People still made fresh goat cheese, and at first goat's milk was more popular as a drink than coffee. As long as the animals were plentiful, milk from sheep and goats was used in breads, as a drink, and for cheese.

People still picked and used *ch'il 'ahwéhé*. wild Navajo tea, but Mormon tea was no longer reported. People still used wild vegetables and a few wild seeds, including *waa'* (beeweed) and several wild berries. The use of the bitter wild potatoes declined; they were most often replaced by the potatoes available at trading posts. In small gardens the Navajos grew corn, squash, melons, cantaloupes, pumpkins, and beans; wherever possible, they also grew peaches and apricots and either ate the fruit fresh or dried it for later use, reconstituting it by boiling. At the stores people bought coffee, wheat flour, and raisins. For a while both sugar and candy were expensive and hard to get, although by the late 1930s both were liked and were being purchased at least by some people. There is also evidence that some trading posts were attempting to stock locally requested items; for example, baby bottles and nipples were stocked in areas where they were used for raising orphaned lambs (Russell 1991).[10]

The Stock Reduction Program, mandated by the US government on the Navajo reservation in the 1930s, reduced access to fresh meat and milk; in terms of the subsistence diet, the loss of the formerly ample supply of both animal protein and minerals from organ meats sounded another kind of death knell. In more general terms, as Eldridge (2012) noted, the program destroyed family subsistence and wealth and increased dependence on the US government.[11]

By the late 1930s, Wolfe (1984) found, the Navajo diet was a mix of native wild game (such as deer, prairie dogs, and rabbits) and domestic animals and crops (such as sheep, goats, and, in some places, cows and horses). Meat from domestic animals started to replace wild meat, a trend that continued into the 1950s. Gathering was abandoned by many because wild plants and animals became increasingly difficult to find. This affected some cooking practices, such as the making of ash. Two types of cornbread seemed to disappear: *nanoyeeshi* (poured bread, which was baked in ashes and eaten without removing the ashes, which were seen as protective), and *tsé'ást'éí* (paper-bread).[12] Frybread and tortillas were very common. Many people in this period started buying cornmeal instead of drying their own corn at home and then hand-grinding it. Even hominy could be bought; then it was soaked in lye and frozen. When it was produced at home with ash less available, some people cooked it in baking soda and water, but they reported that the results were not as good as when ash was used. Goat's milk was used wherever it was available, but canned (cow's) milk was increasingly available.[13] Other popular items at trading posts were wheat flour, potatoes, sugar, salt, coffee, and lard, although according to Wolfe, canned shortening did not become a preference until the 1950s. White corn replaced corn flour in many kinds of bread. Potatoes and white flour, rather than corn, became staples, and mutton became increasingly popular.

In the 1930s dry farming was common except where rivers, both small and large, and river basins made irrigated farming possible. The irrigation projects on the San Juan River are but one example. Sometimes wells and springs also provided water, as did rain. The heyday for these farms was before the 1940s, when men began to leave for railroad jobs, when welfare checks and commodity foods became available, and when pickup trucks, which couldn't be used to clean ditches or plow, replaced horses and harnesses. Wheat was grown, being waist-high in some areas, and was popular allegedly for frybread (Bingham and Bingham 1979). Flour mills were built, such as the one at Round Rock, and Chinle had a horse-driven corn grinder set up on Presbyterian Hill near the former Gorman Trading Post for community use (Mitchell 2001, 224, 250, 464n21). In river basin areas, as well as in some canyons, it was also possible to grow apple, peach, and apricot trees. Extended families often planted small gardens of corn, beans, squash, pumpkins, and/or melons; many of these crops were planted deep and were spaced well apart in groups.[14] Some people also grew tomatoes, cucumbers, sweet corn, onions, radishes, and pinto beans; potatoes, cabbage, chili peppers, carrots, and lettuce might also be found in gardens. At least in earlier times, Tall Woman's home area of Chinle had a growing season of 120–150 days, but like the residents of other areas, Chinle's inhabitants depended on water from melting snow coming down the washes in the spring (Bingham and Bingham 1979, 14). People constructed ditches, dams, and other means of controlling this water and releasing it into their fields. Horses, scrapers, and hand tools were involved, and the ditches had to be cleaned annually and the dams repaired whenever necessary.

By the late 1930s native plants were included in the diet only occasionally; McDonald (1965) identified these as wild spinach (beeweed, or *waa'*), sour berries (*chiiłchin*, or sumac berries), cactus fruit (mainly prickly pear), wild onion, wild rhubarb, pinyon nuts, yucca fruit, Navajo tea, and maybe other tea plants. More staple items came from the trading posts. During the first round of store shopping, the Navajos chose baking powder, cornmeal, potatoes, sugar, wheat flour, coffee, lard, and salt. If additional purchases were possible, then pinto beans, squash or pumpkin, melons, canned tomatoes, canned peaches, canned milk, soda pop, and candy were added. There was still a lack of electricity, running water, and refrigeration.[15]

Reh's (1983) careful research in the 1930s in the Navajo Mountain area, a place usually considered more traditional than other places in Navajoland, led to a publication focused on the 1939 consumption habits in District 1, which also provides much clarification of the ways of living at that time.[16] One-third of Navajo income at that time was in the form of food, grown or produced and consumed at home. The rest was cash or trade credit from the sale of farm and livestock products, pinyon nuts, rugs, and wages, and it was turned mainly into food. Corn remained the staff of life, although wheat flour, ready to use, was rapidly becoming popular. Corn needed to be hand-milled and then ground on grinding stones. The Navajos preferred green corn and planted two crops, one in mid-May and another in early June. The first batch was ready early in September and lasted until mid-October, which was frost time. People ate the first crop every day and consumed most of it.

The time of roasting ears was also the time for Enemyways and some other appropriate ceremonies, for which the family having the event needed help with donations of sugar, coffee, flour, and sheep. When the frost came, the people picked unripe corn and roasted it in green husks in outdoor stone ovens (Reh 1983, 6).[17] After roasting, the corn was removed, husked, sun-dried, and shelled, then hung in sacks in the hogan or the storehouse. This corn could be boiled with water or milk at any time of year. One could also cut off the soft kernels, grind them into a dough, and make them into large tamales, which were rewrapped in green husks and baked in ashes. Then these were unwrapped and dried in the sun. Any hard shrunken pieces of corn were left in the sacks to be cooked later with milk or meat. If the corn was being used for making tortillas or tamales, first the ashes of cedar needles were leached with boiling water. The hard pieces of corn were then soaked in this water to soften them before grinding. Ashes from sagebrush or greasewood could be used as substitutes, and sometimes people traded ash for chili peppers.

THE 1940S AND 1950S

Steggerda and Eckhardt (1940) state that by 1940 wild plants were no longer significant in the Navajo diet; cultivated foods, such as corn, squash, and melons, which could be eaten either fresh or dried for wintertime consumption, were the popular foods. Wild game had become scarce, being displaced in many areas by mutton, goatmeat, horsemeat, and beef by 1955. When Darby, Salsbury, and McGariety (1956) published the *first* nutritional study of Navajos (conducted in Ganado and Pinon, Arizona), it was clear that sheep or goats were being butchered for meat, and corn, melons, squash, beans, and potatoes were grown wherever possible. But wheat flour from the trading posts had become a staple, and coffee, tea, and soda pop had displaced the earlier herbal beverages. A typical diet of the time was described as featuring mutton—roasted, fried, or stewed with potatoes and onions—bread, and coffee or tea. If milk was used, it was mainly canned evaporated milk from the store.

By 1940 anthropologists were clearly becoming interested in diet and cooking as topics during their Navajo fieldwork. That year brought Flora L. Bailey's famous essay, "Navaho Foods and Cooking Methods," published in the *American Anthropologist* and based on her association with Clyde Kluckhohn, Leland Wyman, and others. Bailey (1940, 272nn5–7) cites the following sources on Navajo foods extant at the time of her work: Washington Matthews's *The Night Chant*, the Franciscan Fathers' *Ethnologic Dictionary of the Navaho Language*, Willard W. Hill's *Agriculture and Hunting Methods of the Navaho Indians*, Francis Elmore's "Food Animals of the Navaho," Edward Castetter and Morris Opler's "Uncultivated Native Plants Used as Sources of Food," and Gladys Reichard's *Social Life of the Navajo Indians*. Emma Reh's *Navajo Consumption Habits (for District 1), 1939* was not yet available.

Other events in the 1940s and 1950s included stock reduction; range management policies with the permit system; World War II and its military service choices as well as the off-reservation jobs connected to it; the shift to a wage economy from a livestock-based subsistence economy; increased awareness, since the 1928 Meriam Report, of the need to increase educational opportunities for Navajo youth, especially by building more day schools; an increase in paved roads; the increased use of automobiles and pickup trucks instead of wagons; relocation programs; and continued dietary changes involving further adaptation to non-Indian foods.[18] White (1983) shows that in the 1930s home-produced foods provided the largest part of the Navajo diet, but within two more decades some Navajos had become completely dependent on federal programs for sustenance.

Wolfe (1984) found that the use of wheat flour increased and the use of milk from sheep and goats decreased in the 1940s and 1950s. Her data on the typical diet of the time showed that cornmeal mush, blue bread, and pancakes from goat's milk were still popular, as was dried or roasted meat eaten alone or in stew. Cornbread or cornmeal mush, mutton stew with potatoes, and hominy mutton stew were also popular. In this period Wolfe's sources starting talking about frybread, usually made from part corn and part wheat flour and fried in sheep tallow (fat). Pinyon nuts were being enjoyed, as was parched corn.[19] Some goat cheese was still being made.[20] Peaches and grapes were picked in season, dried, and then reconstituted by boiling. Food items purchased during trips to the trading post by wagon included wheat flour, sugar, potatoes, coffee, chewing gum, canned tomatoes, and candy.[21] These trips also included lots of visiting, exchanging news, and retrieving the mail besides shopping for groceries, clothes, fabrics, dishes, tools, utensils, and whatever else was needed. Canned shortening was just starting to replace sheep fat for frying.[22]

Although boarding schools started much earlier than the 1940s, Eldridge (2012) identified them, along with relocation programs, as influential in destroying traditional foodways among the Navajos.[23] By stressing a Western diet and ways of cooking, eating, setting the table, and serving, these schools taught many Western ideas about food, domestic life, and culture. The unspoken messages, of course, were negative—namely, that Navajo foods were dirty, backward, unhealthy, and not as valuable as Western ones. Relocation programs in the 1950s that pushed the Navajos into cities also put them in foreign environments that were full of Western ideas about everything.

THE 1960S AND 1970S

Wendy Wolfe gives the 1960s and 1970s limited discussion, and Alford and Nance (1976) claim that there were no changes in dietary patterns from 1955 to 1976, yet there are some studies and events that should be mentioned.[24]

In conjunction with the Navajo-Cornell Field Health Research Project based in Many Farms, Arizona, from 1956 to 1962 (Adair and Deuschle 1970), publications were developed for home health workers that considered diet (Navajo Tribe 1963; Loughlin 1963). In addition, a large nutritional study was done in the Lower Greasewood Chapter of the Navajo Nation from December 1968 to January 1969 by the University of Pittsburgh (1969; see also Kopp 1986). It showed that mutton and corn continued to be staples in the Navajo diet and that most families ate organ meats and some native plants such as cactus and yucca fruits, pinyon nuts, wild spinach, onion, and rhubarb.

But as expected, the study also showed an increased dependence on external food sources since the 1950s through meals at schools (both boarding and day), and the federal Commodity Food Program (see appendix A). Since the data demonstrated a high risk of inadequate intake of iron, protein, and vitamin C, additional smaller surveys among children and pregnant or lactating women were done, and then several nutritional support programs were developed on the reservation (Butte, Calloway, and Van Duzen 1981; Van Duzen et al. 1969; Van Duzen, Carter, and Zwagg 1976). Calloway, Giauque, and Costa (1974) demonstrated that some of the commodity foods were inferior to the traditional foods they replaced and that the people in the Lower Greasewood Chapter study area, although they had more food, lacked adequate meat sources. There was less reliance on the land, mutton, and farming, but 71 percent continued to raise and grow at least some of their own food, including sheep, goats, cattle, chickens, corn, squash, beans, potatoes, and yucca. The economy appeared to still be in transition from a subsistence economy to one based on wage labor, and the trend of more reliance on the purchase of commercial food products was clear. For instance, Donovan (2012) claims that the late 1960s is when the first Navajo taco was created—by Louis Shepherd, who, with his wife, operated the Window Rock Lodge for more than ten years.

As Bailey and Bailey (1986, 271) and others show, by this time the relationship between traders and the Navajos was changing as employment opportunities increased, credit became less important, and automobile and truck transportation became more common. People began turning to off-reservation stores in the late 1960s and early 1970s, and even on the reservation, trading posts had new competition from supermarkets. First Fed Mart opened a big store in Window Rock in 1968 (Aberle 1969, 247); shortly thereafter Imperial Mart opened in Chinle (Navajo Tribe 1974, 31). In time some trading posts became local convenience stores or shifted their focus in other ways; others went out of business (Bailey and Bailey 1986, 271; Powers 2001).[25] Kelley (personal communication, 2015) noted that the interviews done for the Trading Post Encyclopedia project suggest that the "great divide for trading post survival seems to have been 1980."[26]

Another development was the beginning, in 1962, of a tribal irrigation farming project, the Navajo Indian Irrigation Project in the Farmington, New Mexico, area. Bingham and Bingham (1979) provide excellent details about this and other irrigation projects. With the development of the Navajo Agricultural Products Industry (NAPI), the Navajo Nation went into the business of large-scale irrigated farming, producing a number of foods labeled NAVAJO PRIDE, as well as alfalfa and other crops. NAPI eventually became a source of foods (mostly onions and potatoes) donated to the Navajo Nation's chapters.[27]

A major influence in this period was the Commodity Food Program, which had begun on the reservation in 1959 (see appendix A). Information about diet and food availability during the 1960s and 1970s is now readily available in different sources such as community studies, ethnographies, life histories, and autobiographies (Downs 1972; McCullough-Brabson and Help 2001; Lamphere 2007; McCloskey 2007).[28] The institutional limitations of the Commodity Food Program restricted distribution to canned or dried foods, so it never included fresh vegetables or fruits. In time and with program changes, other sources of food aid became available to some, including general assistance or welfare, Supplemental Security Income, Social Security, Aid to Families with Dependent Children, food stamps, Women, Infants, and Children (WIC), and school lunch programs.[29]

In 1972 the Navajo Health Authority (NHA) was chartered by the tribal council to develop programs to improve the health and well-being of the Navajos. One of the programs established was the Navajo Ethnobotany Project, to compile all the previously published Navajo ethnobotanical information and make it available to the Navajos themselves. The result was a well-illustrated work entitled *Nanise': A Navajo Herbal* (Mayes and Lacy [1989] 2012). By agreement, medicinal and ceremonial information was limited in the work.

THE 1980S AND 1990S

Wolfe (1984) comments on a number of food changes that were taking place by the 1980s. The most common diet items continued to be coffee, tortillas and frybread (made from unleavened wheat flour, possibly with the addition of powdered milk from the commodity foods), potatoes, and sugar. Mutton continued to be popular, but beef and chicken were also well liked, coming from both on- and off-reservation supermarkets and trading posts because people who had transportation now shopped wherever the prices were best. People had mostly given up eating horsemeat, and horses were no longer being butchered. Cattle were often sold instead of being butchered at home, but people readily bought and ate beef in all kinds of cuts. Some men, especially those with pickup trucks, continued to hunt deer, usually with friends; venison remained popular in season and was considered a treat worthy of sharing when available.

According to Wolfe (1984), by the 1980s a typical morning meal was fried eggs, fried potatoes, a flour tortilla or toasted store bread, a fruit drink, and coffee. Some preferred to have hot or cold cereal with milk, or pancakes, usually made from a store-bought mix. For lunch, a stew of mutton with potatoes, carrots, celery and/or onions was popular, as were beans, hominy, pigs' feet, and some kind of bread, such as a tortilla or frybread. Other options were store bread with Spam, bologna or other processed lunch meats, hot dogs, sausage, fried chicken, and baked potatoes. Coffee, fruit drinks, and soda pop were common beverages. At night the meal often copied lunch or else consisted of broiled or fried beef and baked potatoes. Fresh or canned vegetables were often part of this meal, and sometimes people also had canned fruit.

Wolfe (1984) also notes that by the 1980s potatoes and white wheat flour had become staples, more so than corn. With one exception, wild plants and berries were almost never gathered unless people lived in rural areas. The exception was *neeshch'íí'* (pinyon nuts), from the pinyon tree. Navajos love the flavor of these nuts, which bring high prices when in season, and groups of people still gather them each fall. Milk had become more available through the WIC program and school lunches. Many were adding powdered milk to frybread and tortilla batters and even to Navajo pancakes. One woman told Wolfe that she used it to make the traditional goat cheese. The use of coffee had increased; the wild Navajo tea, *ch'il 'ahwéhé*, was still being gathered and used in areas where it was available, but *tł'oh 'azihii* (Mormon tea), which was more common in 1910–1920, was seldom used at all by the 1980s.[30]

The area of the diet that Wolfe (1984) found to be the least changed by this decade was that which included bread and corn foods. Poured cornbread, or *nanoyeeshi*, and paperbread, or *tsé'ást'éí*, had almost disappeared unless one bought them or traded to get them. She attributed their disappearance to the fact they were more difficult to make than blue bread and cornmeal mush. Poured bread was traditionally baked in the ashes of a fire and then eaten without brushing or rinsing off the ashes, as was usually done for any kind of bread baked this way. In 1980 Wolfe's collaborators still believed that eating ash protected them from disease and other bad events. The literature suggests that poured bread was used ceremonially to prepare warriors for battle. Perhaps the belief in the protective powers of this bread stemmed from this, since one could be protected from enemies as well as any disease they might be carrying. By the 1980s it was known that ash contained some important nutrients, but whether it was viewed as adding strength or health to warriors was unclear.[31] It had already been established that ash was too strong for babies even though they ate cornmeal mush. Besides not eating too much ash, if any at all, babies were also not to eat *chiiłchin*, or sumac berries; if a nursing mother ate these berries, people said her milk would cause the baby to have diarrhea.

In terms of grains, by the 1980s people spoke of frybread hunger and tortilla hunger. Both of these breads were made from white wheat flour and some powdered milk and were craved. Although it was common to see numerous cornfields on the reservation in the 1940s, by the early 1980s very few people were still planting corn. In earlier times people had used fresh corn—corn on the cob, cut off to be boiled in stew or processed immediately to make kneel-down bread and many other dishes. In the 1960s and 1970s it was still common to see people planting, growing, harvesting, drying, and hand-grinding corn with grinding stones in the northeastern areas of the reservation, but by the 1980s few people were doing any of these activities.[32] This probably varied by area; Eldridge (2012) said that in 1980 "many Navajo families still farmed, raising corn, squash, and melons as the most popular foods; gardens were mainly small and did not provide a major source of food for many families." She added that one study (no source given, but probably Wolfe and Sanjur 1988) claimed that "many of the traditional foods were rarely if ever consumed."

From my observations, there were many reasons for the decline in farming. People worked in a cash economy and were not available to farm. In some families, sections of land went to others when the elders who had farmed passed away, and the new inhabitants chose to build on the land or put a mobile home on the space instead of continuing to farm. In some cases, the infestation of grasshoppers and then a spreading green noxious weed ruined the gardens several years in a row, and people just gave up. Drought conditions were another factor for some. Corn, of course, was still being used; one could purchase it, already ground, at the store. Even hominy (already lye-soaked and frozen) could be purchased if one wanted to make hominy at home; many cooked it in baking soda and water instead of continuing to use the traditional method of culinary ash and water to soften the dried raw corn kernels. Although baking soda does loosen the outer skin of dried corn kernels so it comes off, it does not have the same nutrition-enhancing effect as ash (Wolfe et al. 1985) and may actually cause the loss of certain nutrients in the corn by destroying them. Also, by 1980 many people had moved out of rural areas, far away from juniper trees or other plants from which culinary ash could be made, so it was harder to obtain this ash.

Unlike ash, sugar was readily available by the 1980s, and many were adding it to their coffee and tea. More and more adults and children were also eating candy and drinking soda pop, getting both on trips to stores and even gas stations. Eldridge (2012) said that by the 1980s soda pop and other sweetened drinks, store-bought bread, and milk were common in the Navajo diet, and frybread, tortillas, potatoes, mutton, and coffee were staples.

Wolfe's (1984) summary of the Navajo diet as of 1980 identified the following as the most common items: coffee, tortillas and/or frybread, potatoes (either boiled in stew or fried), and sugar in coffee or tea. Coffee became popular when it was made available through the early trading posts. Before then, wild teas were gathered and consumed, and the Navajo tea *ch'il 'ahwéhé* was still popular though not readily available in some areas. The types of bread were variations of the same homemade unleavened wheat-flour dough. Even though tortillas and frybread were already viewed as traditional, they became common only after the arrival of wheat flour.[33] Of the two, tortillas were more common, but both were often made with instant nonfat dry milk obtained through the Commodity Food Program. Liquid milk was used most often in coffee, raising the question of a possible lactose intolerance, which Wolfe could not research. However, she did note that sheep's milk and goat's milk have more fat in proportion to lactose and are thus more tolerable than cow's milk. Whole milk, canned evaporated milk, reconstituted nonfat dry milk, and goat's milk were all still available and in use in 1980. The Navajos were also using both fresh eggs and dehydrated egg mixes, the latter coming from the Commodity Food Program.

In terms of meat, Wolfe (1984) correctly noted that in earlier times it was taboo to eat fish, fowl, and eggs. However, by the 1980s chicken and turkey were being consumed, and eggs were no longer taboo. Fishing as a sport was enjoyed by many at the various lakes on the reservation, but reportedly it was still rare for people to eat what they caught. Mutton remained popular; although it could be fried or roasted, perhaps the most common way to eat it was in stew, where it was boiled with potatoes, onions, and maybe carrots or other vegetables. Various sheep organs continued to be eaten at the time of butchering, with some, such as 'ach'íí' (sheep intestines), being particularly popular and sought after. Beef was also popular and was prepared by frying, roasting, boiling it in stew, or eating it as ground beef.

Other foods available through the Commodity Food Program retained their popularity in 1980, including commodity (i.e., processed) cheese, spaghetti and macaroni, canned vegetables, numerous types of beans, and canned or bottled orange juice.

Only a few seasonal wild plants identified by Wolfe's sources were still occasionally being used for food in the early 1980s. Environments differ in what might be available, and not everything in any environment is eaten. People learn that some plants are poisonous, cause sickness or vomiting if eaten raw, are too strong, or have a bad taste. Some plants that are inedible in their raw state can be used if cooked, dried, or eaten with *dleesh* or a culinary clay. *Dleesh* was also mentioned as being used with wild wolfberries and wild potatoes to make them sweet enough to eat.[34] But *dleesh* should be in the category of substances that both go with other foods and have medicinal qualities. Some plants can be eaten only if they are very young, perhaps before toxins develop (Wolfe 1984).

The seasonal wild plant foods identified by Wolfe's sources were as follows, although it is unclear if the foods are the same as others identified with different names: wild sumac berries, which were eaten both as berries and in a pudding (the same as wolfberries, eaten with *dleesh* as a sweetener, and sour sumac berries, or *chiiłchin*); desert yucca and sweet mountain yucca fruit (the same as wild Navajo banana); wild potatoes (with *dleesh* as a sweetener); wild onions; wild celery, which reportedly can also be made into a soup with wild onions; wild spinach, or *waa'* (Rocky Mountain beeweed); *tł'oh deesk'idí* (green amaranth); *tł'ohdeeí* (falling seed grass, amaranth, goosefoot, or pigweed); and cactus fruit, mainly prickly pear.

Since her 1984 research, Wendy Wolfe has remained active and continues to be concerned with issues relevant to the Navajos, such as food insecurity and diabetes; see, for example, Wolfe et al. (1985), Wolfe and Sanjur (1988), and Wolfe (1994). (Later researchers have worked on these problems, too, such as Pardilla et al. 2013 and Gittelsohn et al. 2013).

Of particular importance since Wolfe's work is a study from the 1990s. The Navajo Health and Nutrition Survey, a comprehensive survey of the nutritional status of a representative sample of 985 Navajos living on or near the reservation, was conducted between October 1991 and December 1992. After presenting preliminary results to the Navajo Nation and the Navajo Area Indian Health Service staff (NAIHS), the researchers published the findings as a supplement of the *Journal of Nutrition* with supportive funding from the IHS and the Centers for Disease Control and Prevention (Ballew et al. 1997). The data base was supplemented with six Navajo food ingredients: blue cornmeal, juniper ash water, Mormon tea, two kinds of Navajo tea, and North American pinyon nuts. Navajo recipes for frybread, tortillas, blue cornmeal mush with and without ash, kneel-down bread, Navajo cake, and sumac pudding were also added to the Food Intake Analysis System, along with a variety of soups, stews, and mixed dishes (2086S).

The survey indicated that the current Navajo diet exceeded the recommended 30 percent total fat content and 10 percent saturated fat content, even with the likely underestimation of saturated fat and cholesterol intake. There were some slight differences between the results of this survey and the University of Pittsburgh study (1969), and elders over sixty appeared particularly at risk; but in general, in the early 1990s the Navajos remained at risk of inadequate intake of the same key nutrients: vitamins A and C, folate, calcium, and iron. Although there are ways to improve intake, the study noted that three major limitations affected dietary choice among the Navajos surveyed: cost, availability, and shelf life. The researchers' dietary recommendations included the following: fortified ready-to-eat cereals, an improved consumption of fruits and vegetables in canned versions if fresh weren't available, canned and boxed orange juice with an extended shelf life, and the increased use of nonfat dry milk and traditional blue cornmeal foods made with ash—which, as has been known for centuries, provides substantial amounts of calcium.

The researchers concluded that an increasingly sedentary lifestyle, the erosion of traditional dietary practices and patterns, and an increasing dependence on a few refined and processed foods may be major factors in the higher incidence of obesity and chronic diseases among the Navajos in the past fifty years. "Diet is an important behavioral risk factor for all chronic diseases and is susceptive to intervention within the limits of the resources available to a population," the study concluded (Ballew et al. 1997, 2092S).

SUMMARY

It is clear that of all the foods eaten by the Navajos over time, both corn and sheep have retained a special place in Navajo culture. Home-ground corn continues to be preferred for both the Girls' Puberty Ceremony and weddings, although commercial cornmeal will do, if absolutely necessary. Hot roasted corn on the cob remains popular at fairs, dances, and concessions set up at some traditional ceremonies, such as the Enemyway. Some Navajos told Wolfe (1984) that they viewed certain foods as "strong, including blue cornmeal, white cornmeal, cornmeal with kind unspecified, mutton, pork chops, beef, ribs, cornmeal mush, and goat's milk." The original Navajo tea, or wild tea, can still be found in the mountains in the summer and dried for later use. Preferences for the seasonal usage of two animals continue to be known: one should eat rabbits in the winter and prairie dogs in the spring or fall, when these animals are fat.

With so much cultural change, the use of traditional foods, including wild foods, has certainly declined. There are, however, some still in use; people prepare them for their own consumption or for ceremonies. Older Navajos have knowledge about them, but the younger Navajos who are interested in them know little, be it concerning their location; how to harvest, dry, store, and reconstitute them for later use; or how to create beverages or dishes for consumption. Wolfe (1984) and just about everyone else who has written about Navajo dietary changes agree that people need to be encouraged to use the traditional foods, which were clearly more nutritious than today's highly processed foods. Ash is a good source of calcium, and using powdered milk for tortilla or frybread adds carbohydrates, calcium, and thiamin. Wolfe and Sanjur (1988) show that the Navajos' usual diets are low in vitamins A and C, and the use of dairy products is very low. The worst deficiency is in calcium, with iron and phosphorous shortages coming in second and third.

Wolfe's (1984, 213–224, 287–296) sources had no trouble identifying their favorite native foods. In the category of corn dishes they named blue corn-meal mush with ash (in several varieties), yellow cornmeal mush, cornmeal mush (type unspecified), blue dumplings, steamed corn (including steamed Indian corn on the cob), and sweet cornmeal tamales. Others were hominy corn, parched corn, blood sausage (made during butchering), goat's milk (most often only for ceremonies now), and milk mush. The bread category included the very popular kneel-down bread; some named a combination of kneel-down bread with blood sausage or blood pudding. Other breads listed were blue bread, paperbread, Navajo cake (mainly for Kinaaldás, the Girls' Puberty Ceremony, but at least annually, according to most), poured bread (*nanoyeeshi*) and Navajo pancakes. In addition to both goat's milk and sheep's milk, which some claimed not to like, the only beverage was Navajo tea, *ch'il 'ahwéhé*. Pinyon nuts and even pinyon nut butter were mentioned, along with acorns. Fruits included prickly pear cactus fruit, *dit'oodí* (apricots), dried peaches, *didzétsoh dík'ǫzhí* (wild plums), dried cantaloupe, and wild currants.[35] Berries mentioned were cedar or juniper berries, choke-cherries, and wild sumac pudding or berries. Seeds listed were goosefoot, pigweed, *tł'ohdeeí* (which were often ground and used to make dumplings), and *'ostse'* (tumble, tansy or hedge mustard). Sweeteners mentioned were culinary clay, *dleesh*, and *biínídoot'aal* (sucked cornmeal whose starch has been converted to sugar by saliva enzymes). Some people said there were only two traditional ways to sweeten foods such as cornmeal dishes: with *biínídoot'aal* or with *dleesh*. Traditionally, *łeeyáán*, the white crusty alkaline surface scraped off some soils, was the source of salt.[36]

When contributing food to a ceremony, people took coffee, bread, mutton, potatoes, or the ingredients from which to make bread in large quantities (flour, sugar, baking powder, powdered milk, and salt), as well as candy, soda pop, or cookies. My observations suggest that the list remains much the same to this day, with the addition of paper towels, napkins, dishwashing soap, toilet paper, paper or Styrofoam plates and cups, plastic utensils, and bottled water. The foods people get hungry for and seek out at concessions (at

Enemyway and Nightway ceremonies or at fairs, rodeos, powwows, and parades) are frybread, kneel-down bread, tortillas, tamales, mutton stew, ribs, coffee, roasted corn, and paperbread. Elders in nursing homes often crave blue cornmeal mush, fixed in several different ways, mutton (even if it has to be ground up), and the usual native breads.

Although common and favorite foods are not difficult to research, specific nutritional deficiencies have been hard to study for all of the reasons cited in Kopp (1986, 15–22). People's vitamin A levels were normal when they were still eating organ meats, but Vitamin C levels were usually below normal range, and the rates of growth and maturation were slower than among middle-class whites. Malnutrition, given the records, is as hard to study as the general nutritional status of Navajos. Yet even by 1980 it was sadly clear that the Navajos were using a poorer nutritional quality of foods and that a return to more of their traditional foods and ways of preparing them would be beneficial, not only for health reasons but also to support self-sufficiency and cultural integrity. It should come as no surprise that the DPI's study of food sovereignty (discussed below), released in April 2014, reached similar conclusions.

The Twenty-First Century

There have been a number of developments in the last sixteen years that deserve discussion.[37] One is the burgeoning consumption of fast foods on the reservation, which, of course, coincided with the proliferation of fast-food franchises there.[38] Given numerous decades of work in Chinle, I decided it would be worthwhile to map out what I have been able to learn about the topic in this community and to include it in this book as appendix B.

Interest in native Navajo foods and transmission of the knowledge about them through the generations is alive and well today on the Navajo reservation. The tribal newspaper, the *Navajo Times*, prints many articles, often illustrated, on how to make various foods and on fairs and competitions. Another great resource is *Leading the Way: The Wisdom of the Navajo People*, a monthly magazine published in Gamerco, New Mexico, which frequently features illustrated stories on traditional food preparation and use. This magazine has included discussions of farming, tools, and all kinds of other topics relevant to those interested in native foods.

Cookbooks are available from all over the world, and many specialize in a single tradition or a single popular food item. Many cookbooks focus on Native American cuisine of the US Southwest and thus include the Navajos' neighbors, such as the Zuni and Hopi Pueblo Indians. See, for example, Cox and Jacobs (1991), Dahl (2006), Edaakie (1999), Fergusson (1945), Fischer and Fischer (1983), Franklin (1995, 2002), Hardwick (1993), Hesse (1998), Kavena (1980), Keegan (1987), Kuehlein, Calloway, and Harland (1979), Niethammer (1974, 1999, 2011), Noble, Lowell, and Cook (2013), Nusom (1999), Swentzell and Perea (2016), and Taylor (2007). Navajo cookbooks are available that have been assembled at different times for different reasons and with different goals in mind; see, for example, Office of Navajo Economic Opportunity (two undated works); Brzezinski (1993); McDonald (1965); Lynch, Lynch, and McCarty (1986); and US Department of Agriculture (2003).[39]

Professional journals and publications from academic and more popular presses identify current interests and trends. The botany of the Southwest, native plants with potential nutritional value or medicinal properties, and the field of ethnobotany are well represented in the literature, starting with Matthews (1886) and continuing with Wyman and Harris (1941, 1951), Pesman (1967), Harrington (1976), Mayes and Lacy (1989, 2012), Mayes and Rominger (1994), Dunmire and Tierney (1997), Tilford (1997), Nabhan (2002, 2016), Turner and Turner (2008), Salmón (2012), Nazarea (2014), Rogers (2015), Jordan (2015), and Middleton (2016), to cite just a few. Likewise, issues such as scarce resources and water rights are of growing concern (d'Elgin 2016).

The Rise of the Food Sovereignty Movement

Research on the Navajos' diet and health continues from many different perspectives (e.g., Kunitz 1983; Davies 2001). The Navajo Nation Council asked the DPI, located on Diné College's Tsaile campus, to research the food sovereignty movement, which started as a grassroots movement but had grown into an international one. The DPI was established by the Navajo Nation Council and the Diné College Board of Regents in 2005 as a research institute that could blend Western research with traditional Navajo values and natural, traditional, customary, and common laws and then provide technical assistance and advice to the policy makers by making presentations to the council. The DPI has addressed a number of topics to date, including leadership and development, Western methods of policy analysis, the brain drain on the reservation, the pros and cons of establishing a Walmart on the reservation, the establishment of a constitution, and the pursuit of various kinds of government reform. In June 2016 it began the Healthy Office Initiative to combat sedentary work environments.

The concept of food sovereignty was born in 1993 when an "international peasant movement" called La Via Campesina (2016) formed in order to address issues of concern to farmers and other rural and agricultural workers. La Via Campesina grew into a global movement of marginal and poor people to gain control of land, seeds, and the production of healthy food. La Via Campesina is now an international coalition and advocacy network that coordinates more than 150 million farmers, fishers, foresters, and agricultural workers on five continents and promotes family farm–based sustainable agriculture. The food sovereignty movement exists to address the indignities of the current global food system, in which small farmers around the world cannot earn a fair price for what they grow while more than 1 billion people go hungry every day.

Given the ongoing global struggles over the control of water, land, food, and livelihood, the food sovereignty movement "calls for policies that are ecologically, socially, economically, and culturally appropriate for their circumstances" (Grassroots International 2016). The food sovereignty movement promotes the recognition of climate change, environmental justice, biodiversity, and agroecology (indigenous knowledge-based farming systems) and is opposed to transnational corporations, GMOs, land grabs, the use of pesticides and other chemicals, and monocropping (the agricultural practice of growing a single crop year after year on the same land). It has attracted small farmers, fishers, indigenous peoples, consumers, environmentalists, and landless workers—those who are the most affected by poverty and global hunger. All seek to define their own labor, fishing, food, agricultural, and land policies.

Some sources say that the term *food sovereignty* was coined at the First World Food Summit in 1996 by La Via Campesina. In time the grassroots movement expanded to showcase the need for democratic food systems that include input from citizens as well as producers. The First International Forum for Food Sovereignty was held in Nyéléní, Mali, in 2007. Most people now use the definition of food sovereignty found in the declaration from that forum (US Food Sovereignty Alliance 2016):

> Food sovereignty is the right of peoples to healthy and culturally appropriate food produced through ecologically sound and sustainable methods, and their right to define their own food and agriculture systems. It puts the aspirations and needs of those who produce, distribute, and consume food at the heart of food systems and policies rather than the demands of markets and corporations.

Pedal and Plow (2016), defines food sovereignty as follows:

> [The] right of peoples and sovereign states to democratically determine their own food, agriculture, livestock, and fisheries systems and policies.
>
> In a nutshell, food sovereignty is the right of peoples, communities and countries to define their own policies regarding their seeds, agriculture, labor, food, and land. These policies must be appropriate to their unique ecological, social, economic, and cultural circumstances. Food sovereignty includes the true right to food and to produce food.

The goal is to incorporate the following six principles into national and international trade and agricultural policies so they become visible in local communities:

Food for people. The right to sufficient, healthy, and culturally appropriate food for all should be at the center of food, agricultural, livestock, and fisheries policies.

Value placed on food providers. All who grow, harvest, and process food must be valued, including women, family farmers, herders, fishers, forest dwellers, indigenous peoples, and agricultural, migrant, and fisheries workers.

Localized food systems. Food providers and consumers should be brought together for joint decisions on food issues that benefit and protect everyone.

Local control. The right of food providers to have control over their land, seeds, and water must be respected, and the privatization of natural resources must be rejected.

Sharing of knowledge and skills. Local knowledge and skills that have been passed down over generations for sustainable food production should be shared; technologies that contaminate and undermine local food systems, health, and well-being should be rejected.

Harmony with nature. Production and harvesting methods should maximize the contribution of ecosystems, avoid costly and toxic substances, and improve the resiliency of local food systems in the face of climate change.

Some people recognize a seventh principle:

Food as sacred. Food is a gift of life, not to be squandered or commodified. Everyone has a sacred responsibility to nurture healthy, interdependent relationships with the land, plants, and animals that provide us with food.

These principles make it clear that food sovereignty is a political concept and a social justice issue that reaches far beyond the narrow, now outdated term *food security*. The latter exists "when all people, at all times, have access to sufficient, safe and nutritious food to meet their dietary needs and food preferences for an active and healthy life" (Pedal and Plow 2016). Food security refers only to the availability of food and deals only with the protection and distribution of *existing* food systems. (See also Food Secure Canada 2016; Global Food Politics 2016.)

By 2008 some countries began to add food sovereignty to their constitutions or comparable laws; Ecuador was first in September 2008, and Venezuela, Mali, Bolivia, Nepal, and Senegal have followed. This action makes food sovereignty a basic human right. It prioritizes and protects nature and nonrenewable resources as well as the consumption of food produced within the country. It also bans or at least restricts GMOs and discourages monocropping. Knuth and Vidar (2011, 23) summarize this trend as follows:

3.3.1. Explicit and Direct Recognition of the Right to Food
A total of 23 constitutions recognize the right to food explicitly as a

human right. Of these, nine countries recognize the right as a separate and stand-alone right: Bolivia (art. 16), Brazil (art. 6), Ecuador (art. 13), Guyana (art. 40), Haiti (art. 22), Kenya (art. 43), and South Africa (art. 27.1). The Interim Constitution of Nepal recognizes an individual right to food sovereignty (art. 18.3), and Nicaragua (art. 63) provides for the right of every person to be free from hunger.

Ten constitutions recognize the right to food of a specific segment of the population: Brazil (art. 227), Colombia (art. 44), Cuba (art. 9), Guatemala (art. 51), Honduras (art. 123), Mexico (art. 4), Panama (art. 52), Paraguay (art. 54), and South Africa (art. 28.1.c)) have provisions regarding the right to food of children; Costa Rica (art. 82) protects the right to food of indigenous children; while South Africa (art. 35.2.e) also specifies the right to food of prisoners and detainees.

An additional five countries recognize the right to food explicitly as part of a human right to an adequate standard of living, quality of life, or development: Belarus (art. 21.), the Congo (art. 34.1), Malawi (art. 30.2), Moldova (art. 47.1), and Ukraine (art. 48); while the right to food is explicitly recognized in Brazil (art. 7.4) and in Suriname (art. 24) as part of the right to work.

Food Sovereignty Trends on the Navajo Reservation

In the past decade in particular, studies of the environment and reservation lands have become increasingly focused on taking care of Mother Earth, documenting the destruction caused by coal, uranium, and other kinds of mining (both strip and open pit), as well as other kinds of commercial developments.[40] While environmentalists exist on the Navajo reservation (e.g., Diné Care Inc.), to date their numbers are not large, nor is their organization very obvious. A review of the current publications concerned with Navajo culture show public interest in studies about the following: food, identity, protection of the land, worldviews rooted in the land, environmental knowledge, critical land-use issues, water rights, ways of knowing, land disputes, relocation, removal, partitioned lands, encroachment by Western values, devastating mineral extraction, the Black Mesa region, contested cultural landscapes, the intimate connection to land, tribal conservation, and food traditions. For those interested in native foods, researching the connections between food and identity remains of major interest (Salmón 2012). Another idea that is now being considered by some Southwestern groups, such as the Hopis, is developing tourism through agricultural tours (Fonseca 2011).

On the Navajo reservation, interest in traditional foods is a focus of the Miss Navajo competition, in which the contestants have to butcher a sheep within an hour and, as of 2017, prepare some of the meat, and both describe (in Navajo) the history of Navajo traditional foods and then make one of them. The ideas for the changes came from the outgoing 2016 Miss Navajo, Ronda Joe. Various other fairs around the reservation, however, still have frybread contests for both women and men, and at the annual Utah Navajo Fair there is a chili cook-off. The *Navajo Times* covers these events, discussing the competitions, winners, and techniques. It also occasionally features other traditional foods such as pinyon nuts and pinyon nut picking (Yurth 2012; Beyal 2013) and the making of *ntsidigo'í* (kneel-down bread) (Allen 2012) and *'alkaan* (corn cake for the Girls' Puberty Ceremony) (Jimmy 2013).[41]

The Diné Policy Institute's Food Sovereignty Project

In 2011 the issue of food sovereignty gained attention and importance, including coverage by the *Navajo Times*, when the DPI began to study and analyze the subject with the goal of making recommendations to the Navajo Nation Council. Although the addition of this area to DPI's agenda was briefly mentioned at the fall 2011 Navajo Studies meeting in Crownpoint, New Mexico, I learned more about the project the following year through a PowerPoint presentation by Dana Eldridge (2012), then a DPI research assistant.[42] This presentation made it clear that the goals of the project were to examine the effects of modern food production on the environment, the economy, health, and Navajo culture; to determine where the Navajo originally obtained their food and how that differs from today; and what role colonization and food play in current health, social, and economic issues. In time a broader framework was added to the project that incorporated the global concepts of food insecurity and food deserts as appropriate descriptors of the reservation—a place in the industrialized world where healthy, affordable food is difficult to obtain. Worldwide food deserts are typical of low socioeconomic minority communities with various diet-related health problems.

Eldridge's (2012) holistic analysis began with the fact that plants are grounded in the Navajo creation stories and emerged in the Fourth World (the present world), where the Navajos' Fundamental Law was also established (Austin 2009). The Holy People divided plants into five groups: poisonous, ceremonial, medicinal, "different animals' vegetations," and "no use plants," but one of Eldridge's (2012) illustrations shows the five as poisonous, ceremonial, medicinal, animals' natural food, and food for humans. Plants, like animals and humans, have minds, bodies, spirits, and souls, and thus they are life forms that can feel and hear and that have purposes; one has to learn about them, however, because some are dangerous. At the Emergence, four main plants were noted: corn, beans, squash, and tobacco. Eldridge then presented a list in Navajo of "all of the corn-based foods."[43]

More extensive work with Eldridge was possible after her presentation at the Food and Wellness Policy Summit in Window Rock on June 13, 2013. Our conversations (especially on June 18) answered some of my questions about her study, and I share what I learned with her permission.[44] The Diné Food Sovereignty Initiative was funded by a Native Agriculture and Food System Initiative grant through the First Nations Development Institute with support from the W. K. Kellogg Foundation. DPI and the Land Grant Office of Diné College were working to address "the lack of access to healthy, affordable, and traditional foods in the region directly around Diné College and [to] revitalize traditional food systems." Dana told me that the project began in 2011 with a literature review and got a $45,000 grant in June 2012 from a place in Longmont, Colorado, that allowed interns to conduct interviews. The 2011 literature review convinced Eldridge that the problems really started when outsiders (Spanish, Anglos, and others) came onto the reservation. After the scorched earth policy (the destruction of Navajo resources by the US military) and the incarceration at Fort Sumner, the Navajos really became dependent.

Interns began conducting interviews in the summer of 2012, using the "First Nations Food Tool," a food sovereignty assessment tool, which they modified for their own use.[45] The interviews were conducted at fairs and in Bashas' supermarket parking lots in five communities: Chinle, Tsaile, Many Farms, Round Rock, and Lukachukai. The interns held meetings with growers and used focus groups to learn why people were or were not farming, what barriers they faced, and what they thought should be done about the issues. The interns presented data in each of the communities and worked with an advisory board that consisted of two cultural specialists from the

Diné College faculty—Avery Denny (also a Nightway singer) and Wilson Aronilith—and others.

In June 2013 the interns compiled their results; they had conducted 200 consumer surveys and 20 in-depth surveys (10 more were lost because of a computer problem). The data collected were organized by group. The project, which was to end in June 2013, was extended to the end of the summer. One goal, to start a farmers' market in Tsaile, had already been accomplished in the fall of 2012.

By June 2013 Dana's group had identified the Bureau of Indian Affairs (BIA) land permit system of the 1930s as a major problem but had also expanded its horizons to understand that the Navajo Nation's drought cycles were part of global cycles and that studies elsewhere might be relevant to their own work (such as a study of elephants by Allan Savoy in South Africa). Dana also said that talking to livestock owners and farmers was extremely important.

The political situation in the Navajo Nation proved to be a stumbling block, because DPI, the diabetes research group, and Dana's research group could never get admitted to council meetings, despite repeated requests, while big corporations and beverage industries were admitted without any problem. A group of women, fed up with the Navajo Nation Council for doing nothing about diabetes, suggested a tax on junk food to get their attention. It failed, but at least the issue was put on the table and showed that grassroots efforts can make things happen. Dana hoped to educate the council delegates as well as others by starting food system awareness conferences. She said that people need to understand the connection between colonization and Western illnesses and begin to decolonize the food system. She mentioned the work of Milburn (2004) on indigenous nutrition and the fact that today one in three Navajos on the reservation has diabetes.

Dana said that clearly the overarching issue is global problems and food deserts, of which the Navajo reservation is one. She showed me a new Power-Point presentation, which was very inclusive and almost overwhelming, given its identification of "everything that needs to be done, and soon." DPI had already determined that the Navajo Nation's government is complacent and that the system is not conducive to establishing food sovereignty. Dana hoped that people would continue to push for government decentralization and reform. She was also studying how to bring about change. One issue was trying to get electronic benefit transfer cards and WIC program benefits accepted at farmers' markets; her group planned to work in policy development and to meet with chapters, grazing committees, and other local groups.

Dana wanted to see schools, hospitals, prisons, nursing homes, hotels, and casinos committed to serving healthy traditional foods. Among the goals was to get a commitment from the Navajo Nation to support healthy and traditional foods. She told me she wanted to use the Lummi Nation model and build in Navajo food exclusivity clauses. When her group did public presentations, the members made mutton tamales from white Navajo corn and served all Navajo foods. She knew that they needed to raise public awareness, and remembering that knowledge is power, rebuild families and communities by working through the peacemaker courts and land offices. They needed to use an intergenerational approach to regain control over their own food. Dana said she was very aware that public education is crucial to establish community-based programs and to legitimize and empower local people.

The group was working with others studying dry farming and encouraged people to return to small-scale farming rather than engaging in agribusiness with tractors. The group's goals were to get people to work with nature, restore wild lands, and work toward finding a balance between cultivated lands currently under agricultural use and wild lands. The group also wanted to work with local communities and network with other indigenous peoples, sharing models; success stories (such as the Taos County Economic Development Corporation's mobile livestock slaughter unit); water catchment, harvesting, and conservation techniques; ideas being generated by the Native Food Systems Resource Center (2012, 2016); and other data. The idea was to develop standards rather than regulations, since the word *regulations* seemed to suggest rules and colonialism. The group wanted to turn around attitudes on the reservation so that farming would be seen as a good thing again instead of something to be feared. Other goals of the group were the following: addressing the liability problem, given the current litigious and individual capital market system; encouraging the Navajo Nation to subsidize Navajo produce; banning GMOs from Monsanto; and assisting the Navajo Nation in developing its own food safety standards and tests to include traditional foods and to protect seeds.

Dana also wanted to do public outreach, to educate all Navajos about the food systems on the reservation. It was already clear to her that a hands-on approach would be most beneficial and that the land permit system was one of the biggest underlying causes of the current mess. Water rights were also becoming a global issue. She wanted to have a conference on native seeds and set up a planning conference for seed searches and exchanges. She also wanted to make policy recommendations for both the Navajo Nation and the Indian Health Service. She saw a need to develop a guide for nongovernmental organizations and communities that would emphasize culture and tie Navajo identity to traditional knowledge, concepts, and values and empower the people to have and use this knowledge base. The emphasis needs to be on native seeds and indigenous foods, with environmentally sustainable farming despite desertification. As of June 18, 2013, Dana's advisory group had expanded to include Robert Johnson, then from the Navajo Nation Museum, Sheila Goldtooth from Round Rock, and Ida Yazzie and Roy Kady from Chinle.

After going through the new PowerPoint presentation and discussing it with me, Dana willingly shared several specific findings from some of the interviews.[46] Very few participants mentioned blue cornmeal mush, squash, or melons as foods they ate today, and it was clear that by that time, both fruits and vegetables were being eaten less than once a day. In today's world, Eldridge identified fried potatoes, frybread, tortillas, sugary drinks, and processed meats as the most frequently consumed foods, and tortillas or frybread as the "only traditional food" consumed on a daily basis. She said that even sheep are declining in Navajo eating patterns in the twenty-first century.

Today on the reservation, where most food is now purchased rather than made, there continues to be limited access to stores. The general trend has been a decline of precontact foods and an increase of nonnative foods. Today's Navajo diet is like the diet of the rest of the United States, with soda and other sweetened drinks, processed meats, and bread being the most common items consumed. Also like elsewhere, on the reservation the health issues on the rise are obesity, heart disease, hypertension, some cancers, and the ever increasing rate of diabetes. The Navajos' loss of food sovereignty and concurrent dietary changes, Dana explained, were fostered by American interventions and policies, forced removal, livestock reduction, boarding schools, relocation, food distribution programs, and the lifestyle changes inherent in the shift from a subsistence focus to a wage-based economy.

In her Navajo Studies Conference PowerPoint presentation, Eldridge (2012) also considered food as medicine. For instance, the traditional Navajo diet included juniper ash, which is high in calcium (one teaspoon of ash has as much calcium as one cup of cow's milk), as well as organ meats and native corn, which is high in protein. The American diet now consumed by the Navajos, she noted, consists of dairy products, processed meat, popular cuts of beef, and commercial corn, which is high in starch and sugar. Food is being emphasized now in mental health work, gardening and farming in prisons and among troubled youth is having positive results, and studies show that community-based agriculture keeps families and communities together. Switching to a list of corn and GMOs, Dana asked, "What's sacred anymore?" Money is the bottom line, with *bigger* and *faster* being pushed and with food production characterized by herbicides and pesticides, GMOs with gene patents, monocropping, industrial food complexes with factory farms, processed food, and a few food companies controlling most of the food. After briefly mentioning NAPI, environmental effects, and the issues of race, class, and labor, Eldridge ended with two definitions of food sovereignty and the question, "Now what?" She quoted the renowned Native American activist Winona LaDuke, who said that the recovery of a people is tied to the restoration of traditional foods.

Articles in both the *Navajo Times* and *Leading the Way* confirm Eldridge's statement that an interest in relearning food traditions and growing one's own food is increasing in many areas and many contexts on the reservation. A concurrent political development also attracted attention in the spring and summer of 2013. Navajo Nation President Ben Shelly wanted to introduce ideas about desert farming gathered on a trip that he and his wife had made to Israel in December 2012. Shelly hosted a two-day conference (April 9–10, 2013) for farmers in Shiprock, New Mexico, saying in the *Navajo Times* that Navajo lands can "'bloom' like Israeli deserts" (Bitsoi 2013d, 2013e). Eldridge (2013) responded with a letter to the editor calling for the use of homegrown expertise instead and announcing that the DPI initiative she represented was sponsoring a free Spring Planting Conference at Diné College on April 22–23, 2013. In the same issue of the paper Allen (2013c) covered a workshop in Tuba City, Arizona, "Planting Seeds for Healthier Communities," which was designed to help the Navajos grow their own fruits and vegetables. Among the sponsors of this event was the Navajo Nation Department of Agriculture.

Clearly the *Navajo Times* is following environmental news now, covering Earth Day and recycling events in several communities as well as reporting on the long-term drought that must be confronted (Bitsoi 2013b). As the summer of 2013 progressed, the coverage of relevant issues continued. Several reports (Allen 2013a, 2013b; Ramirez 2013a, 2013b; Bitsoi 2014a–f) focused on the attempt by the seventy-member Diné Community Advocacy Alliance (DCAA) to win support for a 2 percent tax on all junk food sold on the reservation; an elimination of the 5 percent sales tax on fresh vegetables and fruits, seeds, nuts, and water; and the use of the resulting revenues for wellness projects. As of December 31, 2014, the sales tax on fresh vegetables and fruits—which had gone into effect in October despite President Shelley's veto—was eliminated. The companion Healthy Diné Nation Act of 2014, which imposes a 2 percent sales tax on junk food (food with minimal or no nutritional value), was presented to the Navajo Nation Council *four* times before it was passed on November 14 by a vote of 10 to 4 during a special two-day session (Bitsoi 2014c).

Earlier attempts had failed for a variety of reasons, despite support by the Navajo pro golfer Notah Begay III. In April 2014 the council had tried but failed to override President Shelly's veto of the bill. As of August 7 the proposed act was still awaiting consideration by the Law and Order Committee (Bitsoi 2014d). After the DCAA put an increased effort into educating the council about the diabetes epidemic on the reservation, the necessity to combat it and the obesity epidemic, and other findings of the DPI's Food Sovereignty Initiative, the Healthy Diné Act was finally passed, signed into law by President Shelly on November 21, 2014, and implemented on April 1, 2015. The revenues collected by taxing junk food were to be deposited into the Community Wellness Development Projects Fund, administered by the Division of Community Development, to promote healthy living and establish wellness projects at the local level.

A major article by Bitsoi (2013c) provided detailed coverage of the June 13, 2013, Food and Wellness Policy Summit in Window Rock (see also Bowman 2013). In another article, Bitsoi (2013a) discussed GMOs, the need to plant heirloom seeds, and the need to work with a group called Native Seeds/SEARCH. Other related coverage included updates (Landry 2013) about congressional work on various versions of the US Farm Bill, which called for the reduction of $4 billion in the Supplemental Nutrition Assistance Program

(SNAP). Congress was supposed to pass the Farm Bill by September 30 but did not do so until late February 2014—and then it cut $8 billion from food assistance programs.

Research projects and discussions continue in the newspaper about obesity, diabetes, junk food, food insecurity, food deserts, food hunger among children and the elderly, and advice on how to return to a healthy diet. Yurth (2014b), covering the community of Fruitland, reported that the agricultural census for 2012 showed that farms were growing on the reservation, although they were getting slightly smaller and the farmers were aging. Other articles report on farmers' markets, hoop houses and gardens, crop rotation, raised beds, drip agriculture, natural pesticides, composting, rainwater harvesting, and other techniques to improve individual and community farming. It is hoped that the talking and reporting will lead to productive actions in the future.

In sum, the ongoing reports and presentations that Eldridge and her team gave on the Diné Food Sovereignty Initiative, along with the final report (DPI 2014), provide a new framework for ongoing food problems and stress the need for the Navajos to return to localized agricultural and livestock-rearing practices in order to reclaim food sovereignty and address serious health, nutrition, and economic problems. The project used many different perspectives, including a historical review of Navajo food systems, and it related the food problems of the Navajo Nation to larger global issues such as food deserts, where the lack of access to nutritious food pushes people into buying unhealthy foods, which then lead to obesity, diabetes, and other problems.

The Navajo Nation, despite its beginnings and its sovereignty, no longer has a self-sufficient food system. Using community-based and grant-supported participatory research, Dana Eldridge and her team acquired input from more than 200 people in five communities. Their study shows how the concept of k'é teaches kinship and reciprocity among humans, food, plants, and animals.[47] Their strategies and recommendations (DPI 2014, 65–83) are numerous. To name just a few: the creation of new access points for traditional and healthy foods, such as farmers' markets and mobile grocery stores; community-supported agriculture; public education; partnerships with local institutions to purchase locally produced food; food standards; and the reform of land policies (i.e., the assertion of control over land from the BIA and the centralized Window Rock government). The Navajo Nation Department of Agriculture (NNDA) was put in charge of implementing the recommendations. The report did not comment on the draft of a rangeland improvement act newly proposed by the NNDA (Yurth 2014a, 2014c).

2 | Subsistence Practices in Tall Woman's Family

BEFORE I PRESENT Tall Woman's recipes, some other particulars need to be discussed: what people ate; what equipment, if any, was needed for finding, growing, and processing food; and what methods were commonly used for preparing, eating, and storing various foods. What the Navajos ate depended on when and where they lived.

Subsistence through Foraging

In earlier times the Navajos ate everything they could find, and almost all of them spent much of their time working and helping to find food. Men and some boys went on extended hunting trips, often in the fall when the animals were fat, and the boys left at home trapped gophers and wood rats, among other things. Women and girls gathered wild plants—seeds, roots, bulbs, greens, fruits, and berries—and prepared them to eat and, when appropriate, for drinking, chewing, and smoking.

The Navajos ate wild turkeys, ducks, chickens, doves, prairie dogs, gophers, weasels, badgers, porcupines, chipmunks, jackrabbits and other rabbits, squirrels, beavers, skunks, otters, field rats, locusts or cicadas (*wóóneeshch'įįdii*), small yellow birds (*'ayááshiłtsoii*), other small birds, and, according to Tall Woman's parents, dogs and rats during the incarceration at Fort Sumner.[1] They also ate antelope, deer, elk, buffalo, horses, mules, burros, and donkeys; Tall Woman said donkeys had white meat that looked and tasted like pork. Some people say they also ate wildcats, mountain lions, mountain sheep, geese, groundhogs, and wolves, but others disagree. Tall Woman said that after the Fort Sumner incarceration until her children were small, Navajos did not eat dogs, coyotes, bears, fish or any other water dweller, or any crawling things like turtles, snakes, lizards, or frogs (which were seen as bringing rain). They also did not eat crows, buzzards, or eagles. In addition, certain birds and animal parts were used only ceremonially or for medicine. For example, bluebirds were gathered only for ceremonial use; a skunk's gall bladder was used to treat coughs, sore throats, and sores; and beaver skin was used to make the hair tie used in the Kinaaldá, or Girls' Puberty Ceremony.

Women and girls mainly used their hands to gather wild plants, seeds, and pollen; dig roots and bulbs; and collect greens, fruits, and berries. Tall Woman said that she always took plenty of sacks—burlap, gunny, or other kinds—and whatever else might be necessary, such as sticks, shovels, wooden tongs, and sometimes gloves with her when she went out looking for food, because she never knew what she might see or find. She went on foot or on horseback when she went alone, but when the children were with her she took the wagon. Her favorite riding horse was a bay-colored one named Jaa'i, for its big ears. For long trips she rode with a saddle, saddle blanket, and bridle; otherwise she might ride bareback.

In earlier times they often took a donkey along to use as a pack animal. And if they were going to places where rain had made the berries and other foods plentiful, they'd take sheepskins to sleep on overnight. They might be gone for three or four days gathering foods. If they were going to pick pinyon nuts for several days, Tall Woman might build a brush shelter for them to use and take along a tarp or an old blanket to spread on the ground where they were picking. Sometimes when wild foods were on the ground or fell on the ground, she would hit them with a stick before brushing them off. For prickly pear cactus fruit, she removed it with tongs and then used a brush she made from a plant with soft leaves that she bound together on-site for that purpose.

It was during these trips that Tall Woman taught her children where to look for clay used with certain wild plants and how to gather foods and plants for other reasons. Her daughter Augusta said the following about Tall Woman:

She knew what plants could be used for medicines for yourself, for healing illnesses, sores, cuts, stomachaches, headaches, or other things you might suffer from. She also knew which plants the medicine people gathered to use in the curing ceremonies. She taught us which ones were just ordinary weeds, which grasses could be used in bundles to make hairbrushes or the brushes for the grinding stones; which wild grasses had seeds you could eat raw, or grind into flour for bread or mush, or use to flavor soups or other dishes, which plants to use to keep snakes and bugs away, which ones helped in dyeing wool different colors. She showed us stones that might work as grinding stones, but those weren't very common. Of course, there were some wild plants and fruits and berries that we could eat and like her own Mother and other women, she passed that knowledge along to us as her children. She taught us about some of those wild foods, like *chiiłchin*, *'ostse'*, *tł'ohdeeí*, prickly pear fruit, peaches in the canyon, pinyons, wild carrots, wild onions, wild potatoes, wild spinach, wild celery, yucca fruit, the plants you could use for making tea, and other things, like *nímasii dleesh* [light-colored clay used as a sweetener], that you needed to use when fixing certain kinds of berries. She knew where to find them, what they looked like at different times of year, when they'd be ripe, how to prepare them by using the grinding stones and other things, and what you needed to do to store them and save them for later use.

According to Tall Woman, women didn't usually go hunting, even for small animals. If Tall Woman came across a porcupine or a badger while she was out gathering, or she came near to its hole or another place where it lived, she'd have whoever was with her chase it away or else corner it, catch it, and kill it. She always had others do that, though; she would not do it herself. She usually said to the small animals she saw, "I know you are there, and I will not harm you. Don't harm me or hurt me, either. I'm not here to hurt you." When she got home, she would tell others about any tracks she had seen. But if she was out gathering by herself, she never captured or killed an animal.

Seya was the main hunter in the family; Tall Woman's father, Hastiin Delawoshí (Man Who Shouts), was Seya's main teacher about those things. Hunting deer and other animals has to be done the right way; it's surrounded by a lot of rules and traditions, and the hunters must have a ceremony before they start. The food they take with them and even the butchering has to be done a certain way. Howard, Seya's brother, went with Seya to keep him company, but because he had a bad eye he didn't hunt very much. Later Seya taught his nephew Cecil Jr. (a.k.a. Dino, one of Augusta's sons) to hunt, and now he's the main hunter in the family.[2]

The tools and practices involved with hunting varied with the prey, and people always used as much of the animal as possible after it was captured. Hunting was supposed to be respectful and often involved songs and prayers, other ceremonial practices, tracking, and even disguises and decoys. A club was necessary to hunt prairie dogs and sticks, stones, special clubs, or even slingshots for rabbits; Navajo hunters also used bows and arrows (originally double-curved bows and stone arrowheads), rocks, knives, and other methods. For example, prairie dogs were often captured by pouring water down their holes. Men and boys might push a stick down a rabbit hole and twist it, hoping to catch the animal's fur in it.

The women were in charge of any meat the men and boys brought home; if the meat wasn't going to be eaten right away, the women usually made jerky (cut it into very thin slices and hung it up to dry) as a way to preserve it. Different ways of preparing meat are discussed later, but they varied according to the animal. For an example, if a porcupine was caught and killed with a slingshot, the whole animal was skinned with a knife to remove the quills and the hair. The animal's insides were cleaned out, and then the animal was cooked in a hole dug in the ground. A similar procedure was used with a prairie dog: the entrails were removed, salt was sprinkled on the inside, and the animal was closed up, thrown on the fire, and covered with embers to cook. The hair was removed with a knife just before the meat was eaten. Some women also fried bits of meat in a pot. Besides eating the meat of the animal, people used the skin, fur, teeth, claws, sinew, bones, feathers, gall bladder, and other parts of specific animals for various purposes.

Subsistence through Farming

In time the Navajos added farming to their ways of procuring food. This was true in Tall Woman's life, and as her story (Mitchell 2001) makes clear, farmwork consumed a big part of her days. After the incarceration at Fort Sumner some seeds and some basic farm tools initially came from the US government. However, seeds were undoubtedly also available from the Navajos who did not go on the Long Walk, as well as from caches that people hid before being rounded up and then retrieved upon their return. In addition, trading was already ongoing with the Hopis and other Pueblo groups, and it seems reasonable to think that this trading might have included seeds as well as other items.

Livestock

The Mitchells did not have a lot of farm animals, as some of their neighbors did. For instance, they never raised cows, pigs, or chickens (although some of their children did later raise chickens). Frank always said cows were too much work, even though Uncle John Mitchell had them and kept them up on the mesa. Now people pay a fee to have their cows kept in Colorado. Mary Alice Begay's father's oldest brother had pigs. Old man John Gorman down the road and his wife, Ruth, had lots of animals, a big farm, and a nice wagon. He had everything imaginable, including ducks, geese, turkeys, bees, fruit trees, watermelons, corn, squash, and plenty of chickens. Those animals could be heard calling at night, especially the sheep, goats, cows, horses, and donkeys.[3] He was a cousin of Nelson Gorman's; they were all from the Kiyaa'áanii clan (Towering House People), and were Presbyterian, but despite the Protestant-Catholic hostility at the time, they were nice to Catholics.[4] When Ruth and Augusta would come home from Myrtle Begay's (Mary Alice's mother's) place, they would go to old man Gorman's to buy eggs for fifty cents a dozen.[5] He'd tell them to come in and eat, and usually he'd give them a bowl of soup made from a sheep leg cut from the second joint, boiled with corn, and served with a tortilla. When his wife went to the hospital, he stopped eating unless he had company, so people always tried to stop by to encourage him to eat.

Over the years the Mitchells mainly had horses to use in farming and also for riding, as well as sheep and occasionally one or more goats. Sheep (fig. 1) and goats provided meat, milk, wool, skin, and a variety of body parts used for tools. Given the Navajo premise that "sheep is life," one's well-being was in part assessed by the size and condition of one's flock. Frank always taught his children that they had to take care of any animals they had and understand them. They needed to learn all the songs that went with them. All

FIGURE 1. Sheep enjoying watermelon rind, May 2015. Photo by Cecilia Sandoval.

animals have to have food and water, all of them have names given to them by the Holy People, and all of them must be treated with respect.[6]

SHEEP AND GOATS

Sheep (*dibé*) and goats (*tł'ízí*) were taken out at dawn so they could eat; on the way back they stopped at ponds, creeks, washes, dams, or any other place they could drink. In the early days there were no windmills. The sheep just lay in the shade or bushes; they were not put in a corral. Even the goats learned to stay like that.

When the ewes or nanny goats were being milked for human use, their lambs or kids were taken away at night to a separate place so that the mothers could be milked in the morning. The other method that Tall Woman's family used to prevent the baby animals from nursing was to make a paste of *chąą'* (feces) by mashing it up and mixing it with water. This was then smeared on the mothers' teats and udders in the evening. In the morning, a rag and warm water were used to wash the feces off the udders and teats, and then the mothers were milked. Milking was done every day. For some time Tall Woman would send both Ruth and Augusta over to Myrtle Begay's place to get goat milk; Myrtle's husband worked in Barstow, but Myrtle was usually home. Augusta was already out of high school by then; she and Ruth would stop by to see *Cheii* (maternal grandfather) John Gorman on their way back. He would always boil the hoof part of a sheep leg with roasted corn and make *neeshjízhii* (a stew with dried steamed corn) for them.

After Augusta was married and had several children, her brother Seya gave Tall Woman a beautiful milking goat; she had to be milked twice a day because her udders were huge and would become very heavy (fig. 2). Finally that goat became sick; one of her legs swelled up, and we learned that she had been bitten by a snake. We don't know what kind it was, but Tall Woman called it *diyóósh* (bull snake) because it always brought the wind, and that's how it got its name. It could be identified by the black zigzags on its back. The goat was given a shot, and a year later the veterinarian said the family could start drinking her milk again. Later a medicine man who disagreed with the animal doctor attributed many of Tall Woman's sicknesses to the milk from that goat even after it had gotten well. One time a hand trembler (Navajo diagnostician) said that a snake had caused Tall Woman to get sick and that she had gotten the sickness from that goat's milk. Everybody was drinking that milk, however, and nobody else got sick. An herbalist cured Tall Woman that time, and eventually Frank sold the goat.

In Tall Woman's time, people put diapers on the rams and the billy goats from mid- to late summer to prevent them from mating; then in the fall they would take the diapers off so the animals could start breeding. Some people still do this; others just keep the males penned up away from the females. A man around Cottonwood, Arizona, near Red Rock keeps people's rams for them in a huge fenced area where he feeds and waters them and lets them graze. He gets paid per animal. That was being done in the 1940s and maybe even earlier. People who had more than 100 ewes would need only three rams, so it was fairly easy to keep them separate until the right time. Different people would do that as their job. Augusta said she used the same man her mother did, near Red Rock, for two to four years, paying him ten dollars a month per ram. Lambs were always born in May, so the rams would be pastured with one of these people for July, August, and September. Thus, she would pay thirty dollars to

FIGURE 2. Geneva, Mae, and Josephine Mitchell milking a goat, July 1964. Photo by author.

pasture one ram for three months. Now she just diapers her (one) ram, because she doesn't have very many sheep anymore. Tall Woman tried to teach her children how to use the moon, stars, and the constellations to figure out when the lambs would be born, but none of them ever learned how to do that.

Tall Woman would start checking the ewes' udders and stomachs to know when they would lamb. She used to be a midwife so she knew that if the udders were hard, lambing would begin soon. She also knew whether the head of the lamb fetus was facing the mother's tail, as it should be. She would check every night, with a lantern or a flashlight, and when it was close to the time of birth she would check three or four times a night. She always had a separate place for the pregnant ewes and the new mothers and babies, just like a maternity ward. She said to leave them alone after they were born unless the mother rejected the baby. Then she would ask one of her sons to hold the mother still, get a cloth and pick the baby up with that, and let the mother sniff its head. She also would rub the baby on the mother's back end or in the placenta and then put it back up to the mother's face again. That's the way the mother learned that the baby was really hers.

Sometimes if the mother doesn't have enough room or has multiple births and not enough milk, she will crush her babies. Tall Woman went out every few hours to check on things. If a lamb was orphaned, she'd bring it into the hogan and put it by the fire. She considered sheep "soul food." She would give that orphan milk out of a Coke bottle; I think these were the first bottles at the trading post. She would also buy nipples when they finally started selling them, but before that she would just take a glove finger, fill it with milk from a sheep or a goat, and let the baby suck from that.

Sheep, of course, have to be sheared, and in the old days they had no tools for that. Tall Woman said that her great-grandmother and great-grandfather used a sharpened shoulder-blade bone, or scapula, from a sheep or a cow to remove the wool. Later they used sharp pieces of tin from tin cans. When knives became available, they used those, and finally they shifted to shearing scissors or clippers, which were available from the trading posts by the early 1940s or even the 1930s in a few places. When Augusta took home economics in school, her Navajo teacher taught them how to sew, weave, and shear. Tall Woman always used sharp, small scissors, almost like surgical ones, to shear around the eyes and faces of the sheep.

HORSES

Tall Woman always said that taking care of horses (łįį́) was a man's job, unless the men were away for wage work or traveling for some other reason and the girls were old enough. Men and boys usually took care not only of the horses but also of the cows and donkeys, if a family had those animals. Although everybody learned how to ride, usually bareback, it was boys who were supposed to know how to harness the horses to the wagons, plows, or other farm equipment. In Tall Woman's family, however, everybody learned how to do those things, just as everyone learned how to hoe, weed, and plant. Tall Woman told her children to learn the story of the horse from the Horse Songs in the Blessingway and to learn to sing those songs. Augusta was the only one who tried, but she never could learn them. Tall Woman also taught her children to talk to their horses; the horses understand people, and people need to understand them. Do not mistreat them; take care of them. Frank said people should have a lot of horses so they can be rotated for the various jobs, like traveling, pulling the wagon (fig. 3), helping with

FIGURE 3. Horse and wagon transportation common in an earlier time, June 1963. Photo by author.

farming by pulling the plow or the baler, or just being ridden to go check on the livestock.

Frank kept the horses up in the Black Mountain area, which had much more vegetation than around Chinle, for most of June and into the summer, and he would travel around to check on them. Later, when it was time for Enemyway ceremonies, he would bring them back down and keep then near home so people could borrow them. Of course, the horses they used with the wagon were kept around all the time. Frank worked as a judge, and while he was traveling around for this, he would always look to see where the winter feeding places might be the best for the horses.

Tall Woman always rode a horse she called Jaa'i; it had great big ears and was a bay color (łíí łchí'í). She used the round female saddle, not the western saddle used by men, along with a saddle blanket and a bridle. She rode her horse all over until she got much older, and then she just hitched up the wagon to go places. When she rode that horse in her younger years, she was really tall; that's why she got the name Tall Woman.

The family grew its own alfalfa hay, and when it was time for the first cutting, the horses were brought back home. They stayed in the field to the east of the hogan. That field belonged to Ruth's first husband, John Shirley. It was fenced at one time, but the flood of 1964, which washed out the bridge in Chinle and killed some people driving across it, took out a lot of the fences. Before then, everything had been fenced. The hay was kept in front of Ruth's house in an old shack, which was divided down the middle so that Frank could put the feed hay on one side and store hay and corn on the other side, where the horses didn't eat. The stored corn husks were covered with tarps or other materials. The family kept a big pile of corn in there, and Tall Woman would often go out in the morning, take the husks off, separate the ears into good and bad corn, and spread the husks out to dry (fig. 4). The bad corn went into a sack to be hauled in the wagon to the grinder on Presbyterian Hill, to be ground into winter feed for the horses and stored in sacks. The good corn was ground by hand by the women and girls for food.

Even though Tall Woman knew a lot about herbs and treating illnesses,

FIGURE 4. Tall Woman sorting corn, June 1969. Photo by author.

she did not nurse any newborns for horses or try to heal those that were sick. However, some women who had that knowledge did so. After Frank brought the horses down from the Black Mountain area for the summer, he would drive them over toward Chinle and put them in the field near Uncle John's place; there, a road went back to the wash; it was cleared out all the way to the Canyon de Chelly Wash.

Although Frank had made a big pond for the horses and other animals down in the wash area toward the west, in the late 1940s or early 1950s, after the government had put up the windmills and they were working, the tribe started putting in shallow wells. Howard and other family members worked on those projects. The shallow wells were put in not only for the horses and other live-stock but also for people, so they would have good clean water to drink. There were six wells in the area, and Augusta used to water the horses at three of them frequently. Now a lot of those places are dried up. The Mitchells had other places they got water from, too, besides those shallow wells and the windmills. They went to the Franciscan mission, Garcia's Trading Post, or to the Chinle Boarding School in the wagon with containers to get water from the faucets.

Butchering

Part of taking care of livestock involved knowing how to butcher. Sheep and horses were butchered at home, and those who had pigs or cows also butch-ered them at home.

BUTCHERING SHEEP

There are many accounts detailing how to butcher a sheep (fig. 5), a practice that is considered part of Navajo culture and is still required of Miss Navajo contestants.[7] The account below came directly from Tall Woman, whom I saw butcher sheep many times. The sheep was always needed for food when it was butchered, perhaps because of company, a ceremony, a celebration of something, or just because people were "hungry for mutton." Everybody always said that sheep and goats are butchered the same way and that the animal chosen should be fat. People now know that the internal organs are very high in protein, minerals, and fat; the Navajos eat almost every part of the sheep, except maybe the hooves and the skin.

FIGURE 5. Isabelle Deschine and Mae Mitchell butchering a sheep, June 1963. Photo by author.

Here is Tall Woman's description of how to butcher a sheep:

It usually takes two people working together to butcher a sheep; the same is true for a cow, but that is much more work. I never butchered a horse by myself, but I helped Frank and others do that. We did eat horsemeat, and some used it as a remedy for coughing. When you are going to butcher, gather everything you will need, like a very sharp knife, a rope, one or more dishpans, and maybe some rags. Then choose the animal; you check how fat the sheep are by feeling under the breastbone. After you pick out a fat animal, keep it quiet; if it starts struggling, that makes the meat tough. First tie its legs together and put the animal on the ground, a table, or in a wheelbarrow. Put a pan underneath the neck to catch the blood. Then quickly cut the throat through the neck all the way through to the spinal cord. Catch the blood in the pan, saving it to make blood pudding, blood sausage, or other things later. Next cut the skin open by the chest bone, first making a slight slit; then cut the skin first between the back legs and then between the front legs. Remove the hide, working slowly from side to side. Start at the second joint of the leg and cut, peeling the skin off from that joint on all the legs. You can have several people working on this together, pulling carefully on each side. You want to pull the skin off all the way to the backbone, the tail, in one piece. Cut the tail open and take off that skin, too.

You remove the head after all the blood has drained out; remove the skin around the neck. Cut the neck open very carefully where the meat is; you want to get to the throat, neck, and windpipe under the jaw. Take those things and pull them out a bit from the neck. You can rub some of that with a knife because it has a meatlike skin on the top. Pull those things down and tie them two times to prevent everything in the intestines from coming out right there. The skinning is finished when all four legs and the back have been skinned and the neck has been tied. Then hang the skinned animal upside down by its feet from a hook, a chain, or a wire in the shade.

People have different ways of doing things; some cut the front legs before they open the stomach; some cut them after they open the stomach. Whenever you cut the legs off, you separate them at the hip bone, cut down the backbone, and cut the ribs off of that. All of that meat will be cut up for cooking, roasting, use in stews, and other things. In my parents' time, they used the socket where the front legs come off for a spoon. The backbone is cut apart at each joint; sometimes a saw or even an axe might be needed to do that. You cut through the leg joints near the hooves and break off the feet. Later those leg parts have to be pounded until the hooves come off, and then you skin the rest of those legs. Those pieces are either hung up to dry or boiled.

You want to open up the flesh to remove the organs: the stomach, intestines, heart, liver, gall bladder, bladder, and kidneys. Most of the organs get baked immediately, roasted on an open fire you already have going. Some people say the heart should be boiled and the liver roasted with stomach fat. The liver (*'azid*) is a real delicacy. You spread it out thin and then roast or fry it after wrapping fat you've already cooked around it. The bladder and gall bladder have to be removed carefully; if the bladder (*'alizh bizis*) breaks, it will ruin the taste of the meat. Bile (*'atł'izh*) is used by some people to lose weight; the bitter taste of it stays in your mouth forever. Feces were also used by some people to stop foot odor, body odor, and athlete's foot, and they were applied while still warm. Some people use the bile as medicine and dry those organs for later use.

You work your way down when you are looking for the stomach, cutting every bone in the sternum, using two fingers as a guide, and splitting the area open just far enough to allow you to remove the stomach and intestines. You take the stomach out before removing the meat from the chest. You have to be very careful doing this, and it's best to run two fingers in front of the knife as a guide while you cut. Put the knife in the stomach so its tip comes out even with the top of your two fingers and cut the skin upward. The stomach and other stuff will come out, and you will need to clean the stomach and both intestines, the big one and the small one. The waste matter is in the neck and throat, and you don't want to burst that, so when you remove those, put them in a separate pan.

But before cleaning the stomach and intestines, you remove a small piece of meat from the top of chest area, the breastbone (ʼayid). The chest meat or chest blanket is called ʼayidítsíʼ, the stem meat. Some say the upper chest area is the best part of the meat, the prize meat, the butcher's piece, the sheepherder's special. This piece of meat goes to the one who did the butchering. If the butchering was done at home, this is the first piece of meat that is cooked; usually, everybody who is around helping also eats a piece of this. That way nobody will go hungry in the future. If the one who did the butchering is stingy with this, that person will starve.

The stomach and intestines get separated after they are removed so they can be washed. The stomach is covered with fat, and you have to remove that, too, as soon as possible, after the stomach is taken out so it doesn't stick. People hang that fat up to dry on a wire or hang it over the sides of a wheelbarrow, if you're using one. That fat is very, very sticky and looks like white lace. People eat it with the liver, or use it to make ʼachʼíiʼ.[8] The stomach is used in making sausage, náshgǫzh. Cut up the kidney, liver, and heart, add onions and yellow cornmeal, put it in the stomach, and boil it.

Another kind of sausage is blood sausage, made with blue cornmeal, diced potatoes, spices, and blood (dił) from the animal just butchered. Some people prefer to use up old corn that was coarsely ground when making this, instead of blue cornmeal. The blood immediately clots in the pan or dish it has drained into during butchering, and because these

clots do not mix with the cornmeal and other ingredients, they have to be
removed by straining. Some people add flour, chili peppers, and pieces of
the heart and kidney, too. You mix everything up, put it in the stomach
or other casing, and boil it until it is done. Blood sausage is known to be
much higher in iron than commercial sausage.

Someone has to do the dirty work of cleaning out the intestines. But
those are very important in making two foods: blood sausage and 'ach'íí'.
You save both the large and small intestines when butchering, holding
them back until you are ready to make blood sausage. The large intestine
gets turned inside out to make 'ach'íí', and the fat won't fall off during
cooking if you wrap the small intestine around the large one. That way
the 'ach'íí' is juicy inside and crunchy outside.

You can also use a cow's intestine for making the same thing. I always
got the big intestine to make sausage with. I'd add fat, white cornmeal,
onions, potatoes, and meat; it's the same thing as blood sausage but without the blood. Some people now like to add chili peppers to that, too. You
can make sausage by using either the stomach or the big intestine.

To make 'ach'íí' you need to take the fat off that covers the whole
stomach, after you hang up the sheep. You have to cut the fat open very
carefully and remove that in one piece, if possible, without tearing it. You
remove that with your hands, or, if it's really tough or thick, you can use
a small knife. When you hold that up, it looks just like lace. You let that
dry out by hanging it over a wire or line, after you cover the line with a
cloth or dish towel to prevent the fat from sticking to the line as it dries.
You cut a piece of fat off the edge; the middle part is thicker. Then cut it
into strips and squeeze the fat together in your hands, or roll it. The small
intestine gets wrapped around the fat. Be careful when roasting that,
because it's very greasy, and if the grease drops into the fire, it can make
a big flame flare up. This 'ach'íí' is considered a real treat; nutritionally,
it is rich in vitamins. This is the first thing that goes on the stove or the
grill, right next to the mutton from the front of the sheep, the meat from
the bone in the front of the sheep, the 'ayidítsị', the chest meat that goes to
whoever did the butchering. You also cook the liver and browned fat from
the 'ach'íí'. Put the fat over the liver and eat that between tortillas. I always
fixed that for Frank because it was one of his favorites. You also eat the
heart and the windpipe that way. You clean everything first and then cut it

all into small pieces and fry it with onions. If you have a meat grinder, you can also grind it up instead of cutting it. The fat and the marrow pieces you get can be saved and used as grease when you make paperbread and other things. My daughters tell me it's like the spray called Pam.

The head and organs should be baked immediately, roasted on an open fire. Both the head and the hooves have to have the hair or wool singed off; you turn those around while they are being singed so it's evenly done. Then they are cleaned up with a knife. You have to hit the hooves with a hammer, the head of an axe, or something else until they come off. The head is cleaned after the wool is singed off; then some people dry it thoroughly in the sun and store it in a sack for winter. You can also cook the head right away, after you singe the hair off and clean off the ashes, burnt hair, and other things. In early times we wrapped the head in wet paper sacks or newspapers; now a lot of people prefer to use tin foil. The head is slowly roasted in the ground; it might take two and a half or more hours to roast it, depending on how big the head was and how hot the ground was from the fire you had made earlier. You cover the wrapped head up with hot ash and then build more fire on top of it. Some people eat every part of the head, and others don't. People say that eating the brain will help you in your thinking; some say the tongue and eyes taste like chicken. The eyeballs are kind of hard, but the tongue is soft and tasty, something like a hot dog or a hamburger patty.

The hooves can be cooked and eaten, too, just like the head. Both of those have to have the hair or wool singed off first. Then you clean and remove the hooves, as mentioned earlier. The remaining part of the leg is hung up to dry; then you can store it in a sack for the winter, when you can fix it with hominy or in other ways. My daughters Augusta and Ruth always told me that old man Gorman had lots of those legs hanging around drying, with the hooves that had been removed drying, too. In earlier times we used sheep, goat, cow, and horse hooves. You had to singe off the hair first and then pound them on a board with something or take a piece of metal to get those off. Sheep hooves break off the easiest of all of those; inside them there is a tiny bone. You can use those leg pieces where the hooves were in the winter, if you dried them out and saved them. They give soup a good aroma, and you can also put them in with beans and roasted corn.

The hide or skin should be dried out after the butchering is finished. You clean it, dry it out, and then use it as a bedroll. The sheepskin or goatskin is stretched on the ground and nailed down. It dries in the sand, and you need to put dirt over it to keep dogs and cats away from it. That's why you also try to get all of the meat off the skin. When the People only lived in hogans and ramadas, they would nail the skin to the ground so they could watch it while it was drying. You need a really hot, dry day for that to dry right; it may take several days if it's too hot or if the wool is too thick on the skin. It's easiest to get the skin to dry quickly if you butcher right after you shear. Some people use the brain to soften the inner side of the pelt. You want to get the fatty layer under the skin, so as the skin dries you peel that layer off, softening it with water if necessary. Then you put that on a cloth so that you can rub that on your grill and use it as grease. We saved all of the fat from butchering because we use it in skillets, Dutch ovens, and other cooking things. We never used Crisco or other lard from the trading posts.

There's even a food called 'akágí that you can make from the sheepskin, if you have a fresh one; we use pieces of that as a snack, something like jerky. You heat up the sheepskin by putting it around a big Navajo pot that we kept on top of our barrel stove. I used to have one of those big old Navajo pots, much bigger than anything around here today. It was really heavy, too, and I'd put it on top of the barrel stove and keep hot charcoal close to it when I wanted to do that to a sheepskin. That skin had to be very fresh. You keep turning the skin around and around and that wool really comes right off. When it's about half done, I cut some of the finished part off. Then I wash that skin and cut it into strips. When you heat those strips, they curl up. There are two ways to make that food: you either let the strip coil on itself, or you add a layer of sheep fat before letting it roll up on itself. Then we roast that coil on charcoal and eat the little pieces like that. 'Akágí can be made either with or without fat.

The rest of the sheep is then cut up for cooking. The meat cuts best if it's cold or frozen already; when it's fresh it's hard to slice up. You will need to have your fire going, the grill hot already, so the meat doesn't stick. You can hang the meat in the shade to dry before cooking it, or if you have electricity, maybe you could put it in a refrigerator or freezer. You can roast pieces, keep them for later, or make them into a stew. We boiled, grilled, roasted the meat by itself, or added it to stews. We also dried it for use later. We always ate just about everything from the sheep.

BUTCHERING HORSES

In earlier times horses (*łį́į́*) two years old or younger were sometimes butchered to supplement the diet of wild game and mutton. That was usually done in the wintertime, when the horses were fat. People believed the meat was better then, and of course it was easier to keep it from rotting when the weather was cold. Many people ate horsemeat to protect themselves from colds or to help themselves recover from a sickness. Tall Woman helped butcher horses usually while the children were at school. Frank would kill a young male colt; they had lots of horses, and he wanted to control the number of males, so he always had one of those butchered. They did this the same way they butchered a cow. They took the skin off but didn't use the hooves or anything below the second leg joint. They also never ate a horse's head, according to Tall Woman, the way they ate the heads of sheep, goats, and cows. But the meat and the insides were cooked and eaten. They also used horsemeat to make regular sausage, blood sausage, and jerky. Tall Woman helped her sister (who was known as Small Woman, Grandma Zhinii, or Grandma Black) a number of times to butcher horses. When they were done, Tall Woman would bring back a whole leg of the horse. When people butchered a horse, they always gave parts of it to their relatives, which wasn't the case when they butchered a cow.

BUTCHERING COWS

As with horses, it was best to butcher cows (*béégashii*) in the late fall or the winter. People believed the animals were fatter then, were easier to butcher, and had more flavorful meat. There were also fewer flies at that time of year, and the meat kept longer unrefrigerated. Cows are butchered like sheep, and most parts of them are eaten. The head is baked. The feet are hung up to dry after the skin is pulled off, and when they are ready, they are boiled. As with sheep, the cow's intestines are cut into really small pieces and used to make sausage. The meat can also be made into jerky and thus kept a long time. Tall Woman said that sometimes it seemed that people were less willing to share cow meat than freshly butchered horsemeat. She thought that maybe some of them liked the taste of beef better or thought that cow meat was more valuable.

BUTCHERING PIGS

Tall Woman also helped when people living nearby butchered pigs (*bisóodi*). She was often the one who took the skin off for the others. First she would take off the hair with hot water, then she'd skin the pig and cut up the meat; she always came home with all kinds of cuts of pigmeat—ham, bacon—and the skin, too.

When Tall Woman was ready to cook the meat, she usually boiled it in a big Dutch oven; sometimes, though, she'd fry it and make gravy, too. When she boiled it, sometimes she would add beans. Whenever she cooked pig-meat, she would collect all the fat or grease in a big cast-iron skillet and cook it over the fire with a little water added. When it was done and still warm but not hot, she'd pour it into a big #10 can that she used for storing lard. Even when she boiled the meat, she would strain the water she had used into that can to make her own shortening that way. The family stored the lard in the ground storage pit with the meat and corn. Once a cat got in there somehow and was trapped. When Woody Davis, Tall Woman's son-in-law, opened the pit to get corn to shell for seeds for planting, the cat jumped out. Woody laughed and said that the cat must have used up eight of its nine lives being stuck in there over the winter.

Tall Woman went to the dairy at the Chinle Boarding School when they butchered pigs; Seya was working there at the time and would tell her when they were going to do that. She helped there and brought home some of the meat and grease from there, too.

The Farming Process

Although the Mitchells farmed, they were not known for having lots of different kinds of animals or a big farm, compared to John and Ruth Gorman, some clan relatives down the road who had everything. The Gormans were very nice to the Mitchells, even though, as noted earlier, the Mitchells were Catholic and the Gormans were Presbyterian. Their farm included fruit trees and bees along with the usual corn, squash, and other crops.

According to Wolfe (1984) and illustrated by Tall Woman's family farm, Navajo farming traditionally was small-scale dry farming with very little irrigation. Sometimes when the washes ran, ditch irrigation could be used in the Canyon de Chelly area. Given her life in and around the Chinle Valley, with periods in the summer at sheep camps near Fluted Rock, Tall Woman was usually cooking in places about 5,000 feet in elevation and up to about 8,000 feet at the sheep camp. Although the elevation can get above 10,000 feet on the reservation, Tall Woman said she never made any adjustments in food preparation because of the altitude. The dry farming the Mitchells practiced was mainly an extended family affair and very labor-intensive.

The focus was on raising corn, pinto beans, and alfalfa hay, but squash, watermelons, and potatoes were also added in some years. I remember that the Mitchells' farm included fields of corn, squash of different kinds, beans, potatoes, melons, cantaloupes, and watermelons, what Wolfe (1984) termed the "core crops" that were hand-cultivated. Wolfe also noted that a second layer in gardens might include tomatoes, cucumbers, sweet corn, onions, radishes, and pinto beans; a third, and the last, would be devoted to potatoes, cabbages, and chili peppers, as well as carrots and lettuce sometimes. I was occasionally in Chinle at the right time to help plant; the corn, squash, and melons were planted deep and spaced well apart in groups. The family also grew alfalfa hay. I never knew the Mitchells to plant pumpkins, but they did grow the gray squash that has a wrinkled skin and is orange inside, known as *naayízílbáhí*. Some young people called these "the best pumpkins" in English, preferring to use them for pies in later times.

Since Tall Woman's farm produced food for the extended family, it was expected that whoever was available would help. In addition to this labor pool, until wage work became common, people in similar geographic areas used to help one another, moving in groups to prepare the ground, plant, and harvest. Workers were fed by the family whose fields were being planted or harvested. Tall Woman's story (Mitchell 2001, 246–51) describes the process in detail, including the two ways the People planted entire fields: in circles or in rows. Like many families, they saved seeds in jars for planting the next year. Sometimes seeds were prepared by soaking them in water, and occasionally greasewood leaves were mixed in. Initially, families kept most of the crops they grew for themselves, but sometimes they traded with others for things they did not have, such as peaches or apples. They also traded their produce at the store for coffee, tobacco, or sugar.

According to Tall Woman, it was men's work to prepare the field while the women were cooking and feeding whoever came to help, in the old days when everybody helped one another. Tall Woman's father, Hastiin Dela-woshí, would ride up and down the Chinle Valley calling people to get the planting started. Clan relatives from the canyon came to help Frank in the same way he helped others, and some would stay a few days. The men would plow section by section and mound the earth up along the edge of each section. They would each have two horses and a plow. Some sections would have to be replowed so that mole holes could be packed down. Some people had more problems with moles than others.

Then the men would fix the irrigation ditches. They would go to the water source, like a wash, and from there clean out the ditches that brought the water down and into each section. They had ways of blocking the ditches off, and all of them had to be checked and repaired, if necessary, so that they could irrigate section by section. At least one of the Mitchells' fields was close enough to the Nazlini Wash to allow the men in the family to construct hand-dug ditches, which were then used to divert water into these fields with a system of opening and shutting gates, also handmade. The work of digging and repairing these ditches, monitoring them daily, and keeping them clean was done by Tall Woman's sons if they were around; if not, it became women's work.

The Mitchells had one huge section, to the northeast of their hogan, that included two to four fields. That's where the corn and other things, like pinto beans, were planted. Squash, both the gray and green kinds, were planted in the same fields but in separate places. They also had a big long field by the wash, which is where all the alfalfa was grown.

Beans were planted between the corn because those two crops ripen at about the same time and could be harvested at the same time. One crop did not affect the other. One time they tried planting corn and pinto beans over at Mary Davis's (the Mitchells' oldest daughter's) place. Those crops, like alfalfa, didn't need to be checked on very often, at least early in the season. But other crops—such as watermelon, other melons, and squash—were more apt to be stolen, so they had to be planted near the hogan, where the family could keep an eye on them.

The Mitchell children's families lived apart from their parents and from one another, but all were in the same area. There was also an island in the Nazlini Wash that Frank got the Bureau of Land Operations to block off. The Mitchells built jetties toward the wash all the way down and fenced in that whole area, too, since it was theirs. The flood of 1964 took out the jetties; now only one cedar tree is left, and there is sand all over. David, Frank and Tall Woman's oldest son, did all the planting there; he planted a lot of peach trees and took care of them. They really produced well because the soil was so good there, just as it was at Mary Davis's place. However, when David got sick and passed away, nobody took care of those trees, and they all died. In those days there was a road only at the top along the wash, nothing going through it. That wash was very deep then, just like the pond Frank dug with the scraper, which was eight feet deep.

When the ground was ready, it was time to plant. The only seeds that Tall Woman soaked before planting were the melon seeds: watermelon, honeydew, cantaloupe, muskmelon, and others. Some people believed in soaking their corn seeds, too, but Tall Woman always said that doing that was apt to make the plant weaker or make it break before the corn matured. So her family didn't do that. They did soak the melon seeds in a mixture of manure and water. Tall Woman took sheep or horse manure, mixed it with water, added some dirt, and put the seeds in, and then stored the container in a warm place. She checked on those seeds all the time. It usually took about a week for them to sprout; once they did, she planted them right away. The time of planting also depended on how wet the ground was where she intended to plant them.

Women and children helped put the seeds in the ground. Augusta described it as follows:

Every four plows covered up where you put them, so you had to pay attention to stay ahead of the plows and watch what you were doing. They were planted about one yard apart; if you did that too close, the seeds would not produce right. Mom told us to take three long steps to measure that out and to be quick, stay ahead of the plows. We were supposed to put about six seeds in one place, but she said don't count them out. She carried seeds in a bucket, a bag, or a sack. She told us to always put a stake or stick at the end of the row when we were done planting in it. That told the person running the two horses and plow where things were. Any seeds that were left over when the group was done were given to the next person to take to the next area where they were all going to keep helping each other.

As Tall Woman explained, different colors of corn were planted separately. It could be done by rows, by sections, by fields, or by larger areas, if one had the land. The different colors would be harvested separately, too, and the rows would be marked wherever a different kind of crop started. People had blue, yellow, white, and multicolored corn. Red corn was very rare in the Chinle Valley. Tall Woman said that her family usually planted white corn for their own use; they would exchange that or other things for blue corn, which some other people planted.

"Sometimes we just bought bags of blue corn, already shelled and cleaned, from people we knew," Tall Woman explained. "If it was twenty-five pounds, it usually sold for five to ten dollars in early times; later it might be twenty-five dollars for twenty-five pounds. We also planted yellow corn to use in making offerings."[9] Sometimes the pinto beans were planted at the same time the corn was planted, and sometimes the beans were planted after all the corn was in the ground. "We always put sticks at the end of the rows where the corn was planted; sometimes people would plant the beans in the middle, between those sticks. When people plowed, they always marked the places where they had prepared the ground for planting the corn."

Living with Tall Woman, I learned that she checked on the garden areas daily by walking around in them to check on the progress of certain crops, to determine what needed water, weeding, and other kinds of attention. When she returned, she would share her findings and often assign the necessary work to specific family members. At certain times during the growing season, people would have to carry water to the young corn, beans, or other plants, preferably early in the morning but sometimes early in the evening. This was done by hand, using pans, buckets, or other containers to transport the water and then pouring it on with cans or dippers. When it was time to weed, this too was done early in the morning in the summer, by hand, hoe, or both. Just after daylight was also the time some preferred to gather the corn pollen, or *tádidíín*; however, harvesting was done later in the day, after the dew was gone.

When the plants started coming up, Tall Woman would go out and check on them to see how they were doing. She would also check that all her tools were sharp and ready to use and that there were enough buckets and bags around. When the weeds started to grow, she would wait until the crop was big enough that the children could distinguish the food plants from the weeds. Then she would sharpen the hoes and tell them to start early in the morning to weed. They carried water with them, too, for themselves and for the plants that needed it.

Weeding the watermelons and squash had to be done *her* way. Tall Woman would get a glove, go out there, and move the vines gently so they weren't tangled around each other. She also said not to hoe too close to the center of the plants. She weeded those kinds of plants by hand with a glove on, reaching into the center of the plants and then moving her hand very gently around the vines.

Once the plants started blooming, they might need water every now and then. Tall Woman was always checking to see how the plants looked, and she would haul water from the wash in buckets to the plants. The time to water plants, especially melons and squash, is in the evening. The children usually did not haul water to the corn or beans. Tall Woman would check the ground to make sure it wasn't getting too dry, but it also couldn't be too muddy because that would block the plants trying to come up. She might let a little irrigation water in, if it were available later in the summer from the canyon and the corn or beans needed it, but if so, it would be only very little, compared to the early irrigating. Rain was always wonderful, and a sufficient amount meant that there would be no problem.

Augusta planted a garden near her home for several years. First she removed the topsoil and raked the area. Then she borrowed a cultivator from a relative, turned up the ground, and raked it again. She added mountain dirt, which she had collected from Wheatfields in eight five-gallon cans, and worked it in so it was well mixed. Then she used a garden hose to irrigate it. She was able to grow tomatoes, squash, green peppers, jalapeños, and chili peppers.

Tall Woman had been very unhappy to see that their farmland was not being used after Frank passed away in 1967; she said that the ground was hungry for planting—it had rested for too long, and it needed to be planted. So she was really happy to see Augusta planting a garden. Earlier, Augusta and Howard had decided to grow corn and beans in a field across from Mary Davis's hogan; they got more than 100 pounds of corn and the same amount of pinto beans from that field that year!

In her discussions of harvesting, Tall Woman chose to start with corn, given its importance to the Navajos:

When the corn starts to get its silk, barely has any silk, the 'azóól, or corn tassel, comes up. That has the tádidíín, or corn pollen, on it, and it happens before the corn really starts forming well. It's when it's barely starting. Dá' azóól refers to when the tassels are growing; when the tassels emerge and stretch out, the pollen is getting ready to shed. It's best to gather that in the morning, after the dew has dried off the tassels. But if the weather is too hot or too dry, there won't be very much pollen.

Tall Woman would go out and check it every day. When it starts to form, on a very clear, calm day, it would be time to gather the pollen. Some people went out before the sun came up, but many others waited until daylight, because then the dew that comes in the night would have time to dry off first. Tall Woman would take a big pan and a dishcloth or dish towel with her so she could cover it up when she was done gathering it. She continued:

You put the pan under the 'azóól and tap on the corn, *not* the 'azóól. That way the pollen falls into the pan. They say if you aren't serious about gathering it, you won't get any. Sometimes men have more luck collecting pollen than women. It just depends on how you think about the whole thing. Keep your mind on the prayers and how you are going to use the tádidíín after you gather it, when you return home. When you come back, put it through a strainer to get any sticks, bugs, or leaves out of it. You can also remove bigger things you see in it by hand. Then you need to dry it inside the hogan, where there is no draft. Stir it with your hand to check its dryness. When it's thoroughly dry, test it by taking a teaspoon of it and seeing if it sticks to your finger.

Tall Woman always told her children to bless themselves with the corn pollen when it was finished drying before they put it in a jar and stored it in a safe place.

Tall Woman said there were four stages to corn (these will be discussed in chapter 3). She was always in charge of stage one, when the ears were tiny and the kernels were very, very small; she'd go out to the fields and bring some tiny ears back in, boil them, and make all the children taste them. She told the children to say, "*Ayaazh* [tiny corn kernel], I am putting you into last year's little bag" (meaning their stomachs) just as they were ready to eat it. After that, everybody was allowed to help her. She would go out to the fields in the wagon when the corn got fully ripe.

If Tall Woman wanted to make kneel-down bread, she needed a lot of corn to do that, at least one or maybe two wagonloads. She also needed a lot of wood, and she sent the men and boys to get that. She had to build a fire in the ground to heat the ground pit first, and then add wood so it would cook all the way around, on all sides. Sometimes the men would take the wagon and go into the mountains and bring back at least two loads of wood if she said she was going to be roasting kneel-down bread in the ground. The women had to grind the corn by hand for that.

Tall Woman would announce when each of the four stages of corn needed to be addressed and what was going to be done. She was always the director of that, and she told her children how to fix it, too; sometimes she fixed it herself, but she also explained how to do it so others could help her. The small children were told to pick up the husks, the leaves for use as a liner in the bottom of the fire pit or for making kneel-down bread.

When the corn was harvested, the long, big ears with lots of kernels were always separated from the small ones with few kernels. The small ears, and any ears that had bugs or worms in them, were put in a gunnysack and taken up to the community grinder behind the Presbyterian Church. One person would walk a horse around and around to make the grinder work and coarsely grind that corn. Then Tall Woman or Frank would mix that corn with oats bought from the store and use that as horse feed. If she planned to use the corn to make food for the People, it was the big ears, ground by the women and girls on the grinding stones. The feed corn for animals was always planted separately and taken to the community grinder for processing.

Corn was always the first crop harvested, and then Tall Woman would have everybody go and pull the bean plants out of the ground and put them in sacks. Even after all the bean plants had been harvested and the children thought they were done, Tall Woman would make them go back and check the field all over again to see if they had missed any plants or dropped any. They picked up any they found, so the field was really empty when they were done. Tall Woman was always concerned that some beans might get lost, so she carried a bag with her, pulled up the whole plant, and put it in the bag. It was important to be careful because the ripe beans would split, the shell would burst, and the seeds would spill all over the place.

Beans had to be harvested before they got too dry. When everyone got home, Tall Woman had all who had helped empty out their sacks on the ground, where she had spread a canvas or other kind of cloth. The beans were left out there to dry, covered up with another piece of cloth or something. Then she would hit the beans lightly with a stick to make them jump out of their shells. She'd have all her children do that, too. Then Tall Woman would winnow the beans with a pan or a basket to make sure that the leaves, stems, and sticks that came out with the beans were separated. After winnowing, she put the cleaned beans in sacks for storage.

When it was time to harvest melons, Tall Woman said she could tell if a watermelon was ripe by tapping on it; it would sound hollow if it was ripe and very dense if it was not. The other melons, like cantaloupes and muskmelons, would get yellow when they were ripe; she could also tell by their smell that they were ripe.

After corn, the other crop the family grew a lot of was hay (tł'oh), because of the animals. Most of what they grew was used for their own animals, but Frank sold any extra hay they had to people he knew or at the trading post. When it was time to start cutting the hay, Frank made everybody in the family help clean the alfalfa fields before the hay was cut. Frank would put all of the kids in a line and have them walk both ways in the field, stopping to pull up any weeds by hand to keep them out of the hay. Tall Woman helped with that, too, and they put those weeds off to the side of the field and burned them later. That way their hay (alfalfa) was weed-free, and people really wanted to buy it.

Howard was put in charge of running the hay cutter and would always do that (fig. 6). After the hay was cut, it would be left on the ground for three or

FIGURE 6. Horse-pulled hay cutter or mower, August 2016. Collection of early Navajo farm equipment at Hubbell Trading Post, National Historic Site, Ganado, Arizona. Courtesy of National Park Service.

four days to dry. How long that took depended on the weather and the thickness of the hay. Whoever planted the alfalfa had to be careful and really pay attention so the seeds weren't too thick or too close together; that made the hay grow too thick, and it would be hard to turn over with the cutter and the rake when it was time to start harvesting it.

After the hay was dry, it would be raked again with a two-horse team. Howard would rake it into big piles, and it would stay that way for at least a day. Then the whole family came with the wagon to put the hay in it. Here extra helpers were really needed; the hay had to be stacked right on the wagon, with a man on the top making sure it was, while the kids on the ground tossed it up from the piles with three-pronged pitchforks. Men who had horses were usually very happy to help because they wanted the hay as pay.

The Mitchells had to use someone else's baler because they didn't have one of their own. Nelson Gorman, who was John Gorman's cousin, had a baler, so they used his at first. The balers were run by one horse, and someone had to lead that horse around and around (fig. 7). Augusta said she did it only

FIGURE 7. Horse-pulled hay baler, August 2016. Collection of early Navajo farm equipment at Hubbell Trading Post, National Historic Site, Ganado, Arizona. Courtesy of National Park Service.

once because it made her too dizzy. This person had to take the wagon to where the baler was. Frank usually paid ten cents a bale; first the hay was baled with wire, then later with twine or cord.

Most of the people who owned balers charged the same price to make a bale. This process took at least four people: one or two on the wagon, throwing the hay into the baler; one leading the horse around to make the baler work; and two to run the baler with the stakes, blocks, and wires. These two would be on the side of the baler to adjust the blocks and wires. Then the hay would be measured for length, and a piece of metal was put in to hold the first block of the four they made. One man added the block from the first end and then fed the wire in. The second block was put in when the first one was getting ready to come out. It had to be wired when the next one was about halfway out.

Tall Woman was always there, raking up every little piece of hay she could find to put into the next bale or to put back on the wagon. The next load would always be waiting in line for processing.

For more information on the Mitchells' farmwork, see Mitchell ([1978] 2003) and Mitchell (2001).

FARM EQUIPMENT

In the early 1960s the Mitchells were still farming with horse-drawn plows, rakes, cutters, and hay balers. As Bingham and Bingham (1979) document, in earlier times people planted in groups, with each person using a *gish*, a planting stick that was arm's length, sharp on one end, and about three fingers wide. This stick, which could be curved or straight, was fashioned from greasewood (*díwózhii*), and was well taken care of. A group in which each person was using a *gish* could reportedly plant ten acres in a day. Some people say that the *gish* could be made from either juniper or oak and should include an extension that allows the person to push it into the ground, making a hole for seeds. (A picture of a Zuni *gish* may be found in *Leading the Way* 11 [5]: 23.)

The Mitchells had draft horses (which were sometimes used in teams), harnesses, a plow, a wagon, a mower (or cutter), a rake, and a variety of other tools, including an axe, a scythe, a sickle, three-pronged pitchforks, knives, hoes, shovels and spades, ropes, big sticks (used to swish through the corn and hay to alert snakes of the human presence), containers (for hauling water to plants, storing seeds, and harvesting), and clippers. Baskets and pans were used in winnowing; sacks, often homemade, were used for storing seeds and harvested foods. Pails, buckets, and pans were used for harvesting, storage, and hauling water to the crops; a big barrel was used for hauling water with the horse and wagon from the nearest windmill as often as necessary. Pans were also used to catch blood while butchering an animal, and knives and axes were used for butchering and cutting the ribs apart.

THE STORAGE AND PRESERVATION OF CROPS

Although some Navajos used storage pits for storing pumpkins and squash, by the time I met the Mitchells, those days were past in their family. Tall Woman reported having a big storage pit in the ground near the area where her daughter, Mary Davis, and her family lived in the early 1960s. It reportedly kept things very cool as well as protected from the rain, which was much more common then than it is now. In those days many people, including the Mitchells, did not have running water, electricity, or refrigeration.

As we discussed storage pits further, I learned that even though Tall Woman's children knew that their parents had used such pits while they were growing up, the only one that any of them remembered seeing was the big one fashioned by Woody Davis, Mary's husband. They suggested that the floor of the pit was lined with "a layer of dried cedar bark, not juniper. In the early days, only cedar trees were hauled back for this purpose."[10] The bark had to be removed first, sun-dried, and then put in the pit so it covered the entire floor. Vegetables could be put on top of that, and then, if one wanted, a piece of canvas. More bark was added to cover the canvas. Whatever crops were put into the storage pit, they reportedly were covered with more bark, then very thin rocks, then a layer of dirt. Then a repeat of the layers could be added. Tall Woman noted that the corn must be thoroughly dry, with the husks off; it should have been sun-dried for two to three weeks before being put in the pit. More than two layers of corn should never be put in, and the ears should not be touching each other. She also said that only the immediate family knew where the storage pit was.

Navajo archaeology proves that both storage pits and caches were used in earlier times, the latter mainly when traveling. Reh (1983, 7) provides descriptions of the big, bottle-shaped underground pits that were used in District 1 in the 1930s to store matured dry corn. These pits were usually located near winter hogans but were sometimes right in the cornfield. Reh learned that some people with large crops would sell their surplus to the trader and then buy it back later, when needed. If they had two successful crop years in a row, they would clean out the pit to make room for the new crop and sell the old corn to the trader, or if it was not in the best condition, they would feed it to their livestock. All the pits that Reh saw were dug into hard, dry earth, eight to ten feet down and four to five feet across. The top opening was squared off with timbers, being just wide enough for a ladder to be put down inside. Once the crop was in, people would close the opening with logs, then cedar bark, and then earth. Such a practice leaves a slight mound above the earth. The pits would be opened whenever corn was needed. Fodder left in the field after harvest was cut and used for horses, or else other animals (except for sheep) were allowed to graze in the field area.

Besides using storage pits, the Mitchells and other Navajos preserved food for later use by sun-drying it. Tall Woman often used the roof of her home or a daughter's home, putting food up there to dry while being protected from other people (especially children) and dogs. She sun-dried apples, peaches, and apricots given to them by relatives who had trees in Canyon de Chelly. These fruits and others, such as berries they picked while traveling, as well as squash and melons, could be cut into slices or strips or dried whole, then reconstituted with water later, when needed for consumption. Even corn could be sun-dried, either on the cob or after being scraped off the cob. In addition to being put on a roof, sometimes, especially in the case of freshly butchered meats, food was hung on clotheslines of wire or rope to sun-dry.

In the winter Tall Woman continued to use the roof for preservation, but then the object was to freeze what she put there or to use the roof as an outdoor refrigerator until mealtime. Hay was stored for family use in an abandoned barn. Sometimes ears of corn, not shelled, were kept in other unused buildings, either in large sacks or covered containers. Tall Woman would check these frequently for evidence of rodent attacks.

According to Augusta, her mother mainly stored things in sacks. She had lots of long, big, heavy sacks around home, mainly two feet wide; these were not gunnysacks but instead were thicker than flour sacks. She also would hand-sew two or three cloth sacks together, get them wet, fold them up on top of her head, and wear them that way in the heat. These big heavy sacks were sewn with red thread, and she made them with red seams on each side. She called them *bidichíí*—literally, "red mark on the thing."

I was able to see several of these sacks in June 2013; one (fig. 8) was made of very heavy fabric and was almost three and a half feet long and eighteen inches wide, with a one-and-a-quarter inch hem on the bottom. Tall Woman reportedly had at least two of these sacks. They were used to transport gifts such as bread or meat for the stick receivers during an Enemyway. The sacks would be filled, put over the horse's saddle, and taken to the camp. The end was gathered up or folded like an accordion and then tied with twine or rope. From the sacks I was shown, it was clear that Tall Woman took care of her sacks and mended them over and over again.

The front of one sack showed an eagle perched on top of a circle that said FULTON A SEAMLESS, with the words EXTRA HEAVY underneath. The circle was about eight inches in diameter.[11] Some sacks were plain other than for this logo. Other sacks (not shown) had this logo and a pattern of a blue line

FIGURE 8. Fulton A Seamless feed sack with eagle logo, one of Tall Woman's old heavy-duty feed sacks saved by the family, June 2013. Photo by author.

with two red lines on each side of it. The lines (but not the logo) were on both the front and the back of the bag. Another of Tall Woman's sacks still extant in 2013 reportedly came from the place that sometimes ground corn for ceremonial cooking, City Market in Gallup. Sacks such as these, which were plain and narrower, were used to haul corn in from the field.

Cooking

Cooking, to the Navajos, is not just an ordinary physical activity but a spiritual one as well. In addition to the prayers that both Tall Woman and Frank offered with white cornmeal to the east upon arising at dawn each day, Tall Woman offered prayers at certain times while cooking. These were individual, private prayers of thanks to the Holy People for a variety of things, such as wood for the fire, the fire itself, the food that had been cooked and made available for the family, or the continued well-being of all. The two times that

I know she always offered prayers were when she finished using her stirring sticks and when she had finished cooking and was using the fire poker to move the charcoal or ashes back to the center of the cooking area. If Tall Woman gave the stirring sticks to others to clean off, they too were expected to give thanks.

COMMERCIAL COOKING EQUIPMENT

Despite her own mother's daily use of Navajo pottery, Tall Woman had different practices; she never used Navajo pottery for preparing or serving food unless doing so was required in a specific ceremonial setting. Her regular or daily cooking equipment consisted of both store-bought and traditional tools and utensils. The former included cast-iron stew pots, cast-iron skillets (different sizes that she called thin and thick), griddles, and cast-iron Dutch ovens. She had a favorite big cast-iron pot that was round without any feet. It had belonged to her mother, and Tall Woman used it for boiling water. Her grinding stones were also from her mother. She had another cast-iron pot with a lid that someone had added wire to for a handle. She also had a cast-iron teakettle; it was left on the woodpile for a long time after she passed away. Her stone grill was greased with sheep marrow and used for making paperbread, or *tsé'ást'éí*. Reportedly, no one in the family knows who got it after Tall Woman died, but it is now gone and we have no pictures of it.

Other store-bought items used for food preparation were shovels, pickaxes, and hoes for digging cooking pits; ropes for butchering animals and suspending the carcasses; several large pieces of tin; some other kinds of metal; and pieces of woven wire or racks with horizontal wires (like today's oven racks) used as a grill for outdoor cooking. By the early 1960s Tall Woman owned a variety of metal grills that were used for making bread, roasting corn, and cooking mutton. Some of her grills were homemade (fig. 9), created by resting pieces of plain wire on stones, built up to the height she needed for cooking. When necessary, these were repaired with other pieces of wire. All the grills were used either on top of fires built beneath them or in a ground pit (fig. 10).

Tall Woman had different sizes of axes, used mainly for chopping wood but sometimes for cutting ribs apart. Her tools included several knives, especially a big one that she used specifically for butchering. Smaller knives were used to skin the sheep and do other cutting tasks, such as slicing vegetables

FIGURE 9. Homemade half-barrel grill on rims from truck tires, August 2014. Photo by author.

and fruits. At least while I was there, Tall Woman kept her knives very sharp by rubbing them on her grinding stones.

In the early 1960s Tall Woman often served food from a common bowl, and people ate with their fingers most of the time—for stew, however, there were usually spoons. By the mid-1960s the family started increasing its supplies of store-bought utensils and dishes, first with plain white enamelware dishes and later with speckled enamelware. Tin, ceramic, or aluminum plates, bowls, and cups were also purchased, along with silverware. By the 1970s many of Tall Woman's store-bought pots, pans, and coffeepots were enamelware, mainly blue and white. She always had a big coffeepot on her stove or fire. She told me that before they bought such a pot from the trading post, she had used large #10 cans from either trading post purchases or commodity food supplies like canned peanut butter, milk, juices, and raisins.

In time other store-bought items were added, and they often had multiple uses. Her large aluminum mixing bowls, for example, were used for making

FIGURE 10. Ground pit with grill base resting in the pit, and grill racks resting on a table, August 2014. Photo by author.

or storing bread dough; catching blood while butchering; serving food such as ribs, mutton, or sliced melons; and even for hauling hand-washed laundry outside to the clotheslines. One bowl was always reserved for use as a dish-pan, and another to hold water for hand washing before eating, with a bar of soap and a towel nearby, right inside the hogan door. One of the buckets the family owned was used to hold water for drinking; that too, with a tin ladle (or earlier a gourd) for dipping, was kept right inside the door.

Eventually, Tall Woman began using some plastic containers and big bowls; today her daughters have a mix of plastic, paper, Styrofoam, and ceramic plates; plastic and glass drinking glasses; ceramic mugs; and metal and plastic silverware. Big containers frequently carry their owners' initials marked on the bottom with paint or nail polish so they don't disappear dur-ing group get-togethers.

Another crucial store-bought item was some kind of barrel for hauling water. Tall Woman had several of these, which her family would put in the wagon and take to the windmill to fill with water when necessary. The barrels were covered with either cloths or metal lids and kept outside the hogan door.

To gather foods, such as wild berries in the Red Rock area, Tall Woman often used buckets from the trading post or containers saved from the Commodity Food Program; the ones she found most useful were the coffee and lard containers. Sometimes a cardboard or wooden box served as a substitute.

TRADITIONAL COOKING EQUIPMENT

Since so much cooking was done outside, a few comments are necessary about the wood needed for cooking. It was usually the men's job to gather and bring home wood, for heating the hogan as well as for cooking. Frank and his sons or grandsons who were old enough to help would go up in the mountains with the horse and wagon to chop wood and bring back a wagonful. In time, of course, pickup trucks replaced wagons, and the Navajo Nation started a permit system for cutting wood. Now many Chinle people buy it by the truckload, either from someone who has provided their wood for years or from a person who sits in a truck full of wood over by one of the stores in the Tséyi' Shopping Center's public parking lot.

In Tall Woman's day both pinyon and cedar were commonly used, and in earlier times, when supplies were plentiful, also oak and greasewood. Oak is a hard wood and takes longer to cut with an axe, but it makes a good, long-burning fire. Reportedly, the number of oak trees decreased because people cut them down for ceremonial use. Augusta said that now they can sometimes find someone with a truckload of oak for sale, but it will cost more. One local man jokingly calls it "peyote wood." Greasewood has always been easy to gather since it used to grow all over and can be snapped off the bush by hand without needing an axe. People often use greasewood today for grilling, preferring it to the charcoal now available commercially in bags. Everybody knows that greasewood makes wonderful charcoal because, like oak, it burns for a long time, so the People are always watching for it as they move around. Tall Woman usually got her own while coming back in the wagon from Black Mountain.

According to Tall Woman, in the early days, before the Navajos had cast-iron skillets, they boiled everything. They put the result in a bag and hung it somewhere to let it cool off. Then it could be used "like cold cuts today." They also roasted things. There was no frying, and, as she noted repeatedly, at that time the Navajos were neither fat nor sick. There also was no soda pop and no junk food. They didn't suffer from obesity or diabetes.

Although Tall Woman considered three pieces of equipment traditional— her cast-iron teakettle, her mother's cast-iron pot with no feet, and the cast-iron pot with the lid and wire handle—some people would not agree with this characterization because those items originally came from the trading post. Thus, from another point of view, Tall Woman's traditional cooking equipment included a number of sets of stirring sticks; a pancake turner; sets of grinding stones for grinding corn, seeds, and other substances; and a grinding stone brush (often a bunch of the same grasses as those used for the traditional hairbrush, only shorter). Some also use the grinding stone brush as a strainer when working with culinary ash or other foods with lumps to be removed. Other tools include a cedar turner for making paperbread; a sharpened cedar stick used like a fork; and a basket, often the traditional Navajo wedding basket, although sometimes a pan or big dish was substituted for this. The basket was used for winnowing or as a container for serving bread, covered with a cloth. Tall Woman also had a very large, heavy Navajo pot that she said was from her mother. The only stone cooking implement she had was a stone grill that was used for making paperbread. Some called it *bíkáá'at'eesí*, saying that this word is for any kind of a stone grill, but *tsé* is stone, and *tsét'ees* is a stone griddle.[12] Tall Woman never washed her stone grill but instead cleaned it with a rag or brushed it off.

It is unclear where Tall Woman's cooking tools went after she passed away. Various women in the family have a set of grinding stones (fig. 11), greasewood stirring sticks (fig. 12), gourd dippers (fig. 13), a traditional hairbrush (fig. 14), and a brush for the grinding stones (fig. 15); all agreed to my photographing them, even though they were not Tall Woman's.[13] Gourd dippers were used before metal ladles and measuring cups became available, for retrieving drinking water from its container and for pouring batter onto cooking surfaces. Rolling pins were never part of the inventory because bread dough and other things were shaped and rolled by hand.

I have no idea if there was a traditional practice of creating the items we call pot holders and dish towels, but what Tall Woman did while I lived with

FIGURE 11. Set of small grinding stones, June 2013. Photo by author.

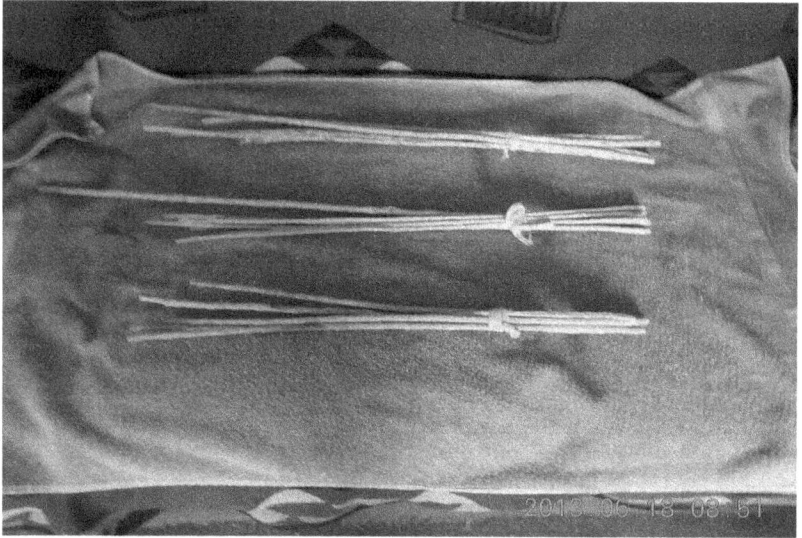

FIGURE 12. Three bundles of greasewood stirring sticks, June 2013. Photo by author.

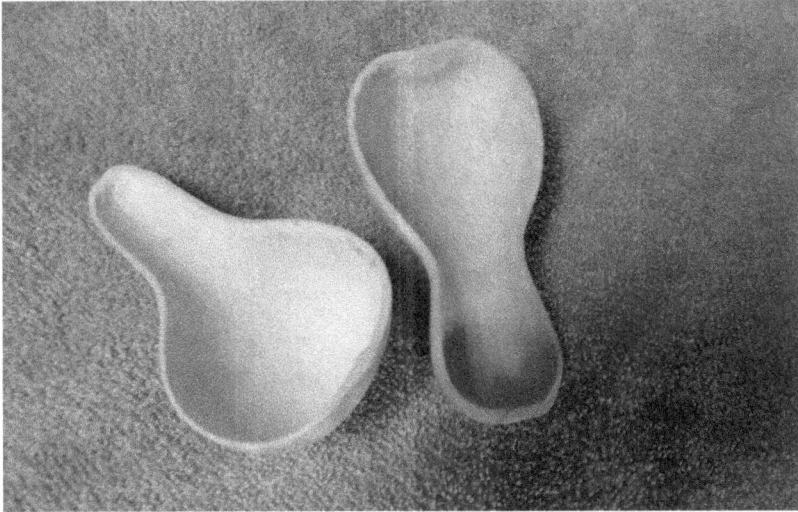

FIGURE 13. Gourd dippers, June 2013. Photo by author.

her was to tear pieces of material into the right size for use as pot holders or to employ several old sacks from store-bought flour that she kept around in piles. She also had several other pieces of fabric she kept around; one she called *łeets'aa' béjołí* (dishrag), and another, which she kept for cleaning cast-iron skillets, Dutch ovens, and similar items, she called *łeets'aa' bee yit'oodí* (dish towel).

Tall Woman had two or three sharp cedar sticks, each with one end pointed and the other end sharpened flat. Sometimes her son Howard made them for her, but she also made them herself. When preparing the sticks, she cleaned them, smoothed them, and flattened one end to make it wide, thin, and spatula-like. She referred to them as *tsé'ást'éí*, the same term she used for paperbread, maybe because she used them while preparing that bread.

Her stirring sticks, *'ádístsiin*, were made from greasewood; when I asked other elderly women about this, they all said that these sticks had to be made from greasewood, but no one could give me a reason for this practice. Tall Woman frequently collected these sticks and also fashioned them when she was by herself; she said that fall was the best time to do this and that prayers were necessary when you gathered them.[14] She also had her mother's stirring

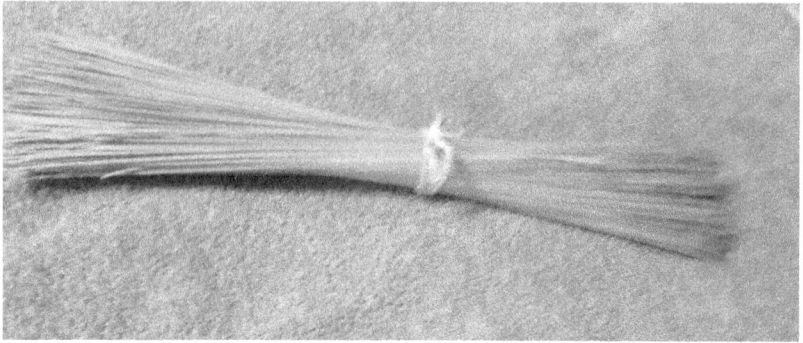

FIGURE 14. Hairbrush made from "under the pine tree brush grass," *ndíshchíí yaa bé'ézhóó*, June 2013. Photo by author.

FIGURE 15. Grass brush for grinding stones; also used as a strainer, June 2013. Photo by author.

sticks and kept them tied in a bundle with a cloth, separate from her own; occasionally she used them in addition to her own. These stirring sticks were mainly used for stirring cornmeal mush; when she was finished, Tall Woman would shake them off and give individual sticks to whatever children or grandchildren were around, reminding me of how we share the attachments of the electric mixer after we have mixed batter. Each child would clean the stick off with his or her finger and offer a short prayer while doing so. Tall Woman expected her daughters to try to make their own stirring sticks and brushes, but not in front of her.[15]

In some of the traditional narratives about the Emergence (see chapter 1), credit is given to the *nádleeh* (a transvestite or a hermaphrodite) for making certain cooking tools in the Lower Worlds (Goddard 1933, 128; Matthews 1897, 70–72; Haile 1981, 33–34; Reichard 1963,140–41). These tools included gourd dippers, stirring sticks, hairbrushes, grinding stones, pottery, water jars, earthen bowls and spoons, and baking stones. Others, however, learned different explanations. Some learned that *only* stirring sticks came from the Lower Worlds. For example, according to some, the first stirring sticks were made by the deity Salt Woman. She made them from greasewood, or *díwózhii*, because, according to Steven Begay (personal communication, 2016), "that was the only wood not involved in the Holy Way ceremonies." Salt Woman made them to stir *"gad 'ádin*, raw cornmeal mush, for the Twins. After she made that, she decided to show the boys how to roast meat and add salt on top of it to make it taste delicious." She made the stirring sticks in odd numbers "because the main stick represents the *kinaaldá*, then the four days of her [own] ceremony; hence there are at least five sticks in a bundle. Then you may add two sticks at a time to represent the things you want your daughter, niece, aunt, or sister to have: hard and soft goods, sheep and horses, and so forth."

Other ceremonialists have different ideas. One told me that the original stirring sticks had seven in a bundle, representing seven female deities, all viewed as "our grandmothers: Changing Woman, White Shell Woman, Sun Woman, Moon Woman, Water Woman, Mountain Woman, and Salt Woman." Others said seven stood for the seven days of the week. But now people bundle them together in both odd and even numbers. Some people believe that women should have two sets, one about one foot long for regular tasks, and the other about two feet long for ceremonial use.[16]

As is true of the other traditional tools, the stirring sticks pass from mother to daughter and are the sole property of women. Viewed as *k'aa'* (women's arrows), they offer protection from Poverty People and the monster Hunger. Sometimes a woman prefers to leave the set from her mother tied together and hung on the wall in the hogan or in the kitchen of another kind of home, as if on display. Then she uses only a set that she herself has made.

Traditionally, these stirring sticks are made in the fall; after offering corn-meal to the bush, one harvests the straightest sticks one can find by snapping them off at the bottom or cutting them with a knife. The outer bark is removed, either with a knife or by burning it off over the fire, and the sticks are rubbed with a rock to smooth them. Then they are tied together and hung up to dry for a few weeks before their first use.

The main use of the stirring sticks is in preparing corn foods. The woman is supposed to pray each time she uses them, both when starting to make the food and when finishing. These prayers are supposed to be for more food in the future and for a good life and blessings to come to the family, its land, and its livestock. Today the sticks are most often seen in use at the Girls' Puberty Ceremony when the corn cake batter is prepared. Each woman is expected to bring her own stirring sticks to help make the batter. They are also used to make the mush prepared for traditional weddings. A few people mentioned that occasionally the white corn used during sandpainting is stirred with them. As discussed in chapter 3, these sticks were also used to prepare mushes made from wild berries and yucca fruit. In those instances, they were sometimes used more for mashing up substances than for stirring them. A different kind of use for the *'ádístsiin* is for massaging women's bodies, either before they start to stir food with them or during the Kinaaldá; in the latter setting, the young woman may be massaged with the sticks as well as with the hands of the ideal woman attending her.

When a woman finishes stirring food with the sticks, she cleans each one off with a finger, eats the mush obtained that way, and prays when she is done; then she feeds the children. In earlier times the stirring sticks had songs and prayers associated with them; some say the songs were sung only while preparing food or using the sticks during the Girls' Puberty Ceremony. (Whether this is still done, I do not know; although I have witnessed and helped with many Kinaaldás in the past fifty years, I have never heard these songs used.) Now some say that the *'ádistsiin* are like prayersticks, because a woman can use them to bless herself, others, and the foods prepared with them. She can also bless all these with cornmeal, corn pollen, and prayers.

Another traditional tool made by the *nádleeh* in the Lower Worlds that is considered essential for life and viewed as a protector is the grass brush, or *bé'ézhóó'*. Others disagree, saying that there were no brushes in the Lower Worlds. The hairbrush and grinding stone brush are made from a tall grass known as *ndíshchíí yaa bé'ézhóó'*, "under the pine tree brush grass," accord-ing to Steven Begay. From 2010 to 2016 a lot of people told me that this grass was no longer around in the Chinle Valley because it's too dry and there is no rain. But people who live in moist areas can still find the long, tall grass used to make the hairbrush. They now make these grass hairbrushes and sell them at flea markets for ten dollars each (the price in 2013). Some say that one can simply break off juniper branches and use them as a brush or a strainer.

Other grasses used to make the hairbrush and the brush for the grinding stones that Tall Woman mentioned are broom grass, rabbit bush, and desert grass (see chapter 3). Until fall the stems of these grasses are green and pur-plish; in the fall, as the stems start to dry, they turn golden. Although beliefs differ about when to make the brushes and how to treat the stems in the pro-cess, most people say that anyone who wants to can make a hairbrush by collecting the grasses in the late fall; when they have dried, they can be easily broken off or cut with a knife. Many people also remove the outside cover-ings on the stems and then let the grasses dry. When they are dry, the stems are put together and the bottom is made even by tapping them on a flat sur-face. The bundles are usually about two feet long. The grasses are tied together about six inches from the bottom with a strip of cloth and then again about eight inches above that. Just before the bundle is used, the second tie is removed so that only the one nearest the base remains.

Like other traditional tools, these brushes have songs and prayers associ-ated with them. In earlier times it was common to have more than one hair-brush per household and for the brushes to be used daily. Now the *bé'ézhóó'* is used as a hairbrush mainly while fixing a girl's hair during her Kinaaldá.[17]

Except for length, the hairbrushes are the same as the brushes used to clean off the top and bottom grinding stones (*tsédaashch'íní* and *tsédaashjéé'*, respectively) after corn or other foods have been ground on them. Some prefer to call these brushes, which are eight to nine inches long, *tsé bąąh naalzhóó'*, "swept off the stone." Johnson (2011) said that using the grass brush to clean the stones after they have been used for grinding renews and rejuvenates the stones. Then the brush's name becomes *tsébee' nálzhóól*. Any brush that has been used to clean the grinding stones or to brush the ashes off food baked or roasted in the ashes in ground pits is no longer used as a hairbrush. Women might have several of these smaller brushes among their tools, for these were also used as sieves and strainers, to remove lumps or clots from liquids, and to clean up any cornmeal that has dropped on cooking surfaces.

Another traditional tool was the fire poker, or *honishgish*, which was viewed by many as sacred; it was most often made from cedar and could be either narrow or several inches in circumference. The growing end is the poker end. Tall Woman said that besides being used in cooking, it protected the home and thus was kept by the hogan door or, when in use for cooking, by the stove, the grill, or the fireplace to show the poker respect. It was used daily to push charcoal or ashes back while a woman prayed at the cooking fire after she had finished cooking. After praying with the fire poker, she set it aside.[18]

As mentioned above, some traditional accounts say that grinding stones were among the tools made in the Lower Worlds by the *nádleeh*. Others say that the first ones were made by the Holy People and brought by them to the surface of the present world, Mother Earth, for use by the Navajos. Still other ceremonial practitioners say that there were no grinding stones in the Lower Worlds; instead they were created on the Earth's Surface, in the present world, by the Holy People. One ceremonialist told me that Talking God and Hogan God gave White Shell Woman her first grinding stones at her puberty ceremony. Traditionally, every household had at least one set of grinding stones (also called metates and manos—milling stones) and a brush with which to clean off the stones after use. However, it was not unusual for a family to have several sets of different sizes. As a set, the stones serve as protectors against the monster Hunger, personified by Hunger Man and the Dichin Diné'é, or Hunger People. Collectively the stones are seen as Lady Warrior; many say that *tsédaashjéé'*, the bottom stone, is the woman's bow, and *tsédaashch'iní*, the top stone, is her bowstring. The corn kernels or whatever else is being ground are *k'aa'*, the arrows. Just as an animal is seen as taking away hunger, it is said that with the grinding stones, a woman can overcome hunger and poverty, just as a man traditionally did with his bow and arrows. Together the woman and the man plan how to fight hunger and prepare to do so with complementary actions.

Many people say the grinding stones are like a mother. The stones were made from a special hard rock found at or near a volcano lava flow bed. Once located, the stones were pounded so they would not crack or change shape. In earlier times, some say, this was the job of a stonecutter (Browne 2008).

But women could and did make their own. After finding a special hard rock, they hit it with another rock to make it the right shape. Thus the stones were frequently *dich'íízh* (rough). Like other traditional tools, they and the brushes associated with them are owned by the women and are passed down from mother to daughter, sometimes at the time of marriage. If there were none to be passed down, then men could be asked to make them. Today it is also possible to find traditional-culture classes on how to make grinding stones.

Grinding is viewed as a female job, although once in a while a man may be asked to do it for a medicine person who needs a substance ground up by a helper. In earlier times grinding stones were used in daily life to prepare food, but also in the Kinaaldá and other ceremonies. Their ceremonial use continues today. Grinding is done either inside or outside, with a sheepskin or goatskin being put down first, the hair side against the ground or floor. Some put a flat stone or a spruce tree branch under the bottom stone, at the thinner end, which is closest to the person doing the grinding, so that the stone slopes away from her. Although it was most often corn that was ground, people also ground berries, seeds, and other things, including some substances used as medicine.[19]

Since the surface of the stones frequently contained numerous tiny indentations, constant cleaning was necessary. This was done by the small brush discussed above. In earlier times, when the Navajos often moved with their animals to sheep camps or relocated for other reasons, the grinding stones would sometimes be buried in a field near the homesite, to be retrieved upon return. They are now occasionally found when land that has been unused for a long time is prepared once again for planting. There is reportedly no rule against using grinding stones acquired by finding them.

Just as with other cooking tools, there are prayers and songs associated with the grinding stones. The Corn Grinding Songs are still heard today, but mainly during demonstrations of grinding during various competitions (Johnson 1964). There are also Corn Songs that belong to the Blessingway.[20]

Although I never saw it, Tall Woman's daughters told me that in earlier times she had had a big, heavy set of grinding stones. She also had a another set, equally long but thinner (about four inches), which I saw in use. Tall Woman told me that grinding stones varied in size and thickness; she said the lighter, smaller ones were made and kept around so that children could help prepare foods and learn to grind. They were also easier to take along when traveling. Sometimes women passed the sets of grinding stones to the next generation of females in the family, but Tall Woman never mentioned having her mother's, and after Tall Woman's death, no one seemed to know what had happened to either of her sets. According to Tall Woman, women usually made their own grinding stones, often watching for the "right kind of stones" while traveling around, herding sheep, gathering foods, or visiting others.[21]

I have no idea how many sets Tall Woman had during her lifetime, but I do remember that at least once Frank brought home from his travels what he considered to be an appropriate stone that she would like for making a grinding stone. People rarely if ever loaned their grinding stones outside the immediate family, and some even took time to hide them if they were going to be absent from home for a while. Tall Woman reportedly used the heavy grinding stone set most often during her lifetime.[22] That was the first kind used right after the harvest. The thinner one was taken out for use when finer, more powder-like results were desired. Tall Woman laughingly suggested that if you were making food for people who had no teeth, you would use the fine grinding stones a lot of the time.

Pinyon nuts, corn (both fresh for kneel-down bread and not newly picked), wheat, and (earlier) some berries and seeds were all ground. Tall Woman never did have a food grinder, a meat grinder, a blender, or any such appliance. Grinding was done after the *tsédaashjéé'* (bottom stone) was placed on a soft goatskin or sheepskin; those around were always urged to help or to learn. Tall Woman said she always kept her *tsédaashch'íní*s (top stones) sharpened, often spending a whole day on this job. If both stones started to get too smooth or dull, she pounded them all over very, very slowly, using a hand-sized rock to hit them repeatedly.[23] The same procedure was applied to the bottom grinding stones by lightly tapping them all over their surfaces very slowly. That roughened the surface on the stones, made them sharp and "gave you teeth all over so you could grind things very fine," said Tall Woman.

MEASURING

Since Tall Woman measured everything with her hands and fingers and rolled things with her hands, she did not use rolling pins, measuring cups, or measuring spoons. As noted earlier, before cups became available commercially, gourd dippers were used for water and pouring batter. For a while Tall Woman still had such a dipper with her cooking equipment, but after 1970 I no longer saw it.

WATER FILTERS AND WATER BAGS

An item I did not know about and had not heard about from Tall Woman emerged while I was reviewing my fieldwork data and manuscript preparation with her daughter, Augusta. How common it was I do not know, but it seems appropriate to include it here. I will call it an early water filter or purifier. Augusta told me that her father, Frank Mitchell, had seen Garnett Bernally's father, Tom Scott, create a filtering system when he dug a well east of his hogan about ten feet deep and lined it with rock about halfway up the sides. Before that well, people would get water from a big ditch or the Canyon de Chelly Wash, but it would be muddy. After seeing how Tom Scott's well worked, Frank thought it would be a good idea to make such a system for his family, too. Using a gunnysack obtained either from the trading post or from government-issued rations (but not flour sacks), he put used charcoal (saved from fires) in it, then he lowered the sack into the water. The charcoal made the water clear up, so it could then be used for cooking and drinking.[24] Frank also made these water filters by putting wood and charcoal in an old blanket; it worked the same way. In any case, as soon as this homemade filter was put into a well, the water cleared up.

Tall Woman also had another way of clearing up the water from the irrigation ditch, which was always muddy and brown. After she had her children bring some ditch water back to her in whatever kind of container she had around, she would make a mixture of one-fourth cup of goat's milk to about two tablespoons of ditch water in a big can. Then she would pour the mixture down the well into the sack that had the charcoal in it. Frank also used this method in an area that he scraped out to create a big pond behind Augusta's house so she could plant.[25]

Near his newly created pond, Frank dug a hole about four or five feet deep and pounded a barrel into the hole. Then either he or Tall Woman gathered charcoal, put it in a gunnysack, and lowered that into the hole, followed by the milk-water mixture. The resulting water was very clean instead of muddy. When they applied this same process to the muddy water in the Canyon de Chelly Wash, it cleared it right up, so everybody could drink it; wash their clothes, their hair, and themselves in it; and bring their animals to drink it.

Before the time of trading posts and government rations, Navajos fashioned water bags from goatskins, and some families made and used these until the early 1920s. It was common to butcher animals carefully and save the skins for later use; sheepskins became bedding, among other things, and goatskins frequently became water bags. Water was put in through the neck area, and the legs were tied together with 'ats'id, the ligament from a sheep's backbone that was peeled off and dried for future use. Frank reportedly made plenty of these goatskin water bags when his children were small, and it was common to see people with these bags slung over their horses' backs or over their saddles when they rode on horseback to bring their livestock to drink at water sources.

INDOOR COOKING METHODS

When Tall Woman prepared food, most often it was cooked. The methods she used were boiling, roasting, baking, barbecuing, and frying; "stove-type" equipment included both outdoor cooking sites and those inside the hogan or inside one of her daughters' houses. The indoor site would be either a woodburning stove, handmade by a family member from a barrel, or a small commercial caboose-type cast-iron stove (fig. 16). Later it would be either a gas range, with bottled butane or propane supplies delivered or hauled in by family members with trucks, or, in a few cases, an electric range, once the family was connected to electricity.[26] Of these inside types, Tall Woman much preferred the woodburning stove, given her great familiarity with it over time. She used a variety of styles and sizes. Most often the men in the family were responsible for hauling water as well as securing wood, chopping it, and bringing it inside for her to use, but many times I saw her chopping and splitting wood with an axe herself. Most of the cooking on these stoves was either boiling or frying.[27]

Several elderly women I talked with during 2010–2015 reported having had a number of barrel stoves through time, although not any more. Tall Woman credited her son Seya with making an indoor stove for her "that

FIGURE 16. Woodstove inside a ramada, June 2001. Photo by author.

really worked well." He was working at the Chinle Dairy at the time and was able to secure a fifty-five-gallon drum or barrel from there.[28] It was not an oil drum, nor was it sticky or dirty inside; apparently it had previously been used as a water barrel. Seya cut the barrel in half in the middle and left the top on so that it could be used as a cooking surface and for heating up coffee and other things. Near the back of the top, whoever made these barrel stoves usually cut a cross or a star-shaped or multi-pronged hole and bent the pieces back so a stovepipe would fit over the folded back points and go up through the hogan's smoke hole. The cut-edge bottom of the barrel rested on the ground and could be moved all around. Tall Woman carried hers outside, inside, into the ramada (a roofed shelter with an open front), and elsewhere. On the side near the bottom there was another cutout, a rectangular doorway through which people put wood for heat, for making charcoal, or whatever. Cooking (roasting and baking) was also done inside the stove.

OUTDOOR COOKING METHODS

In earlier times, before barrels became available, cooking was done directly on the ground: a small indentation was made in the earth, rocks were piled around it to shield the fire from wind, and food was cooked over the fire (fig. 17). Tall Woman cooked outside whenever possible, using a variety of methods. Perhaps the easiest way was to set up an outdoor grilling area: she usually marked a circular place on the ground by lining the edges with rocks; then she added stones, cinder blocks, or rocks held together with mud to create some height; and finally, she put a mesh wire screen or a grill on the top (fig. 18). Under this grill she would build a fire, and she would cook either on the grill, over coals or hot ashes, or in the fire itself, depending on what she was preparing. Much of the food was roasted; for example, a sheep's head, a real delicacy, was cooked right in the ashes, being singed first and then occasionally turned while being roasted in the pit. Food could also be boiled in pots placed on top of the grill or reheated if cooked earlier. When Tall Woman cooked outside, she always kept old towels or rags around to use as pot holders, and she had one or more "poking sticks" that she used to turn food over and to rearrange hot coals or pieces of wood. She had no special name for these sticks, calling them "just plain sticks."

Tall Woman said she had a *tsét'ees*, a stone grill, but I never saw it. She described it as being about thirteen and a half inches long, eleven inches wide, and one and a half inches thick. It was "as smooth as glass," although she did not know what kind of stone it was. She was very careful to grease this stone grill with only one of two things: the spinal cord or the brain of a sheep. When butchering, she often saved these parts and dried them for later use; then they were reconstituted with water. She said that since Frank used the brain when tanning skins for making moccasins, she might not always have one available. Her stone grill was her mother's and was given to her before her mother passed away.

"That was the only way you could inherit things," she explained, "if people gave them to you before they died. Otherwise, their things had to be gotten rid of, disposed of in some way." (Tall Woman inherited her mother's weaving tools, too.) She used this grill only for making paperbread, and she said, "I didn't do that very often because it took a lot of wood to make it. Then too, your hand had to move very, very fast over the surface of the stone grill, in both directions so you didn't get burned. My daughters were afraid to try

FIGURE 17. Tall Woman cooking a meal in a ground pit, with Isabelle Deschine (seated in front of sheepskins hanging out to air) and her son, Jerry Mitchell, July 1966. Photo by author.

FIGURE 18. Outdoor fireplace, with a grill rack on legs beyond the left wall, May 2014. Photo by author.

doing that." Now no one in the family knows what happened to her stone grill.

Sometimes Tall Woman preferred to dig into the ground to create a pit in which things could be cooked, most often by baking. The size, shape, and depth varied according to what was being prepared. The biggest pits I ever saw her make were those used for the all-night baking of the *'alkaan*, the traditional corn cake prepared for the Girls' Puberty Ceremony, or Kinaaldá. The pit was made anew each time, and whenever the ceremony was going to be held at her home, Tall Woman was the one who measured the pit (fig. 19), outlined where it should be dug east of the hogan, and then helped dig it (fig. 20) with a pickaxe and shovel (Frisbie [1967] 1993, 40; Mitchell 2001, 280).

Another use for such pits was to roast corn. They were most often used by people who did not have a *bááh bighan* (a small outdoor earth or mud oven, described below). First they dug a big deep hole in the ground, about six feet in diameter, and built a huge fire in it that was kept going all day. Then they brought a wagon (or later a pickup truck) full of green corn, nearly ripe, to the hole. Once the hole was hot, they put the fire out and left some charcoal in the hole, which they filled with corn and then sealed with damp earth. Then another fire was built on top. The husks were left on the corn while it was being steamed, which made it really sweet. People said that the best way to roast corn was in this kind of pit, although you could also do it in a skillet. Tall Woman often mentioned making *ts'áálbái* (a coffee creamer made from corn) this way and said that after the corn was roasted it should be ground fine like flour.

The other kind of outdoor cooking place that I know Tall Woman used was a small, round, flat-topped adobe oven called a *bááh bighan* (literally, "bread, its house"). Frequently this was made on the left (north) side of the hogan, but once she built one farther away, to the northwest, where her daughter Mary lived. Tall Woman said that these temporary outdoor ovens could be built anywhere; there were no rules about where they were put. She built them by herself, as did others; if she wanted a bigger one and one of her sons was at home, however, he might help her.

The *bááh bighan* (figs. 21 and 22) was often the height of an adult arm, and rocks or whatever else was around were used to shape it. It had a dirt floor unless there were flat rocks to use for that; the wide doorway faced east, and a smoke hole was made on the top. The Navajos made either a flat or domed top. Clearly the larger Navajo outdoor ovens were like the Pueblo outdoor

FIGURE 19. Measuring the pit for cooking the 'alkaan, the corn cake for the Girls' Puberty Ceremony, June 1963. Photo by author.

FIGURE 20. Digging the pit in which the 'alkaan will bake overnight at a girl's puberty ceremony, June 1963. Photo by author.

FIGURE 21. Chester Begay's *bááh bighan*, earth or mud oven, back view, with a barbecue grill made from a barrel on a wheeled stand, August 2013. Photo by author.

bread ovens, sometimes called "beehive-shaped" or by their Spanish name, *hornos*. Mud, dirt, and water were mixed to make them, and they had to be patched with mud plaster or adobe when they needed repairs; the mud always had to be thick enough to keep all the steam inside. These ovens were not only easily repaired but also easily replaced without too much effort. When the oven was being used, hot rocks were put inside it along the edges to make it stay hot for a long time. After the oven was filled with food, such as bread or corn, the smoke hole was covered with a flat rock and the doorway was covered with a piece of metal or a round or flat rock, then often sealed with mud or clay. Tall Woman, like others, used this kind of outdoor oven for making kneel-down bread, but whether she ever processed green corn right after it was harvested and brought in from the field in this kind of an oven, I do not know. Her daughters said that as far as they knew, she used this oven only for making kneel-down bread.

FIGURE 22. Chester Begay's *bááh bighan*, front view, August 2013. Photo by author.

Although I never photographed the flat-topped small adobe oven while living with the Mitchells, Augusta and I did visit several Pueblo outdoor ovens in Chinle in 2013 (figs. 23 and 24). One was definitely of the larger bee-hive type; the others were smaller and in various stages of disrepair. All were reportedly used for both baking bread and processing green corn. Reh (1983, 6) provides a good picture of a round, flat-topped oven similar to the kind made by Tall Woman. Terry Reynolds (personal communication, 2012), who edited the Reh manuscript, told me that this particular oven was made from stones piled up, with mud applied both inside and outside and a final plaster coat of mud on the outside. When Reynolds sat down beside it, her shoulders and head were higher than the top of the oven. Reynolds reported seeing them in Sheepsprings, and Klara Kelley (personal communication, 2013) said she may have seen some in the Four Corners area during archaeological survey work. Others mentioned additional archaeological sightings; for example, David Brugge (personal communication, 2011) said he saw two styles of ovens during the Chaco Project: the usual beehive type and a smaller, flat-roofed one. Although some people claimed that these were each used for different purposes, he doubted it. Others suggested that the Spanish actually got this kind of oven from the Moors, perhaps during the Roman period, on the Iberian Peninsula.[29]

Two recent pictures are found in Gorman (2013) of a mud oven made in 2005 and used for steaming corn and baking bread. Gorman is shown making a mud oven and then standing behind a finished one. She said they made it using half sand and half clay, with some straw and water. She credited the idea of adding straw to a class they took on building an adobe house. The mud oven does need to be replastered occasionally.

Farm Pests

When we discussed the troubles faced in growing crops, Tall Woman said she should probably mention something that happened occasionally to some people. Sometimes crops were stolen by other people, not animals. Her family experienced that a few times, and it seemed to always be different kinds of melons and squash that were taken, not corn or beans. Tall Woman said that this was why she tried to check their fields every day; some people also planted their squash and melons closer to where they lived so they could keep a better eye on them.[30] As far as Tall Woman knew, nobody was ever caught for stealing crops from the fields, but everybody was aware that it might happen.

Turning to other sources of trouble in the fields, Tall Woman said that she viewed crows as the worst garden pests around. "They always managed to show up when the corn was ready to be eaten," she said, "and they knew how to pick it at just the right time." Of course, she did not use the ears ruined by crows as food for her family; instead she left the husks on and set them aside as food for the animals.

While I was living with her, we made scarecrows to put up in the corn-fields (figs. 25 and 26), and we hung cans with rocks in them, too—anything to make noise to scare the crows. The scarecrows were nothing fancy: we just took two sticks, crossed them, tied them in place, and then draped a shirt on that, letting the sleeves wave around. When we saw the crows starting to circle and gather, we would chase them away while we were hoeing. Both

FIGURE 23. Pueblo-style oven, front view, at Eugene Peterson's residence, August 2013. Photo by author.

FIGURE 24. Pueblo-style oven, back view, August 2013. Photo by author.

FIGURE 25. Navajo cornfield in Chinle with two scarecrows, May 2015. Photo by author.

Howard and Seya sometimes killed crows with slingshots or BB guns and then hung them upside down on crosses in the field, jokingly calling that "crucifying the crow."

Rabbits reportedly didn't bother the Mitchells' gardens very much, but sometimes cottontail rabbits got into the melons. Tall Woman said they didn't bother the corn much. "Sometimes we would tie a dog in the garden to bark and chase both the crows and the rabbits," she noted. Moles (*na'agédí biza'azis hólóní*) were a different matter; they caused a lot of trouble even when the men were plowing and trying to get the fields ready to plant.[31] They'd find mole holes all over, and sometimes they had to go back and plow the fields again to get rid of those holes. Some years it seemed like everybody had trouble from moles. Seya finally obtained and set a metal trap, Tall Woman explained:

That was very dangerous because all of us had to remember where he

FIGURE 26. Navajo cornfield southwest of Fort Defiance, with a shallow well pump, September 2016. Photo by Klara Kelley.

put it. It seemed like the main time moles would come out was when we were irrigating. Once water got into their holes, they'd come out, just like prairie dogs. Way back, gophers (*na'azísí*) also used to eat the corn. People used metal traps for them, too, but those were usually small traps; sometimes, however, they used regular big rat traps for them. A lot of people preferred to pour water down their holes and make them come out that way and then just kill them by hitting them over the head.

Squirrels didn't cause people any trouble unless they were trying to grow crops in the mountainous areas. Tall Woman said that in the Chinle Valley they just didn't see any around. The same thing was true about the big rats; those were in the mountains and often ate garden crops there. However, some of the people who lived in Wheatfields, Arizona, had rats in their houses and their summer camps, too; at times they also had mice. Because of that they couldn't leave any food at their houses if they weren't there all the time.

Another thing that caused problems was grasshoppers, *nahachagii*. One year a long time ago they were really bad, especially in the summer. The people had to fight them, and that one time the government gave the Navajos some poisoned grain mixed with something sweet. Each person who had a field got a barrel of that and was told to put it along the edges of the field, along the irrigation ditches in each section, and on all of the mounds in the field. The poisoned grain really stank, and the people were told to wear gloves and cover their noses so they wouldn't inhale the smell. The grasshoppers seemed to be able to smell the corn and know that it was ready, so they just moved in overnight. Sometimes none of the corn crop was saved because the grasshoppers chewed on it while it was young. The people dried those ears and used the husks for sheep food.

At noon, the worst time of day for the problem, the fence posts would be solidly covered with grasshoppers. Tall Woman's family did not plant any beans that year because the ground was covered with grasshoppers. In 1969 or 1970 the government finally sent a plane to spray the whole Chinle Valley. It didn't tell the people exactly when the plane was coming, but such spraying was usually done in the morning. Once a plane crashed in a field right after the pilot had sprayed the last field to the south; when he turned around to do it one last time, he crashed. All the adults rode their horses over to see the crash, and the kids ran over there, too. Tall Woman told her children to stay home because there might be dead people in the plane, but it turned out that the pilot was okay. That spray did do some good.

Another plane sent to spray landed near the police station across from the Catholic church (the station's 1970 location). The pilot might have been looking for the old airport and misjudged his location. Unfortunately he was killed in the accident, but that spraying also did some good. After that there were grasshoppers for a few more years, but not as bad as before the first spraying. The grasshoppers finally moved to some other place and crawled underground.[32]

Seya said that when he was in school in Albuquerque (1929–1933), the same problem with grasshoppers happened there: they just showed up in a thick cloud and ate everything in the fields. The school officials bought chickens and ducks, and the kids chased them out into the fields so they could eat the grasshoppers. Since the eggs are in the soil, some people say that if they cultivate in the fall they can get the eggs out. People stopped irrigating after the grasshopper problem began, so then the weeds grew. Tall Woman was always out in her fields checking for grasshoppers. Any time she saw tiny things jumping around, she'd come back home and say they were starting to come out again.

There were other kinds of insects, too, such as locusts, but they didn't bother the garden and were not viewed as pests because they can be eaten. The Navajos hunted locusts and removed their heads before eating them. There were also problems from a strange-shaped green insect called *to'iłchííhí* (I am not sure what its name is in English). This pest attacked the squash plants on both the top and the bottom of the leaves. Tall Woman mixed chili powder with water, and sprinkled it on the leaves of the squash plant. That bug really stinks. Caterpillars, *ch'osh ditł'ooí*, didn't cause any trouble in the gardens. There were big furry ones and also the kind that hang in the trees in nests like long bags.

Some kinds of animals also bothered the crops. Raccoons were not a problem, but skunks were. They were as bad as crows and acted just like them, getting into the corn. Howard and Seya shot at them with guns or slingshots, and sometimes that helped. Dogs and coyotes could also be a problem, but mainly for the sheep—a pack of dogs could quickly kill all the sheep. That happened to Tall Woman's daughter Mary, and she was so upset that she never replaced the sheep. If the dogs and coyotes were really hungry, they would get into the corn and eat that, too.

Sometimes it was really just the soil that was the problem in the fields: it was just too full of clay. Tall Woman liked to mix sand and mountain dirt from Wheatfields into her soil when she could.

Snakes, *tł'iish*, could also be a problem, especially in the corn, in the alfalfa fields, and among the watermelons. Tall Woman always carried a big stick with her and told her children to do the same thing. She said to "swish back and forth with it so that those snakes would know you were coming and get out of the way." Tall Woman always talked to the snakes as she walked, swishing her stick. She put *nabííh*, a plant that wards off snakes, around the house, both inside and outside, if she found a nest of snakes nearby; she also put it by the corral and other places. The main kind of snake she talked about was called *diyoołish*.[33] There were water snakes around too; they would show up during irrigation or when the washes were running.

There were two other kinds of pests that bothered the corn. One was *dá'áchaan*, black stuff on the cornstalk that some people call smut. If people found that on any stalk, they would separate the ears from that stalk and use them only for the animals. The other thing was *naadą́ą́' bich'osh*, a worm that would get inside those ears. When people found that, they would throw those ears into the animal food pile, too. The worms themselves could be fed to chickens, if people had them.

The Decline of Farming

Farming declined throughout the reservation for many reasons, not the least of which were a lack of adequate rain, ground that was too dry and hard, and the need to haul water for the farm as well as for the household. Tall Woman and others in her generation all reported that in earlier times the reservation got "*lots* of rain!" In the Mitchell family, the availability of people capable of helping with the various tasks involved in farming declined, too, as people found wage work and were not at home full-time. Furthermore, as people, including Tall Woman, aged and started having more physical problems, cultivating crops, even alfalfa, became increasingly difficult and was finally abandoned. Today the areas used earlier in farming that are still in the family are either covered with noxious weeds or have become homesites for the next generation.[34] Occasionally a household might try to grow tomatoes near the house in an area fenced to keep out sheep, goats, dogs, and wandering horses and cows, but success continues to be minimal.

Beliefs about Food

The last topic Tall Woman and I discussed before we got into specific foods and recipes was some of the beliefs that she and others had about foods. These often came up first as asides during discussions about other things. According to Wolfe (1984) and many others, at least in earlier times Navajos had as many beliefs about food and its preparation as they did about other activities, such as weaving, pottery making, and hair combing. Although unfortunately I did not devote much time to this topic while working with Tall Woman, I would like to include some of the beliefs she mentioned. For example, it was commonly believed that cows, horses, and donkeys should be butchered only in the winter. Obviously, the cold weather preserved much more of the meat and kept it from spoiling in days before refrigeration became available. But it was also believed that these animals were the fattest in the winter and easier to butcher when fat. Some also said that in the winter these animals were not as "fishy," or strong tasting, as they were in the summer. Likewise, many believed that since it was more common for people to be sick in the winter, people in general needed more meat, especially horsemeat, to protect them from colds at that time of year.

It is not surprising that there were many beliefs accompanying sheep and goatmeat. For example, it was a shared belief that one should eat the sheep intestines, 'ach'íí', to bring good health. They are rich in vitamins because the green grass and excrement remain in them when the animals are butchered. These contents are thoroughly removed, and the cleaned-out intestines are considered a prize delicacy to this day. Another special part was the sheep's head after it was cooked, including the eyeballs. Both Tall Woman and Frank told me repeatedly that the eyeballs were always given to an honored guest, and indeed they followed that practice. Tall Woman also thought it was important to eat boiled sheep or goat lungs because they are soft. Some people said that eating sheep brains helps the human brain, but others said that the brains of these animals should not be eaten because doing so stretches the stomach.

Different families had different ideas about which organs were considered delicacies. Tall Woman prized the lungs, heart, kidney, and liver; a neighbor disagreed, saying that the lungs and trachea were generally not liked because they had hardly any fat or meat on them. In general, eating too much fatty meat was believed to cause stomachaches, laziness, and stomach distention.

Steven Begay (personal communication, 2016) said there were lots of these beliefs.[35] He added that as children, they had been taught that neckbones (especially the first one) and the tailbone of sheep should be eaten only by very old women and men; young people who ate them would develop poor complexions and deformities. Boiling backbone pieces in a stew would make the rest of the meat disappear. Steven was also taught that only old people can eat the fat and the little bit of meat on the sternum; if young people do that, it will make their faces sunken. Bone marrow should never be sucked out of boiled bones; instead it should be pounded out—and once again, only by old people. Fatty marrow with lots of salt was considered delicious, but that food too was only for old people; if young people ate it, it would cause them to be lazy.

Some people in Begay's grandparents' generation used cooked bone marrow like hair gel. Boys and men were told never to eat mush off the stirring sticks because that was only for women. Children were forbidden to eat the thin film of cornmeal mush that dries on top of mush that is setting or is sticking on the sides of a container; should they ignore this belief, they would get speech problems, like stuttering. The cure for this was identical to the practice that Seya reported his mother, Tall Woman, and her mother had done to him before he went to school: coming up behind him, his grandmother surprised him by hitting a clay pot with a stick so hard that the pot broke and the pieces fell all over his head (see Mitchell 2001, 159).

Begay recently mentioned a few more beliefs that he had been taught; for example, women who had recently given birth should not eat *naayízí* (squash) or melons; if they did, their newborns would have upset stomachs. Likewise, these new mothers should not eat intestines or other internal organs; if they did, they would not heal.

As noted earlier, some people believed that those who ate the meat of little yellow birds would have nice-looking children. Food beliefs associated with the Girls' Puberty Ceremony can be found in Frisbie ([1967] 1993). Elsewhere in the Navajo ethnographic literature there is plenty of information about rules and beliefs surrounding food before, during, and after hunting, pregnancy, childbirth, weddings, trips to the sacred mountains, and all other ceremonial events.

3 | Defeating Hunger by Making Something from the Earth

Cooking with Tall Woman

INTRODUCTION TO THE RECIPES

As explained in the introduction to this book, the Navajo Origin narratives include accounts of the activities of the twin sons of the deity Changing Woman. Among their adventures, the Holy Twins traveled the world, killing monsters that were destroying Mother Earth and making the earth uninhabitable. While most of the monsters were eradicated, a few among them were spared, including Old Age, Poverty, and Hunger. As the narratives relate, Hunger was allowed to live to remind humans or Earth Surface People that it was up to them to be actively involved in their own well-being and to work the land and utilize its resources without waste to maintain their own health and achieve the desired state of *hózhǫ́*. Through time, it was a major responsibility of generation after generation of Navajo women to keep Hunger at bay. This they achieved by acquiring and then fully using an in-depth knowledge and understanding of the environment, its diversified resources, and specific tools such as grinding stones, stirring sticks, brushes, and pottery. This chapter explores what Tall Woman chose to share about how to survive. Discussing a variety of Mother Earth's resources and the practices she learned in order to use them most efficiently, she reveals the many ways she knew to ward off starvation and hunger.

A quick glance at the following pages will show readers that this chapter is not like an Anglo, or Bilagáana, cookbook. Just the categories recognized, as well as their names, make that obvious in an instant. In Tall Woman's collection of recipes, one will not find any hors d'oeuvres, appetizers, salads, entrées, side dishes, desserts, salsa recipes, and the like. There will also be no pies, cookies, brownies, pastries, or cakes, except for one, the 'alkaan, which in Tall Woman's time was made specifically for the Girls' Puberty Ceremony, or Kinaaldá. As already mentioned, much of the cooking was done outside over a fire, in a pit, or in an earthen oven quickly made by whoever needed to use it.

The recipes that follow are presented in seven sections, as organized by Tall Woman's remaining children in 2014–2015. The categories and the contents of each section were established by them according to their perspectives, not mine. No claim is being made that these categories would be universal among the Navajos if outsiders were to elicit paradigms or taxonomies that Navajos have of "traditional food." It was no surprise that just discussing with other Navajo friends how Tall Woman's recipes were being organized made it instantly clear that diverse ideas existed.

Other elements to note include the following: none of the recipes are for high-altitude cooking, given the elevations in which the family lived. Likewise, there has been no attempt to rewrite the recipes for possible creation in a microwave oven, which was of course unheard of in Tall Woman's day. Occasionally someone from the family added the required temperature and time settings if preparation was to be done in the oven of a gas or an electric stove, but such stoves were never important to Tall Woman. Most of her cooking was done over a wood fire, either inside a woodstove in the hogan or outside on a grill or a baking sheet, in the ground or in a mud or earthen oven. Similarly, as might be expected, Tall Woman talked about "a pinch of this," "a little bit of that," or "maybe a handful or two" of whatever. She did not use measuring cups or measuring spoons when cooking, nor did she own any. Although she occasionally used a gourd dipper to pour batter onto a grill for pancakes, she mainly used her hands for everything else involved in food preparation, including rolling, shaping, stretching, and flattening tortillas, frybread, and other foods. Where measurements have been provided, it was mainly Augusta Sandoval, a professional cook in her own right, who did so.

Sometimes, when discussing how to use different kinds of food resources, Tall Woman talked informally about what the Navajos did with them, where and when they found them, and so forth, rather than itemizing the different steps of a recipe. At other times she shifted to a recipe format, describing ingredients item by item. I have left the presentations as she gave them to me in all seven sections. Some sections include a mixture of both styles; others, such as sections 2 and 7, do not use any recipe formats in the conversations.

At times there are multiple recipes for one item; this is because she herself mentioned a variety of ways of making something or because her daughters reported that she had taught them variations she hadn't mentioned to me. All agreed to have the variations identified and included. Then too, not all her daughters knew how to make all the foods she talked about because they had lived in different places during their lives. Initially they were all at home, of course, but then some went to boarding schools, some married and set up their own households in separate hogans and homesteads nearby, and some left for military service or wage work through on- or off-reservation employment (Mitchell 2001).

As noted earlier, Tall Woman's daughter Augusta Sandoval was a major help in assembling the recipes. Although we did not test each recipe together, she has made all the recipes herself over the years, now including even the few she hadn't learned about earlier from her mother. The area that was the most difficult to pursue was the wild foods, mainly the plants used in earlier times. Many of these plants are no longer found where the family or other relatives live, as Tall Woman herself often noted when traveling with me to search for them and when talking about their importance in earlier times.

Finally, despite Tall Woman's vast knowledge of ceremonial foods and the medicinal properties of various things in nature, especially in the plant and animal worlds, none of this has been included even though Tall Woman was well-known for it. Much of this knowledge is now considered intellectual property and is therefore restricted to its rightful owners by the Native American Graves Protection and Repatriation Act, the federal law known as NAGPRA. The research permit process on the Navajo Nation is designed to uphold this law; it is understood that anything considered to be sacred, or to be intellectual property of any kind, will not be included in publications.

Section 1 | Wild Foods

Animals, Birds, and Insects; Nuts; Plants,
Including Greens, Bulbs, and Roots, Leaves,
Seeds, and Wild Grasses; Wild Vegetables;
Berries; and Other Fruit

Large Wild Animals

Tall Woman and her family ate meat from large animals that were hunted by the men, especially venison from deer, antelope, and elk. In earlier times the methods, procedures, and required personal behaviors involved were well-known and usually adhered to, in order to make the hunt successful. (See Hill [1938] for a classic study of Navajo hunting.) Venison was prepared mainly like beef and mutton—baking on live coals or boiling was often the preferred method of cooking it. Sausage and jerky could be made from these animals, and since the techniques were also used with domesticated animals, the making of both sausage and jerky will be covered in section 5.

DEER

Deer (*bįįh*) meat was and continues to be highly prized, and deer, along with antelope and elk, are still hunted in the mountains to the north of the reservation, in Lukachukai, the Chuskas, north in Colorado, and elsewhere. The hunters go in parties—earlier they went on horseback with offerings, prayers, and many ritual and behavioral requirements; now they use pickup trucks in order to cover as much distance as possible. According to Tall Woman, as soon as the hunters kill the deer, they butcher it and cook the meat by frying or boiling it, like mutton. She said that the deer's head and internal organs are seldom eaten. Before the men return from the hunt, any meat that is left is hung up to dry and turned into jerky (see section 5). Unlike mutton jerky, venison jerky must be pounded and soaked in hot water before it is eaten.

BEARS

Tall Woman said that only under dire circumstances, when people were starving, would they kill and eat a bear (*shash*). There were all kinds of rules to follow for that, such as sacrifices to make before killing it, and only small pieces of its meat would be eaten. Most people believed that bear meat had special protective powers, she said, but they also feared that eating it would make people mean. Tall Woman herself had never tasted it, but she knew people who had.

Small Wild Animals

Several small animals were also hunted for food. Tall Woman mentioned rabbits, squirrels, pack rats, and prairie dogs. Badgers were also eaten, in earlier times, she added, but that was a *long* time ago. Although she taught her children what badgers looked like, she never discussed how they were prepared as food.

RABBITS

Both the cottontail rabbit (*gałbáhí*) and the jackrabbit (*gahtsoh*) were common on the reservation during Tall Woman's lifetime, and they continue to be plentiful in undeveloped areas. Rabbit (*gah*) meat was commonly baked, boiled, fried, or dressed and boiled with cornmeal and salt; it was also eaten in stew. Rabbits were commonly eaten before domesticated livestock became prevalent, and even later people continued to eat them. Some families even raised rabbits for a ready source of food rather than as pets.

Children commonly caught rabbits while out herding and brought them home so Tall Woman could cook them. Sometimes the children went on horseback, either alone or with just a few others, to chase the rabbits down. They would take a greasewood branch and roughen its end so that it had a small fork at the tip that grabbed the fur when the stick was twisted. The children pushed the end of this stick down a rabbit hole and turned it a few times to catch a rabbit's fur and skin on the stick. Then they pulled the stick out carefully and clubbed the animal over the head or slung it down on the ground to kill it.

Sometimes people hunted rabbits at night with flashlights. It continues to be common, at least in some families, to hunt rabbits with slingshots, even when traveling for other reasons, such as to find wood, plants, specific herbs, or types of juniper. Some elderly men say that the only thing that made them quit hunting rabbits was the loss of their eyesight; all still seem to enjoy the taste of rabbit meat.

Tall Woman loved rabbit stew (see section 6), but she also fixed rabbits other ways whenever anybody brought her some. She described how to roast or fry them as follows: Skin and clean the rabbit. Singe the meat if desired. Stuff it with potatoes, onions, or other things if preferred. Then dig a pit and roast it whole under wet dirt and hot coals. Sometimes people would wrap it up in burlap if any was handy. It can also be fried in a skillet with grease over hot coals, with or without a grill. Rabbit meat was always eaten fresh.

SQUIRRELS

Another animal that was hunted and eaten was the squirrel (*hazéí*). Tall Woman's family all liked squirrel meat, and people used a slingshot to catch long-tailed ones, usually the gray squirrel (*tseek'i nástánii*). Like rabbits, the squirrels were cleaned and cooked by either frying or baking them in coals with the fur still on. Tall Woman said that although squirrels were really common when she started raising her children, eventually (sometime in the 1940s) they seemed to disappear, and as a result people didn't eat them very often anymore; instead they ate wild rabbits and prairie dogs.

PACK RATS

Pack rats (*łé'étsoh*) were eaten more frequently in earlier times, mainly so people wouldn't starve. Like rabbits and squirrels, these were cleaned, and like squirrels, the fur was left on during cooking. Usually people added salt and baked the meat in hot coals until it was tender. Even in the 1960s and 1970s some people still liked to eat pack rats, but by then, reportedly, they were already really hard to find.

The last wild animal that Tall Woman talked about eating was the prairie dog (*dlǫ́ǫ́'*). Prairie dogs were easy to find and were frequently seen near the family's home. It was very common for boys to hunt prairie dogs while they were out herding or walking; Tall Woman didn't know of any girls who had tried it. She and her family really liked to eat prairie dogs, so she was always happy when the children brought some home so she could fix them for a meal.

After a prairie dog was killed, the insides were cleaned out. Then a hole was made in the ground and preheated with wood. When the pit was hot enough, the fire was removed. Some people preferred to singe off the prairie dog's hair before cooking it, whereas others did that later. According to Tall Woman, either way was all right. The animals were roasted in the shallow ground pits after the fire had been removed. The meat was salted first and then put in the pit, covered with hot coals, and roasted slowly until it was fully cooked. It tasted like horsemeat or squirrel meat, she said. A really special dish was made by washing out the stomach, filling it with vegetables, and then putting the stuffed prairie dog back in the roasting pit to bake the whole thing. For Tall Woman and her family, stuffed roast prairie dog was "a real treat."

Birds

Only two birds were mentioned by Tall Woman as among the wild things that her family captured and ate: turtledoves (*hasbídí*) and the small yellow birds, *'ayááshiłtsoii*, mentioned in the previous chapter. Birds were often hunted with slingshots if they were small; elaborate traps were used to catch larger ones, such as geese, ducks, and wild turkeys. Doves were very tasty; they might be brought down and killed, or they might be already dead. The feathers were plucked, the chest was opened up, the insides were removed, and the remaining carcass was baked on live coals. Sometimes a grill was used, but at other times the meat was salted and fried on the end of a stick.

The small yellow birds were a frequent target of Tall Woman's son Seya; he always carried his slingshot, and while he was out herding with his sisters, when the sunflowers were blooming it was common for him to catch these birds. He liked to open them up from top to bottom, remove their guts, break off their heads, peel off the skin, and save the wings and heads. Then he'd flatten out whatever was left with his hand or a small stone. After he had caught four or five of these, he'd roast them together. Seya liked to carry a small grill with him while he was herding, and he was always telling his sisters stories about why they needed to eat whatever he caught. He claimed that they would have very nice-looking children if they ate small yellow birds. Tall Woman just laughed about that.

Insects

Tall Woman mentioned three insects that could be used as food. The first, 'ásaa' neiyéhii, was a blister beetle; she was told that it had been a food source in the early days, when people were starving, but she had never eaten one herself. When I tried to learn more about it, I discovered that the adult beetles produce cantharidin, a highly toxic substance that remains active in their blood even after death. It is reported to cause severe skin irritation and blisters in both humans and horses. These beetles liked to hide in alfalfa hay. Tall Woman, who knew these beetles were toxic, did not know how they would have been prepared as a safe food source.

The second insect was the tsís'ná, a black and yellow bee. These bees were always around the irrigation ditches that people dug for their crops, especially in places where small sunflowers and wild spinach were numerous. Sometimes they could also be found where hummingbirds were common. Tall Woman told her children that they had to be very careful when catching the bees, which could attack and sting them and make their arms and faces swell up. She taught them that there was a clear honey sack or bag inside the bee's body; if they caught a bee and used their mouths to break the sack open, they could get the honey out. Doing that, of course, killed the bee.[1]

The third kind of insect is wóóneeshch'įįdii (locusts or cicadas), which are commonly used as food. Summer is when they are plentiful. They are caught by hand and then roasted or browned in ashes. Some people prefer to remove the legs, heads, and wings after the roasting is done, if they haven't been burned off, but some prefer to do that first. Some say that by about 1940 only children were eating them, but others disagree and report that these locusts are still eaten today. They reportedly taste like roasted peanuts. Apparently some people ate them for medicinal reasons; they have been said to cure stomachaches and prevent sore throats as well as smallpox, measles, and other contagious diseases.[2]

Nuts

Pinyon nuts, or *neeshch'íí'*, from the pinyon tree, are the only nuts that Tall Woman mentioned using as food, but I have heard other Navajos talk about acorns (*chéch'il bináá'*) and walnuts (*ha'ałtsédii*). Pinyon nuts are oily, sweet, and good to eat raw by cracking the shell or thin casing with one's teeth. It's like eating sunflower seeds. Navajos love pinyon nuts, and most say they are best roasted. They can be eaten plain, unroasted, or roasted in the shell; they can also be ground into a meal or ground with something else, especially parched corn. They can also be made into pinyon nut butter (*'atłish*) and pinyon nut oil (*neeshch'íí' bik'ah*).

Picking pinyon nuts has always been a social activity.[3] Families travel to where they know or hear that the nuts are plentiful, usually up in the mountains in thick wooded areas, and then camp out in groups for a long weekend or even longer, staying under the trees in quickly constructed juniper enclosures while they pick the nuts. The crops vary in size and abundance over the years. One area will often get a big crop of pinecones every two or three years. Before they are ready, the cones look like tightly closed wooden flowers; under each petal there is a seed, about one-half inch long, in a thin covering. In the fall and early winter the cones open up, and the seeds are ready to fall. You have to walk a lot to gather them, and people usually pick up only the big ones. Everybody enjoys the social time as well as the results because, as Tall Woman pointed out, "pinyons are the only nuts that Navajos gather to eat and also to sell or trade." People can gather, shell, and eat or gather and roast. The nuts are high in protein, potassium, magnesium, iron, and zinc and also rich in fat. In earlier times in the summer, if people were nearly starving, they would sometimes eat the inner bark of the tree with salt.

The individual fallen nuts are gathered off the ground and put in sacks or cans; sometimes the crop is so thick that a person needs to use both hands to gather the nuts. People often take an old blanket, a shower curtain, canvas, or tarp, spread it out under a tree, and then shake the tree.[4] When they are done, they rake the ground and put everything into a fine mesh screen that is handmade for this purpose. That is shaken to remove the debris, and the nuts are picked out. Some people also like to raid rats' nests because rats stockpile the nuts if they get the chance.

To roast pinyons, use a dry pot, pan, or skillet over a low fire and stir the nuts until they are a bit darker and the inner nut meat is crispy but not burned. Then sprinkle the nuts with salt, let them dry, and eat them while they are still hot by first cracking the thin casing with your teeth to remove the nut meat.[5] Sometimes the roasted nuts would be cracked between rocks or on the bottom grinding stone by rolling the top stone over them, then eaten without salt. If the nuts are cracked or lightly ground while they're warm, they must be taken outside and winnowed using a basket or flat dish. Tall Woman said she poured the nuts back and forth many times while winnowing to get all the shells out; any she saw after that, she removed by hand. Then she ground the nuts again on the grinding stones. Nevertheless, even after they had been ground again, tiny pieces of shell might remain that you could feel in your mouth. Nuts that are put away to eat later should be roasted first so they don't turn rancid.

Pinyon nut butter, 'atłish, is not hard to make. The nuts are very oily, so nothing has to be added to them after they are ground to make them stick together. Pinyon nut butter, like peanut butter, can be spread on tortillas or even eaten by itself.

Family members told me that Tall Woman also made a mixture of cracked or shelled roasted pinyon nuts, parched corn that was ground really fine (like the corn for ts'áátbáí, powdered corn creamer), and salt, which they ate like "popcorn and peanuts." They did not know what she called this nor did others I asked.[6] To make this, Tall Woman reportedly roasted pinyon nuts and parched corn together on a screen over an open fire. Then she strained the result into a basket, put it on a sheepskin outside, and winnowed the results so that any remaining shells blew away. Another version of this that she made, but not as frequently, was to grind unroasted (raw) nuts with parched corn and shape the resulting meal into balls, which were then eaten by themselves. Again, no one knew what she called these.

Wild Plants

Today's Navajos face ever declining knowledge about their wild foods because environmental changes have made it difficult to pass the knowledge along. People have to be able to find the plants and other wild food resources on the land in order to teach and learn about them. The knowledge is multifaceted and includes where they grow, what they look like before flowering, when they are edible (e.g., before or after flowering, the point of ripening, or the effects of a frost), which parts are edible, and how to harvest and process them into sources of food for immediate or later use. All the plants require specific habitats, many of which have been destroyed by continuing drought conditions as well as overgrazing. Although a number of wild plant books now exist that include pictures of some of the plants important to Navajos as food, these resources are of no use when the plants can no longer be found. Some Navajos claim that if people hadn't stopped using them, the plants would still be here. In any case, most of the wild plant foods that were originally part of a healthy Navajo diet cannot be bought today in a store, either on or off the reservation.[7]

The plants included in this section are important for different reasons. Some have seeds that can be processed and eaten, and some have bulbs or roots that can be dug up and eaten. Some provide seasonings enjoyed with other foods, and some provide berries and other fruit. I have included only the plants mentioned by Tall Woman; having no training in botany myself—and not being able to hire a botanist to photograph, collect, classify, and study the plant resources she told me about—I can present only what she shared with me while sadly acknowledging that it will not be of great importance to botanists.

GREEN PLANTS
'Atsá Ch'il, or 'Atsá 'Azee'

Tall Woman told me that *'atsá ch'il*, also called *'atsá 'azee'* (its English and scientific names are unknown to me) was used mainly for flavoring, either when fresh or dried, and that it tasted like peppermint. Reportedly grayish green in color, it grows in low sandy desert lands and has small lavender flowers. The top part of the plant was picked when tender and boiled in soup, or it was soaked in water and then sprinkled on parched corn. Sometimes people added the dried form to squash seeds before eating them.

Ceremonialists call it Eagleway's mint, but I was unable to find anyone who knew the English name for this plant.

Shíínaaltsídí

Shíínaaltsídí ("afraid of the sun") is another plant whose English and scientific names are unknown to me. Tall Woman said that this is probably the very first wild green that shows up after winter; it's very common and is the first thing to ripen. It must be gathered right away, when the shoots are very young, because it quickly turns very bitter. People told her grandmother that only desperate people ate this plant, either raw or cooked. They called it the same thing they called young tumbleweeds: "desperate hunger food."[8] Some said this plant got its name because it dried up too fast and became too old to use. Tall Woman said this green could be eaten raw or boiled, just like spinach and other greens. It could also be dried and used later. Some people liked to thicken it up with sheep fat and make something like a soup. The plant could also be dipped into *taa'niil* (thick cornmeal mush).

Pigweed or Green Amaranth

One type of pigweed or amaranth is known as *tł'oh deesk'idí* and is variously translated as heaped grass, green amaranth, rough pigweed, careless weed, or grass with humped seeds. This plant comes in many species and has many English names. Tall Woman said that it was *one of two foundational plants the Navajo depended on for food before corn.* The other plant was goosefoot (*tł'ohdeeí*), or grass whose seeds fall. These two plants were foundational because the big seeds of each could be processed to make breads and mush. Pigweed or amaranth was important both as a plant and for its seeds. It was very similar in taste to wild spinach or beeweed, *waa',* when boiled. The stems are reportedly like asparagus, but the leaves are large.

The young plants are gathered in the spring, just like spinach, and they (especially the leaves) are boiled for about one hour. Salt and maybe half a cup of sheep fat are added. "We used to use this a lot for flavoring," said Tall Woman, "but I think it was in the early 1940s that it started losing its popularity." People sometimes liked to make *tł'oh deesk'idí* with another species of amaranth (see under "Seeds" below).

BULBS AND ROOTS
Wild Onions

Tall Woman said that the Navajos still gather wild onions (*tł'ohchin*) and keep the roots for winter. These onions are easy to find on the mesa; people who were herding would check near the washes, in the rocky soil on hills, and in other places. The roots of the kind called crow's onions (*gáagii bitł'ohchin*) are slender, and a lot of people don't like them; they say to just leave them for the crows, which might be how they got this name. Crow's onion is used in rabbit stew. The plant smells like an onion and has a flower cluster; the bulbs that look like onions are small (one-half to three-fourths of an inch in diameter).

People gather these wild onions early in the spring, from March through perhaps the end of April, by digging them out with a shovel. They can be used either fresh or dried, the whole plant or just the bulb can be eaten, and they are used either raw or cooked and either alone or added to something, like soup, stew, or gravy. When it is added to soup, wild celery and maybe some other herbs are also added for flavor. The wild onion's leaves can also be eaten, often by being chopped up fine and added to soup or stew. Wild onions can be sun-dried and kept for the winter. Before a dried one is eaten, it is reconstituted by soaking it and then boiling it. Some people like to bake wild onions on hot stones.

Tall Woman said that wild onions can also be roasted under hot ashes. The bulb can be singed in hot ashes or roasted quickly just to remove the strong taste. Some people prefer to remove the outer skin and then tie or braid a bunch of onions together to make a chain. They would make a hole or opening in the ashes, put the onion chain in, cover it up with hot ashes, roast it for five to ten minutes, remove it, shake it off, and brush it with a Navajo grass brush. They would eat the onions right then or else cook them longer. Drying them usually works better if they are braided together first and quickly roasted; they seem to dry quicker that way.

Lilies and Cattails

"In the early spring," said Tall Woman, "while we were herding or out looking for other foods, sometimes we found these lilies (*'iiłtsínii* or *'iiłts'ínii*),
and then we would dig them up, peel the bulbs, and eat them raw." There
were several kinds, such as Mariposa lily and Sego lily. Although some people like to eat the whole plant, Tall Woman said her family only used the
bulbs when she found them. The bulbs look like small onions, maybe an inch
in diameter, and are deep (at least six inches underground), thick, and scaled.
The plant has erect stems, from four to twelve inches long, and at the top are
large, white to yellowish flowers. They are found only early in the spring by
spotting the flowering stems and then digging deep. Remove the bulb from
the ground, peel off its outer husk, and eat the white inner part raw, just as it
is found. Tall Woman said everybody liked them because they were crisp and
nutlike, sort of like a raw potato; others said they were sweeter, more like
pomegranates.

Cattails (*lók'aa'*) were among the hunger foods Tall Woman mentioned.
If people were starving, the insides of the tender young stalks that appeared
in the early spring could be and were eaten.

Wild Carrots

Wild carrots (*chąąsht'ezhiitsoh* or *chaasht'ézhíí*) seem to have several different names, including wild onion, wild mountain celery, and Queen Anne's
lace, but Tall Woman insisted that what she meant was different from these
things. However, she did say that when she prepared wild carrots as food, it
was like using wild onions and they tasted like celery.

Wild carrot was gathered early in the spring (March and April), when the
plants were young. The roots are eaten like carrots. Some people confuse the
plant with *haza'aleeh* (wild celery, wild parsley, or biscuit root). *Chaasht'ézhíí*
has a single stalk with fernlike, flat, light green leaves and purple flowers.
"Some people think that's like wild parsley," said Tall Woman, "but that's
different." One must dig deep to get the white root, which is covered with a
tough bark; they grow bigger during the summer. The covering on the root
is removed, and the root can be eaten raw, baked, or boiled in soup. Wild

carrots can also be ground into flour. To keep them for winter, people would bake them on hot stones, sun-dry them, and store them. To reconstitute them people would soak them in water and add them to soup or meat stew or just eat them by themselves.

Wild Potatoes

Wild potatoes, especially the gopher or small globe-shaped potato (*nímasii yázhí*), were very common and could be found all over, especially near the canyon wash and other sources of water. They were dug up and cooked by either baking or boiling. They were peeled after they were cooked and could be reheated later. People fried fresh wild potatoes in fat or cut them into pieces and sun-dried them for the winter. They can also just be picked and kept for several months. Wild potatoes can be boiled into a pudding, ground into flour and mixed with water for griddle cakes, or mixed with goat's milk to make porridge.

These wild potatoes have a sour taste; although children ate them raw, adults added *dleesh* (light-colored clay) mixed with water to them when boiling or baking them to remove the bitter taste and to prevent poisoning. Boil them for twenty to thirty minutes, then peel them and mash them with your hands. Dissolve about two tablespoons of *dleesh* in about one cup of water and mix it well. Add salt if desired. Then mold the mixture into small loaves and serve hot or cold with mutton broth or goat's milk.

Wild Sweet Potatoes

Tall Woman said that the wild sweet potato (*nahooyéí* or *nímasii likaní*) was a root that was dug up and eaten in earlier times, either raw or boiled. People ate a lot of it in her parents' time. It could be dried to be saved and then reconstituted by being soaked in water. The dried roots could also be ground into flour.[9]

SEEDS

Numerous wild seeds were used in earlier times. Many were reportedly ground and added to other things to make bread dough. Mayes and Lacy

(1989, 139–44) give a recipe for native weed seed bread that uses beeweed seeds, and they also provide the nutritional composition of goosefoot, prickly pear fruit, pinyon seeds, purslane leaves and stems, and sunflower seeds.

Pigweed or Amaranth (Prostate)

Another kind of pigweed or amaranth is called *naazkaadii.* Tall Woman said the following about it:

> This plant was very common while I was raising my children. It's very low, mainly about six inches tall, but some grow to one or two feet with long stout stems; it spreads all over the place. Earlier I talked about using its leaves, but this plant is also important for its seeds, which are small, black, and shiny. We gathered as many of those as we could, and then after we got home, we heaped up the plants on a sheepskin and beat them with a stick to loosen those seeds, thresh those plants. You can sun-dry and store the seeds or grind them into flour. If you do that, you can make that into dough by adding water and then shape your dough into long loaves to bake in hot ashes. Some people prefer to add cornmeal or store-bought flour to that if they are making bread. In my family we just usually used the flour made from the ground-up seeds. Some people like to make that into mush. And sometimes- people just parched a handful of seeds and ate them, saying they tasted like sugar.

Sunflowers

Children and young adults ate sunflower seeds; others ground them with corn into cakes called *ndíyíliitsoh,* which means big sunflower. The sunflowers that grow along the roads are small; they are called *ndíyílii.* The sheep really liked to eat them. The big sunflowers grow along drainage ditches and the washes. Tall Woman's family picked the heads of the big ones and then either sun-dried or boiled them. They are bitter, but mashing them with *nímasii dleesh* removes that taste. Even then, some people still find them too tart to eat. The result can be spread on a tortilla, or the tortilla can be dipped into it. Some people say the sunflowers taste like dried peaches, with or without brown sugar. To prepare the seeds for eating, sometimes the whole head of the sunflower was steamed before it was sun-dried; that was said to shrink the kernels. Drying it first and then parching it was said to enlarge the seeds.

Mustard

The mustard plant in all its varieties is called *'ostse'*. According to Wolfe (1984), tumble mustard and tansy mustard are more abundant and used more today than hedge mustard. Tall Woman said that there were many different types of this plant, which was very important to all the Navajos for its seeds. The mustard plant grows long, slender pods, which are very, very full of tiny seeds. The pods were picked in mid- to late summer, after they had dried on the plant. Some people liked to do it sooner, gathering the pods fresh and letting them sun-dry. To free up the seeds, people rubbed the pods in their hands over a pan, a dish, or a sheepskin. Parching the seeds made grinding them easier, and grinding them created a very greasy mixture, almost like peanut butter. Lots of dishes can be made with that, such as gruel or mush on its own, or it can be added to cornmeal mush, to cornbread, or to other flours to make bread. Use about two table-spoons of the mixture each time.

If the seeds are thoroughly dried, they can be stored whole. People say that they have lots of protein in them.

WILD GRASSES

"We always gathered wild grasses while we were out gathering foods to eat," said Tall Woman. "We'd get lots of broom grasses, rabbit brush, and desert grass to make into bundles so we could make hairbrushes or the brushes we used on the grinding stones. These were plentiful around the Nazlini and Chinle Washes, and they grew wild in the cornfields close to the Catholic church. We also found them on the way to Black Mountain, over the mesa, or more toward Round Rock, Wheatfields, Window Rock, Moaning Lake, Seya's Rabbit Hunting Rock, and other places."

The wild or uncultivated plants or grasses that Tall Woman talked about in relation to providing foods are described below.

Indian Rice Grass, Bunchgrass, and Millet

Tł'óh dééhí—Indian rice grass, bunchgrass, or millet—grows in clumps two or more feet tall; it seems to grow best in sandy places, even on sand dunes. Early in the summer its rice-like grains ripen and it gets small, dark seeds at the tips. In time these seeds get large and plump. They have two close-fitting outer scales covered with very fine white hairs that have to be removed before they can be ground to use the seeds for food. The seeds are bigger and the grass plants are bigger than scorched grass.

Scorched Grass

Scorched grass is called *ndidlidii*. It is hard to use because you have to burn it to expose its seeds, which can then be ground into flour. It looks a lot like baby's breath with its puffs of small seeds. Tall Woman used to hold bunches of the stems over the fire so that the hairs would burn off and the seeds would drop into a pan or onto a rock below. The seeds can also be parched by putting charcoal in a pan and shaking the stems. Then the seeds are ground and added to cornbread for flavor.

"If you have lots of seeds," said Tall Woman, "you can make small cakes or bread from them; you can also grind them and mix them with goat's milk to make mush. Those seeds will keep for a long time if you roast them first."

Sweetgrass

Sweetgrass is called either *tł'óh niłchíín* or *ndetlidi*. It was the seeds of sweetgrass that were used as a source of food. People ground them with their grinding stones into a powder after gathering them, although some preferred to burn the seeds to ashes before grinding them. The resulting powder could be used to make bread or mixed into milk to create a drink.

Goosefoot

Goosefoot, or *tł'ohdeeí* (which includes Freemont goosefoot, white goosefoot, and lamb's quarter) is called the "plant with horns" or "horned grass" in English, and some say the leaves of the two-foot goosefoot plant look just like a goose's foot.

Tl'ohdeeí seems to include any uncultivated plant that spreads out and provides food through its leaves and its stems as well as its seeds, which can be eaten whole or ground into flour to make bread or mush. Like pigweed or amaranth, *tl'ohdeeí* is a foundational food for the Navajos—of major importance in the diet *before* corn, since it produces big seeds that can be processed into mush or breads.

According to Tall Woman, *tl'ohdeeí*, or goosefoot, was very common in earlier times. The plants were usually large, with up to five-feet-tall whitish-green stems. The Navajos gathered them early in the spring as soon as they came up, boiled the young shoots, cut them up, and ate them just like spinach, or *waa'*. Tall Woman explained as follows:

> Some said to boil them longer than *waa'* and change the water at least once after thirty to forty minutes, but I didn't follow that. These plants were very mild tasting. You can eat that plant alone or with stew; some people say it's salty, but my family liked it. You could also dry the young shoots for winter if you boiled them first. It's really like *waa'*. The shape of the leaves reminds people of the footprint of a goose.
>
> In the late summer or early fall, we harvested the seeds by shaking them off the plants. One plant might have many clusters of tiny seeds on it. After you gather the stems you need to thresh them to get the seeds off. You can heap them on a sheepskin, cover it with a cloth, and beat them with a stick. Or you can put all of them into a cloth sack and walk on them. Then you winnow the results to remove bits of chaff and grind the seeds into flour. People then roasted those seeds; sometimes they just put burning charcoal embers into a basket and shook them around in there.
>
> These seeds have many uses; one of them is flavoring. We mix them with cornmeal to flavor many cornmeal dishes. You can make a mush from it and use it like cornmeal or *k'íneeshbízhii*, dumplings. You can mix the roasted seeds with water to make a dough and then pat it into cakes and bake them on a hot stone as a griddle cake [called] *tl'ohdeeí ɫees'áán*. Or you can make a cake out of it and bake that in a pit oven in the ground. You can mix the seeds with milk, pour it onto a greased rock

griddle, and make [the] griddle cakes [called] *'abe' bee neezmasí*. The roasted seeds also stored well for winter use.

Tall Woman described the following two kinds of goosefoot:

Tł'oh dahikaałí (witchgrass or rustling grass). This is a tall wild grass. When it is fully grown and the seeds are ripe, it sways back and forth, making a rustling sound that tells people that the small black seeds are ready to be gathered. This kind grew only in certain places, such as Blue Canyon. Tall Woman said that there used to be two different names, *tł'oh tsááhíí* (rustling grass) and *ch'il dabááhíí* (witchgrass), but by the middle 1960s rustling grass was rarely seen or used. The Navajos gathered the grasses, winnowed the seeds, and then parched or roasted them. The whole dried seeds could be stored, but usually the seeds were ground into flour after being roasted. This was added to other breads for flavor (maybe about two tablespoons per loaf or per three cups of cornmeal).

Tł'oh ts'ózí (narrow-leaf grass). This is another very common and important plant that Tall Woman gathered frequently, especially after her children were in school, the Civilian Conservation Corps and the stock reduction programs were under way, and Frank was serving as a judge (the 1930s and 1940s). She gathered the seeds in the spring and then ground them on the grinding stones. Once the seeds had been ground, they could be used like cornmeal: cooked into a mush, made into breads, or mixed with goat's milk and served as a drink. This plant spreads out just like goosefoot and witchgrass. It reportedly had a red taproot, was between one and five feet tall, and produced shiny black seeds. In the spring Tall Woman gathered the young shoots and stems and boiled them for ten to twelve minutes with salt. The whole family liked those cooked greens; they were mild and had a pleasant taste. She also made them into soup by boiling the leaves for about an hour and adding some sheep fat, maybe one-half cup, and some salt. Sometimes she would add cornmeal flour to that to make a gruel or mix that with corn flour to make bread or dumplings. Chewing handfuls of the roasted seeds created sugar in the mouth, and that was sometimes considered a meal. Tall Woman said she stored both the seeds and the greens after boiling them like *waa'*.

WILD VEGETABLES

In addition to the wild onions and wild carrots mentioned above, Tall Woman described some other wild plants that are like wild vegetables.

Asparagus

Ch'il deeníní (whose English and scientific names are unknown to me) resembles asparagus and was very common in the local area.[10] Tall Woman said the following about it:

All around where we lived, all the people gathered it and ate lots of it. You picked the young shoots in the early spring or maybe the first week of May. You had to watch, because as the shoots get bigger, they get tough and bitter. After you gather it, you boil the young shoots and eat them plain or add them to stew or soup. If you want to keep them for later, you boil them first and then sun-dry them just like spinach. Even the animals like to eat this plant when it is young and tender; you have to watch them, though, because if they eat too much of it, they will bloat.

Wild Celery, Wild Parsley, and Biscuit Root

Haza'aleeh is the name variously used for wild celery, wild parsley, and/or biscuit root.[11] This plant is used both as a seasoning and a flavoring, and its fernlike leaves, which are close to the base of its short yellow stem, are also used for food. Tall Woman talked about using this plant mainly as a flavoring. She said it tastes like celery and has to be dug before it gets its yellow blossoms. She most often gathered it in the early spring, usually March, and then cooked it. Some say it tastes like garlic, but others say it's more like chili pepper; it is used mainly to flavor soups and corn dishes. It is often eaten with *taa'niil*, a thick cornmeal mush, or *tóshchíín*, a thick blue cornmeal mush.

The entire plant—roots, stems, and leaves—can be chopped and boiled to make a soup or a mush, but it is very important to wash the leaves first, which are covered with a film of dirt and dust that makes them taste very strong. To dry *haza'aleeh* and store it in paper bags for wintertime use, peel and slice the roots lengthwise after washing the leaves. Then spread those out on a sheepskin or goatskin to dry completely in the sun where they will not be bothered by animals. (Tall Woman used to put them on top of the ramada or storage shack.) Some people prefer to roast the fresh shoots a bit in the fire first before sun-drying them. Others prefer to dry the leaves and the roots separately. The plant is very salty whether fresh or dried.

Tall Woman said that sometimes when she talked about *haza'aleeh*, she didn't mean wild celery; she meant biscuit root, another plant that likes to grow in sandy, rocky places. Although I did not get a separate Navajo word for biscuit root, Tall Woman was adamant that the plant was *different* from wild celery or wild parsley.

There used to be a lot of this plant on the open plains, often in dry sandy places, on rocky hills, and on the mesa under sagebrush. The biscuit root plant was also part of the parsley family, like wild celery; it had many species. Its blossoms are a variety of colors, from white to yellow to pink to purple, and they only last a few days. The plant grows very close to the ground in sandy places, acting like a ground cover, and it must be picked before it blooms.

At first its young fleshy taproots are sweet and tender. They can be peeled by hand and eaten raw or cooked. Or after they are peeled and baked, they can be dried and ground into a coarse, starchy flour. The roots can be chopped up to make a sauce or gravy, and the leaves and stems can be used as a substitute for parsley. The plants that Tall Woman's family usually found had yellow flowers, and its flat leaves were dark green. It is related to *chaasht'ézhíí*, the long white carrotlike root mentioned in the Wild Carrots section; the two plants are like siblings.

The biscuit root plant was common and frequently used while Tall Woman was raising her children, but she said that after the rain stopped coming, it couldn't be found in many places anymore. In the mid-1960s, about the only place she knew where it was still growing was around Cuba, New Mexico.

Wild Spinach

There are several types of Navajo spinach, or *waa'*, and it is called by several different names in English: Rocky Mountain beeweed, beeplant, gumweed, and wild spinach. According to Tall Woman, this used to be a common plant; it was tall, with branching woody stems and purple, purple-pink, or white flower clusters. It was most often found by drainage ditches or washes and was gathered in the spring and early summer, when the shoots were still green, young, tender, small, close to the ground, and not too tall and bitter. The young stems, leaves, and shoots were all eaten; the small leaves were washed and then boiled until tender. Some people suggest changing the water several times while boiling, then squeezing the water out and draining it on the ground, to remove the bitterness. Boiled *waa'* can be eaten itself or added to stew with meat, wild onions, and wild celery.

To save it for wintertime use, after boiling it and pressing the water out, spread it thin on anything, even a screen, and let it dry in the sun. When it is dry, roll it into balls for storage and pack them in a can. Add just small pinches to a winter soup. Each ball can also be soaked in water, boiled to soften it again, and then boiled with venison or mutton fat, fresh or dried fried mutton, or any kind of stew or soup.

Like some other plants, *waa'* was also valued for its seeds. In earlier times people gathered the seeds and ground them fine to make bread or mush. Tall Woman described using two large ears of Indian corn, which she had shelled and finely ground, mixed with *waa'* seeds, then molding the mixture into cakes that she baked in the hot ashes in the ground. This was just a kind of corn cake, with no special name. As of the late 1960s, many areas didn't have any wild spinach left.[12]

Swiss Chard

Swiss chard (*tsą́ą́'bíí*) was similar to wild spinach but with very large leaves on a three-foot stalk. It is gathered early in the spring and is said to be one of the very first edible greens to appear after winter. It was reportedly very popular a very long time ago. The greens are rinsed and then boiled by themselves to remove the bitter taste. Swiss chard is eaten by itself or added to mutton or hominy stew after it has been boiled. It supposedly tastes like spinach when cooked. To dry it, boil it first and then sun-dry it in clumps.

Berries

In the early days, when people were starving, they frequently gathered and ate berries raw, even the sour and bitter ones, such as juniper (*gad*) and mistletoe (*dahts'aa'*). There were lots of berries, such as wild raspberries, strawberries, rose hips, squaw berries, salt berries, sour berries, hackberries, and service berries.

SUMAC BERRIES

Sumac berries, or *chiiłchin*, were very popular in earlier times and still are, even though it's harder to find them. (*Chiiłchin* might also include squaw berries, salt berries, skunkbush or squawbush, sour berries, and three-leaf sumac.) They add color and are used as a seasoning. There used to be lots of sumac berries near Round Rock. The sumac bush grows low on the ground or on tree stumps. The berries, which are small (about one-fourth inch long), red, and somewhat flat, are covered with hairs and have a large seed; they usually ripen in July, but they can still be picked after they have dried on the bush, if the birds haven't taken all of them. They have a distinct smell and are very sticky and sour. Wash them to remove the bits of leaves and stems, then sun-dry them whole. They can also be dried over a fire; stir until they are all dry and all of the sticky juice has dried out. Sumac berries keep well and can be stored whole, then ground very fine when needed. The dry ones can be used for a long time, but they don't have much of a berry taste later.

There are a variety of things you can make from *chiiłchin*. Among them are two drinks that Tall Woman told me about (see section 7). Some people grind the dried berries and mix them with sugar and water to make a jam; others even ground the bark in with the berries for jelly, and in earlier times people ate the bark with salt. Now young people say you can also make a pie using the whole berries. If you boil the berries and mix them with flour and sugar, you can make a pudding, as in the following recipe. This can be eaten with a tortilla or by itself with a spoon; it's not runny.

Chiiłchin (Sumac Berry) Pudding

3 cups dried berries, ground
4 tablespoons flour
2 ½ cups boiling water
⅓ cup sugar

Mix the berries and the flour. Stir the boiling water into the mixture and boil for about ten minutes. Add the sugar before serving.

Sumac berries, either fresh or dried, can also be used to make a mush. If the berries are fresh and you grind them with the seeds and all, you can add sugar to that and eat it uncooked. If you want to remove the seeds, they will sink in water. If you are using dried berries, grind them and mix in a small amount of water, cornmeal, and sugar, then boil the mixture until it thickens, as in the recipe below.

Tóshchíín with Chiiłchin (Blue Cornmeal Mush with Sumac Berries)

½ cup dried berries, ground
1 ½ cup white cornmeal
1 cup or more cold water
4–5 cups boiling water
Sugar (optional)

Mix the berries and white cornmeal. Add the cold water until the mixture is moist, and stir to get rid of any lumps. Slowly stir in the boiling water and boil the mixture until it thickens, maybe for half an hour. If you want it sweeter, add sugar; if you want it thinner, add more water. As an alternative to the sugar, you can mix fresh berries with cornmeal and use that as a sweetener. If you use a lot of berries, the mixture will turn pink.

You can sweeten the berries by mixing them with *dleesh*, too, as in the recipe below.

Chiiłchin with Dleesh (Sumac Berries with Clay)

3–4 cups fresh or dried berries, mashed and boiled
½ cup water
1 tablespoon dleesh (see section 2)

Strain the berries, then mash them again. Mix the water and the dleesh. Add that to the boiled berries and stir. Eat by itself or with a tortilla.

CHOKECHERRIES

Chokecherries (*didzé dík'ǫzhí*) are small black or dark purple cherries that grow on shrubs or small trees in the mountains. When fresh they are bitter, but when dried they are sweeter. They can be eaten fresh (the pit must be spit out), or they can be sun-dried, stored, reconstituted by being soaked in water, and mixed with other foods. Tall Woman said chokecherries were used in Mountaintopway and Beautyway ceremonies.

Breads, cakes, and other things can be made from chokecherries. Grind the raw berries, pat the result into a cake no bigger than two and a half inches in diameter, and dry that in the sun. To make a sauce, soak the dried berries in water, then mix them with wheat flour or corn, sugar, and water. For mush, simply boil the berries with cornmeal. Drinks can also be made from them (see section 7).

WILD CURRANTS

The term for wild currants, *k'į́njįł'ahí*, includes wax currants, wild gooseberry, and squaw currants. These berries, which are a bright to deep red, grow wild on a bushy shrub that flourishes in moist places in pine forests. The berries are sticky, and some people say they don't like their smell, but other people grow them. They can be eaten fresh and raw, but Tall Woman said to be careful not to eat too many, because they act as an emetic (i.e., cause vomiting). Sun-dry them for later use; then when you want to use them, boil them in lots of water until they are puffy and soft, about thirty minutes. A mush can be made by adding two tablespoons of cornmeal to the boiled berries; eat it with tortillas.

Tall Woman did not use wild currants to make jelly, jam, or pie, but younger people, such as her daughters, were interested in doing so. Boil lots of berries with lots of water, then mash them and squeeze out the juice, saving that to drink. Some prefer to add one to three tablespoons of sugar and more water, then strain. For jelly, strain out both the fruit and the seeds, and for jam or pie filling, strain out only the seeds and leave the fruit in.

HACKBERRIES

Hackberry (*jiłhazhí*), including desert hackberry, is an orange-red berry that ripens in late September, when a lot of other wild fruits are no longer available. Hackberries are very sweet and can be eaten fresh, ground or mashed and made into cakes, or sun-dried for later use.

JUNIPER BERRIES

Juniper (*gad*) berries turn dark, almost purple, when ripe and are good to eat raw; most people prefer to spit out the seeds while chewing them. They can be mixed with raw shelled pinyons. "Sometimes when we gathered enough juniper berries," said Tall Woman, "we removed the seeds and ground the fruit. Then we mixed it with water, and with our hands made patties to cook on the grill. Those were thin, maybe one-fourth inch thick. My whole family liked to eat those."

SEEPWEED

Seepweed (*łichí'íí*) is a small thorny desert bush that produces seedy red berries.[13] The berries are bitter if they're not ripe, but they can be sweetened with *dleesh*. Tall Woman's family picked them while herding and either ate them then or brought them home for grinding. They often mixed them with *dleesh* and water to make a fruit mush. The seeds can be boiled whole to make a gruel or mush, or they can be mashed in water and then strained for juice; add sugar to the juice to make a drink. The berries can be saved for later use by being sun-dried whole; they can then be eaten like raisins or stored in sacks for use in the winter.

SERVICEBERRIES

Serviceberries (*didzé dit'ódí*) are soft berries that grow on shrubs or small trees, and they are purplish red or black when ripe. Tall Woman's family gathered them either when they were fresh or after they had dried on the bush. They can be eaten raw or dry, like raisins, or boiled to make a sauce. They can also be used to make a drink (see section 7).

YELLOW BERRIES

Tall Woman said that the yellow berries, which were common in the early 1960s, came from the leaf pocket plant, which grew one to two feet tall and produced berries that turned yellow when they ripened.[14] There were lots of these plants around her home. Yellow berries (*tadiłchoshi*) are sweet but extremely seedy; they can be eaten raw. The leaf pocket plant got its name because the leaf has a little covered pouch or bump on it; inside that pouch is the berry. If the weather has been dry, the berries are very sour. They can be sun-dried and then boiled later. Some of Tall Woman's daughters made jam from them; they can also be eaten plain or with *tóshchíín*, blue cornmeal mush. Another way to prepare them is to cook them until the skin comes off, then strain out the water and eat what remains alone or with meat.

WOLFBERRIES OR TOMATILLOS

The Navajo name for the wolfberry or tomatillo (also called rabbit thorn, matrimony vine, or box thorn) is *haashch'éédą́ą́*, which means "food of the Gods and offerings." According to some, the name implies that this berry is used in ceremonies, such as the Nightway and the Fire Dance, and was brought by the Holy People. Others disagree, saying that the wolfberry is an old food that must be eaten with *dleesh*, but it is not a ceremonial food.

Wolfberries grow on a thorny shrub that is usually shorter than five feet. The flowers are greenish white, and the berries, about three-eighths of an inch long, vary in color from reddish purple to orange and have a whitish waxy outer coat. Some people call them tomatillos, or baby tomatoes, because they look like them. Wolfberries were gathered in the summer, although if it had rained a lot, they'd be ready in May or June. They need a lot of water, and they grow quickly and easily, like greasewood.

Tall Woman always found wolfberries around Round Rock and Red Rock, at the base of some mesas (like Red Rock Mesa), or along the banks of certain lakes (like Moaning Lake). They also grew along the banks of the washes and sometimes even near the windmill at Cottonwood, Arizona. She always took empty cans and buckets with her in her wagon to use as containers for the berries. One time she thought she'd try to bring home an entire plant and grow it near their hogan. She picked a big plant, dug it up carefully, replanted it at home, and watered and watered it—but it didn't make it.

Some of the places where wolfberries grew became gravesites, so now nobody goes over there to bother them. One of those places is along the wash where the Presbyterian preacher, Robert Gorman, buried people who died during the 1918 flu epidemic. Also, in time the winds blew and spread sand and salty weed all over the area. This made the wolfberry bushes die out along the washes.

Wolfberries can be used fresh or dried. They are very bitter, sour, and tart and cannot be eaten without mixing them with *nímasii dleesh*, the special food clay. People who forgot to mix that clay in would get really sick. Today there are almost no wolfberries left, so anybody who has them uses them very sparingly.

Wolfberries can either be sun-dried whole or be boiled first and then sun-dried by spreading them out on rocks or on a sheepskin's underside. People liked to wash off the stickiness first, and if they boiled the berries they drained the juice off before sun-drying. The berries can also be dried by heating them in a warm skillet until the stems and leaves come off. Once they are dried and cooled off, they are prepared by grinding them, boiling them, and adding the *dleesh*. Some people like to take the seeds out before adding the *dleesh*, and some prefer to add sugar as well. The dried berries can be soaked in water to make a syrup.

To make a mush or a side dish, take dried berries and boil them in water for about half an hour, stirring the mixture with stirring sticks. Add sugar if desired, and taste the mixture to see if it's too sour. Remove the reconstituted berries and grind them. Add *nímasii dleesh* and water to make the mush the desired thickness. To use it as a side dish, do not add more water; just eat it with wild potatoes or add to soup.

To make jam, put about one and a half cups of berries into one-fourth cup of water in a pan. Boil it, then strain it (save the liquid) and grind the results. Tall Woman's family used the grinding stones for that, but some people preferred to mash the boiled berries between stones. In a separate container, add about two tablespoons of *dleesh*, broken into small pieces, to the water and stir. When that looks creamy, put the ground berries into a bowl, add the creamy *dleesh*, and then add the strained liquid. Some people like to add about one tablespoon of sugar at that point and mix everything together. You can eat this like jam, spreading it on tortillas or other breads or dipping the tortilla or bread into it. Keep this in the refrigerator; you can also freeze it.

Like other berries, the *haashch'éédą́ą́* could also be made into a drink (see section 7).

SILVERLEAF NIGHTSHADE

Naaltsoii (or, according to Tall Woman, *hosh beldei'hééh*) was identified by Wolfe (1984) as the silverleaf nightshade or white horse nettle. The plant has purple flowers and yellow berries; it goes way back, Tall Woman said, and in the 1970s was one of the few old plants that remained. The berries or seeds are used in one of the three ways of making cheese (*géeso*), from the milk of sheep or goats (see section 2).

Other Fruits

CACTUS

There are many kinds of cactus (*hosh*) available where Tall Woman and her family lived, such as barrel, hedgehog, ball, and fishhook, but the one she mentioned specifically and most often was the prickly pear cactus (*hosh nteelí*).[15] Much of the time they found that cactus while herding by watching the birds and the goats, which knew when the fruit was ripe. The cactus often grows in places where it's hidden; the fruit ripens in the late summer or early fall, turning red or purple. Some kinds of cactus have fruit that stays ripe for a long time. The fruit can be eaten raw; some people eat the seeds, but others spit them out. As of the early 1970s, it was not clear where this cactus could still be found—a few plants were in the flower bed near the back door of the Chinle Catholic church rectory. Tall Woman wasn't sure, but she thought there might also still be some in Canyon de Chelly.

To gather the prickly pear cactus fruit, people had to protect their hands from the needles; if they didn't, their hands would swell up. To pull off the spiny fruit, people used a *hosh bee wóbéhé* (cactus fruit picker): a forked stick, tongs, or two sticks put together like chopsticks. Sometimes people just covered their hands with lots of wild weeds. Others wore gloves.

There were at least four ways to clean the picked fruit: use a Navajo brush, rub the fruit with a heavy cloth, peel off the skin and needles by hand (very carefully!), or use another plant to clean the cactus fruit. Tall Woman said that most people preferred the latter way; she called the plant *hosh bee yildéhé* (cactus brush plant), but others called it by slightly different names.[16] The cactus brush plant is gray, about one foot tall, and has a soft stem and soft leaves that pull the needles off the prickly pear cactus fruit. The cactus brush stems and leaves are tied into a bundle and, as the name implies, used as a brush. The cactus fruit is put on a flat surface—such as a stone or a cloth on the ground—and the fruit is rolled back and forth over the brush. All the prickly needles come off on the leaves, but it takes a lot of work to do it thoroughly.

Even then some needles will remain stuck to the fruit, but those will come off when the fruit is boiled, the water is strained off, and the fruit is washed again. People who wanted to eat the fruit as soon as they found it would rub it in the dirt and then carefully peel it. As they ate the flesh, they spit out the seeds.

The cactus fruit can also be dried. After removing the needles, sun-dry it whole or after cutting it in half and removing the seeds. (This is the same way to sun-dry peaches: cut them in half, remove the pits, and put the halves in the sun to dry.) Some people slice the fruit around and around in circles, leaving the seeds in there until later. Dried cactus fruit keeps for a long time. To use it, first boil it in water. It can be eaten plain or boiled with something else, like dried peaches. The juice can also be squeezed from it after boiling; some like to drink that without adding anything to it, but others make a syrup from the juice by adding sugar. Some people make jelly out of the juice, and others cook that fruit into a mush. However, in earlier times, if people wanted to make jam or jelly from any wild fruits or berries, they had to haul water in for that and have enough wood to build a large fire outside.

GRAPES

Although wild grapes (*ch'il na'atł'ó'ii*) grew in some places, Tall Woman said that the only grapes they ate were raised by friends in the canyon.

PLUMS

Tall Woman said that there were some wild plums (*didzé* or *dzidzétsoh dik'ǫzhí*) in the area, and when she found ripe ones and brought them home, people either ate them right away or the plums were split open, the pit was removed, and the fruit was sun-dried for later use. Like other fruits, they were reconstituted in boiling water; depending on how sweet they were, people might add sugar after mashing them up.

RHUBARB

Wild rhubarb is called *ch'iłt'óó'íí* or *jiłt'ooí* (the former name also includes curly dock). Tall Woman said that she collected the stems, which were one to three feet tall, but not the large leaves or the blossoms. The stems had to be young; she gathered them in the early spring, cut them into pieces, and boiled them to make a mush for her family. Sometimes her children would suck on the stems, either raw or cooked, to extract the juice.

YUCCA FRUIT

Yucca fruit in general is called *hashk'aan*. The desert variety of yucca, *tsá'ászi' ts'óóz*, has a narrow or slender leaf; the mountain banana variety, *tsá'ászi' nteelí*, has a broad leaf that is about two inches wide. The latter is sometimes called the Navajo yucca.

Early researchers such as Matthews (1897) noted that at one time the yucca plant was a staple and thus very important to the Navajos as well as other Native Americans. Both the wide- and narrow-leaf species are found on the reservation and are used in numerous ways, including to make the soapsuds used in some ceremonies and the equipment used in the Moccasin Game (Frisbie 2015).[17] Yucca fruit could be called the Navajo banana. The fleshy fruit is very sweet and is usually gathered in early October. It overripens quickly and falls off the plant, and because animals like it, too, it is necessary to watch the fruit carefully as it starts to ripen. People eat it raw like a banana but also bake it in hot ashes, boil it, make it into sticky rolls or jelly, sun-dry it, and (after roasting and reroasting it) store it for winter use. Tall Woman also added it to cornmeal mush as a flavoring or spice.

Tall Woman and her daughters picked lots of wild bananas and used the fruit from both the wide-leaf and the narrow-leaf yuccas.[18] Sometimes they would put them into a Navajo pot and mash them with stirring sticks. Then they would fashion what they had mashed into a loaf with their hands and put a stick through it to turn it around during cooking. Everybody in the family reportedly loved this food.

The desert variety, the narrow-leaf yucca, was said to be common around Tuba City. Tall Woman said that many people thought its fruit was bland. It is gathered in the early fall when the fruit is dark green and ripe. If it's not ripe, it's very bitter. It is cooked in the ground after the pit has been heated up and the fire removed. After the fruit is put in the ground, it is covered with hot ashes and sand and bakes for one to one and a half hours. Then the skin is peeled off, the fruit is sliced in half, and the seeds and inside casing are removed. People like to eat the fruit with salt; many say it tastes like cucumber. Others mash it up after it's been baked and eat it like mashed potatoes. It can also be eaten like baked potatoes instead. The desert variety of yucca fruit does not dry well, so it is not stored for winter.

The fruit of the wide-leaf yucca, the mountain variety, is very sweet and mushy when it's ripe. Some bilingual Navajos told me that the wide-leaf yucca's fruit is called wild bananas and is preferred by many of the People. Tall Woman reported that there were lots of yuccas near the roads to Moaning Lake, Cottonwood, and other areas in Arizona where she took her daughters and went gathering. Besides gathering berries there, the family picked bunches of wild bananas; these were short and fat, yellow at first and white when ripe, and full of black seeds. By the time Tall Woman was sharing her recipes with me, however, she said it was already getting harder and harder to find the wide-leaf yucca.[19]

The fruit looks like a short green banana; it ripens in the late summer and early fall, when it is very sweet and can be eaten fresh. It can be boiled, with frequent stirring, until it thickens into a paste and then eaten that way, or it can be sun-dried, mashed up, rolled by hand, and baked.[20] The dried fruit can be saved to make these logs, or fruit roll-ups, later.

To keep the bananas, cut them in half and dry them on stones in the sun or by a fire. Grind up the dried halves, pat them into cakes, and reroast them. These can then be broken into pieces for more sun-drying, or they can be put on new greasewood sticks and stored; the sticks poking through the middle let the air help dry them. Later, they can be reconstituted by sprinkling them with water. Adding enough water will make them into a gravy or a thick syrup to use with other foods.

Neesdoo' is the name of the dried yucca fruit roll; it is four to five inches long and two inches in diameter. Tall Woman described two ways of making these rolls.

In the first method, rub the outer pulp off with your hands and throw the seeds away. Put the skin and pulp in a pan and cook it over a fire until it gets very brown and as thick as applesauce. Remove, pour it into a different pan, and let it cool. Grind the fruit until it's very fine and sticky. Put a small amount (a few teaspoons) on a flat board and mold it into a small cake. Repeat until all the fruit has been made into cakes. They will be red and slightly sticky. Sun-dry the cakes for about five days. Knead the cakes into hard dough with your hands and shape them into loaves, like bread. Make a hole down the middle of the length of each loaf with a stick. Put a string or some rope on this stick and let these sun-dry on a line for another five days. Store for the winter in boxes or other containers.

The second way to make *neesdoo'* is to cut the fruit in half and sun-dry it or dry it by a fire. Grind up the halves, pat them into cakes, and reroast them. After that, break the cakes into pieces and sun-dry them again. Then sprinkle them with water, run a stick down the middle of several of them to let the air in, and store the results.

When you are ready to use the yucca roll, no matter which way you made it, cut a piece off, soak it in hot water until it becomes like a jam or thick syrup, and then eat it with bread, cornmeal mush, pudding, or other foods. Tall Woman's family often ate it with *tanaashgiizh*, blue cornmeal mush made with juniper ash. You can also eat pieces of the roll like candy or put pieces into cornmeal dishes as flavoring.

Section 2 | Possible Additives

Culinary Ashes, Salt, Sweeteners, Yeast, Baking Powder and Baking Soda, Shortening or Grease, Clay (Dleesh), Gravy, and Cheese

Culinary Ashes

As will become clear in many of Tall Woman's recipes, the use of a culinary ash (łeeshch'ih) is very important. Nutritional studies done among Navajo populations have demonstrated that the ash, like the milk from sheep or goats, is an extremely important source of calcium. Wolfe (1984, 222, 300) and others have demonstrated that culinary ash reduces the mineral binding effect of phytates (phytic acid) and allows a person to get higher amounts of calcium, magnesium, potassium, iron, copper, and zinc in foods such as cornbread, hominy, and mush.[21]

Research has further shown that natural ash fortification ensures mineral adequacy and adds nutrients in a diet of traditional foods. In terms of calcium, one teaspoon of ash has as much calcium as one cup of cow's milk. It promotes bone health and is easily digested by the small intestine. In some recipes, if baking soda (sodium bicarbonate) is substituted for the ash, it will lower the mineral and vitamin A content while also increasing sodium and thus the risk of hypertension. Two tablespoons of baking soda are equivalent to one cup of juniper ash, which is something like baking powder. Tall Woman preferred to use juniper ash in all her recipes for corn, cornmeal, and cornmeal mush. She said it made them taste better.

Although studies show that culinary ash can be made from dried tumbleweed, salt bush, corncobs, bean vines, or greasewood (both gray and black), the most common source is the juniper tree (fig. 27).[22] According to Tall

FIGURE 27. Juniper tree, Canyon de Chelly, Arizona, February 2016. Photo by Cecilia Sandoval.

Woman, the green branches are freshly gathered by breaking them off (fig. 28); she used to put them in an old sack, or on a blanket with the ends tied together, and take them home in the wagon (or later a pickup truck). Then she piled the branches on a small raised grill or on a screen with a wide pan underneath—a skillet, a dishpan, or even a cookie sheet. The grill should be set close to the ground; if the grill isn't big enough, aluminum foil can be added to the sides to make it wider. A fire is started, and as the green branches burn and the ashes fall into the pan below, more green branches are added to the fire (fig. 29). Tall Woman warned to be careful with the fire, because juniper is oily and the fire picks up quickly. Some people prefer to stir the burned residue in the pan with a spoon to make it cool off before they sift it. Only the burned leaves are used; the stems and berries are discarded.

The ash is removed from the pan; some prefer to sweep it up with a cooking brush made from thin sticks of sage or grass tied in the middle. This is the same brush that is used as a strainer. Then the ash is sifted through a piece of window screening to make sure there are no pieces of leaves or sticks in it. People also go through it with their hands to smooth it further, check for lumps, and crush the ashes until they have a really fine texture. Any residue that hasn't turned into ash can be recooked. The ash is thoroughly cooled and then sifted again before storing it for use later. It should be stored in airtight containers in a cool place; coffee cans from the store work well.

It takes a lot of juniper to make juniper ash. Tall Woman always told Howard and Frank to bring back as many juniper branches as possible when they made their trips into the mountains in the wagon to get wood. Sometimes she would go with them to gather juniper branches while they were working; that way she would always have a supply on hand and could prepare the ash whenever she had time.[23]

The juniper tree stays green year-round, so green branches can be picked at any time. Tall Woman pointed out that there are two kinds of juniper, and one makes a more powerful ash.[24] Some say that both the bark and the top

FIGURE 28. Juniper branches gathered for making ash, February 2016. Photo by Cecilia Sandoval.

FIGURE 29. Burning juniper branches to create culinary ash, February 2016.
Photo by Cecilia Sandoval.

of the leaves differ on the two kinds; others say that the difference is just on
the leaves, where on one kind there will be little red speckles right on the tips.
Today, reportedly, it is the other kind that grows near the highway. "That's
the common one that doesn't have the red speckles," said Tall Woman. "If
you use that to make ash, you will need to use more ash because it's not as
strong. The one you want has juniper bunches on it, the yellowish kind, not
the one with blossoms or berries. You pick the whole branch." People try to
avoid picking juniper near the roads because they claim it smells from all the
cars and other vehicles, and the ash will smell like that, too.

Some people use juniper ash only with blue cornmeal dishes, to turn them
blue or grayish blue.[25] They claim that otherwise the blue cornmeal will
cause heartburn. Babies, the elderly, and the sick, however, should not eat
anything made with juniper ash. To use it, add it to either cold water or boiling water, whatever is called for. Ash can be used with any color of corn when
making cornmeal dishes. It turns a white cornmeal mix light blue or purple

and a yellow cornmeal mix green. Ash is commonly used in making *tsé'ást'éí* (paperbread), *nanoyeeshi* (poured bread), *tóshchíín* (blue cornmeal mush), and many other foods, such as mush, dumplings, and tamales.

Salt

According to Tall Woman, in the early days people gathered a native salt (*łeeyáán*), which they found deposits of on the tops of rocks; essentially it was an alkaline crust that was often gray. After being harvested, it was ground on the grinding stones. There were other kinds of salt that were used ceremonially but not for cooking. Whether that is still true is unknown to me.

The general term for salt is *'áshįįh*. Tall Woman mainly used the rock salt (*'áshįįh ntl'izí*) that Frank brought back from his trip to the sacred mountains; she ground up little pieces of it as needed. Rock salt is also brought back from the Grand Canyon, Salt Lake City, and other places, such as Jemez Pueblo, New Mexico. Some prefer to go to Zuni Salt Lake to get their salt because, they say, it is white and powdery. People usually go there in groups, make the appropriate offerings, and bring back big chunks to give to people. At least one member of Tall Woman's family continues to get her salt through friends who go to Zuni Salt Lake. Of course, people can also buy commercial salt at a supermarket or sometimes get it with commodity foods.

Sweeteners

Before the Navajos were introduced to sugar by the army, the government, traders, and others, they used other things found in the environment as sweeteners.[26] Some of these things were plants that were used to sweeten tea and coffee as well as food. Some were the same plants that produced berries that were mashed into juice. For example, *chiiłchin*, sumac berries dried and then ground very fine, were used by some as a sweetener. Tall Woman also named some plants that used to be common, such as *ka bizhi*.[27] Describing it as a tall plant, she said she gathered its leaves, boiled them, and then strained the resulting juice to get a sweetener. She also dried the leaves for later use as a sweetener.

Tall Woman also used juices as sweeteners; the ones she mentioned while describing how to make poured bread (see section 4) were all included:

juniper juice, squash juice, yucca fruit juice, and prickly pear cactus fruit juice. These juices were all obtained from boiling and mashing the vegetables or fruits or the plants from which they came.

Sometimes the Navajos also chewed handfuls of certain seeds to make sugar. For example, the seeds of pigweed or amaranth, *tł'oh deesk'idí*, were gathered, parched, and then chewed to make sugar. They could even be eaten as a meal in and of themselves.

Certain plants were chewed because when a person's saliva combined with the starch, the result was glucose or a sweet substance like sugar. Small portions of the chewed substance were added to a batter that needing sweetening. Tall Woman talked the most about using this process to sweeten cornmeal, saying that there was a well-known way to sweeten cornmeal that depended on (the enzymes in) human saliva.

Some people were asked to suck on parched corn and then spit into various batters to sweeten them. They might suck on parched white corn kernels that had been coarsely ground, or they might chew on them for a few minutes in the front of the mouth, where the saliva isn't as heavy. They also might suck on a cornstalk (*dá'ákaz*), a practice called *biínídoot'aal*. The foods that were sweetened this way included *'alkaan* (corn cake), *łeehilzhoozh* (large kneel-down bread or big tamales), and *tanáá'niil* (white cornmeal mush). Of course, some found this practice unsanitary or unhealthy, but even they thought it was all right if children were the ones doing it. As time went on, however, more and more adults refused to use this method of sweetening food. Some opposed it because the spitters were cigarette smokers.

Wild honey was another sweetener that people used. When various members of Tall Woman's family were out searching for food or herding the sheep and goats, they always watched for bees. Sunflowers were among the plants that seemed to attract big black and yellow bees. People who found honeybees were often able to retrieve the honeycombs. At least two times bees had moved into storage sheds around Tall Woman's hogan, and she smoked them out to get the honeycomb. Her neighbor, John Gorman, who had a huge farm, also raised bees, and sometimes she bought small jars of honey from him.

The Navajos also added *nímasii dleesh* to certain foods to make them sweeter. Various creamers, made of finely ground cornmeal and added to tea and coffee, acted as sweeteners too.

In time, of course, commercial sugars, both white (*'áshįįh łikan*, literally, "sweet salt") and brown (*'áshįįh łikan yishtłizhígíí*), were introduced and quickly became the most popular sweeteners in use. By the time I met Tall Woman, all the family members were using sugar as well as commercial syrup and honey. Domesticated wheat was also still being used as a sweetener; it was allowed to sprout and then dried before being ground and added to various kinds of batter.

Yeast

Although yeast (*díík'ǫsh*) was available from the trading posts and other stores, Tall Woman never used it; she said she made no foods that required it. However, she and some other elderly Navajo women said that they knew that some people did have yeast before the trading posts came. Tall Woman remembered hearing that it came in tubes, almost like sticks of butter now. "In earlier times," she recalled, "there was something that was rotten smelling that was used to make a bread that was brownish. The bread was called *bááh díík'ǫsh bił 'ál'íní*, meaning that it was made with something spoiled or rotten. Maybe that was the early yeast." This bread was reportedly baked in Dutch ovens over coals, in pit ovens in the ground, or in the big tall beehive-like ovens if there were a lot of loaves.

Baking Powder and Baking Soda

Although Tall Woman didn't use yeast, eventually she did start using baking powder (*bił 'ál'íní*), which was always bought from the trading post. It was one of the items that Frank hauled during his freighting days while bringing goods from Gallup to the trading posts, so she knew about it and had ready access to it. Initially, because it was new, she used it sparingly, mainly to make biscuits. Eventually she started adding a little bit of it to tortillas, frybread dough, and griddle cake batter. Her daughters said that within the extended family Tall Woman became known for making the best baking powder biscuits—which, Augusta said, were "really, really nice and tasty."

The only time Tall Woman mentioned baking soda was during her discussions of culinary ash. She didn't use baking soda as a substitute for juniper ash, but some of the People did, even though it lowered the nutritional values. Tall Woman did, however, learn to use baking soda to address certain gastrointestinal problems.

Shortening or Grease

Tall Woman said she never bought commercial shortening or lard at the trading post when it became available because she always saved animal fat (*'ak'ah*) when they butchered. She saved fat from cows, sheep, goats, and pigs, but not horses, and stored it in #10 cans. With pigs, she first cooked their fat in a Dutch oven or a big cast-iron skillet over the fire, adding a little water and letting it boil slowly. She stirred it constantly until the water had boiled off. Then she strained what was left and let it harden into a lard that was very clear. The containers of grease were stored in the ground storage pits along with meat and corn during the winter.

Some of the People called this grease tallow, but others restricted their use of that English word to the long piece of fat that came from a sheep's spinal cord. This was preserved by hanging it up to dry; when it was to be used for making paperbread, it was soaked to soften it up, and then the stone grill was rubbed with it before the bread was made. Tall Woman always tried to get at least a piece of this when a sheep was butchered. She would either use it immediately or dry it for later.

Tall Woman made several comments about sheep fat. She preferred to use this kind of fat when making tortillas, frybread, and mutton because it made the taste of the food "special." She noted that some of the sheep's organs, like the kidneys, also contained fat. Reminding me that all parts of the sheep were used, she said that the brain (*'atsiighąą'*) and the brain stem (the part right near the hole at the back of the head where the spinal cord passes through) were used as grease, too. She preferred to use the brain stem fat when greasing griddles, skillets, her stone grill, and other pans. She laughed when saying that this was her kind of Pam (a modern cooking spray her daughters were using). She also told me that the only kind of grease she ever used when making paperbread, *tsé'ást'éí*, was the fat from the brain or backbone of a sheep.

The chitin, or adipose fat (*'ak'ahłání*), which is the fat over the stomach, would be eaten spread over some of the organs; much of that fat was thin and lacy. It was cooked carefully on both sides only until it turned tan. Then an organ, most often the liver, was cooked for a short amount of time on a little charcoal or a small fire—just long enough so it wasn't raw. When the organ was done, it could be eaten with or without a tortilla, with the thin part of the stomach fat either on top of it or wrapped around it. The thicker part of the stomach fat and other kinds of fat were saved and used by Tall Woman when she made blood sausage.

Light-Colored Clay

In earlier times the Navajos dug up a light-colored clay, *dleesh* (fig. 30), while gathering wild foods. Many people say it is white, but it also comes in gray and light yellow. When dry, *dleesh* was a powdery substance that was used with foods that were astringent to remove the bitterness. Some call this mineral substance, which can be found on the reservation, food clay. There reportedly are several kinds of *dleesh*; at least two are used for medical problems, and another is used for painting patients in certain healing ceremonies. Yet another kind is called *nímasii dleesh*; it was used as a sweetener with wild potatoes, red berries, wolfberries, seepweed, and sumac berries.

Dleesh was stored in cloth sacks. When she was ready to use it, Tall Woman dissolved a few tablespoons of it in a little water, added it to whatever foods had already been boiled, and stirred the results. She said that some people preferred to do the mixing themselves while eating, by first taking a mouthful of the boiled or baked food and then a mouthful of *dleesh*. At present, some of the People still gather it to use for medical problems or to whiten wool for weaving.

Wolfe (personal communication, 2015) told me about a project that analyzed the food clays used by Navajos: *dleesh łigaaí*, white clay, and *dleesh łibáhí*, gray clay. As part of a broader study, Johns (1985, n.p.) tested the gray Navajo clay with clay used by Bolivian Indians with their wild potatoes and found both clays to have "adsorptive capabilities under digestive conditions that would make them effective detoxicants of the glycoalkaloids found in wild potatoes." They work strongly in the digestive system and less so in the mouth. The clays have a very high mineral content (sodium, potassium, calcium, magnesium, iron, zinc, and copper), but their most important function, which is recognized by Navajos, is to detoxify or remove the bitterness of wolfberries and wild potatoes. "Johns concludes that these culturally

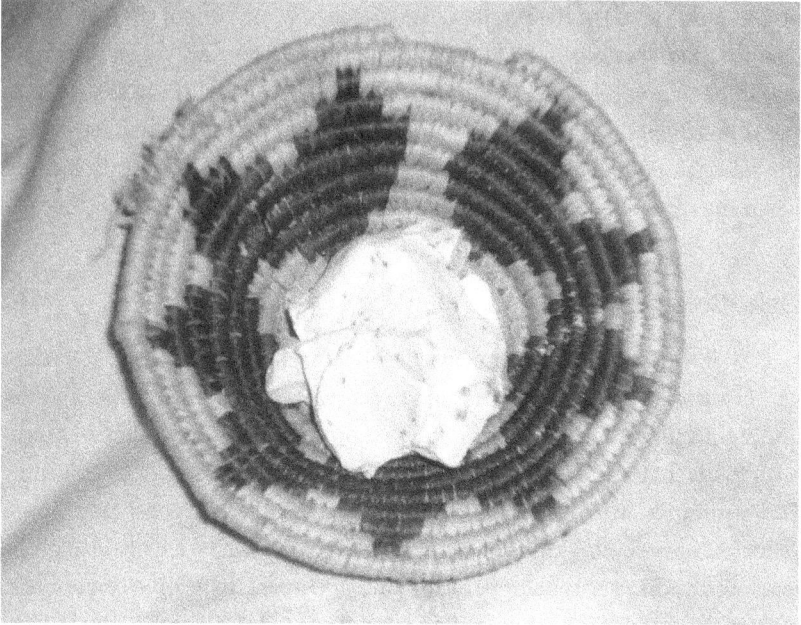

FIGURE 30. *Dleesh*, light-colored clay, February 2016. Photo by Cecilia Sandoval.

maintained geophagic practices [i.e., eating clay] appear highly adaptive for making bitter potatoes palatable and for increasing the resources available for human subsistence" (Wolfe et al. 1985, 340).

Gravy

Gravy (*'ii'ol'éél*) is used to thicken rabbit stew, mutton stew, *tóshchíín* (blue cornmeal mush), and a few other foods. Some things, like cornmeal mush, make their own gravy, and in earlier times *ts'áálbáí*, a corn-based substance now used as a coffee creamer, was used for thickening.[28] To thicken something cooking that is too watery, Tall Woman said, add regular cornmeal that has been ground up. To make gravy for a meat dish, take the meat out after it has cooked and leave the liquid in the pan. Remove part of the liquid, mix ground cornmeal with it, and pour it back in the pan.

Of course, after the stores arrived, people starting using white flour for the same purpose. Mixing white flour or cornmeal serves another purpose as well. "Sometimes we do this to stretch the food that we have, to fill people up, so there is enough for everybody," Tall Woman said.

Cheese

Géeso (probably a loan word from the Spanish *queso*) is cheese made from the milk of sheep or goats. Cottage cheese is *'abe' neesk'ihi*, which means "coagulated milk."

Tall Woman told me about three kinds of cheese made from the milk of goats or sheep. Two did not involve using a wild plant, but the third did; it used *naaltsoii*, or silverleaf nightshade.[29] The first two kinds of cheese were made only during the lambing season and were eaten almost as soon as they were made.

The first kind of cheese is made from rennet, a juice found in the lining of one of the stomachs the animal has. This cheese requires either a newly butchered lamb or kid or one that has frozen to death on a cold night; the animal must be less than four months old and not yet eating grass. The *'ats'ǫ 'asis*, the rennet stomach, is removed; its membrane lining, or rennet, contains gastric juice with an enzyme called rennin, which coagulates or curdles milk. The cheese is made from this juice.

The stomach is rinsed out and put it in a pan of fresh unboiled milk. Some tie it on a stick and stir it into the milk that way. This is left for most of the day to thicken the milk and cause it to form cheese curds. This works because the stomach has a lot of fat in it, and sometimes it even already has something like cheese inside it. Once the curds form, the stomach is removed. If it was attached to a stick, it can be hung up to dry and used again later. Or it can just be thrown away. To reuse it, it is softened up again in a pan of fresh milk, which will start to thicken the milk again. The curds are pressed into round patties and allowed to set a bit longer. These cheese curd patties were usually eaten right away because the People really liked them. Some preferred to grill them in hot grease and then eat them plain with the rest of the meal. Some wrapped a few of them in a tortilla, maybe also including pieces of the cooked stomach, and ate them that way.

The second kind of cheese requires a nanny goat or a ewe that has just given birth. She must be milked right away, or at least on the same day she has given birth. The milk is put in a warm place by the fire or on the stove for a few hours until it thickens. It can also be boiled and stirred until it thickens like cottage cheese. Today people say this cheese looks like and tastes like cottage cheese. It is usually eaten by itself.

The third kind of cheese could be made anytime berries could be obtained from the *naaltsoii*, or silverleaf nightshade plant. "The plant's name is really *hosh beldei'hééh*," said Tall Woman. "It has purple flowers and yellow berries, and it is one of the very few old plants that remains today—one that goes way, way back. There used to be lots of these plants around our hogans and everywhere. Some say this plant is dangerous to horses, and perhaps also sheep; cattle and goats eat it without any problem."

This plant is tall and has many nettles or thorns. The berries turn yellow or white when they're ripe. People say the berries are poisonous if they are not ripe, so even if they are yellow, humans shouldn't eat them directly. Either the berries or just the seeds inside them are used, fresh or dried, to make milk curdle and turn it into *'abe' neesk'ihi*, cottage cheese. If the berries are fresh, they can be used either whole or ground up; if they were dried whole and stored, they have to be ground before they are used. The berries are mixed right into the milk and left there until the cheese forms. Whole fresh berries are usually tied in a cloth, maybe four or five of them together, and the little sack is left in the milk until it curdles. Then the sack is removed and the berries are thrown away before the cheese is eaten.

To use just the seeds inside the berries, dry the berries and grind them. Then put four or five seeds in water and soak them. Later grind them again and strain the result through a cheesecloth. Add this juice, just a little at a time, to fresh milk from either a sheep or a goat. Keep stirring the milk until it gets to the desired thickness. The seeds thicken the milk, and if it sets for an hour or so, cheese will form. After that happens, put the cheese through a screen or a strainer and let the liquid drain out of it. Then squeeze what's left a little at a time, and wrap the resulting cheese in a cloth to keep it that way.

Section 3 | Cultivated Crops

THIS SECTION INCLUDES one cultivated grass (wheat) as well as cultivated vegetables and fruits. The vegetable and fruit sections are each arranged alphabetically. Corn (which is sometimes considered a grain rather than a vegetable) has been separated from the vegetable category and is presented right after wheat because of its importance in Navajo culture and as a staple in the Navajo diet.

Wheat

Wheat (*tł'oh naadą́ą́'*) is a European crop brought to the New World centuries ago by the Spanish along with milling processes and gristmills. David Snow (personal communication, 2014) notes that the Spanish got durum, hard wheat, from the Arabs in the tenth century. The first wheat crop reportedly sown in New Mexico was planted by the conquistador Juan de Oñate's colonists at San Juan in 1598.[30] Miller (1989) presents data about the flour and other foods provided for the Navajos incarcerated at Fort Sumner, revealing the sources, problems, and bad quality of some of the foods used there.[31]

The Navajos have been growing wheat for a long time and taking it to places for milling, especially in Colorado. In New Mexico and Arizona, the earlier wheat-growing areas included Shiprock, Wheatfields, Tsaile Lake, Ganado Lake, and Many Farms.

Wolfe (1984) says that by the late 1930s wheat flour, along with potatoes, sugar, coffee, lard, and salt—all items from the trading posts—had become major parts of the new Navajo diet. White flour, which was really bleached wheat flour, replaced corn flour in many kinds of bread by the late 1930s. It was also in the 1930s that the famous brand Blue Bird Flour, so loved by Navajos, became available (Calvin 2010).[32] Because of more processing, white flour does not become rancid, and it also stores better.

Tall Woman said that in earlier times the term for flour was 'ak'ą́ą́n, a term that covered three kinds of corn flour: blue, yellow, and white. "White flour" thus referred to flour made from white corn in the early days. If you wanted wheat flour in those days, you had to grow the wheat yourself and then grind it into flour. Since wheat takes a lot of water to grow, you had to be able to irrigate it.[33]

Although the Mitchells never grew wheat, they had ready access to it through a man known as Bitter Water Mountain Man, or Tó dich'íi'nii Dziłijini. He lived in the mountains and was a clan grandfather of Tall Woman's. He grew wheat over by Wheatfields Lake, Wheatfields, and Tsaile (Arizona) and harvested it in the fall. He owned part of a small lake in Tsaile (not Tsaile Lake). He and his sons, Mike and Joe, grew lots of wheat in that area because there was a good water supply. Much of that was from the snow in the mountains in the winter. When the wheat was ready, they would send word for Tall Woman to come in her wagon and get it, or he or one of his sons would bring it to her in his wagons. He also brought her huge gray squash. Tall Woman always had Augusta and the other girls grind it, and she would work with them if she wasn't busy doing something else.

When stores started carrying wheat, it was sold already ground. If people got it elsewhere, they had to process it themselves, and they used horses to do that. They harvested the wheat, put it on the ground, and had the horses run on it. Next they shook off the wheat stems and sifted the leaves to remove stems, leaves, and other things. That made more of the wheat fall on the ground. Then they had their horses walk over it again and again. The rest of what they did was by hand. They gathered it up, cleaned it by hand, sifted it again, washed off any dirt that had been picked up, and spread it out on a cloth or tarp overnight. In the morning they roasted that wheat first and ground it with the grinding stones, which worked much better for grinding wheat than store-bought metal grinders did. But grinding wheat that way was much harder than grinding corn, which is why people roasted the wheat first; that made it easier. Wheat had to be ground really fine to make flour to use for tortillas. In later times Tall Woman and others just took their wheat to a mill in Shiprock to get it ground. Now the wheat sold in the stores is bleached.

Only one recipe is given here; the rest of Tall Woman's wheat recipes are included in section 4.

K'íneeshbízhii Ts'ósí (Noodles)

1 cup wheat flour
Pinch salt
⅓ cup fat
Enough water to make thick dough

Combine ingredients and knead thoroughly. Then roll pencil-size coils between the palms of your hands. Break these into two-inch lengths. Drop them into boiling water and cook for half an hour. (To make this a soup, add meat, or one tablespoon of fat, and some black pepper for seasoning.)

Corn

For the Navajos there is no food more important than corn (naadą́ą́'). Originally obtained from the Pueblos, it is a New World plant first found around 6000 BCE in its wild version in the Valley of Mexico. In time this plant, teosinte, was domesticated and spread, becoming one of the three "sisters" in the Southwest: corn, beans, and squash. People often planted these three together in a mound. Corn was viewed as capable of answering all needs—of animals, humans, and the spiritual world. As a basic food it was grown and eaten daily in one form or another. With its arrival the Navajos adopted the bigger oblong Puebloan grinding stones to use in processing it instead of continuing to use the smaller circular grinding stones with which they processed wild seeds.

The Navajos cultivated corn of many different colors: blue, white, and yellow were the main ones, but gray, black, red, and multicolored (fig. 31) were also known. Tall Woman mentioned that red corn was rarely grown in the Chinle Valley, but she did not say why. Corn was usually harvested in the late summer or early fall (Manolescu [2010]; Gorman [2013]). It is important to remember that Navajo corn is *not* sweet corn; however, in some places

FIGURE 31. Native multicolored corn resting on the rim of a Navajo basket, February 2016. Photo by Cecilia Sandoval.

now—such as Shiprock and Tuba City—Anglo or white people's corn, *Bilagáana binaadą́ą́*, which *is* sweet corn and is viewed as small and glossy, is grown by Navajo farmers. But the People continue to say that they prefer "Indian corn" because it makes them stronger and is much better for them if they are sick.

People had diverse ideas about what color corn should be used for the different foods they were making. For ceremonies, both white and yellow cornmeal and corn pollen were used. Blue corn was preferred for making most of the traditional foods, and when blue cornmeal is combined with culinary ash (see section 2), the nutritional value of the food is noticeably increased.

The farm equipment needed to grow and harvest corn has already been discussed. But some other things that are required for processing corn should be added: knives, baskets, sieves, grinding stones, containers or sacks, grills, stone griddles, many kinds and shapes of pans for different cooking methods, stirring sticks, brushes, a stick with one flat end, shovels to dig cooking pits, axes to chop wood for cooking, mud (and perhaps straw) for making the small earth oven known as *bááh bighan*, and storage pits.

Corn was hand-ground with grinding stones (fig. 32) into a meal, with the food being made determining the level of fineness needed. Corn grinding was viewed as women's work, and Tall Woman often spent much of her day on this task, sometimes assisted by her daughters. She said that it was possible to make the work easier by first roasting the corn kernels all the way through and letting them dry. Then they were easier to grind.

Eventually, with the arrival of trading posts and the railroad among the Navajos, the European crops of wheat, barley, and other grains were introduced, and store-bought wheat flour (bleached white flour) began to replace corn flour as a mainstay in the Navajo diet. At first that flour came in very small bags in the store, not like today. But many Navajos still preferred to use

FIGURE 32. Isabelle Deschine grinding corn with traditional grinding stones, June 1963. Photo by author.

FIGURE 33. Ground white cornmeal, February 2016. Photo by Cecilia Sandoval.

ground white, yellow, or blue corn when making specific foods, or at least to add home-ground white corn and homegrown and hand-ground wheat to store-bought white flour when making frybread, tortillas, biscuits, and the like. Tall Woman noted that by adding some finely ground white cornmeal (fig. 33) to the store-bought flour, people were able to stretch their food supplies. Some foods required ground-up wheat sprouts as well. People gathered corn pollen, *tádidíín*, usually in the morning, to use in their daily prayers and offerings.

The foods made from corn were numerous and are therefore found in later sections of this chapter, such as *k'íneeshbízhii* (dumplings), *náneeskaadí* (griddle bread or tortillas), and *'alkaan* (the big cake baked overnight in a heated ground pit for the Girls' Puberty Ceremony). Corn could be prepared by numerous cooking methods: boiling, steaming, baking, roasting (on a grill, in hot coals, or in various kinds of outdoor ovens), parching, frying, broiling, and sun-drying. Although corn was usually eaten, either hot or cold, right after it was harvested, it could also be dried and set aside for later use. Tall Woman said that steaming fresh corn or roasting it in a pit were the most common ways of fixing corn to eat or to dry it for winter. Parching was said to enhance the flavor, and steaming it saved water when that was scarce.

Corn was also stored in large quantities in pits for the winter. People usually sun-dried it beforehand, leaving the unbaked corn on the stalk or leaving the husk on at first. Then they would usually pull back the husk, or remove it completely, and continue to let the corn dry in the sun. They also sun-dried corn that was already baked or roasted; that made it easier to cook later. Sometimes it was frozen with the husks on.

To process corn that had been dried and put away, if it was still on the cob it could be boiled, if it wasn't too dry, or the kernels could be scraped off the cob and boiled with other things. If the corn had been stored as dried kernels, they could be cooked first or ground to make specific foods.

People had different ideas about many things connected to corn, such as how many stages it went through, how many kinds there were, and what each kind should be used for. (A review of even a few issues of *Leading the Way* will quickly illustrate this.) Tall Woman taught that corn has four stages:

1. When the corn is still just tiny kernels, she would tell her children to say, "*Ayaazh* [tiny corn kernel], I am putting you into last year's little bag" (meaning their stomachs) just as they were ready to eat it. She believed that boiling and eating tiny kernels would bring more corn. Her daughters said she liked to fry tiny kernels in grease or, later, butter.

2. When the kernels are fully formed but still small, they can be cut off and ground to make a batter that is not very doughy; this is used in making *nanoyeeshi*, poured bread.

3. When the corn is fresh, young, and green, and the kernels are fully ripe but still milky, this is the time to make the much-loved kneel-down bread, *ntsidigo'í*.

4. When the corn is fully ripe and the kernels are very hard, it can be roasted right on the cob in a pit in the ground or in one of the outdoor ovens, or it can be singed in charcoal. After it is roasted it is eaten right away or dried. It can be stored, either as kernels or still on the cob, as long as it is thoroughly dry. Then later it can be cooked in boiling water, or the kernels can be ground to make mushes and

sweeteners for tea and coffee. The kernels can also be soaked overnight to use in making hominy or stew.

Corn Recipes

As mentioned above, since corn is a major staple in the Navajo diet, dishes
that contain it are found in most of the sections in this chapter. Here the
focus is on the two basic ways to prepare corn, *łee'shibéézh* (corn that is pit
roasted or steamed in its husks) and *neeshjízhii* (dried steamed corn), followed by recipes for hominy, parched corn or popcorn, and *dahaastiin*, the
frozen ground-roasted corn known as "Navajo ice cream."

The first basic way to prepare corn, *łee'shibéézh*, is pit roasted, baked,
steamed, or cooked in ashes. Either fully ripe corn or what Tall Woman called
"fresh ripe green corn" can be used to make *łee'shibéézh*. Traditionally, fully
ripe corn that is hard, *naadą́ą́' shichi'ili*, is roasted in an outdoor oven, in either
a ground pit or the earth oven, *bááh bighan*. (If there is a lot of corn to roast,
the latter will be used.) The outside pit should be about five and a half feet deep
and twenty inches in diameter on the top (but larger underneath).

Make a fire in the oven or pit in the morning and keep it going all day, adding wood as necessary; also heat up some rocks in the fire. In the evening,
when the pit or oven is hot enough and the charcoal has burned down, remove
the fire and the hot coals with a shovel but leave the rocks in there. Add the
corn, either with or without the husks. Put two or two and a half layers of corn
in the oven, spread out. If you are using the big beehive-shaped oven, put at
least two wagonloads of corn in it at a time. Also put some water in there,
maybe half a bucket, to make sure the corn steams. Others say to sprinkle
water over the corn; cover it with corn leaves, wet dirt, and hot coals; then close
the oven tightly.[34] Some say that if the husks are moist, water isn't necessary.

After you have filled up the oven, make sure that it is sealed very tightly.
Cover the door with a piece of metal or a big metal lid. Seal it with more mud
if necessary, especially on the top and around the doorway, and let it steam
or roast all night. If you are using a pit oven, put the husks right on the hot
coals, turning the corn now and then as it roasts. Some people put a metal
cover over that and build a small fire on it, keeping that going all night to
roast the corn in the pit.

Tall Woman noted that there was another way to make *łee'shibéézh* that doesn't involve either kind of oven. In this method the corn ears are roasted in hot charcoal while they are still in their husks. Turn the ears while they are roasting, using your hand, a wire, or a stick. This is basically quick roasting, because you keep turning the ears over quickly in the hot charcoal. Try to singe the husks until they get brown. Then brush off any black charcoal spots or scorched places on the husks, scrape off or tear off any burned parts, and put the ears in the sun to dry.

After roasting the corn overnight in either a ground pit or an outdoor oven, remove the łee'shibéézh in the morning and husk it. You can eat it right away off the cob if you want, or you can make it into neeshjízhii, dried corn. Remove the kernels first before sun-drying, or leave it on the baked cobs for sun-drying for wintertime use. To sun-dry, you can either remove the husks and lay the corn on a clean surface or pull the husks back and hang the corn by them. Some prefer to dry the corn on the baked cobs, scraping the kernels off later when they are ready to use the corn. Some people prefer to scrape the ears together to loosen the kernels—this is called shelling—and then winnow the results. Spread the cobs out to dry in the sun for one or more days.

To check if the cob is thoroughly dry, break it in two. When the corn is thoroughly dry, clean off the cobs; you can either shell them, removing the kernels right away, or leave the kernels on the cob. If you shell the cobs, winnow the kernels when you are done to make sure they are clean. Grind the roasted corn right away and use it for hot drinks and other things (see section 7). Or put the roasted corn, either shelled or still on the cob, into a clean dry container—such as a burlap sack, a twenty-five-pound flour sack, or a large cloth bag—and store it in a cool dry place.

When you want to use the corn in the wintertime, scrape off the kernels if necessary, add them to boiling water to reconstitute them, and cook them for four to five hours. For ways to use neeshjízhii, see sections 6 and 7.

HOMINY

Hominy (bił ha'nigáhí) is made from steamed corn that is roasted or baked in a ground pit or a big beehive-shaped outdoor oven. Some people (such as Young and Morgan 1980) use the terms haníígaii and posole as synonyms for hominy, but Tall Woman said that haníígaii means to "cook a long time." Haníígaii is actually a stew made from a backbone and dried corn; in other words, the backbone has to be there in Tall Woman's understanding of the meaning of that word.

Hominy is usually made in the winter, and according to Tall Woman there are at least two ways to make it. The first one, the traditional way, uses *naadą́ą́' shichi'ili*, fully ripe corn that is hard. Traditionally this corn is roasted in an outdoor oven, either in a pit in the ground or in the *bááh bighan*. The second way to make hominy is to use corn that has just become ripe; this is variously described as corn that is hardly ripe, green corn on the cob, corn that is not too ripe, or corn that is not fully ripe and hard. In both cases you are starting with *neeshjízhii*, dried steamed (or roasted) corn kernels.

Tall Woman said that the traditional way to make hominy is to use white corn that has been dried, either removed from the cob or left on the cob. If you have stored the corn on the cob, the first thing to do is to take the dried cobs and remove the kernels by hand or by rubbing two ears together. Then winnow the kernels (fig. 34). It's easier, of course, if this has been done ahead of time.

Once the winnowing is done, the dry corn kernels are soaked overnight. Then change the water, put the kernels in clean hot water, and boil them. About two hours after they have started boiling, add about one-half cup of juniper ash; this will start to loosen the skins in another half hour. As we have seen, ash adds flavor and acts as an alkaline treatment, infusing the kernels with calcium, trace minerals, protein, and niacin while altering the amino acid balance of protein to increase its quality and nutritional power; it also raises the calcium, magnesium, phosphorus, iron, zinc, and copper content of the food.

After the skins have been loosened and removed, drain the water, rinse the corn, and wash the skins away. Change the water and cook the corn for another two hours or until the kernels are tender. One of Tall Woman's daughters added that if you are using an electric or a gas stove inside your home, put the dried corn in a large pot of water, cover the pot, and cook for four to five hours over medium heat. Then drain the water off the corn and season it with salt and pepper to taste.

Changes in Hominy Preparation

While discussing hominy with me in the late 1960s, Tall Woman said that some Navajos were already using baking soda instead of juniper ash when

FIGURE 34. Ruth Shirley Yazzie winnowing hominy, June 1964. Photo by author.

making it. She believed that this was happening because it was getting really difficult to find juniper or to make the culinary ash to prepare hominy the traditional way. Although these people claimed the hominy was just as good this way, Tall Woman had tasted it and did not agree. Clearly baking soda does tenderize the corn and make it puff up, but it has very little nutritional value and thus removes all the nutritional advantages of using culinary ash. Some say it actually causes nutrients to be lost; it is known that baking soda lowers vitamin A and various minerals and increases sodium and thus increases hypertension. Tall Woman insisted that hominy made with baking soda was not true hominy—not only was no ash used; the corn was also done in an hour.

Another shortcut she reported was making hominy by boiling dried corn. By the late 1960s stores were selling dried corn that was advertised as already roasted or steamed. People claimed that they didn't need anything to soften the corn, like ash, because the corn had already been cooked before it was dried. Because of that, it takes a much shorter amount of time to soften the corn when it is boiled. Again, according to Tall Woman, doing it this way does not produce traditional, true hominy.

Tall Woman provided several other comments about using hominy. She said that if you want to make hominy stew, during the last one or two hours of cooking the kernels, add pieces of meat. Another thing that some people liked was hash. To make this, grind up dried meat and then grind that again with dried corn. Then the result is dried, and it's called Navajo hash. She said you can also make refried hominy: After fully cooking the hominy, drain the water and then grind the cooked kernels on a grinding stone or in a metal grinder. Take the result and fry it in fat. Hominy corn cooked that way looks like refried beans. Although Tall Woman had eaten that, she said she had never fixed it, but other family members had.

PARCHED CORN

Parched corn (*naadą́ą́' sit'ee'*) is comparable to popcorn. While discussing this, Tall Woman mentioned two ways of eating it: alone or with pinyons.

Take dried corn kernels and parch them in a frying pan over a hot fire, stirring constantly. Some say to add sand to prevent the kernels from burning, but Tall Woman said that if you pay attention to stirring, it won't burn. Next, sieve the results and rinse with water. Then add salt and eat that like popcorn. People have different ideas about what color corn makes the best popcorn. But unlike Anglo popcorn, this kind does *not* pop. Everybody loves this corn, saying the roasted dried corn kernels are really sweet. Tall Woman reportedly used to make batches of this beloved food for her children to take back to boarding school with them.

The popcorn can also be mixed with shelled, roasted pinyons. Tall Woman said that if she had any *'atsá 'azee'*, a wild herb that some thought tasted like peppermint, she would soak a bit of that in water and sprinkle it on the parched corn or on a mixture of parched corn, salt, and roasted pinyons. She called it "popcorn and peanuts."

NAVAJO ICE CREAM

One of the foods that Tall Woman said was a family favorite, especially with the children, was *dahaastiin*, which family members called Navajo ice cream. To make *dahaastiin*, start with corn that has been roasted on charcoal, in a ground pit, or in the *bááh bighan*. After it is roasted the corn is dried and thoroughly ground. This kind of corn is the basis for many dishes, including creamers, *tóshchíín* (blue cornmeal mush), and cakes. Tall Woman said that the recipes for *tanaashgiizh*, blue cornmeal mush with ash, or *tanáá'niil*, sweetened white cornmeal mush, can also be used to make Navajo ice cream.

Add a little milk (although some say water will work) to the finely ground roasted corn. The resulting mix is like pancake batter but thinner. The batter for *dahaastiin* is not too thick and not too watery. The big difference between it and pancake batter (besides the milk) is that the *dahaastiin* batter always has a sweetener added to it. Today most people just use sugar, but Tall Woman preferred using juices from plants. She mentioned *hashk'aan* (yucca fruit) juice or *hashk'aan* pieces, or boiling the fruit and then mashing it with the corn. Juice from squash, juniper, or prickly pear cactus fruit will also work. (Of course, you have to remove the thorns from the cactus fruit first.) Any of these plant juices will make the batter sweet.

According to Tall Woman, in earlier times *dahaastiin* was made in the winter because it had to be put outside in a shallow pan—but up high, like on the hogan roof, so animals could not bother it.[35] In the morning it would be frozen, and she would take it off the roof, bring it inside, and cut it into square pieces so everyone could have some. If it thawed too fast and got too watery, people would squeeze the square with their hands, like a sponge, before they ate it. Sometimes children would get into the *dahaastiin* during the night, but if that happened, they got in trouble in the morning. One woman told me that the pan she was using on top of the hogan roof was tipped over during the night, and in the morning she was greeted by a long *dahaastiin* icicle hanging by the hogan door. She laughingly reported that it was "really sweet."

Tall Woman said that even though more and more of the People were getting electricity in the Chinle area by the late 1960s and early 1970s, fewer were making Navajo ice cream, even though with refrigerators and freezers they could have made it at any time of the year.

Besides making *dahaastiin* from the two variations described above, Tall Woman mentioned two other ways to make it. One, the simplest, is to omit the sweetener and just mix the finely ground cornmeal with water or milk and then freeze that. The other way is more complicated: First make *tanáá'niil*, sweetened white cornmeal mush. Then mix ground *chiiłchin* (sumac berries) into it and freeze it. This produces a red *dahaastiin* with a sour flavor.

Cultivated Vegetable Crops Other Than Corn

BEANS

Of the many kinds of beans (*naa'ołí*) recognized—kidney, white, green, pinto, and many more—Tall Woman's family reportedly grew only pinto beans, *naa'ołíłbáhí*, on its farm. These beans were among the very first crops to ripen, and they were harvested by pulling up the whole plant. After placing these on a sheepskin, a big cloth, tarp, or something comparable, family members beat the plants with sticks until the bean pods broke open. Then the beans were gathered up and winnowed in a basket to remove dirt and other chaff.

To prepare them for eating, beans were usually boiled. After being winnowed, they were soaked in water and then boiled until the water turned dark. Tall Woman said that the water should be changed several times when fixing beans to make them taste better. After the second or third change of water, the beans were ready to cook by more boiling. They can be eaten by themselves, with salt, or they can be reheated to eat later. Although some people liked to fry beans in fat, Tall Woman rarely did so. Another common way the People used pinto beans was to add them to the sheep's backbone if they were fixing mutton. Tall Woman also liked to "give them a good flavor" by adding pigskin, pigs' feet, or some other kind of pigmeat, plus bacon grease or salt pork, to the beans while fixing them.[36]

BEETS

Although Tall Woman's family didn't grow beets (*nímasii łikaní łichíí'í*), family members got them from others, including John Gorman and another neighbor, Hastiin Tsoh (Big Man), who grew them every year. The beets were dug up, cleaned off, sliced, and prepared by boiling.

CARROTS

Tall Woman also didn't grow carrots (*chaat'ínii*), but Leo Shirley, a son-in-law, did. He used to bring huge carrots from an area near Flat Rock, Arizona, on the Nazlini Road, to share with the family. Tall Woman washed them, cut them up, and boiled them. They were also eaten raw, after being washed.

CUCUMBERS

Tall Woman didn't grow cucumbers (*ta'neesk'ání dik'ǫ́zhí*), either, but she was often given cucumbers by those who did. She washed them off, sliced them in various ways, and ate them raw. Some people said they were too salty. In time people started frying them in sheep fat in Dutch ovens after dicing them. Tall Woman tried this, but she preferred to eat them raw, as did most of her family.

POTATOES

Like many other people, Tall Woman grew her own white potatoes (*nímasii*), to reduce dependence on both the wild ones, which were reportedly bitter, and those sold at the trading posts. After digging the potatoes up and cleaning them off, she might eat them raw, but she added that there were also many ways to cook them. They could be roasted whole in hot coals or baked in Dutch ovens or, later, in store-bought ovens. They could also be boiled (peeled or unpeeled, sliced or whole) and eaten by themselves or boiled with mutton or goatmeat. A mush could be made with them by adding water to the boiled potatoes and cooking them further. Some liked to fry them with fat, adding onions and salt. According to her children, Tall Woman enjoyed them both raw and cooked in all the ways she mentioned here, as did the whole family.[37]

PUMPKINS

In Tall Woman's family, at least, there was a terminology confusion between pumpkins and red squash (*naayízíłchii'*). Some relatives did grow pumpkins, *naayíziłtsooí*, along with squash, beans, corn, and different kinds of melons. Others said that the family didn't grow pumpkins but instead grew a gray squash, *naayízíłbáhí*, that had a wrinkled skin and an orange interior and was called a pumpkin in English. Tall Woman grew the gray squash, not pumpkins.[38]

SQUASH

Although many kinds of squash (*naayízí*) are grown by the Navajos, Tall Woman said she only ever planted two kinds: the green striped ones and the hard gray ones with the wrinkly skin mentioned in the previous section. Although some people called the gray squash pumpkin because it was orange inside, she said it was Indian squash, not real pumpkin. Gray squash had to be harvested before it got too big. Tall Woman planted squash separately, not with the beans and corn.

The green striped ones were always picked before they got too hard. They were cut up, boiled or fried, and eaten that way alone or as part of a stew, or they were sliced vertically and the pieces hung up for drying. These could be stored for wintertime use in stews or soups or to be eaten by themselves.

Tall Woman liked gray squash better because it was sweeter than the green striped kind, but she sometimes added sugar even to the gray squash. Tall Woman let gray squash get really ripe, or hard on the outside, before harvesting it. Gray squash was usually harvested later than other kinds of squash and could be stored whole for wintertime use. Sometimes she also got gray squash from Mountain Man, a clan relative. He would bring lots of gray squash in his wagon and sell it to people near the Chinle Boarding School.

When the gray squash was ripe, Tall Woman picked it, cleaned out the seeds, cut it into small pieces, and then steamed the pieces in a pan over the fire. She never made soup out of this squash, but some of the People did. She also would put the whole squash near the fire and bake it by turning it around and around. When it was done, she would cut it up and serve it that way. Tall Woman never ate the squash rind but always scraped the pulp out, mashed it up, and added commodity brown sugar to it before boiling it all together. When she made that, she served it to be eaten by itself. Sometimes she did not add sugar if the pulp tasted sweet enough by itself.

Different kinds of squash are used for different things. For example, the green striped ones are used for frying and cooking with mutton. Both white scallop squash and yellow crooked-neck squash are peeled, sliced, blanched, and dried. Of course, all the varieties of squash had different names; for example, summer squash was *naayízí yázhí*. Even today, Navajos like many different kinds of squash, and if they are growing crops they will usually grow more than one kind of squash, such as acorn, summer, spaghetti, large round fat ones, and little gourd-shaped ones.

Squash is like melon in the sense that both are still eaten either fresh or dried. It's common for people to cook meat with squash; first they pick and clean out the squash, then they dice or cut it and boil it alone. Next it's mashed up and boiled again, with meat. Fresh squash can also be roasted on the fire. The green striped ones are usually salted before serving; acorn squash, when fresh, is cut in half and then baked or roasted over an open fire, in hot ashes, or in an oven. Squash can also be peeled, cut into thin strips, and fried in mutton fat or baked on coals.

If people had lots of squash, they would store it whole, because like melon, squash keeps for several months in a cool dry place, like a storage pit. Squash can also be dried for wintertime use. To do that, peel the squash, remove the insides, cut up the squash, and dry the pieces in the sun. The green striped ones were often cut in circles or spirals (*náhinist'as*), dried in the sun, and then tied into packages to store. Tall Woman said that if you did this right the squash would last for years. The strips just had to be boiled briefly to be used later. Summer squash was usually sliced thin and put on a screen to sun-dry, peeled or unpeeled. Large winter squash was usually cut so that its meat could be hung in the open air on a wire or string. It dried better in the sun if it was cut into half or whole circular or spiral strips that were long and thin. The strips could be suspended from sticks to dry. Sun-drying might take several days; it was very important that anything being sun-dried did not get wet. Small squash remained fresh for three to four weeks; then it would be cut into long spiral strips. Gray squash was not cut in circles to make curly strips.

There are many ways to fix dried squash, according to Tall Woman. Boil it, add sugar if desired, and eat that. Make jam out of it by adding a lot of sugar. Scorch it on hot coals, boil it, and add cornmeal flour to make soup. To reconstitute dried squash, just add it to mutton stew, to another stew or soup, or to meat along with dried onions. Tall Woman believed that squash was important to have around, because if meat or other food was in short supply, squash could be added to it to stretch it so everyone could be fed. Whether fresh or dried, squash really filled people up.

Navajos also used other parts of the squash plant besides the squash itself.

For example, some preferred to save squash leaves and use these instead of corn husks when making kneel-down bread. They said that squash leaves made it easier to do the wrapping involved in making this kind of bread. Other people liked the seeds, *naayízí bik'óó sit'é*. They roasted them, added salt, and ate them just like sunflower seeds. The seeds had to be cleaned first, dried either in the sun or over hot coals, and then sprinkled with water and salt. Some people, including Tall Woman, liked to add *'atsá 'azee'* (a seasoning) to the seeds.

A major part of the squash plant that some people, including Tall Woman and her family, used was the blossoms, *tá'iitsóhii*, which people collected and ate. People used them as seasoning and also ate them fresh or dried, or baked and stuffed. Tall Woman never stuffed them for her family, even though her mother did that and had taught her how. Tall Woman taught her children that it was very important to pick the older squash blossoms, because the more of those that were picked, the more new squash there would be.[39] Today nobody in her family uses squash blossoms as food, but when they did (and when she fixed them), they often ate the blossoms by themselves after washing them. Some said they tasted like corn pollen.

To dry the blossoms for later use as seasoning, Tall Woman strung them on a wire, dried them in the sun or the shade, and then stored them. When she wanted to use them to season soup, stew, or meat, she crumbled them up. She would also boil them in mush or soup, adding cornmeal or sheep fat.

When people stuffed the blossoms, they usually used blue cornmeal and milk, no ash, and maybe some white wheat flour. Even though Tall Woman didn't make stuffed blossoms, she told me the way she had learned to do it from her mother. Gather the blossoms, wash them, and let them dry. Stuff them with a thick dough made from cornmeal or white flour and a bit of goat's milk. Then bake them. There were also a few other ways to make them. One was to stuff them with a mush made from blue corn flour and goat's milk. Another was to use baked corn flour, white wheat flour, and goat's milk. That mixture was boiled into a thick mush, and then the blossoms were filled with it. Those were turned upside down in hot ashes and covered with some kind of pan, more hot ashes, and sand, and then they were baked for thirty-five to forty minutes.

Cultivated Fruits

In addition to using the wild fruits that were plentiful at one time and frequently gathered as food, the Navajos eventually started growing some fruits as well. These included various kinds of melons and some fruit trees, at least for some people; a few also planted grapes but continued to call them wild grapes. Tall Woman's family never planted those.

MELONS

Tall Woman said that most people liked to grow melons of one kind or another; watermelons, muskmelons, and sugar melons were common, and people grew them "way back, before the traders came." Some were striped, and some were red, pink, or yellow inside with black seeds. Some were smooth outside, and some were rough. People disagree over what kinds were bought from the traders, because nobody grew them; some said they were mainly honeydew, muskmelons, and cantaloupes, but others disagree. Tall Woman talked mainly about cantaloupe (*ta'neesk'ání*) and said that if it was the kind with a rough skin, it was called *ta'neesk'ání dích'ízhí*. This was orange or yellow on the inside, and she preferred to grow this kind. When a sweet yellow cantaloupe splits open because it's ripe, the term *deestálii* refers to the split-open state. A cantaloupe can be sun-dried after being peeled and sliced into strips, then reconstituted by boiling.

Tall Woman said she could tell that a melon was ripe by tapping on it and hearing a hollow sound, seeing that it had turned yellow, or smelling a sweet odor. People enjoyed melons fresh but also dried them for wintertime use. Sometimes people also ate them during the day as a snack. Some people grew a lot of melons and traded them for other things. Tall Woman grew only enough for family use, however—mainly plain green ones, either long or round, and mainly yellow on the inside.

WATERMELONS

There were many kinds of watermelon (*ch'ééh jiyáán*), and they had different names, such as white watermelon (*ch'ééh jiyáánłgai*). This kind was usually huge, round, often a creamy color on the outside, and yellow inside. Some women tried to make jam out of its rind, but Tall Woman never did that.

Watermelons could become very big and were usually pink or yellow inside. There were many different kinds of green ones, and they came in all sizes. Watermelons were very popular and were eaten fresh in the summer and the fall. They retain their popularity today. Most people cut them into large pieces, but some just scoop the flesh out with their hands; the seeds, except for the black ones, are often spit out. Many save the black seeds for replanting. Tall Woman said that she had never heard of seedless watermelons when she was farming.

Like other melons, watermelons could be sun-dried. To do that, the red part was cut into pieces and dried like pumpkins or other melons. Some liked to cut the melon on the end, scoop out its seeds, slice it from top to bottom, and then hang strips up to dry for use in the winter. These would be steamed later to reconstitute them; the rind would be cut off and given to the sheep to eat (see fig. 1). Some preferred to cut the watermelon into circular strips like a squash. Then the strips were hung up to dry in the sun. Some preferred to wrap the strips around a stick to dry and then wrap them around each other for storage. Later they were reconstituted by boiling them until they were soft, adding sugar if wanted, and serving them like other melons. The fruit mush can be eaten alone or with a cornmeal dish. People also stored watermelons whole in their underground storage pits for months at a time.

Fruit Trees and Fruit

Before Fort Sumner and the Kit Carson roundup, the Canyon de Chelly area was known for fruit trees, especially apple and peach trees, which grew in the bottom of the canyon (Jett [1974, 1979]). These fruit trees were shown in the Franciscan records to have continued into the early 1900s. Eventually, however, some of the orchards were let go and fell into disuse. Some of the vegetation, planted originally by the Civilian Conservation Corps and the Works Progress Administration to stop erosion problems for the farms in the canyon, became detrimental, spreading and sapping precious water away from the remaining fruit trees. Recently the National Park Service was able to get funding to successfully eradicate both tamarisk and Russian olive trees in this area, and now families are replanting fruit trees. When new owners, the Ortegas, took over the Thunderbird Lodge in 2013 (with a contract that ended in December 2015), they not only changed the lodge's name to the

Sacred Canyon Lodge, they had Navajos who farmed in the canyon plant twenty peach trees on their farms. They said they were having this done to reclaim the lost Navajo heritage and to help heal the historical traumas associated with the canyon (Yurth 2013).

Although Tall Woman and her family did not raise apples or plums, for a while they did grow peaches, and in any case they had access to all three of these fruits through their relatives (Mitchell [1978] 2003; Mitchell 2001, 242–43).[40]

APPLES

Tall Woman and her family always enjoyed picking apples (*bilasáana*) and either eating them on the spot or bringing them home from the canyon in their wagon. At home they sliced them or ate them whole as fresh fruit, but they also mashed them up and ate the mush as a side dish. Like other fruits, apples were sun-dried by being sliced and set on a screen out of the way of animals. Dried apples are called *bilasáana biskąą*. For Tall Woman's family, apples were as popular and important as peaches.

PEACHES AND APRICOTS

Peaches (*didzétsoh* or *dzidzétsoh*) were enjoyed both fresh and dried. Reportedly, both peaches and apricots (*dit'oodí*) were introduced to the Navajos and the Hopis by Spanish priests who planted them in the 1600s. Both fruits became favorites, and families started planting them in nearby fields and canyons. There was also a busy trade of mutton or beef for dried peaches, watermelons, and apricots from the Hopis, who did more farming than the Navajos. People ate the fruit right in the canyon, while picking it, or took it home for drying.

A close friend and clan relative of the Mitchells gave them an area in the bottom of Canyon del Muerto that was filled with peach trees. Tall Woman made it clear to me that there was a lot of work associated with having those trees and taking care of them. Her family members had to clean up around them, irrigate when necessary, prune, harvest the fruit when it was ready, and bring out the peaches by wagonloads. Then they had to split them open, remove the pits, eat some, and sun-dry the rest to store the fruit for wintertime use. Even the hogan roof was used for sun-drying. Some people saved the seeds or pits for planting. Others liked to remove the pit, roast that, and eat it.

When the peaches were dried, they were stored in a sack for the winter. When people wanted to eat them, they heated them up with a little water; after the peaches softened, they could be mashed by hand or with a spoon. The peaches could also be soaked overnight in water, cooked in the morning, and eaten with a hot tortilla or with *tanaashgiizh*, the thick blue cornmeal mush, either mixed in or placed separately on the side. Tall Woman recounted that finally they had to return that land to the owner (apparently in the 1950s) (Mitchell 2001, 242–243, 462n11). The men were all away working, and it was hard to go back and forth caring for the trees. The sands in the canyon made it hard to get the wagons in and out, and they also needed people at home herding and watching the farm and the hogan.

PLUMS

Another relative, Uncle John, planted plums (*ch'il na'atł'o'iitsoh*) very near where they all lived in Chinle rather than down in either Canyon de Chelly or Canyon del Muerto. Lots of other people tried planting them, too. These trees did fine as long as they were irrigated; in some places the ground was hard clay, and when the trees were irrigated it got very muddy. As long as the plum trees had a lot of rain or were irrigated enough, the plums would grow big and sweet. Everybody in Tall Woman's family ate the plums when they ripened. They ate them whenever they were hungry during the day, either whole or sliced. They also sliced them for sun-drying and stored them for winter use. Some of the women also tried making jam from the plums but found that doing so took a lot of sugar if the fruit was very sour.

PROCESSING FRESH APPLES, PEACHES, APRICOTS, AND PLUMS

Apples, peaches, apricots, and plums shared processing techniques. They were eaten fresh while ripe, either whole or sliced, or were dried for winter. The fresh fruits could be stewed before eating or boiled with a small amount of cornmeal mixed in to make a mush, which could be eaten by itself or with blue corn dishes such as *k'íneeshbízhii* (dumplings) and *tanaashgiizh* (thick blue cornmeal mush). All the dried fruits were reconstituted the same way, by using boiling water and then mashing them up into a mush. Some people liked to add brown or white sugar to the mush. In Tall Woman's family, nobody ever used these fruits for making pies or any fruit-filled pastries.

GRAPES

Tall Woman and her family did not plant grapes (*ch'il na'atł'o'ii*), but others they knew did, especially those living in Canyon de Chelly. Sometimes these people gave her grapes. These were large and different colors when ripe: green, red, or purple. The wild grapes that people sometimes found while herding or looking for other foods were smaller and only two colors: purple or green. For reasons unclear to me, the Navajos I know who planted grapes called them *ch'il na'átł'óíí*, the name for wild grapes. The grapes given to Tall Woman and her family were eaten raw, often shortly after they had been picked from the vines and given to her. The same was true of the wild ones. Sometimes, however, people liked to sun-dry them, turning them into raisins for winter use. To reconstitute them, they were boiled, cornmeal was added, and the mixture was boiled longer to create a jam-like mush. Some people tell their children not to eat too many grapes, whether wild or cultivated, because eating too many or eating them too often causes a stomach-ache. Tall Woman did not mention how to alleviate that.

Section 4 | Cake, Breads, Dumplings and Marbles, Pancakes and Griddle Cakes, Flour Tortillas, Frybread, Poured Cornbread, Kneel-Down Bread, Paperbread, and Wheat Bread

Cake

Tall Woman told me about only one kind of cake, *'alkaan*, the corn cake originally associated with the Kinaaldá, or Girls' Puberty Ceremony. At present this is made in secular contexts as well, but to the best of my knowledge it continues to be the only traditional cake the Navajos make. Recently I learned that in some places there is now another kind of *'alkaan*, a small individual corn cake called *dítł'ógí' 'alkaan*.

Although the traditional cake is known by several names, I have always followed Tall Woman's preference in calling it *'alkaan*. In her day, and for at least a decade after she passed away, making this cake was an integral part of the Girls' Puberty Ceremony. It involves the girl whose womanhood is being celebrated as well as many family members, neighbors, clan relatives, and others. Both women and men have responsibilities associated with the cake, specific jobs to do during its creation. However, it is the women who prepare the batter and who often dig the ground pit in which the cake will bake all night. Men gather the firewood and chop it, if necessary; they also supervise the all-night baking so the results will be satisfactory (Frisbie [1967] 1993, xv–xxii, 38–46, 362–66, 411–12; Roessel 1991; Begay 1983: Keith 1964).

As continuing discussions about this cake in *Leading the Way* (Kaibetoney 2009) and the *Navajo Times* illustrate, people have different ideas, traditions, and recipes for making *'alkaan*.[41] Whether these vary by family, region, agency, clan, or other larger groupings, I do not know. But the women involved determine how large the cake will be, how the batter will be made, what will be added to it, if anything, and so forth. The size of the cake determines how much batter and how many corn husks have to be prepared and how big the ground pit must be. The cakes I have observed and helped with over the years have always had the pit dug to the east of the hogan's doorway, which itself faces east.

Nowadays some claim that preparing the 'alkaan is "way too much work" and that "this is why the ceremony is declining or fading away." Yet my own observations and experiences suggest the opposite: although changes have been and are taking place, as would be expected, the ceremony is alive and well, and even though making the cake does take physical labor, people are usually having a good time while doing so (see Frisbie [1967] 1993, xviii–xx, for some of the changes I witnessed between the 1960s and the early 1990s).

Perhaps one of the major changes I have seen since the mid-1960s is the fact that now the cake can be and is made outside the traditional Kinaaldá ceremonial context. Wolfe (1984) found that this was already true in the early 1980s, but I didn't see it until the early 1990s. Women who were doing this told me that they often "get hungry for the cake, or somebody in the family gets hungry for it," so they just make it. People like its taste and like to have it around. Some say that they let the cake cool off, harden, and be dried for later use, that it's better at that point because when it's hot, freshly cooked, and just removed from the ground, it's often mushy. In the nonceremonial context the 'alkaan is "just a cake," comparable to pound cake or chocolate cake (but no packaged mix—yet!).

When it is baked outside its ceremonial context, it can be made either outside or inside. To make it outside, in the ground pit already heated beforehand by burning a fire in it, use a Dutch oven, a cast-iron pot with a lid, a skillet, a heavy enamel pan, or an old metal dishpan. Line the pan with corn husks and then put the batter in it. Cover it up and build another fire on top of the pan. People say that baking it outside in a pit like that would probably take twenty-five to thirty minutes. Some people use an inside electric or gas oven, putting the batter in a nine-by-thirteen-inch pan lined and covered with aluminum foil. The cake is baked very slowly at low heat—about 250°F for about four hours.

Other changes I've noticed are pieces of 'alkaan being sold for five dollars each, both at flea markets and along parade routes, and the cake being made with extra ingredients. Raisins were being used earlier, but now some add a sweetener of brown or white sugar or even syrup (one cup per cake). Some omit the sweeteners that were possibly used in earlier times, such as ground dried wheat sprouts, or the practice of having children chew on ground corn-meal and then spit into the batter to add salivary enzymes to it. Some people now say that both blue and yellow cornmeal should be used, or only white cornmeal.

Since Tall Woman talked only about the 'alkaan made for a Kinaaldá, that is the focus below. She began by identifying all the things one needed to have on hand to make the cake (even though she knew that I had already helped make several in ceremonial contexts by the time we were discussing tradi-tional foods): ears of corn (whatever color is preferred), dried corn husks, one or more sets of grinding stones, sheepskins or goatskins to put underneath the grinding stones, brushes for the grinding stones, stirring sticks, buckets and washtubs, sweeteners (such as wheat or wheat sprouts ground into a fine powder and/or raisins), a shovel and an axe for digging the pit, juniper branches and a grass broom, firewood, water, sand, and possibly brown paper bags and boards to place around the pit.

Tall Woman said that traditionally the kinaaldá, the girl having the cer-emony, spent hours grinding either white or yellow corn by hand using the grinding stones, usually with help from her female relatives. Then she parched the resulting cornmeal and dried it in a skillet, if necessary. Since the cake bakes in the ground overnight during the bijí (the final night of a ceremony, with all-night singing) of the traditional four-day ceremony, the third day is usually when the grinding is finished and the batter is made for the cake. While some women work on this, others fill up buckets of water and put them on the fire to boil. Someone digs the pit in the ground after the discussions are finished about the size of the cake to be made and where the pit should be located. People build a fire in the pit and keep that going for at least four hours, if not overnight. If overnight, then this is done on the cer-emony's second day so that the pit will be ready when the batter is, on the third day. When the pit is hot enough, the coals are raked out and juniper branches are used as brooms to brush the bottom before anything made from corn husks is placed on it.

Once the water is boiling, about six handfuls of white corn flour (parched and ground earlier by the girl and others) are stirred with the stirring sticks

FIGURE 35. Preparing *'alkaan* batter with greasewood stirring sticks, June 1963. Photo by author.

into about half a pail of boiling water. Women bring their own stirring sticks with them to help add the ground corn into the boiling water, and they gather in the hogan so that a number of buckets can be processed (fig. 35). They keep adding the ground corn and stirring until the batter thickens, or starts to get thick and tough; then the bucket is removed from the fire and set aside to cool for ten to fifteen minutes. If white or brown sugar is to be added, it is dissolved in boiling water, and a pan full of that is divided among the buckets containing the batter, with about half a cup of sugar water being put in each bucket. Earlier, people, often children (following the practice called *biínídoot'aal*), were asked to spit into the batter after sucking on parched corn to let the enzymes in their saliva convert the starch to sugar.

If ground wheat flour is being used, the women stir about one cup of it into warm water and then divide this wheat water among the buckets holding the batter. This has to be *dínéísá*, wheat that was allowed to sprout and then dried before being ground. In other words, the wheat sprouts were grown specifically for this purpose.[42] It is supposed to make the mush or batter liquefy and taste much sweeter. Some people like to add a sprinkle of corn pollen and mirage powder to the batter at this point.

While the thickened batter is cooling, women use their hands to stir the mush, rubbing it against the sides of the pail, and removing any lumps they find in the batter by squeezing them between their hands. This process continues until all the buckets of batter have been stirred, cooled, rubbed, and declared lump-free; it may take thirty minutes or more.

Meanwhile, others in the hogan are working on the dry corn husks that have been saved and brought in where the batter is being made. These will be moistened briefly by being held under water in a bucket; then they are removed and their ends are torn about half an inch in five or six different places. That done, the husks are flattened out. These will be used to line the pit, and two crosses will be sewn together to use on the bottom and the top of the pit. Some also sew together a circular mat for the bottom of the pit.

When these things are ready, the pit should also be ready and the coals removed. People usually put boards, wet brown paper bags, or newspapers around the edges of the pit so they can kneel beside the hot pit without

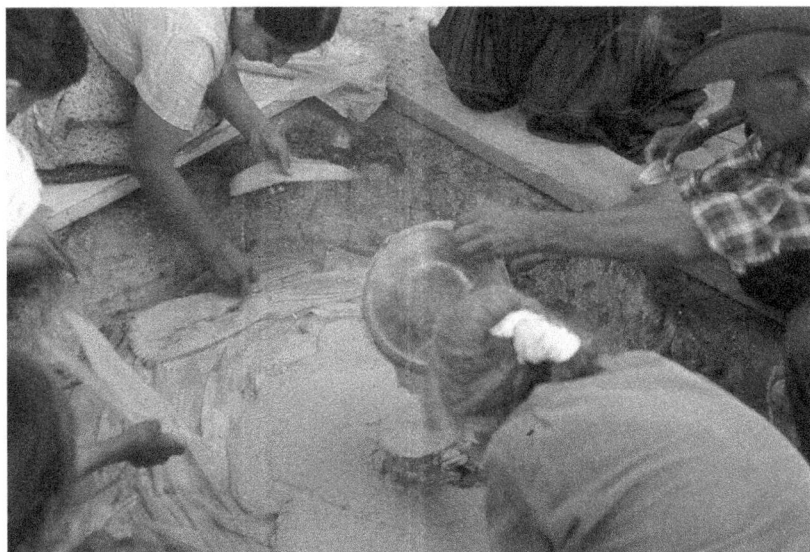

FIGURE 36. Pouring 'alkaan batter into a ground pit, June 1963. Photo by author.

getting burned. Corn husks are brought from the hogan, one of the crosses is put on the bottom in the center, and the bottom is covered and the sides are lined with husks, with the ends being tucked under those on the bottom. Some prefer to use a corn husk mat instead of the bottom cross. Both women and men start bringing the buckets of batter from the hogan. Then, kneeling around the edges of the pit, people pour the batter in (fig. 36), at the center first and adding corn husks along the sides as necessary so the batter is in contact with the husks, not the hot sides of the cooking pit.

When all the batter is in, the second corn husk cross is put in the middle of the top, and the cake is blessed with cornmeal from east to west, south to north, and all around in a sunwise fashion (i.e., clockwise). Then the top is covered with another layer of corn husks, a layer of dirt, and hot coals or firewood. Some people prefer to substitute a layer of brown paper bags on the top, covering them with a thin layer of sand and then hot ashes or coals. Finally, a fire is built on the top of the cake and allowed to burn all night. Someone is assigned the responsibility of watching the cake and making sure that the fire is adequate and continues to burn throughout the night so the cake cooks correctly.

After the all-night singing is completed, with the Racing Songs that accompany the *kinaaldá*'s final run followed by the Twelve Word Song, it is time to remove the cake (fig. 37). All go outside to the cooking pit; first the dirt or sand and the ashes are removed with grass brushes and juniper branches.

Then the cake is cut from the center, known as the heart of the cake. According to many, the *kinaaldá* is supposed to give the first piece to the main singer and the next pieces to his or her helpers. Pinches from all four directions are taken from around the heart of the cake and are buried in the pit as an offering to Mother Earth. Other pieces of the cake are cut and usually put on newspaper or paper bags until they cool; these will go to all who helped in one way or another. The cake hardens as it cools; many like it to do that before eating it. Then they break it up and eat it with stew. Some people prefer to dry it for later consumption.

SMALL INDIVIDUAL CORN CAKE

While working on Tall Woman's recipes in 2012–2014, I heard about another kind of traditional cake, *dítł'ógí' 'alkaan,* or small individual corn cake. It

FIGURE 37. Removing the finished 'alkaan, July 1963. Photo by author.

seems to be identical to what Tall Woman called *nanoyeeshi*, or poured bread, which is discussed below. I was told that to make *dítł'ógí' 'alkaan*, the *nanoyeeshi* batter was poured into a heated ground pit lined with overlapping corn leaves, not husks. The edges were also lined the same way, and another layer of corn leaves was added after some batter had been poured into the pit. Asking Navajo friends about this kind of *'alkaan* was not fruitful until I asked Steven Begay. He told me (personal communication, 2015) that this is a small, individual-size corn cake with a sweet flavor like *'alkaan*. He thinks it is sweetened with chewed and fermented cornstalks. He also remembered that it "had a bland, dry taste with a hint of sour sweetness."

Breads

The Navajo words for bread are different in Arizona and New Mexico. In New Mexico *łees'ááh* means bread baked in an outdoor oven or in ashes; it can also mean rolls. In Arizona bread is called *bááh*, the Navajo pronunciation of the Pueblo word for bread baked in an oven. The two words, though different, mean the same thing. Traditionally bread was made from flour that was ground on grinding stones, either from corn that was homegrown or from wheat that was homegrown or acquired from those who raised it. After the trading posts were established, the Navajos could also buy white flour, which was bleached wheat flour.

Since Tall Woman did not use yeast, *díík'ǫsh*, there are no recipes for yeast breads in this section. After baking powder became available through the trading posts, she did use that for some things, as shown below. She preferred to use white corn, which the Navajos grew and which was home-ground for everything, from tortillas and frybread to biscuits and various kinds of corn-bread, unless the item was made only from blue corn. The recipes she gave me for wheat breads are at the end of each section.

BISCUITS

Tall Woman's daughter Augusta talked with me about biscuits (*bááh nímazí*) and her mother making them. She said that her mother used the recipe for tortillas but added more baking powder. Augusta said you can use the same measurements as in the blue cornbread recipe (below) from her 1974 workshop (Sandoval 1974). "But just don't pat it as firmly as you do for blue cornbread; make it looser," she instructed. "You make biscuits on a greased cookie sheet by dropping spoonfuls of the dough on it and sticking them in the oven. Don't roll the dough or cut it into any shape; just drop it on the cookie sheet."

When Tall Woman started to use baking powder from the trading posts, she made biscuits in an old skillet in a ground pit. First she heated the shallow pit by building a fire in it. Next she put the skillet with the dough inside it right on top of the charcoal. Then she put an old metal dishpan over that for a lid and made another fire on top of the lid. "She always seemed to know when the biscuits would be done," Augusta explained, "because they always came out nice and brown but not burned. She just knew when to remove them."

Bááh Nímazí (Biscuits)

2 cups flour
1 ½ to 2 teaspoons baking powder
¼ cup grease (sheep or cow fat)
Enough warm water to mix the dough

Mix the flour and baking powder, add the grease with a fork until the mixture is blended, and stir in the warm water. Let the mixture rest for fifteen minutes. Using a spoon, drop dough by the spoonful onto a greased pan. Bake ten to fifteen minutes in a very hot oven (about 450°F) until golden brown.

BLUE CORNBREAD

Blue cornbread, or blue bread (*bááh dootł'ízhi*), can be made in any shape: a round loaf, a long loaf, as biscuits, or as dumplings (*k'íneeshbízhii*). The recipe below is basic; follow it for whatever you are making and then just pat the dough into the shape you want. Likewise, it can be baked in a ground pit, in ashes, on a grill, or in an oven. If you bake it in a ground pit or directly in ashes, brush the dirt or ashes off with your hands when it's done. Some follow that by washing the loaf with warm water in which they have dissolved some salt. That softens the crust and adds a salty flavor to it. If you make a long loaf, let that stand on its side to dry. Some people wrapped their loaves in a towel.

The recipe is named for the culinary ash, *łeeshch'ih*, that is added to the blue cornmeal mixture to turn it blue. The ash is mixed with boiling water, strained through a grass brush like that used to clean the grinding stone, and added to blue corn flour to turn the dough, batter, or mixture blue. If the brush clogs up with the ash, clean it off and strain the mixture again. Sometimes Tall Woman strained the mixture through an old thin flour sack (see culinary ashes in section 2).

Blue Bread Baked in Loaves

Tall Woman said that the name *bááh dootł'ízhi* implied round loaves. Wolfe (1984) reported two kinds of blue bread made from the same batter, both common through the 1940s because wheat flour was seldom available: small loaves baked in ashes, and flattened round patties that were fried on a lightly greased griddle. Most of the time these were eaten warm, but they were also good cold.[43]

Bááh Dootł'ízhi (Blue Cornbread)

7 ½ cups finely ground blue cornmeal, sifted

⅔ cup powdered juniper ash
4 ⅓ cups boiling water

Put the sifted cornmeal into a large bowl. In another bowl mix the ash with
one-third cup of the boiling water until most of the ash dissolves. Add two
more cups of the boiling water to the bowl of ash, mix well, and strain it into
the cornmeal with a sieve or similar tool. Mix with a spoon, not your hand,
because it will be *very hot*. Add the remaining two cups of boiling water into
the bowl where the ashes were mixed, and strain this into the cornmeal
mix, too. Mix with a spoon until the dough is soft. Then knead the dough
by hand until all the water and cornmeal are mixed together. The dough
should be very soft and firm, not crumbly. Shape the dough into a round
loaf, a long loaf, or dumplings. Bake in hot ashes in the ground pit for about
an hour. Remove, brush off ashes, and serve.

Bááh Dootł'ízhi Variation 1

6 cups blue cornmeal
1 cup juniper ash
4 ½ cups boiling water

Mix the ash with one cup of the boiling water and strain into a pot with the
remaining three and a half cups of boiling water. Stir. Add the blue cornmeal
and knead the dough until it is soft but firm. Shape it into two or three
loaves or small patties. For loaves, bake covered in hot ashes for about one
hour. Remove, brush off the ashes, wash off the loaves, and serve warm.
For patties, place on a hot greased skillet and heat until browned on both
sides. Dip into salt water and serve with coffee.

Bááh Dootł'ízhi Variation 2

6 cups blue cornmeal
1 cup prepared culinary ash
1 cup water (either cold or boiling)
3 ½ cups boiling water

Stir the ash into the cup of water. Then strain through a Navajo grass brush
into the boiling water in a large pot. Stir. Slowly add the blue cornmeal. Knead
the hot dough by hand until it is soft but firm. If it gets too dry, add more
boiling water; if it is too moist or sticky, add more cornmeal. Shape the warm

dough into small loaves and bake in hot ashes for one hour. First make an opening in the ashes and put the loaves in it, then cover them with hot ashes. When the loaves are done, brush the ashes off with a grass brush and eat the loaves, or first quickly rinse them in salt water if preferred.

Blue Bread Baked in Ashes

Tall Woman also mentioned another blue cornbread that is cooked in ashes this way but is called *naadą́ą́' łees'áán*. The recipe is almost the same as the one above, but just hot water is used to dissolve the ash. Strain the ash through a grass brush and then add it very slowly to two cups of ground blue corn flour. Use your hands to knead that to make a heavy dough. Shape the dough into flat oblong cakes, about five inches long by one inch wide by half an inch thick, and bake those in the ashes for at least an hour. Tap on them with a stick to see if they're done; they are finished when they sound hollow. Remove them, brush the ashes off, and wash them to remove any remaining ashes before serving.

Blue Dumplings or Corn Marbles

The name for dumplings, *k'íneeshbízhii*, means "braids twisted off one by one," "braids twisted on each other," or "broken braids." There are many ways to make these, but essentially they are made from the basic recipe for blue bread baked in ashes. You can also make them from a recipe for tortillas (see below) or for the thick blue cornmeal mush known as *tanaashgiizh* (see section 6).[44] All you have to do is form the dough into dumplings or marbles.

When Tall Woman was raising her children, she made blue corn marbles or dumplings daily. But when the stores came and the Commodity Food Program started, people brought her food, and she stopped making them so often. There was one exception to that, however: in her family *k'íneeshbízhii* were always viewed as special, so she would make them on special occasions—for instance, when a medicine person came to visit with Frank, or when an elderly medicine man came to do something for somebody in the family. Those who knew ceremonies or even those who were trying to learn them were always very grateful if they were served foods "from way, way back," that had been common a long time ago. They always thanked Tall

Woman for cooking these foods for them, and they complimented her on her knowledge of the special foods used long ago and on her ways of preparing them.

Augusta recalled the joking that occurred between her parents about *k'íneeshbízhii*, which she said became almost like "soul food" when it was no longer common. Her dad, Frank, who was a Blessingway singer, "used to tease [Tall Woman] a lot, saying, 'Make *k'íneeshbízhii* every day for me.' She'd always laugh and tease him back by saying, 'Fine, if you want them, then you have to grind everything I need for that on the *tsédaashjéé'* [bottom grinding stone] and *tsédaashch'íní* [top grinding stone].' They were always teasing each other."

Tall Woman told me that by the late 1960s these blue corn marbles or dumplings were not being made very often. In earlier times, when they were common, they were usually made from *tł'ohdeeí*, goosefoot flour, instead of corn. Traditionally they were made to serve in a thin mush or as a side dish with stew or boiled fruit. They were often eaten from one large bowl by everybody who was present.

Even in earlier times the People had different ideas about the sizes of various kinds of dumplings. For example, some said that while *k'íneeshbízhii* were small, they were larger than those made from *tanaashgiizh*. And some claimed that over time dumplings have become longer and skinnier, being called *k'íneeshbízhii ts'óózi*. Dumplings could vary in shape as well as size, and some people believed that the shape of their dumplings could affect the weather: round ones could bring hail, and those shaped like teardrops could bring rain. Tall Woman said that she herself didn't know if this were true. Allegedly, today's dumplings are longer and skinnier than the earlier ones.

In the recipe below for *k'íneeshbízhii*, the initial steps are the same as those in the recipe for *tanaashgiizh* (see section 6).

K'íneeshbízhii (Dumplings or Blue Corn Marbles)

3–4 cups (or large handfuls) blue cornmeal

½ cup juniper ash

7 ½ cups boiling water

A little flour (optional)

Stir the ash into one cup of the boiling water in a separate container. Strain that mixture into three and a half cups of the boiling water through a Navajo brush or strainer. Stir. Add the cornmeal gradually, stirring in slowly. Simmer over a slow fire or low heat for thirty minutes or more, stirring occasionally until it becomes very thick.

Remove from heat, stir, and then roll the dough between your hands into slender, fairly long strips, strings, or coils. Pinch or twist small pieces off the strips; roll these into the shape and size of marbles, forming oblong or thumb-size small dumplings about two inches long; or cut up the long strips of dough. Drop these into the final three cups of boiling water and thoroughly boil them, or drop them right into a boiling stew. Add a little flour if a thick gravy is desired. Stir so the dough pieces sink and cook for about thirty minutes.

If you are adding these dumplings to a stew, wait until the stew is almost done—after you have added any meat, because that needs to cook first. If you don't wait, the long dough strings will be too mushy by the time the stew is done.

There are many variations to making dumplings, some of which Tall Woman explained. For example, some people prefer to flatten the dough instead of making marbles; then they sprinkle the pieces with cornmeal, shaking them to coat each piece. They say this prevents them from sticking together while they are boiling and helps them to make their own gravy. Some people say you can make dumplings without juniper ash, but many prefer to use both ash and salt. Many claim that the ones without juniper ash have no taste. Some prefer to add saliva glucose to the dough; others prefer to use parched ground cornmeal and make the dumplings really big, almost the size of apples. You can use either white or blue corn, but it has to be ground up and then parched or dried out in a hot skillet until it turns a light tan. You can store it that way or use it right away. (Now some say to just use white flour instead.)

You can also make just one big thick dumpling. Bring water to a boil on the fire, then add the cornmeal to that. Keep stirring with stirring sticks (or a big slotted spoon), because this will get really thick very quickly. Add flour to make a thick gravy. Cover the pot and cook the mixture until it's very, very thick, much thicker than oatmeal. Remove the pot from the fire and let it cool. Then, using your hands, fashion a big round dumpling, or roll the dough into a long roll (like a noodle). Then cut that roll into small pieces.

K'íneeshbízhii Variations

Add juniper ash directly to a large pot of boiling water, stirring it in with stirring sticks. Then strain any lumps of ash out with stirring sticks or a grass brush.

or

Put flour from parched corn on the surface of the boiling water, but don't stir it in. Cover the pan and let the contents cook for about twenty minutes in steam. Remove the pan from the heat and then mix the flour into the liquid. The flour will be thoroughly steamed.

or

Just mix cornmeal flour, juniper ash, and boiling water.

or

Mix cold water with the cornmeal flour first, before adding the hot water.

or

Mix white flour, salt, warm water, and sheep fat and drop the dough into about three cups of boiling water, simmer for about thirty minutes, stirring occasionally. Then add to stew or soup. Some call these *k'íneeshbízhii ts'óózi*, long skinny dumplings.

or

To flatten the dough, rotate bits of it in the pan and shape it into patties. Drop these into boiling water and cook for about one hour.

Marbles with Gravy

Set aside half a cup of dough after making it, as above. Shape the rest of the dough into thumb-size pieces and drop these into boiling water. Cook for about twenty-five minutes. Mix the saved dough into one cup of cold water, as if you were going to make gravy. When that dough is dissolved, add the marbles that are still cooking. This makes a thick gravy. Lower the heat and simmer for about five more minutes. Cool and serve.

Marbles with Gravy Variation

1 cup juniper ash
7 ½ cups boiling water
6 cups blue cornmeal

Mix the juniper ash and one cup of the boiling water. Strain into a pot of three and a half cups of boiling water and stir with stirring sticks. Add the cornmeal slowly and knead the dough until it's firm but soft. Shape the dough into thumb-sized pieces and add them to the last three cups of boiling water. Cook for about twenty-five minutes, stirring occasionally. The dough makes its own gravy. Serve hot.

Pancakes or Griddle Cakes

There were differences of opinion about the Navajo name for pancakes or griddle cakes. In addition to *'abe' bee neezmasí*, griddle cakes or pancakes made with milk, some use *łees'áán dit'ódi* to mean pancakes or hotcakes, literally, "bread that is soft and pliable." There are also some who use *nae-mazi* to refer to the same thing, but only when it's made from green corn; thus, these would be round green corn cakes baked on a stone griddle.[45] And there are some who shorten and slightly change the name *'abe' bee neegáází* to *naagáází*. The variations I know about depend on what kind of liquid is used, whether culinary ash and ground wheat are used, or whether salt is added. Some of Tall Woman's great-grandchildren named these blue corn pancakes, a real favorite, "iron bread" after hearing how much iron blue corn with ash contributes to the diet. I also heard the name *bááh ditódi* for pancakes or soft bread.

Navajo griddle cakes or pancakes are still common today and are enjoyed greatly by all ages. They can be made from either cornmeal or flour, but Tall Woman preferred blue or white corn, ground really fine, mixed with some flour. Add any kind of milk, even diluted canned milk. Others say water can be used, if necessary. If blue cornmeal is used, ash must be added; otherwise ash is optional. In later years, she sometimes also added a tiny bit of baking powder from the store. Some people say that these are easy to make with cornmeal, milk, and maybe some flour.

Five recipes were given to me, one each by Tall Woman and four of her daughters (Mary, Augusta, Isabelle, and Ruth). The main difference is the daughters' regular inclusion of baking powder and sometimes also salt.

Navajo Griddle Cakes (Tall Woman's Recipe)

2 cups milk
1 teaspoon baking powder
½ teaspoon salt

2 handfuls blue cornmeal flour
½ cup wheat flour

Mix all the ingredients, stirring in the flours to keep the cakes from cracking. Grease griddle and heat; pour thin batter on and bake three minutes per side. When the griddle cakes have baked, fold them in half and set them aside.

Navajo Griddle Cakes Variation 1

Use hot water instead of milk and both baking powder and cedar ashes.

Navajo Griddle Cakes Variation 2

Prepare the dough for blue bread you might bake. Instead, while the dough is warm, take handfuls of it and shape them into small round patties, about three inches in diameter and half an inch thick. Put the patties on a hot and lightly greased skillet, a traditional stone griddle, a cast-iron plate, or a modern skillet. Cook the griddle cakes over low heat until they are brown on both sides, about ten minutes on each side. Then quickly dip them into salt water (one teaspoon of salt in one cup of water), allow them to dry, and eat.

Navajo Griddle Cakes Variation 3

4-5 cups corn flour
A pinch to 2 teaspoons baking powder
Liquid, such as goat's milk diluted with hot water

Mix all the ingredients, using enough liquid to make a thick batter. Form cakes six inches in diameter and cook on a greased metal sheet for about three minutes on each side.

Navajo Griddle Cakes Variation 4

1 cup all-purpose flour
2 cups white, blue, or yellow cornmeal
1 tablespoon baking powder
2-3 cups (or more) hot milk (any kind)

Mix all the ingredients into a batter that is runny and spreads easily. Heat a grill, cast-iron skillet, or griddle. Pour the batter onto the cooking surface and use the bottom of the cup to spread it out in a circle so it will stay thin while cooking. Let it brown on the bottom, then turn and cook on the other side.

People continue to experiment with recipes for pancakes. For example, some are now using Bisquick, no baking powder, and no ashes. Those who use flour say that it holds the pancakes together better than cornmeal does.

Flour Tortillas

Tortillas and frybread are the two most common Navajo breads today and are viewed as traditional Navajo food. However, though seen as traditional, these clearly appeared *after* Fort Sumner and the white traders introduced bleached white wheat flour. Both use the same dough and the same slapping method; however, some women now prefer to roll balls of the dough out with a rolling pin, to make it very thin, instead of slapping it. Some even have rolling pins made from pieces of discarded broom handles they found at flea markets. The resulting flat pieces of dough or flattened cakes are then cooked. The only difference between tortillas and frybread is in how they are cooked.

The name for tortilla, *náneeskaadí*, is from *nanak'ad*, to flatten, to slap back and forth, the actions required to make the bread.[46] To make tortillas, put the flat pieces of dough, usually circular in shape, on a lightly greased griddle, cast-iron skillet, metal sheet over a hot fire outside, or stone griddle over hot coals. A tortilla that is baked outside on a wire grill over coals (fig. 38) is called *tsííkáá' bááh; tsííd* means hot coals. There has to be plenty of air beneath the grill to keep the charcoal burning. Tortillas made outside have to be turned over by hand after they cook; depending on how much charcoal is underneath, they might need to be turned in about forty-five seconds. When a tortilla gets a brown spot in the middle, it's time to turn it over.

Navajo tortillas, which are thicker than Mexican tortillas, are a mainstay at any meal. Scrambled eggs, meat, and/or vegetables can be wrapped in them; they can be dipped in a stew or a mush; or they can be eaten alone with or without butter, jam, or other things. Tall Woman said that in earlier times, and even when she was raising her children, it was common to eat them with *géeso*, goat cheese wrapped inside the tortilla, and goat's milk to drink.

If wheat flour was scarce, there were other ways to make tortillas. One was

FIGURE 38. Isabelle Deschine (left) and Garnett Bernally cooking tortillas out-side, May 2010. Photo by author.

to mix different kinds of flour, like a bit of wheat flour with some corn flour. If blue corn is used, ash is not. Even today some people prefer the taste of tortillas made with mixed flours or from different colors of corn. When Tall Woman's children were little (around the 1920s), the People made tortillas from wheat berries that were sold at the trading posts. They were ground into flour. People who didn't have a griddle baked tortillas right in the ashes.

Recipes for tortillas are numerous. Below is Tall Woman's basic recipe, with measurements and comments about today's changes provided by her daughter Augusta. Tall Woman also gave me two other recipes: one for tortillas cooked over charcoal (fig. 39), and one for tortillas made from wheat flour.[47]

Náneeskaadí (Tortillas) Basic Recipe

Makes about 12 tortillas

> 6 ½ cups all-purpose Blue Bird flour (Tall Woman mixed in some wheat flour)
>
> 2 heaping tablespoons baking powder

FIGURE 39. Two ears of roasted corn on a grill with a charcoal-cooked tortilla, February 2016. Photo by Cecilia Sandoval.

> 2 teaspoons salt (Zuni salt may be used)
> ½ cup powdered milk (optional)
> 2 cups and 3 tablespoons hot water

Wash and dry your hands. Mix all the dry ingredients (including the powdered milk, if you are using it) with your hands. Add the hot water; this should be hotter than the hot water from most faucets. Mix with your hands and then knead the dough as you roll it around in the bowl. As soon as the dough is sticky, put it on a floured surface and knead it until it is no longer sticky. (If you use too much flour or knead it too long, the dough will be tough. The air outside will also dry it out. You can make the dough ahead of time and put it in a cooler and then in an ice chest. The dough will stay softer in the chest than out in the open.)

Grease a bowl with lard, shortening, or animal fat; today a lot of people spray it with Pam. Put the dough in there and flip it over so all sides are exposed to the grease. Cover the bowl with a cloth; now people use plastic wrap or foil to make it as airtight as possible, since air dries the dough out. Let the dough set for at least sixty minutes and preferably overnight—the longer, the better for texture.

Grease the griddle or skillet and let it get nice and hot. Tall Woman preferred to use sheep fat or a sheep's backbone to do this; she kept this fat in a cloth wrap. (You could also use a goat's backbone.) Doing this will keep the tortillas from burning. Roll the dough into balls, each about the size of a small orange. Then pat them two to four times, thinning the edges while you are patting. Put the patted dough into the hot skillet; the dough will puff up. If you are using a modern stove, turn the heat to medium high and watch the dough carefully, turning it over before it burns. It should become a motley tan color on each side. If it burns just a little bit when it puffs up, that's all right. Take it off the griddle and put it into another bowl lined with a paper towel or paper bag to soak up any grease. Cover this bowl with a clean dish towel.

Tsííkáá' Yideezí (Tortillas Grilled over Charcoal)

Make your own charcoal or, if necessary, use commercial charcoal. Build a large fire from dry cedar wood or oak; Tall Woman preferred oak because it burns longer, stays hot longer, and gives more heat. Greasewood also works well. Let the wood burn down to good thick charcoals, which should be red. With a stick or a poker, spread a charcoal layer on the bottom of the cooking area. Put a grill over the charcoal layer so it's about four inches above it, if the coals are hot and the charcoal layer is deep.

Make the regular tortilla dough. After patting it, put it on top of the hot grill, which can be a wire rack. It will puff up the same way; the temperature of the charcoal will determine how long the tortillas need to cook. Make sure the tortilla is heating evenly, and turn it over so it browns evenly without burning. Keep the fire going on the side so you can move charcoals over to keep your fire burning nicely as you cook. Put the finished tortillas in a bowl lined with paper, and cover the bowl with a cloth to absorb the heat from the steam.

Náneeskaadí Tł'oh Naadą́ą́' Bił 'Ályaa (Tortillas Made from Wheat Flour)

Make the dough for wheat frybread (see recipe below), but when it's ready to be shaped, roll it into long coils of dough, as if you were making pottery. Then flatten these into large cakes with your hands or with a wooden rolling pin.

Make each cake about four inches long. Bake the cakes on a hot griddle for about fifteen minutes per side, turning them over one or two times.

Frybread

Frybread (*dah díníilghaazh*) dough swells up like a doughnut fried in deep fat. The name may also refer to the bubbling of the boiling fat. Sometimes it is called "fried bread" in English.

Frybread (fig. 40) is very popular among the Navajos and is considered traditional even though it is recent in Navajo history (Keane 2013). Even children know how to make it. Frybread is always for sale at fairs and flea markets, and it has a constant place on the menus of all kinds of restaurants on and around the reservation. The making of it is the source of competitions at regional fairs and, until 2017, it was also part of the traditional segment of the Miss Navajo contest. Now it has been replaced by two new categories: preparing some of the newly butchered mutton to eat, and discussing the history of Navajo traditional foods and then making one of them. These competitions are always well

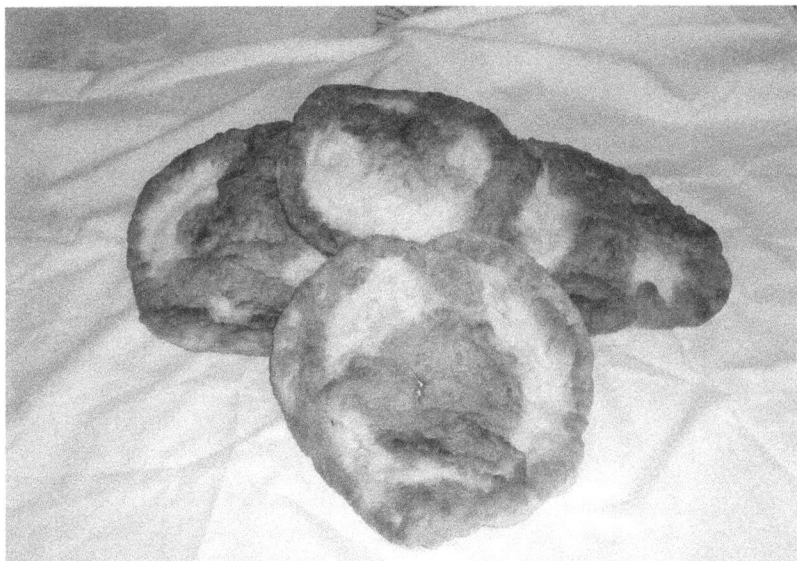

FIGURE 40. Four pieces of Navajo frybread, February 2016. Photo by Cecilia Sandoval.

publicized by the media, with newspapers carrying pictures of frybread contest winners with their "nice golden-brown frybread." Recently some fairs have begun adding a frybread contest only for men.

Given the bread's popularity, it's no wonder that numerous recipes exist. The bread is best eaten warm, either by itself or dipped into mutton stew or something comparable. Thus, people usually make just enough dough for one meal. The dough can be made ahead of time and set on a counter overnight. If it has been refrigerated, let the dough sit at room temperature for at least thirty minutes before you start to make the bread. Given the increasing concern with diabetes and obesity on the reservation, frybread has been labeled "bad" because it is both greasy and fattening (Bitsoi 2013c). However, people continue to "get hungry for it," and many have concluded that "it's good, if you don't eat too much" and "maybe it's all right to have it once in a while." Traditionally it's associated with Blue Bird Flour (described earlier).

Frybread is made in a skillet. Tall Woman used a cast-iron skillet about two inches deep and ten to twelve inches in diameter. She noted that it helps to have a long-handled fork to use when turning the bread over in the hot, bubbling grease. Augusta said that today some people have a skillet they use only for making frybread; some prefer to use a wok, whereas others like a thin metal pan they say is used for gold mining. Tall Woman's basic recipe is given below. Most often she made frybread the same way as tortillas, with the main difference being the amount of fat needed for cooking it. Now white flour is generally used, but traditionally whole wheat flour was used, either alone or combined with corn flour. She added both baking powder and commodity dry or powdered milk to her earlier recipe as she became familiar with these products. Augusta provided the measurements.

Dah Díníilghaazh (Frybread)

4 cups flour
1 teaspoon salt
1 tablespoon baking powder
2-8 tablespoons powdered milk
1 ½ cups warm water
1 cup shortening or lard (enough to produce hot grease that is at least ½ inch deep; 2-4 tablespoons more if you want to add it to the dough to soften it)

Mix all the dry ingredients with your hand. If you are not adding shortening to make the dough soft, just add the warm water and mix by hand until the dough is soft. Then make a ball of soft dough, about three inches in diameter, and pat it with your hands, back and forth, pulling on it and stretching it until it is flat and round, ten to twelve inches in diameter.

If you are adding shortening to make the dough soft, after mixing the dry ingredients with your hands, make a "well" in the middle. Slowly add the warm water and the shortening; do this by kneading the fat and water into the flour very slowly with your hand, working outward from the center in a circular motion until a springy dough is formed. Any flour left in the bottom can be used later to flour balls of dough as they are slapped. After making a ball of soft dough, pat it with your hands, back and forth, always pulling on it to make it flat and round. The dough will be sticky if you use it right away, so cover it and let it stand for about half an hour.

Meanwhile, heat the shortening in a deep frying pan until the grease is hot. Make sure you use enough fat to yield at least half an inch of melted grease in the skillet. Make sure the fire is hot so the grease is hot. Pull off a piece of dough about the size of a tennis ball and twist it into a ball. Pat it flat and then pull it and slap it back and forth between your hands until it becomes a flat cake eight to nine inches in diameter. Some people now use a rolling pin; others like to cut the dough into squares, thus making square frybread instead of round pieces. Some make a hole in the center of the round dough cake before frying it so that the grease will come through and drain out; they claim this makes it easier to turn the frybread while cooking it. (Tall Woman did not follow any of these practices.)

Put the flat piece of dough into the hot grease, tilting the skillet so the hot grease covers all of the dough, all the way around. The bread fries quickly, so in about fifteen seconds turn it over to the other side. Wait until all the dough puffs up and turns light golden brown on the edges before turning it, then flip it right away so it doesn't burn. When the second side is also golden brown, remove the bread with a long-handled fork, making sure that the excess grease drains back into the skillet.

Stand the finished bread up on its edge in a deep container lined with paper towels, newspapers, or brown paper bags so the grease keeps draining off and is absorbed by the paper. You can use a cardboard box, a cooler, a deep dishpan, or a big kettle as the container; it doesn't matter, as long as it's lined. Cover the container with a towel or cloth. Once you have fried all the pieces of bread and drained them, put the frybread into a covered container that is lined with paper towels. Frybread is best served warm.

Dah Díníilghaazh Tł'oh Naadą́ą́' Bił 'Ályaa (Frybread Made from Wheat Flour)

    2 cups wheat flour
    ½ teaspoon salt
    1 teaspoon baking powder
    1 tablespoon shortening
    ½ cup water

Mix the flour, salt, and baking powder. Separately, mix the shortening with the water. Make a hole in the center of the dry ingredients, pour the water into it, and, using your hands, work the ingredients into a springy dough. Pull off a piece the size of a tennis ball; pull and slap it back and forth with your hands until it stretches into a flat cake about ten inches in diameter and half an inch thick. Fry this cake in deep fat for about three minutes per side, turning it once, and then remove it with a fork. It should puff up, making crisp brown bread about one inch thick. Drain the bread on paper towels.

Poured Cornbread

Poured cornbread, or *nanoyeeshi* ("into the ground flowing") is baked in ashes. Some people also called it hurry-up bread, quick bread, ceremonial bread, or war bread. *Nanoyeeshi*, to Tall Woman, meant a poured cornbread that spreads out and bakes in ashes. After grinding corn kernels that are fully formed but still very small (the second of corn's four stages), make a hole in the ground (not too deep), build a fire in it, and let that burn down to charcoal. Once the batter is made, pour it directly into the charcoal ashes, starting in the center, with rolling movements of your hand. Poured bread is usually round in shape when it's done and is, in Tall Woman's words, "like blue cornmeal mush but not as thick, more runny." Compared to *'alkaan* batter, *nanoyeeshi* batter is more watery.

As before, the recipe for *nanoyeeshi* provided by Tall Woman appears first with contemporary changes added by her daughter Augusta.[48] The bread is made from ground dried roasted corn, with a sweetener of choice added. The corn has to be prepared first, of course, and should usually already be available when it is time to make this bread. Grind any color of corn that has already been dried and roasted. A lot of women say that this is one way to use up roasted corn before it gets too hard.

Nanoyeeshi (Poured Cornbread) Basic Recipe

Start a fire either in a pit or under a grill. If necessary, dig a hole in the ground and start a fire in it, because you are going to cook with charcoal. If you are using a grill rack, find an old skillet and put a little charcoal in it when you are ready. If you use blue cornmeal, add juniper ash.

Add some kind of sweetener: juniper juice, yucca fruit juice or yucca pieces that have been washed, boiled, and mashed, squash juice, prickly pear cactus fruit juice, or store-bought sugar. Mix water and salt or łeeyáán (see section 2) to use as a rinse after baking if you want. Mix the sweetener with cornmeal. The batter should be thin but not watery or runny.

If you are baking the bread in a ground pit, make a space or hole in the hot ashes so you can pour the batter in there with rolling movements of your hand. When the batter hits the hot ashes, it spreads out in a way that Augusta said is "just like lava." When it stops spreading out, or expanding, it won't be very high or thick. Cover it with a skillet, a metal pan lid, or aluminum foil. Then cover that with hot ashes, build a fire on top of it, and bake it for about an hour. It's usually round in shape when it's done.

When it has finished cooking, some people say to remove it from the ground pit and eat it as it is, without washing off the ashes, but others say to wash it off with the salt water mixture you already fixed. When Tall Woman cooked bread in a ground pit, she usually washed it off with a salt water mixture before wrapping it in a towel. This softened the crust, she said.

If you are not using a ground pit, you can cook nanoyeeshi by pouring the batter onto a flat surface, like a griddle or a skillet into which you have put a little hot charcoal and then put on top of a grill above the fire. Pour the batter just as if you were making griddle cakes or pancakes. Once you have poured the batter into the skillet or onto the griddle, cover it, and build another fire on top of the cover. When the batter has finished spreading out slowly and has baked, fold the bread in half and set it aside until you're ready to serve it. Tall Woman often made nanoyeeshi inside the hogan.

Nanoyeeshi Variations

Some add a little bit of flour and use milk instead of water. Isabelle uses regular white cornmeal finely ground "plus a bit of baking powder and maybe a bit of regular flour to hold it together."

Kneel-Down Bread

Kneel-down bread, *ntsidigo'í*, is made during harvest season from freshly ground corn wrapped in corn husks. Some people prefer *nitsidigó'í* as the Navajo word, and compound its English words as "kneeldown bread." The name refers to the fact that the ends of the corn husks are tucked in, turned under, or folded back like the legs of a person who is kneeling.

This moist bread with a crispy brown crust is very popular; many people say they make it every day in the fall. Kneel-down bread is now sold at fairs, parades, roadside stands, flea markets, and elsewhere, often at fund-raisers.[49] It's viewed as a delicacy and considered traditional, like blue cornmeal mush.

Some, including cookbooks produced by the Office of Navajo Economic Opportunity (n.d.), call kneel-down bread a Navajo tamale, but Tall Woman never did—nor did she call her kneel-down bread tamales. She made both small and large kneel-down breads; the former was boiled, and the latter was baked in the ground or in an oven. She and I did discuss tamales, and she was aware that some Navajos were using the names kneel-down bread and tamales interchangeably, because to them these things were the same. Augusta provided clarification for me on real tamales, which she and Isabelle make even though Tall Woman never did.[50]

Navajos who call kneel-down bread tamales say there are two kinds, *łeehilzhoozh* (large) and *taajilééhíí* (small); they differ not just in size but also in method of preparation. Some children call them "Mickey Mouse bread." These terms are the same as those that Tall Woman used for her two kinds of kneel-down bread.

The recipe used for making both kinds of tamales is the same cornmeal recipe used to make the batter for the *'alkaan*. Some say that *taajilééhíí* are really the boiled version of *'alkaan*. But unlike the cake, these are individually wrapped, resulting in corn husk packets. Tamales are known by many names among the Navajos I know; besides the *łeehilzhoozh* (which are baked side by side in hot ash beneath a cooking fire underground) and the *taajilééhíí* (which are lowered into boiling water by their tie strings), there are also *be'estł'óní* (tied up in a hair bun shape) and, at least in New Mexico, *nijiło'í* ("carried by its tie string") (fig. 41).[51] People have different ideas about which kind is sweeter, thicker, and so forth. But in any case, for these tamales, the dough (or mush) is individually wrapped in corn husks before being cooked.

FIGURE 41. Plate full of *nijílóʼí*, sweetened blue cornmeal tamales, December 2015. Photo by Steven Begay.

Tamales are made after the corn has been removed from the cob and dried. Most often they are made with either white or yellow corn, but it's all right to use blue corn—as long as the corn is fresh, young, tender, and fully ripe but not hard. A few people disagreed, saying that the corn should be barely ripe (*ʼayaazh*); only then can the kernels make the bread very moist, as is preferred. Tall Woman said the kernels should be fully ripe but still milky (the third of corn's four stages). She preferred to make kneel-down bread from blue corn when some of her children were home from school to help with the work on the weekends. During harvesting the cornstalks were stood on end together in the fields. The family usually harvested enough corn (often filling a gallon-size bucket and a half) to make a dozen pieces of kneel-down bread. It's hard to say how many ears have to be picked to make this, because corn grows in different sizes.

Tall Woman and her daughters (especially Augusta, Ruth, and Isabelle) ground the corn by hand. The boys in the family were never taught to use the grinding stones, although later, if a commercial metal hand grinder was to be used, they were expected to turn the handle or "run the grinder." People were expected to grind the corn really fine for kneel-down bread. Nobody ever sang Corn-Grinding Songs during daily grinding.

Roasting the corn first reportedly made it easier to grind, and some people preferred to use corn already roasted in the oven or in the ground and then grind it. But Tall Woman said she could always tell if a person did that because the corn would dry out too fast and not have any taste. Sometimes dried corn would be coarsely ground and lightly browned in a skillet. Wheat was never used.

Some people sweeten their tamales with about a pound of sugar, either brown or white, but others say to use ground wheat sprouts or the method of *biínídoot'aal* as sweeteners instead of sugar. Today, since some Navajos are using other sweeteners when making *'alkaan* for regular consumption rather than for a ceremonial context, any of those, such as syrup or honey, can also be used to sweeten the tamales. As one woman said while laughing, "Now, it's really become cook's choice when you make those. You just add whatever you want." Tall Woman never added any sweeteners to kneel-down bread.

People differ on which of two necessary tasks should be done first: preparing the corn husks and leaves or making the fire outside. Tall Woman said it made no difference because both have to be done at the beginning. Kneel-down bread is baked in hot ashes over an open fire, in a preheated pit in the ground, in a beehive-shaped oven, or in the earth oven, *bááh bighan*. The ground pit should be eight to nine inches deep and about two feet across. Build a fire in it before you start the rest of the process. Heat the pit by burning wood in it for several hours. The ground must be very hot to make kneel-down bread; check to make sure that the ground is not damp underneath the fire. Sometimes you have to keep a fire going for two to three days to really dry out the pit you want to use for baking kneel-down bread.

Ntsidigo'í (Kneel-Down Bread) Basic Recipe

Cut fresh corn kernels off the cobs or scrape them off. Grind the corn into a creamy mush using grinding stones. Augusta noted that now people use a hand grinder, an electric grinder, or even a metal meat grinder. Catch the juice in a pan or a bowl as you grind, and put it right back into the ground corn to prevent a bitter taste. Crush the little hard kernels inside; the skin will stay with them, and that's okay. Put the ground corn into a pan quickly. (Tall Woman said that if you are too slow doing this, "it will taste funny.") Stir and cover the pan. Add salt or sweetener if you want. If the corn is too hard and not juicy enough, add some milk.

Flatten out fresh corn husks, breaking the base in several places to make

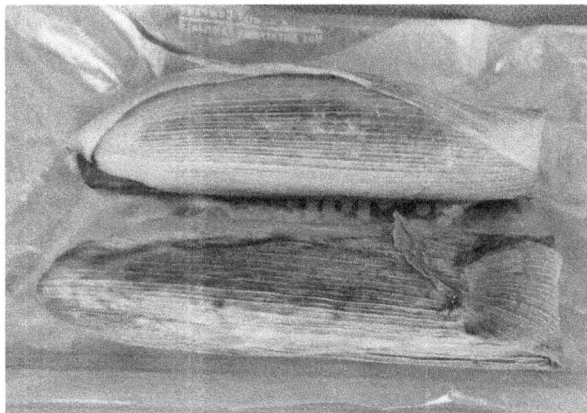

FIGURE 42.
Ntsidigo'í, kneel-down bread, top view, May 2015. Photo by Oliver W. Johnson.

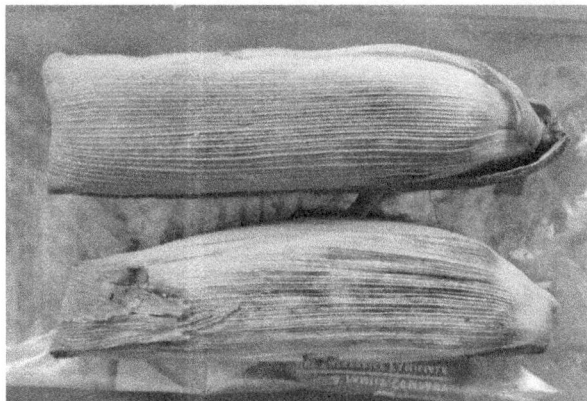

FIGURE 43.
Ntsidigo'í, bottom view, May 2015. Photo by Oliver W. Johnson.

them lie flat. If you are using dried corn husks that you have saved, moisten them and lay them out in pairs with the tip of the upper husk overlapping the butt of the lower one, pointing in the same direction. (Some prefer to shape the husks in a cross, and some prefer to lay out two so that their butts overlap by about four inches.)

Put a handful of mush in the middle of two corn husks to make a small package that is about three inches long, two inches wide, and one inch thick (figs. 42 and 43). Fold the sides of the two husks over the mush and place a third husk on the top. Then fold each end toward the middle. Make all the bread packets this way. For *taajilééhíí*, use wide husks and make smaller packets.

FIGURE 44. Tamales made with deer meat, November 2015. Photo by Cecilia Sandoval.

Some people tie the packets, but Tall Woman never did.[52] For *taajilééhíí*, tie each one in two places crosswise with husk strips; add another husk strip tied lengthwise to make a handle, if you like. For *łeehiłzhoozh*, tie the packet in three places with thin husk strips: at each end and also in the middle. If you add meat to the *łeehiłzhoozh* (fig. 44), some people say you shouldn't tie them at all.[53]

For *taajilééhíí*, put water into a roasting or other long pan and bring it to a boil; then put the packets in the water and boil them overnight. Others say that if the water is really boiling, it only takes thirty to forty-five minutes to cook them.

For *łeehiłzhoozh*, put the bread packets on a flat board, carry them to the fire pit, and scrape out the hot ashes. Place newly picked green corn leaves in the bottom of the pit and put the packets on top of them in a single flat layer. Cover them with freshly picked squash leaves or more fresh corn leaves, overlapping them to help hold the leaves down, and then add hot ashes and slightly moist dirt on top of the leaves. Build a small fire on top and bake for forty-five to sixty minutes. How long it will actually take depends on how big the packets are and how big the pit is, so you should check on them while they are cooking by moving the ashes and the top leaves. If the leaves are slightly brown here and there on both sides, the bread packets are probably cooked. They can also be baked in a conventional oven at 425°F for forty-five to sixty minutes.

Eat the bread packets immediately, while they're fresh, hot or cold, alone or dipped into stew. Cooling them first reportedly makes them both harder and sweeter. You can also cut the packets into smaller pieces and sun-dry them on a piece of string. When you want to use them for the morning meal later, recook them in boiling milk from sheep or goats. Their appearance at this point inspired Garnett to call them "shredded wheat," which became another family joke. You can also boil the pieces in water with meat, or steam them and serve them with salt.

Ntsidigo'í (Kneel-Down Bread) with Sheep's Blood

4 cups sheep's blood
1 ½ cups sheep fat
1 tablespoon salt (optional)

Prepare the cornmeal mush mix as in the recipe above, making sure to remove any lumps with your hands before the stirring is finished. Add the blood, fat, and salt to four cups of the cornmeal mush. Place the mixture in the corn husks, wrapping each one just as you did in the basic recipe. Bake the packets in a pit in the ground that has been prepared by preheating as above. Cover one layer of packets with fresh leaves, slightly moist dirt, and hot charcoal. Cook the packets for about thirty minutes. If you want to use an inside oven, put it on a low setting (275°F) and cook the packets for about an hour. You can also cook these by boiling them over the fire for about thirty minutes. Follow the process above for removing the cooked kneel-down bread, but eat it right away. Don't try to store this kind; sheep's blood doesn't keep. Most Navajos said that they would not add sheep's blood to kneel-down bread that they were planning to sell.

Paperbread

Paperbread (tsé'ást'éí) is a very thin cornmeal bread that many people are afraid to make because they fear getting burned. The process involves spreading the thin batter on a hot griddle with the palm of the hand in one stroke.

Hopis, who call this piki bread, reportedly always make more than Navajos do, and many Navajos buy it from Hopis, if possible. The name means baked on a stone griddle, or *tsét'ees*.[54] Some Navajos have tried to make it using a brush instead of their palms. Tall Woman made her own stick out of cedar that was flat on one end, which she used to remove pieces of paperbread from the stone griddle when they were done.

Tall Woman would make paperbread for special occasions, so it was a real treat for the family. She encouraged all her daughters to learn how to make it, but only the oldest one, Mary Davis, became good at doing so. The rest gave up after getting burned several times. The first recipe below is the basic recipe used by both Tall Woman and Mary. The first variation adds details provided by Mary and Augusta, and the second variation is for a smaller amount.

Tsé'ást'éí (Paperbread) Basic Recipe

Pour boiling water over cornmeal. Stir it until it cools and then thicken it a bit more, if necessary, by adding more cornmeal. The batter should be thin. Heat a stone griddle or a smooth flat stone. Take a handful of the thin batter and rapidly spread it with your flattened-out palm in one stroke over the griddle or stone. Remove the thin bread, fold it twice, like folding a handkerchief. Eat it immediately or keep it for later.

Tsé'ást'éí Variation 1

2 ⅓ cups sifted juniper ash
⅓ cup boiling water
4 ½ cups cool water
5 cups sifted blue cornmeal

Put the juniper ash in a pan; add the boiling water and make a smooth paste. Slowly mix the cool water into the paste, then strain the result into the cornmeal. Mix the paste and cornmeal until they are well blended. Heat the stone griddle. With the palm of your hand, spread this batter on the hot griddle back and forth, once or twice, making a very thin layer. The edges will start to curl up all the way around when it's done. Take a flat knife or a stick with one flattened end and put it under the edges to remove the bread from the griddle without tearing it. Lay the first piece aside flat and put more batter on the griddle with your hand. Remove that piece when the edges start to curl up. Put the first piece on top of the second piece (to hold the moisture in) and fold the first one into thirds the long way. Use the stick and fold the bread under it. The steam from the paperbread softens it, so it should be easy to fold. After making a third piece, put the second piece on top of it and fold it the same way.

Tsé'ást'éí Variation 2

    1 cup juniper ash
    4 cups boiling water
    1 cup blue cornmeal

Using stirring sticks, mix the juniper ash with one cup of boiling water and strain it through a sieve or colander. In the rest of the boiling water, stir in the cornmeal and the strained ashes. Continue stirring, then let it cool. Meanwhile, grease a griddle and heat it on the fire. When it's hot, carefully spread a very thin layer of cornmeal batter on the griddle's surface with the palm of your hand. If necessary, flatten it with a spatula, but do *not* turn it. This should be as thin as a piece of paper. Remove from the griddle as soon as the batter is cooked.

Wheat Bread

In addition to the recipes for tortillas and frybread given earlier, there are two other recipes for wheat bread (*tł'oh naadą́ą́' bááh*) given to me by Tall Woman.

Tł'oh Naadą́ą́' Bááh (Wheat Bread)

Make the dough for frybread and shape it into balls. Then do one of two things: pat these into flat ovals about four inches long and lay them on a baking sheet, or put the balls as is into greased muffin tins, then shape them to match the bottoms of the muffin holders. Bake in an earth oven or a conventional oven at 350°F, turning the oval ones over when they are half done.

Tł'oh Naadą́ą́' Lees'áán (Wheat and Green Corn Bread)

Tall Woman said you need "new wheat," or wheat sprouts (*tł'oh naadáá' dínéesá*) to make this bread. When the wheat is about four inches high, cut it and then grind it. Mix it with freshly ground green corn and shape the resulting mixture into cakes to bake in an oven. Do not make this in the summer, however, because the bread will spoil quickly.

Section 5 | Meat ('*Atsį*')

TALL WOMAN AND her family ate a variety of meats throughout their lives as their living conditions changed. As animals originally introduced by the Spanish— mainly sheep, horses, goats, and cows—became more important to the Navajo way of life, their diet shifted, just as it did when corn arrived and the trading posts introduced flour, commercial bread, and canned goods. Traditional foods declined, as did the use of wild animals and plants for sustenance.

Meat ('*atsį*') was prepared in a number of ways: boiling, roasting, broiling, frying, baking, and drying for jerky. Meat was eaten by itself or in combination with other things, such as in stews or soups and as sausage.[55] No matter how the meat was prepared, people usually added salt and/or other seasonings before eating it.

Since animal husbandry and butchering were discussed earlier, and wild animals as food were included in section 1, this section will focus on meat from domesticated animals, what Tall Woman had to say about how this meat was prepared, and her recipes for making sausage (both regular and blood) and jerky. Comments from her daughter Augusta are included when they update her information by identifying changes and today's practices.

Domesticated Animals

Navajos have eaten meat from donkeys, horses, sheep and lambs, goats and kids, cows, and pigs in addition to the wild animals mentioned in section 1. Tall Woman said that although she had never tasted donkey, her great-grandparents ate it often and said it was white meat that tasted like pork.

Goat and sheep meat is roasted, boiled, broiled, baked, fried, made into stew or other dishes, or dried and made into jerky. The goal was to eat almost every part of a sheep or goat, except for the gallbladder, hair (wool), horns, bladder, and contents of the digestive tract.[56] Some people today grind up mutton to make a mutton loaf or mutton burgers, but Tall Woman never made either of these. In discussing the various parts of a sheep they used, she said that bones are usually boiled with chunks of meat to create a stew; for example, see *haniígaii* (stew with backbone and dried corn) in section 6. The favorite part of the sheep is the chest meat (*'ayidítsį'*) and the ribs. The chest meat is called the butcher's steak; it is supposed to go to the person doing the butchering, but sometimes a child will grab it first. It is roasted right away on a grill over hot coals, as are certain organs, but the chest meat takes longer to cook.

The sheep's head is wrapped in fresh corn husks and baked in coals; this is called *'atsi łeeshibeezh*. The meat roasts that way and is eaten right from the fire. The wool and hair are usually singed from the head first, with care so as not to burn the head. Then the head is baked under the coals or, as some prefer, baked in a heated ground pit overnight. Augusta added that now some people like to wrap the head in tin foil before baking it in an oven set on low heat (275°F) for an hour or more until it becomes tender. Others prefer to put the head in a slow cooker and roast it overnight. When the baking is done, the head is removed, the skin is cut away, and the meat is picked off and eaten.

Just about everybody agrees that the special parts of the head include the eyeballs, the fat around the eyeballs, the cheek meat, and the tongue. People disagree on whether to eat the brains after breaking open the skull; some prefer to use them to tan deer hides. There is also disagreement about processing the feet. Most say to pound off the hooves and wash the feet. Then some prefer to bake them in a heated ground pit for at least four hours with a fire built on top, brush off the ashes, and eat the meat. Others prefer to boil them briefly, pull back the skin, and hang them up to sun-dry. After collecting eight to ten dried feet, they will break them in half and reboil them, eventually adding them to a soup, a stew, or hominy, boiling everything again and then eating all the soft parts.

The sheep's insides can be eaten in a variety of ways. Tall Woman said four organs—the lungs, heart, liver, and kidneys—are considered delicacies; when people butcher, these are the first things eaten.[57] They are either left whole or cut into pieces (not too thin); then they are salted and cooked briefly over the charcoal by roasting, broiling, boiling, or frying them in sheep fat. The organs are eaten alone or with *'ak'ahłání* (adipose fat), the lacy fat that covers the animal's stomach. Of the four organs, the liver (*'azid*) is the most prized; it is not cooked thoroughly, but only for a little bit so the inside is still soft. The cooked organ meats can also be allowed to cool off and then taken along for a cold lunch by those who go out gathering berries or herding sheep. These four organs and others—including the trachea, stomach (*'abid*), diaphragm, and small intestine—after being cleaned out, can be cut up and roasted for eating alone or combined with other things to make sausage. The intestines can also be wrapped in a special way to make a highly prized food called *'ach'íí'*, discussed below.

REGULAR SAUSAGE

When sausage is made from mutton, beef, horsemeat, goatmeat, or venison, the word for it is *náshgọzh*, which refers to the chopped meat (such as little pieces of the heart, lungs, stomach, or spleen) that is used to stuff the entrails of a sheep, a cow, or another animal and then boiled in water. Tall Woman said she never made venison sausage, but her daughters make it. Some people specify the animal to identify what kind of meat they are using; for instance, horsemeat sausage is *łįį́ náshgọzhi*. But many others don't name the animal at all, for sausage or jerky, although they name the organ used—such as the stomach (fig. 45) or the big intestine (*'ach'íídííl*), which is also called the colon (*'ach'íí' łik'aaí*). The organ can be boiled, roasted, or baked on charcoal on an open fire, using a grill and is easily turned into jerky (see below) by pounding it with a hammer to shred it.

One woman I talked with said that to her, *náshgọzh* means cow or beef sausage. "That's exactly like blood sausage from sheep, but it has no blood in it," she explained. Another woman said, "If you don't have an intestine to work with, you can use a cloth sack, even a flour sack, in its place and just stuff and boil that."

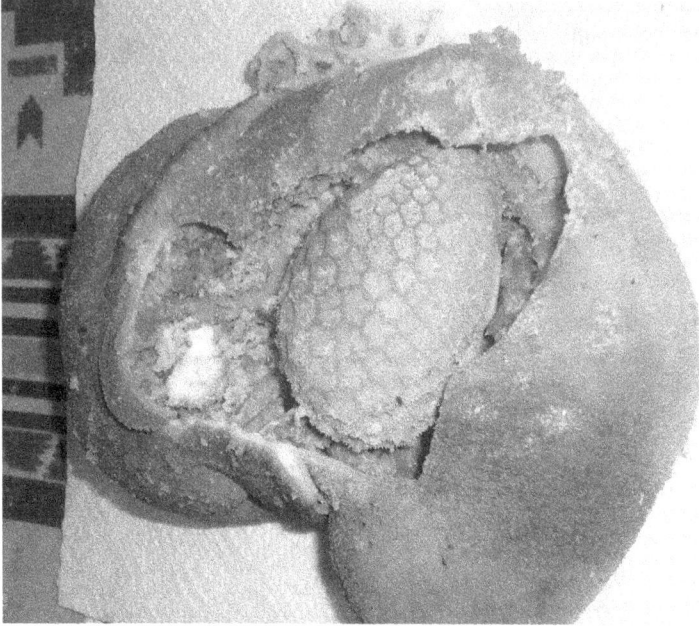

FIGURE 45. Stomach sausage, February 2016. Photo by Cecilia Sandoval.

Náshgǫzh (Regular Sausage)

Cut the meat of an animal (sheep, cow, or horse) into very small pieces. Add potatoes, onions, salt and pepper, and coarsely ground cornmeal to hold it all together. Some people like to add chili. Stuff the mixture into the stomach or intestine of that animal; sometimes extra fat may be needed. Boil it for several hours to create sausage.

BLOOD SAUSAGE

Blood sausage (*'ach'íídííl*) reportedly has a lot of iron in it, much more than store-bought sausage. Some speakers say that *'ach'íídííl* is blood sausage made from the large intestine, and *'ach'ííts'osi* is blood sausage made from the small intestine.[58] Some say that how you cook it determines its name; for example, if you boil it, it's *dił shibéézh*.

If you are butchering the animal yourself, catch the blood from the animal's throat in a pan. Let the blood cool and rest for about half an hour, then squeeze it and stir it with your hands, removing any clots. It should be smooth and thin.

Tall Woman said that in the early days she made blood sausage just from cutting up some meat, usually mutton, and adding it with fat to the blood.

'Ach'íídííl (Blood Sausage) Basic Recipe

1 ½ cups chopped sheep fat, intestines, or other meat already prepared (i.e., liver, lungs, or heart boiled or fried separately on the grill in lacy stomach fat and then diced)

4 cups sheep's blood

1 tablespoon salt

3 cups diced raw peeled potatoes

1 ½ cups chopped onions

1 ½–2 cups yellow or white cornmeal

1 sheep stomach (or large intestine), washed, rinsed, and, if preferred, turned inside out

Boiling water

Optional:

1 teaspoon red chili powder or black pepper

½ jalepeño pepper, chopped

1 teaspoon sage

2–3 cups chopped raw vegetables (such as carrots or celery)

In a large bowl, mix all the ingredients except the sheep stomach and the boiling water. Then put the mixture into the stomach. If the stomach is large, it will probably take two cups of the mixture; a smaller stomach will take only one cup. Tie the ends of the stomach securely with string and then carefully put the stuffed, tied-up stomach into the boiling water. Cover and cook it for one to one and a half hours (or more, if necessary). Keep adding boiling water as needed, and make sure the water keeps boiling while the food cooks. Most people prefer to eat blood sausage warm. It will keep for only a few days.

SPECIALTY FOOD

In addition to sausage, there is a related specialty food, *'ach'íí'*, that is well-liked not just by Tall Woman and her family but also by today's Navajos and even outsiders. It is made by wrapping sheep or goat intestines with or around fat or another organ.[59]

Both the large and small intestines of a sheep are cleaned by running water through them several times. Then a length of the small intestine is wrapped around a section of the colon, maybe twenty-five times. Sheep fat that has been saved from the stomach is cut into thin strips while it is still fresh. The intestine is then wrapped around the fat, or the fat is wrapped around the intestine. It's like a sweetmeat, łikaan, and is very chewy.

Some people prefer to wrap the small intestine around the stomach fat instead of around the colon. Or several pieces of the small intestine can be coiled tightly around the fatter big intestine, with new pieces being added to continue the coil if it breaks or runs out. Some prefer to hold the small intestine in the middle and coil half of it tightly around the other half. This becomes very crunchy when cooked on a grill over an open fire.[60] A pig's intestine can be used to make this, but it can't be wrapped with fat; instead, hold it over the fire with a stick and cook it that way, or cut the meat up and put it on the charcoal.

SHEEPSKIN OR GOATSKIN

Besides the various foods made from the meat of sheep and goats and their inner organs, sheepskin can also be cooked and eaten. Called 'akágí, it was commonly made and eaten in Tall Woman's time, but by the late 1960s many people had decided not to continue the practice because of the work involved in removing the hair, or wool, from the skin. Tall Woman said that people ate this sheepskin delicacy the way that white people eat a snack. It served the same purpose.

Making 'akágí entails pulling the skin off a newly butchered young sheep or goat with tender skin and removing the wool or hair from it. This must be done immediately after all the other jobs involved in butchering if it is to work. If the skin is not going to be used right away, it is folded up and put someplace safe from other animals.

The best way to make 'akágí is to use the skin as soon as it is removed; without removing the wool or hair first, cut a piece of it to make into 'akágí and wrap that around a large, round-bottomed Navajo pot or a big pan. (Tall Woman had such a pot that she used mainly for making 'akágí.[61]) First put the pot on the coals and let it heat up on the fire. Once the pot is hot, put the piece you have cut skin side down against the outside of the pot so that the wool or hair faces out; the heat will make this come right off. After that's done, finish washing the skin and rinse it in water.

Next cut it into strips. Then do one of two things: either coil the strips on themselves or add a layer of sheep fat and salt on top of the strips before you start rolling them up. Work quickly, because they curl up really fast. Roast these on a grill until they get even curlier and shrink in size. Tall Woman used to make at least one strip for each of her children, and they really liked it. Some people prefer to broil a big piece with fat and salt, then cut it into slices or little pieces to eat, but she never did it that way.

JERKY

Making jerky (*'atsı̨́ biskání* or *'ałk'íniilgizh*) was a major way to process meat before the Navajos had access to the utilities to support refrigerators, freezers, and coolers. Tall Woman made jerky out of just about any kind of meat, including deer, elk, and antelope, among the wild game animals, and cow, horse, goat, and sheep, among the domesticated ones. Jerky can even be made from an animal's large intestine and stomach after they are thoroughly washed out and dried in the sun. The organs can be cut into pieces or left whole to be cooked when people are ready to eat them. Since making jerky involves drying fresh meat, Tall Woman made a lot of it to preserve meat, especially in the summertime. Jerky is very nutritious if it's not too salty.[62] It's also very handy to have when people are traveling, camping, or just hungry for a snack or "a food from home."

People had different ways of making jerky, and how they did it depended on what kind of meat they were using. In any case, the meat had to be fresh. Organs could be left whole, but the meat and any fat with it was usually pounded with a rock, hammer, or stone to chop or shred it, then sliced very thin, always cut with the grain so the meat wouldn't be tough.[63] After more pounding, if necessary, the meat was flattened by stretching it out as long and as thin as possible. Garlic, salt and pepper, or other herbs may be added by hand, worked in on both sides of the stretched-out meat. Then the meat was hung up to dry or cure. Tall Woman usually used a wire, a rack, or a line stretched out high enough so that no dogs could get to the meat. Some preferred clothesline rope, but whatever was used, it had to be in the sun.

A lot of people liked to dry their meat for at least thirty days, turning it over after a week. But Tall Woman reminded me that the longer it dried, the tougher it got. She thought that about twenty days was enough for most meat to dry but still be soft. Sometimes it might only take one night. The salt created something like a hard rind on the meat that the flies could not get through. When the drying was finished, the meat was stored in a sack, such as an old flour sack.[64] She always hung the sack high in a cool place so that nothing could get into it, including her children. Some of them called jerky "chew" and tried to find where she had put it so they could take some out to chew on.

When it was time to use the jerky, there were lots of way to fix it. People would roast, boil, fry, or bake it. The most important thing was that it had to be pounded, but Tall Woman said that it didn't matter if you did that before or after you cooked it. She did it both ways, whenever she was ready. Tall Woman sometimes put the dried meat right on live coals to make it pliable again. She also put it on a grill that was over the charcoal. Then she pounded it into small pieces to be eaten after it was cooked. Other times she chose to bake it right in the fat and serve it with hot tortillas. She also liked to boil it and serve it like a soup. But once it was pounded, chopped, and shredded, most often she fried it on a grill in grease or fat.

Her family said she frequently sprinkled water on the strips or put them into water to soak and reconstitute them. Whether she soaked them depended on how dry she thought they were. If she didn't think the meat was too dried out or tough, she just sprinkled it on both sides with water. Then she pounded it again with a stone or a hammer before chopping or slicing it. When that was done, she reheated the jerky in grease so it was ready to eat. She said that "refrying it with grease makes it really, really good." One of her most favorite meals consisted of dried jerky refried with homegrown onions (or wild ones, earlier) and put between two tortillas as a sandwich.

Even in earlier times some of the People preferred to soak the meat in a liquid overnight, setting it in a cool place before hanging it to dry the next day. Today bilingual Navajo- and English-speakers refer to this liquid as a marinade and point out that there are numerous kinds. According to Augusta, however, Tall Woman did not follow this practice; she never made a marinade to soak jerky in before cooking it.

The other things that Tall Woman had to say about jerky were specific to different animals. Beef jerky, pounded and dried, is called 'achǫ.[65] Now people use different marinades when making this, soaking the meat in a marinade overnight in a refrigerator before hanging it up to dry the next day. Tall Woman liked to fry dried beef jerky in fat on a grill, but sometimes she boiled it or roasted it.

Sheep and goats of any age could be used for jerky—both their meat and their organs. If jerky is made from horsemeat, the meat must be cut very thin and dried until it turns dark, then it is chopped up and heated with fat. Some people used this for medicine in earlier times, but others preferred to avoid horsemeat altogether because they didn't like the way it smelled.

In terms of venison, elk meat must be soaked in milk overnight (now in the refrigerator), then patted dry with a paper towel; otherwise the jerky would taste very gamey.[66] Deer meat has always been the most highly prized meat for jerky, according to Tall Woman. Even today deer are hunted in the mountains north of Chinle, in Lukachukai, the Chuskas, and elsewhere. Once the deer is killed and butchered, the meat is cooked by frying or boiling it. Unlike with sheep, with deer it is rare to eat the internal organs or the head. Before the hunters come home, the remaining part of the deer (what the hunters themselves haven't eaten) is hung up to dry so that the meat can be made into jerky. Deer jerky must be pounded and soaked in hot water before it is eaten. In other words, it has to be given more than a sprinkle of water.

Although Tall Woman knew how to make jerky from wild game, she herself preferred not to do that; instead she liked to cook and eat fresh game as soon as possible. As Augusta explained, wild game such as deer, elk, and antelope was rare when Tall Woman was raising her family; it was such a treat that she usually just cooked all the meat right after they got it. They ate all of it within a few days rather than trying to turn any into jerky to preserve it for later use.

Section 6 | Stews, Soups, and Mushes ('Atoo')

STEWS AND SOUPS, collectively known as 'atoo', have always been part of the Navajo diet, as far as we know. Before domesticated animals became part of their way of life, the Navajos made stews using wild plants, with or without wild game. Tall Woman frequently mentioned three plants when discussing these soups: wild onions (*tł'ohchin*), wild celery (*haza'aleeh*), and Rocky Mountain beeweed or wild spinach (*waa'*). Stews that incorporated meat from rabbits or other wild animals were also well liked. In the early days soups and stews were eaten by everyone dipping bread or something else into a single container to soak them up; later, spoons, dishes, and bowls became common.[67]

When the focus of subsistence changed to more of an emphasis on farming and livestock (with sheep, goats, cows, and horses being frequent), these animals were incorporated into the diet, including into stews and soups. For example, Tall Woman said that mutton stews that included potatoes and onions, either wild or domesticated, became equally popular. When trading posts arrived and started selling canned vegetables, and as more and more people adopted farming practices and began growing their own vegetables and fruits, it became common to make stews with additional ingredients, such as various kinds of beans, tomatoes, carrots, and corn. Meat from other domesticated animals was also added at times, including beef, chicken or other poultry, goats, and even calves, kids, and lambs. In earlier times horsemeat was used in stews and soups, but Tall Woman herself had never done that.

Vegetable Soups

The term *bé'élts'éé'* refers to a soup made from wild vegetables (such as bee-weed, onions, and celery) and eaten by dipping bread into it. The following recipe is for one that Tall Woman made often and liked to have available early in the morning, especially in the winter.

Bé'élts'éé' (Wild Vegetable Soup)

Dried wild celery, *haza'aleeh*, ground or chopped
Dried wild onions, *tł'ohchin*
Shortening (sheep, cow, goat, or pig fat)
Water

Put all the ingredients in a big pot, then bring it to a boil over a fire. Continue boiling until the ingredients are tender. Eat it with *taa'niil*, thick cornmeal mush (see recipe below).

Bé'élts'éé' Variations

Chop up onions, fry them in sheep fat, add flour, and make a little soup, then eat this with *taa'niil*, a tortilla, or frybread.
or
Serve it with *'abe' bee neezmasí* or with tortilla, frybread, or *taa'niil*.
or
Make the soup much thicker, like gravy (*'ii'ol'éél*). Add cornmeal and salt to the above ingredients, or add flour browned in mutton grease.

Tá'iitsóhii 'Atoo' (Squash Blossom Soup)

Gather large orange or yellow squash blossoms early in the morning, when they first open, before they become too tough. The flowers of summer squash are the best. Wash them and boil them in water with mutton fat and salt. You can also cut the blossoms up and add them to another kind of soup or a stew by boiling them with the meat, sheep fat, and salt. Lots of blossoms are needed to get a good flavor in soups and stews with boiled meat.

Meat Stews
STEWS WITH WILD ANIMAL MEAT

Tall Woman loved to make and eat rabbit stew and would always fix that whenever anybody brought home some rabbits to cook. The two recipes she gave me for rabbit stew follow. The second recipe makes a more gravy-like stew that some people like to eat in the morning. *Haza'aleeh* (wild celery) should always be used when a stew or soup is to be boiled and has fat or fatty meat in it.

Rabbit Stew Basic Recipe

2 whole rabbits
Wild celery
Wild onions
1 pound shelled pinyon nuts (optional)
Salt and pepper
Boiling water

Skin and clean the rabbits. Cut them into serving-size pieces. Add meat, vegetables, nuts, and salt and pepper to boiling water and cook until the meat is tender. If you are cooking on an inside stove, cook on medium heat.

Rabbit Stew Variation

2 whole rabbits
Boiling water
Salt and pepper
Cornmeal mush
Flour (optional)
Chopped wild herbs of your choice:
Crows' onions
Tumbleweed
Wild celery, either fresh or dried
Wild onion, either fresh or dried
Native salt (*łeeyáán*)

Start boiling the rabbit meat with salt and pepper after preparing it as explained above. Make a regular cornmeal mush, using any color cornmeal (see recipes below). If you want to make more of a gravy, add a bit of white cornmeal to any kind of flour, add water to that until it's the desired thickness, then stir that into the cornmeal mush. It should be like a paste, and it will thicken the mush. Add the mush to the rabbit in the boiling water, then add whatever wild herbs you want. (If you are using tumbleweed, make sure that the shoots are only two to three inches tall and have been picked right after the first summer rain, before they get spines.) Boil for about thirty minutes over a fire, and add more salt (or *łeeyáán*) if preferred.

STEWS WITH DOMESTICATED ANIMAL MEAT

Backbone Stew

Backbone stew, or *haníígaii*, is made with corn, meat, and hominy. Tall Woman said that the name tells you that the backbone is from a sheep or a goat. It was traditional to cook *haníígaii* outside in a big pot; its name, which means "dawn rises on it," means that the fresh whole corn and meat are boiled all night long so that the meat falls off the bone. Some said that the meat should be added only in the last hour. Others said that the name implies overheated or heated immensely. Two ceremonialists viewed *haníígaii* as a strong food and thought that it should be served before the all-night singing started (on the last night of a ceremony), to give the singers the strength to sing all night. Some people think that posole, *haníígaii*, and *neeshjízhii* are all the same food and use the names synonymously, but Tall Woman said that this is wrong because the three are made differently. She gave me two recipes for *haníígaii*, to which Augusta added specific measurements.

Haníígaii (Backbone Stew) Basic Recipe

4 cups fresh corn
4 cups water
10 pieces lamb or sheep backbone
2 teaspoons salt
Boiling water on the side

Put the corn, water, backbone, and salt in a large pot. Stir and then cover. Cook for at least an hour, adding more water from the boiling water as needed. Serve with either tortillas or frybread.

Haníígaii Variation

½ sheep or goat backbone
1 pound hominy
Water
Salt and pepper (optional)

Cover ingredients with water and cook as described above.

Mutton Stew

Mutton stew is one of the standard foods, even at public gatherings. Beef stew can be made the same way just by replacing the mutton with beef.

Dibé Bitsį Bitoo' (Mutton Stew) Basic Recipe

Bone of any cut of mutton
Wild potatoes
Wild onions
Wild spinach
Wild celery
Squash
Squash blossoms, if available
Sheep fat
Boiling water on the side

Put all the ingredients in a big pot over an open fire. Add boiling water as needed. Cook until the meat is tender.

Dibé Bitsį Bitoo' Variations

Add fresh corn scraped from the cob right into the stew. (This is preferred for ceremonies.)
or
Add diced squash and any other vegetables you have grown, such as

tomatoes, potatoes, onions, celery, and carrots.

or

Add chili, store-bought canned whole tomatoes chopped up, and season-ing from the wild plant *'atsá 'azee'*.

Dried Corn Stew

Another popular stew, called *neeshjízhii*, is made from dried shelled corn (*łee'shibéézh*) and fresh or dried meat of various kinds. This corn has been roasted and steamed in its husks in a ground pit or a *báá bighan*. After roasting, it is dried and then shelled. Any color corn that is hardly ripe can be used. Since the corn has been dried earlier on baked cobs, first scrape the kernels off and then boil them with whatever meat is desired to make this stew. In some families *neeshjízhii* is considered a delicacy, a special food to be prepared only for special people or special occasions, such as the conclu-sion of certain ceremonies, after the Dawn Songs.[68]

Hominy Stew

The making of hominy has been described earlier (see section 3). To make hominy stew, add meat, such as mutton or beef, about two hours before the hominy is done. When the meat is cooked, the stew is finished. Add salt and pepper if wanted, and serve hot with tortillas or frybread. At the end of the last night of the Girls' Puberty Ceremony, or Kinaaldá, the last meal the girl feeds people should be hominy with mutton. "That's the favorite thing at that time," said Tall Woman.

Some people like to add the meat right at the beginning of making the hominy so that the meat too gets boiled in the ash water. They say that doing it this way greatly softens and tenderizes really tough meat, "like old jerky or tough jerky made from butchering an old sheep in the fall."

Cornmeal Mush

There are many ways to fix cornmeal mush; thus there is more than one Navajo name for the resulting foods. From my outsider's perspective, it seems that the deciding factor is how much liquid is added; that in itself, of course, affects how thin or thick the resulting mixture is. There are other differences in how the mushes are made, and people also have different names for the same thing. In Tall Woman's view, there are basically three kinds of cornmeal mush: *tóshchíín* (blue cornmeal mush), *tanaashgiizh* (blue cornmeal mush made with juniper ash), and *taa'niil* (thick cornmeal mush), which includes a possible variant, *tanáá'niil* (sweetened white cornmeal mush). The basic idea behind making mush is that cornmeal is stirred into boiling water or milk. Depending on whom you talk to, you may hear that you can make it with any color cornmeal or just white or blue, and with or without culinary ash.

Tall Woman defined the kinds of mush as follows: *tóshchíín* is basically equal parts of ground cornmeal and liquid, usually water. She compared it to white people's Cream of Wheat cereal. It's not too thick; whoever makes it decides how thick and how light in color it will be. If you need to stretch your finely ground white cornmeal when making this, she said, you can add a little white flour or whole wheat flour to it to make sure you have enough. She also called this *'adola* (hot cereal); it's just like the very thin gruel that Spanish-speakers call *'atole*. A family member living in Cuba, New Mexico, said that the Navajos there call this dish *'adola* or *'atole* rather than *tóshchíín*.[69]

The second kind of mush, *tanaashgiizh*, has a consistency "like mashed potatoes," Tall Woman said. The word *tanaashgiizh* can also mean dumplings or marbles; there are many kinds of these, she explained, and *k'íneeshbízhii* are large dumplings or blue corn marbles. *Tanaashgiizh* dumplings are dipped into stews or soups. When Tall Woman made *tanaashgiizh*, she usually boiled it with wild celery, *haza'aleeh*. Her children liked to eat this with boiled dried peaches, either mixed in or separate.

The third kind of mush, *taa'niil*, is the thickest of the three—a cornmeal porridge. Some say the name is a generic term for blue cornmeal mush or porridge, but *taa'niil* can be made from yellow, white, or blue cornmeal. Because of its thickness, it has to be dipped out with a spoon or your hands. The variant, *tanáá'niil*, is reportedly restirred mush made from saliva-sweetened, parched white cornmeal.[70] This mush is made from the same batter as *'alkaan*, the corn cake for the Girls' Puberty Ceremony, but once it is mixed, the batter is boiled instead of baked. Tall Woman preferred to make this in the wintertime.

MUSH WITHOUT CULINARY ASH

Mush without culinary ash is fine for all to eat—even babies, sick people, the "elderlies," women who have just given birth, and people in hospitals or nursing homes. It can be served by itself or with mutton stew, another kind of stew, mutton broth, tortillas, or frybread. "It isn't real tasty," Augusta commented. "It has no flavor, no taste, even if you do use blue cornmeal."

Steven Begay told me about a mush that I thought Tall Woman had not mentioned to me. Being a singer, Begay knows many elements associated with this mush and said it was called *gad 'ádin*, which implies that juniper ash is *not* used in making it. Before I added it to this chapter, I reviewed the mush recipes that Tall Woman had given me. Sure enough; there it was with the heading "Basic Mush without Culinary Ash."

Below is the recipe that Tall Woman gave me, with Augusta again providing the measurements. Variation 2 is from Steven's aunt, Evelyn Sam, and contains some of his commentary.

Gad 'Ádin (Mush without Culinary Ash) Basic Recipe

1 cup cornmeal, any color
1 cup cold water
Boiling water

Mix the cornmeal and cold water and then stir into a pot of boiling water. Cook for about thirty minutes.

Gad 'Ádin Variation 1

3 cups of cornmeal, any color
Cold water
4 quarts boiling water

Mix the cornmeal into enough cold water to make a smooth paste. Then add the paste to the boiling water and stir while cooking it over a fire or medium heat for thirty to forty-five minutes. Keep stirring it. Then remove it and serve the mush in bowls.[71]

Gad 'Ádin Variation 2

3 cups water
1 cup raw unroasted cornmeal (usually, but not always, white)

Put two cups of water in a pan and bring to a boil on the fire. In a bowl, mix the remaining cup of water with the cornmeal. Take the resulting paste and mix it into the boiling water. Doing it this way prevents lumps from forming in the mush. "Lumpy mush is considered a lazy cook's uneducated and arrogant display of character," said Steven Begay. The longer it boils, the thicker it gets—and the thicker, the better.

Eat it when it cools by pinching and pulling out chunks of thickened mush from the pan. Do not add any salt, sugar, or other flavorings. Plain and simple is how this is supposed to be; "when you are hungry, this simple taste is so appetizing and filling."

This mush, which is one of the ancient foods that was first made by Salt Woman for the Twins, can be eaten whenever you get hungry for it. It is also used in ceremonial contexts, especially for traditional weddings and some of the curing ceremonies.[72] When it is made for ceremonial use, Begay said, a traditional Navajo clay pot should be used for boiling the mush. The singer in charge will tell whoever is making it to stir it with only two of the greasewood sticks in her bundle of stirring sticks. The mush is also used to help with some digestive problems.

Tanáá'niil (Sweetened White Cornmeal Mush)

Grind dried white corn into a coarse cornmeal, then parch the white cornmeal. Stir one cup of the parched cornmeal into one cup of boiling water and stir constantly. Sweeten the batter the way you do for 'alkaan: with sugar, wheat sprouts, biínídoot'aal, or a combination of these. The wheat sprouts used for this make the batter more watery; otherwise it's too thick. Some add a pinch of salt or łeeyáán, native salt. Some like to add some sheep fat. Boil this for about thirty minutes and eat it after it cools. Tall Woman said to remember not to store this mush. You can, however, freeze it and turn it into dahaastiin (Navajo ice cream) if you don't make it with sheep fat.

MUSH WITH CULINARY ASH

This mush, or cornmeal porridge—which can be prepared as either tanaashgiizh or taa'niil, since the difference is merely its thickness—is viewed as a traditional food that is easy, tasty, and fast to fix. Thus it is made often. Many say this well-loved food is usually made in the winter and eaten warm, with stew. It can also be served, warm or cold, with boiled fruit, such as dried apricots, dried yucca fruit, or other things. You can also freeze it to make it into *dahaastiin*. Tall Woman gave me several recipes for this. She said you can also use the recipe for blue corn dumplings or marbles (see section 4). In that case just form the dough into dumplings after making the batter.

Tanaashgiizh (Blue Cornmeal Mush with Culinary Ash) Basic Recipe

Use a skillet to dry the blue cornmeal, but don't cook it for too long. Grind the dried meal into really fine flour. Bring some water to a boil, then add juniper ash and continue boiling. Using your hands, squeeze the cornmeal in slowly by the handful. This needs to be stirred frequently, but keep your stirring sticks moving along the edge of the pot, stirring at the edges so the mixture doesn't burn on the top. Then move them into the middle to keep the boiling mixture under water until it's thoroughly cooked. The mixture must be cooked all the way through by the hot water. Do not let it get hard. Do not push it to the bottom, and do not cover the pot—either of these actions will make it burn. Remove it from the fire and stir it. Then dip it out with a spoon or a container, and put it into stew or soup. If it gets too thick or tough, add some boiling water to it and use it like dumplings. You can also freeze this in the winter and eat it at the end of the meal.

Tanaashgiizh Variation 1

½ cup juniper ash
1 cup cold water
3–4 cups boiling water
3–4 cups (or large handfuls) blue cornmeal

Stir the ash into the cold water. Strain the mixture into the boiling water using a Navajo grass brush or cloth. Stir and boil very slowly over low heat or by adjusting the charcoal. Add the cornmeal gradually, stirring in slowly. Keep adding until you get the right amount; the pot should be about half full so there is room for steam to build up in the pot. The steam cooks the mixture and holds it together. Simmer over low heat for thirty minutes or more, stirring occasionally until it becomes very thick, like *k'íneeshbízhii* dough.

Remove it from the heat, stir, and turn over and over with a large spoon.

(This may be hard to do if the dough is very, very thick.) Serve warm or cold, such as with stew or dried fruit. If you want dumplings, just form the dough that way. This does *not* store well, so eat it all up.

Tanaashgiizh Variation 2

Add juniper ash directly to a large pot of boiling water, stirring it in with stirring sticks. Then strain any lumps of ash out with stirring sticks or a grass brush.

Tanaashgiizh Variation 3

Put flour from parched corn on top of boiling water, but don't stir it in. Cover the pot and let the contents steam for about twenty minutes. Adjust the charcoal to keep the pot hot so the steam works all the way through the cornmeal. When the flour is thoroughly steamed above the boiling water, remove the pot from the heat and mix the flour into the liquid.

Tanaashgiizh Variation 4

Use three-fourths cup of ashes and four large handfuls of blue corn flour. (Everything else is the same as in variation 1.)

TanaashgiizhVariation 5

> ½ cup ash
> 1 cup cold water
> 1 cup blue cornmeal
> 3–4 cups boiling water or milk

Mix the ash with the cold water and strain it into a new container. Add the cornmeal and mix well. Slowly stir it into the boiling water or milk. Boil gently, occasionally stirring, until it thickens slightly, about ten to fifteen minutes. If you use milk, the resulting food is called *'abe' taa'niil*, milk mush.

Tanaashgiizh Variation 6

> 1 cup ash
> 4 cups boiling water
> 4 handfuls blue cornmeal

Mix the ash with one cup of the boiling water and then strain it into the rest of the boiling water. Stir with stirring sticks. Add the cornmeal, continuing to stir constantly. Boil for about thirty minutes and stir frequently. Remove it from the fire and stir again. Cool slightly and serve with tortillas or frybread.

Morning Cereal

Some Navajos told me about a cold cereal they made from dried corn silk and milk from sheep or goats, but Tall Woman never gathered and dried corn silk for this purpose and had never made or tasted this food. When asked about cereals, however, she did mention rice. Once the trading posts were established and started making rice available, and once rice was added to the Commodity Food Program (see appendix A), she and others sometimes made rice in the morning, to which they added boiling milk and maybe some white or brown sugar. She said, "We ate it just like Bilagáanas [white people] ate cereal." However, she noted that in her time Navajos did *not* fix rice to eat by itself or to serve as a side dish with meals.

Accompaniments for Stews, Soups, and Mushes

As noted in section 4, sometimes people make marbles, dumplings, or various kinds of bread to dip into soups, stews, and mushes or to serve with them. In addition, Tall Woman mentioned a sauce that could be made to use on mutton stew, soup, *tanáá'niil*, or dumplings. This sauce, which is very salty, is called *dík'ǫ́ǫzh*, and it is made from fresh wild celery, *haza'aleeh*. The herb *must* be fresh, not dried. Mix the herb right into the stew, soup, or mush.

Section 7 | Drinkable Substances (*Dajidlá*)

Water, Juices, Coffee, Teas, Milk, Drinks Made with Milk or Water, and Creamers

THERE IS NO easy label for the remaining group of Tall Woman's recipes, because there is no single word in the Navajo language that means what English-speakers call drinks. Young and Morgan (1987, 827) give *t'áadoo le'é yidlánígíí* or *daadlánígíí* for "beverage." After I had discussed the issue with a number of friends who are native Navajo-speakers, Steven Begay and his relatives suggested *dajidlá*, "drinkable substances." With permission, I have adopted their suggestion as this section's name.[73]

Water

Along with earth, air (or wind), and fire (or light), water (*tó*) is one of the four basic elements of life. Coming from Father Sky, *tó* is provided through natural springs, various kinds of rain, snowstorms, and storms that bring water down from the mountains and hills through canyons and washes—sometimes dangerously rushing as flash floods, but more often calmly, to become available for irrigating fields, crops, and gardens and to fill ponds, lakes, waterholes, and the like for use by all living beings. Although most Navajo farmers practiced dry farming, irrigation was used wherever possible, especially if the snow was deep in the mountains and thus provided a steady spring runoff.

In the early days people carried goatskin water bags with them on horseback and at other times. Tall Woman learned to make these from her mother, and she made many of them well into the 1920s. Sometime in that decade, the Indian Service started programs to install water tanks, reservoirs, and windmills. When her first three children were small (born in 1908, 1913, and 1918), there were no water tanks. Sometimes a group of people dug a well so they would have water for irrigating and other uses, and sometimes just one individual did that.[74] She said it was probably between 1925 and 1928 that the family switched to hauling water in wooden kegs, metal barrels, and other containers they carried in their wagon. Although hauling water was usually seen as men's work, in my own experience in the 1960s it was quite common to see women and children doing this or helping to do so.

Water development before 1930 on the reservation was slow at best, but Young (1961, 174) noted that there were some reservoirs and springs as well as some drilled, dug, and artesian wells. President Franklin Roosevelt's New Deal included programs that constructed dams, windmills, irrigation ditches, water reservoirs, storage tanks, and deep wells with pumps on the Navajo reservation; begun in 1933, these programs came to an end in 1941 when the United States entered World War II. Later, in the late 1940s and early 1950s, there were tribal programs to dig shallow wells (Mitchell 2001, 446-47) and of course some people, including the Mitchells, dug their own wells.[75]

Thus the sources of water expanded from lakes, ponds, springs, ditches, and sometimes washes to tanks with windmills and other kinds of wells. Tall Woman mentioned going in the wagon to a nearby windmill many times, as well as going to the Franciscan Mission, Garcia's Trading Post, and the Chinle Boarding School—other locations where people could get the water they needed for cooking, drinking, washing, and other activities. Sometimes families had to travel great distances in their wagons (and later pickup trucks or other vehicles) to get to the windmills or wells and fill their barrels and other containers with the water they needed.

Tall Woman mentioned a drink that was made by mixing seeds with water and two other drinks made by mixing seeds with milk (see below). The one made with water depended on 'ostse', the seeds of tansy or tumble mustard. These seeds were in the blossoms or pods, which had to be gathered. She rubbed them with her hands to remove the husks and ground them on grinding stones. The seeds were then added to cold water and served as a drink. Unfortunately, I forgot to ask what she called the result.

Juices

Many of the wild plants gathered by the Navajos produced berries, which were picked when they were really ripe and then squeezed and mashed until they became juice, which was strained. Sometimes water was added to the juice before people drank it; sometimes not. Some people also cooked the berries, and others liked to eat the pulp that remained after the process was done. The juices they drank came from mashing sumac berries, wolfberries, currants, seepweed, serviceberries, chokecherries, wild rhubarb or curly dock, and tansy mustard. Once they were mashed up, strained, and ground, some of those berries had to be processed further by adding *dleesh* to reduce or remove their bitter taste. Then the strained liquid was put back in, and the juice was ready.

People really liked to make *chiiłchin* (sumac berry) punch. To do that, grind fresh berries and stir them into water by the handful, probably one handful per quart of water. It's not traditional to add sugar. You can also make this punch from dried berries; first grind them to the consistency of cornmeal, add sugar (as much as desired), and then boil the mixture. Strain that to make a punch that's not too thick. The other drink with sumac berries used goat's milk (see below).

After the trading posts became established and started carrying more than just the canned tomatoes and peaches reported to be favorites, canned juices (apple, orange, pineapple, tomato) became available. Access to them increased in time and in some places through the Commodity Food Program started in 1959 (see appendix A). Another big change was the advent of supermarkets, beginning with the establishment of FedMart in Window Rock in 1968 and followed by Imperial Mart in Chinle in 1974. By then, however, sugar-filled drinks were also available, to the detriment of all.

Coffee

Coffee (*gohwééh or 'ahwééh*) became known to more people at Fort Sumner, although the Navajos had obtained it from the Spanish before 1863 (hence, the Spanish loanword adoption of *café* as well as *'ahwééh*). Stories from the Long Walk document the regularity with which Navajos incarcerated at Fort Sumner were exposed to sugar, flour, coffee beans, and salt. However, just like the flour eaten with water, the coffee beans, which were often green, caused well-documented sicknesses, because the Navajos ate them whole, unground. After the incarceration ended, people's understanding of the purpose of these beans grew, perhaps by observation of how outsiders—such as military personnel, government workers, railway workers, missionaries, traders, and others—used them. Eventually coffee became regularly available through the trading posts. Many people say that early family trips to these stores always focused on getting coffee, flour, sugar, and salt. Later other goods were added, such as tea and rice.

In the early days Navajos reportedly used the small round grinding stones they had for seed grinding to grind coffee beans. But eventually some preferred to process them on larger grinding stones, the *tsédaashjéé'* (bottom stone) and *tsédaashch'íní* (top stone), and finally the trading posts started carrying small coffee grinders as well as coffee that was already ground. The brand most common in the trading posts was Arbuckle's.[76] Tall Woman commonly prepared coffee by putting about one and a half tablespoons of dried ground coffee into the bottom of an enamel coffee pot, adding water, and putting the pot on the fire to boil. Some added a sweetener and/or canned milk before drinking it.[77]

Tea

Tea (*dééh*) was available from both wild plants and the trading posts. *Dééh* is a general label that refers to any of several teas that people may further identify, such as Brigham tea, Mormon tea, Indian tea, and Navajo tea. Tall Woman called Navajo tea *ch'il 'ahwéhé*.[78]

Although some Navajos eventually switched to drinking commercial teas available from the trading posts or provided them for guests either loose or in tea bags, Tall Woman always used native teas.[79] She said that traditionally there were three kinds of wild teas: Mormon tea, or *tł'oh 'azihii*, and two varieties of Navajo tea, or *ch'il 'ahwéhé*—long or big (*ch'il 'ahwéhé nineezígíí*) and short or small (*ch'il 'ahwéhé 'áłts'ísígíí*). Wolfe (1984) reported that all three kinds of wild teas were plentiful and easily available for gathering and drying for use all year long because their twigs stayed green throughout the year. She said that *ch'il 'ahwéhé* is a one- to two-and-one-half-foot plant with thin branched stems, long green stalks, long slender leaves, and yellow flowers clustered in small heads.

Wolfe (1984) also described what was called Brigham tea, joint fir tea, desert tea, or Mormon tea as coming from a stiff shrub that has yellow-green, jointed-looking rigid twigs and stems that were gathered and made into tea. The twigs are boiled whole or chopped until the tea steeps to the preferred taste. The stems could also be dried in loose form for use later. Some preferred to roast the stems first and then make the tea. Many used a handful of stems per cup, letting them steep in a pot of boiling water for twenty minutes or more.

Comparing Navajo tea and Mormon tea, both of which were steeped, Tall Woman said that by the late 1950s many people had stopped drinking Mormon tea because they thought that Navajo tea tasted better. By the time I met her (1963), Tall Woman was gathering only the two kinds of Navajo teas.[80] Both kinds are picked through the summer into the fall when the weather starts to get drier. The smaller tea plants, *ch'il 'ahwéhé 'álts'ísígíí*, come out first, early in June; the bigger ones appear later. The stems and flowers must be gathered right after they come up and are fresh. If they get too tall, they lose their power. Both make a fragrant, clear, amber-colored drink. Tall Woman used both, saying they tasted the same. In time she used more of the small one because there were lots of those plants right around the hogan as well as down in the canyon. The small plants were dried loose rather than put in bundles. Today people report that these plants are "way out there" and not very plentiful because "they need water to grow right."

When I went with Tall Woman to gather the long kind, *ch'il 'ahwéhé nineezígíí*, we picked a number of stalks and put them in small bundles, five or six stalks in each. She liked to fold them into thirds and tie them with another stalk, then hang the bundles on a cord to dry. Occasionally she would dry them by roasting them over a fire. She used the tea bundles either dry or fresh; the dried ones lasted a long time, and both kinds could be reused. When she was ready to make tea, she placed the bundle in a pot of cold water, brought it to a boil over the fire, and then let it boil at least five more minutes to reach the strength she preferred. Sometimes she got the water boiling first and then dropped a bundle into it, leaving it there for just a few minutes. She also made sun tea by putting a bundle into a large jar of water, closing the lid, and steeping it in the sun all afternoon. Some of her contemporaries claimed that their families had never used Mormon tea as a drink or for anything except dyeing wool.

Milk

The milk (*'abe'*) that Navajos drank in earlier times was from sheep (*dibé bibe'*) and goats (*tł'ízí bibe'*). It was a much-needed source of calcium and was readily available until the Stock Reduction Program resulted in massive reductions of these animals. Given the lack of refrigeration, these devastating changes reduced the options for obtaining fresh milk; some switched to the canned evaporated milk available from the trading posts and/or the powdered or dry milk available from stores and various assistance programs. Children were able to receive fresh milk through school programs in some places.

Tall Woman milked her goats regularly and insisted that I learn how in 1963. My attempts caused much laughter until I learned to do it correctly. She always served goat's milk at meals, used it in making certain foods, and made cheese with it. She also boiled and reboiled milk to serve with boiled coffee. I know that she milked her sheep, too, though not as often as the goats.

In addition to drinking milk, people used it to make two of the three kinds of cheese that Tall Woman told me about (see section 2). Milk's other use was in purifying water from newly dug wells or ditches and the like (see chapter 2).

MILK WITH BERRIES OR SEEDS

Tall Woman said that in addition to drinking milk by itself, she gathered several things that could be mixed with milk to make a different kind of drink. One of these was *chiiłchin*, or sumac berries. These could be added, either fresh or dried, to goat's milk after they were ground. The mixture was heated until it boiled and then drunk hot. She also mentioned two plants whose seeds could be mixed with milk. One was narrow-leaf grass, *tł'oh ts'ózí*; its wild seeds were gathered in the spring, ground with grinding stones, and then mixed with goat's milk to make a drink. The other plant was sweetgrass, *ndetlidi*. Its seeds were also ground and then added to goat's milk. Tall Woman said that some people preferred to burn the sweetgrass seeds and add the ground ashes to the milk. With both kinds of seeds, once they were ground, they could also be used to make bread or mush (see sections 4 and 6).

Creamers

Before commercial nondairy creamers appeared in stores, Tall Woman said, there were traditional things that were made to be added to coffee or tea to act like a creamer. She mentioned three kinds, all made from native ground corn. As Wolfe (1984) indicates, the native creamers were more nutritious, having more protein, fiber, calcium, magnesium, and iron and less fat, calories, and potassium than the commercial ones. All three of the native ones also acted as sweeteners. Children might be seen eating these corn creamers after wetting their fingers to get some of the dry creamer to stick to them. This is comparable to seeing children licking their fingers and then sticking them into powdered Kool-Aid or other sweet drink powders from stores nowadays.

Any corn that Tall Woman had that was not destined for some other use she shelled, cleaned, and ground into a powder so it could become a creamer when put into coffee (maybe with sugar), tea, or sometimes even milk. Anglo sweet corn, *naadą́ą́' neez*, which was viewed as sweeter than Indian corn, was roasted in a ground pit and then "ground up really fine." It was much sweeter than comparable powders. The more we talked about these creamers, the clearer it became that they all also served as sweeteners. Since sweeteners are included in section 2, that function is not repeated here, but it should be remembered and included when thinking about what Navajos used as sweeteners. The three creamers Tall Woman mentioned follow; the first two, at least, do not keep well and should not be stored.

The first creamer, *doola*, is a parched corn creamer and is the least sweet of the three. It is made by parching dried white corn kernels and then grinding them fine.

The second creamer, *ts'áálbáí* or *ts'áálbé*, is also a powdered dried steamed corn creamer and can be made at least three ways, according to Tall Woman.[81] First, leftover *'alkaan* can be thoroughly dried, ground very fine, and stored in a jar; some call this *yilką́ą́d 'alką́ą́d* instead of *ts'áʼałbáí*. Or boiled corn can be soaked slightly, parched, and ground. This is then preserved by adding salt and carried on journeys like dried morsels of sweetbread.

Ts'áʼałbáí can also be made from *neeshjíʼzhii*, which is shelled, dried, and baked roasted corn, or steamed roasted corn that has been ground into very fine powder. (It is also the name of the stew made from this corn; see section 6.) Sweet corn and even hard dried corn can be fixed this way. If you are using fresh corn, it has to be roasted, scraped off the cob, dried, and then ground into a very fine powder. If you dried the corn on baked cobs, scrape the kernels off and grind these into a fine powder to use in your coffee or tea. Even though this is already quite sweet, some people still like to add sugar to the drink they have put it in. (The same result can be achieved by browning regular flour in a skillet, putting that in a cup, and then adding coffee or wild tea. If you put the liquid in first and then add the flour, the drink gets too lumpy.) As is true with other creamers and sweeteners, if you make this from dried baked corn that has been ground into a very fine meal, you can make the drink as thick or as light-colored as you want; this is very, very sweet, without adding any sugar.

The last of the three ways that Tall Woman mentioned to make *ts'áʼałbáí* is from dried roasted green corn that has been stored for wintertime use. First shell the *łeeʼshibéézh*, if it was stored on the cob; then grind the kernels into a very fine powder. This can then be put into hot coffee, milk, or tea to act as a creamer.

The third creamer that Tall Woman told me about is *neeshjáhih*, which is made from Anglo sweet corn. In earlier times sweet corn was rarely grown by Navajos, but by the late 1960s, if not earlier, at least around Tuba City and Shiprock, some people were raising it. To make this creamer, cook the sweet corn by baking, roasting, boiling, or steaming it. After it's cooked, dry it thoroughly outside with the husks removed. When it's dry, remove the dried kernels and then grind them into a very fine powder. This is the sweetest of the three creamers Tall Woman told me about. This finely ground, dried sweet corn can be put into coffee or other drinks to serve as a creamer; add as much as you want to make it very light or very thick.

4 | Reflections

NOW THAT ALL of Tall Woman's recipes have been presented in the seven categories that made the most sense to her family, it is time for concluding remarks. Working through the fieldwork data again, and discussing them with members of her family, other elders (in some cases), and some ceremonialists who were interested in helping, has encouraged me to stand back and try to summarize my own thoughts and feelings. These include not just remembering the fieldwork but also contemplating what a review of our work together has shown me about Tall Woman as a traditional Navajo woman. During the work many family stories surfaced again, as did family jokes—even some focused on foods, such as stealing Navajo ice cream from the hogan roof and the grandchildren making up funny names for foods, such as "iron bread"—and the context for these jokes.

Tall Woman was known for her knowledge of the environment and how to find and use the multiple food resources within it. People often came to her to learn some of this knowledge, which she readily shared when they were serious. Tall Woman was also exceedingly well versed in her knowledge of the ancient foods and those used in various ceremonies. She understood that even the preparation of these foods affected the outcome, and thus she was highly respected for her knowledge and her ability to translate it appropriately in ceremonial contexts. As an elderly woman she took pride in telling me that her husband, Frank, often told her how many ceremonial practitioners complemented her knowledge, abilities, and careful correct preparation of the ancient foods, exactly as things were supposed to be done.

Even when preparing food for her family to eat on regular days, Tall Woman always did things properly. For example, she always said a prayer when cooking on an open fire, while stirring charcoal with the fire poker, after mixing blue cornmeal mush with her stirring sticks, or when finishing the preparation of a meal. These were expressions of gratitude for the food and individualized prayers for the health and well-being of the family, the livestock, the hogan, and the current endeavors of all. She also taught her children, or others who might be helping her prepare food, that they should be thankful for whatever food was available to eat and grateful to the person who prepared it. Stirring sticks, for example, should always be wiped clean with one's fingers, then the fingers licked clean. As she repeatedly reminded all of us, in bad times or in earlier times that might be all one got to eat of the meal.

Tall Woman had vast knowledge about how native foods could be used as medicines, cures, therapies for various ailments, and promoters of good health. She used this knowledge on a daily basis to keep her children and the adults in her life, including herself, healthy and active. Well respected as a midwife, she also used her knowledge of food as medicine while assisting women in childbirth and in properly welcoming the newborns.

Tall Woman taught her children to never waste food, to always finish every bit of food put in front of them. She herself was raised in times when people were, in fact, starving: before, during, and after being rounded up and during the Long Walk, the march to Fort Sumner. Raised by parents well versed in ceremonial practices and beliefs, she knew that in addition to Sleep, Poverty, Lice, Jealousy, and Old Age, Hunger was one of the monsters allowed to live on Earth's Surface by Monster Slayer when he was traveling around, destroying people-eating beings. These monsters were left on earth to keep people healthy and aware. Thus Hunger, envisioned as being led by a big fat man who had only a little brown cactus to eat, was left alive: "If we die, people will not relish their food. They will never know the pleasure of cooking and eating nice things, and they will not enjoy hunting" (Reichard 1963, 445). Hunger, then, like Poverty and other monsters, exists "to remind all of us to work the land and know how to survive without any waste." Women—armed with knowledge of the environment and the diverse food resources in it, and with greasewood stirring sticks, grinding stones, grinding stone sharpeners, grass brushes, and pottery vessels—were responsible for keeping Hunger at bay, generation after generation.

As I worked with Tall Woman, discussing foods and various recipes, and much later, while I reviewed her words and thought about them as a whole, several things became very apparent to me. While sharing her knowledge of foods with me, she emphasized how to stretch one's resources—how to always make sure you had enough to feed anybody who might show up, even if your food was in very short supply and everybody in the family knew it. As her story (Mitchell 2001) and that of her husband, Frank (Mitchell [1978] 2003), make clear, given her husband's roles as a well-known Blessingway singer, headman, chapter officer, tribal judge, and early council delegate, it was common for people to come by on horseback or in wagons to discuss matters with him or to request his ceremonial services.

In traditional Navajo culture one does not invite people to come for supper, go out for lunch, or go get coffee and talk; people just come by and stop in, and it is expected that whoever appears will be given something to eat or at least something to drink. Even if all the host has is water, tea, or coffee, that is shared with the guests. To do otherwise is seen as selfish, greedy, and unacceptable—un-Navajo. People are not expected to bring food when they drop in; but if their family is doing well, their garden has produced a surplus, or they have other resources to share, they bring those with them to contribute to the subsistence of the family being visited. This clearly illustrates the Navajo value of reciprocity and the continuation of earlier patterns of people working in groups, helping one another.

Of course, if people are going to a ceremony, then they *are* expected to help out by bringing food and another set of hands to help with the work. They might also donate one or more sheep, a truckload of wood, several large bags of flour, and so forth. And for some ceremonial occasions, they might also donate boxes of Cracker Jacks, sacks of lollipops, or candy to be given away. If a woman is preparing a meal to feed her family when guests stop by, they are expected to stay and eat. So the question arises of how to stretch the food supplies and recipes to feed more people so that everybody has enough to eat and nobody goes hungry.

Stretching food includes never wasting food; people always eat everything that is offered to them; they never leave uneaten food in the bowl or on the plate, saying, "Give it to the dogs" or whatever. Children are taught from an early age not to waste anything, just as they are taught that guests, whether relatives or not, are always fed. By watching, girls in particular learn how their mothers, aunts, and grandmothers stretch food, and they witness the fact that if all else fails, the family will do without so that the extra mouths can be fed. The basic rule, no matter what, is to stretch the resources and be creative so that one can literally make something out of almost nothing.

Occasionally Tall Woman mentioned specific ways of stretching food. For example:

> "Remember that squash really fills people up, so always include that if you have any, adding it to stews or mushes, or serving it on the side."
> "Gravy helps your food go further, so add that in if you need to."
> "*Tóshchíín* itself is very easy to stretch by adding flour, either the same kind you are using, or wheat flour, so you can feed everybody."
> "Remember never to waste anything, even if it turned hard or got old. [For example,] making *nanoyeeshi* is one way to use up roasted corn before it gets too old, too hard. Lots of people make it for that reason."

If you are making hominy stew and aren't sure how many you might have to feed with it, Tall Woman explained, you should add meat at the start of the process so that it boils in the ash water with the corn and other things. That softens the meat and tenderizes it. "This way you could use up really old, tough meat, even old jerky that you had made by butchering an old sheep!" She said the need to always stretch limited resources was part of her reality, part of what she was expected to do to feed her family. She had to know how to extend her resources, never wasting anything and being creative while planning for the future.

Tall Woman was a kind, observant, sharp, astute, generous, realistic, practical, and creative person who was, in fact, the main support of her family. She had a large family and was the wife of a public figure, a highly respected Blessingway singer and a community and tribal leader. Frank had access to wage work and income from his ceremonial knowledge, but he traveled frequently. Her role was that of a matriarch, the leading woman in the settlement, the one whose responsibility it was to make decisions and do all she could to ensure the success of the extended family. Her world was more traditional and more circumscribed than her husband's, and it was filled with different experiences and perspectives. It was her responsibility to be self-sufficient, to preserve and transmit traditional cultural knowledge and practices, and to support the family on a daily basis. Child rearing, running the home, feeding everybody, doing farmwork, herding and caring for the livestock, hauling water, chopping wood, and weaving rugs to sell to support the family—all these jobs were hers.

There are many things that came up during our work together on foods, food resources, and recipes that definitely deserve further study in the future. The plants themselves in the environment require study by a team that includes professional botanists versed in the environments of the US Southwest. Plants have to be identified by their common names in both Navajo and English and by their scientific names, genus and species. They should be presented with line drawings and photographs taken at different times in their cycles.

Finally, botanical information should be presented in a context that includes lists of protected plants on the Navajo reservation in New Mexico, Arizona, and Utah, as well as the specific regulations about collecting them, including permission to be on the land, permits, and regulation tags. I realize, of course, that to do this might not meet with approval from the current Navajo Nation Historic Preservation Department, where applications for research permits are processed. As noted earlier, it continues to be unacceptable to discuss medicinal and ceremonial uses of plants and various foods in print. Another question for future studies is how often, in today's world, plant gathering is approached with prayers and offerings before removal occurs, to show respect and gratitude to Mother Earth. The same question can be applied to planting and harvesting.

There are a number of linguistic issues that require attention; one is linguistic synecdoche, in which a name can mean either the part or the whole. For instance, *tséyi'* means both "canyon" and Canyon de Chelly. *'Ach'íí'* is both sheep intestines and the much-loved specialty food made from them. Kinaaldá (capitalized) is the Girls' Puberty Ceremony, but a *kinaaldá* (lowercase) is the girl for whom the ceremony is being given. Another issue is the fact that many plants appear to have multiple names, in either English or Navajo, or both. For example, *waa'* is wild spinach or Rocky Mountain beeweed; *tł'oh deesk'idí* is amaranth or pigweed, and both are prepared like spinach. Seepweed is known as either *hooch'a'* or *łichí'íí*; tumbleweed can be *tł'ohdeeí naayizí, ch'il deeníní,* or *ch'il 'awóshi.*

With some foods, the name appears to be a generic one, a cover term for many related dishes. One of these is *tanaashgiizh,* which can mean any kind of mush or gruel that is stirred together; according to Tall Woman, it means a thick blue cornmeal mush made with ash, but it can also mean dumplings or marbles made the same way, even though the latter two also have a specific name, *k'íneeshbízhii. Taa'niil,* a well-loved blue cornmeal mush, can also mean *all* kinds of blue cornmeal mush. Nowadays the word for corn creamer, *ts'áálbáí,* includes cereals and *łee'shibéézh.* And what Tall Woman told me was the earlier term for flour, *'ak'áán,* "ground up," was also flour made from any color corn—white, yellow, or blue.

Then there are the practices in which people use words as synonyms when they are not. For example, Navajos I know call both cedar and juniper *gad,* even though these coniferous trees belong to different genera (*Cedrus* and *Juniperus*). As already indicated, other examples of synonyms include wild parsley and wild celery, pumpkins and gray squash with orange-colored insides, wild and domestic grapes, *haníígaii* and posole, and—the one that caused the most trouble in this project—kneel-down bread and tamales. Sometimes the different choices are reportedly related to geography, such as different preferences for the word for bread, *bááh* in Arizona and *łees'áán* in New Mexico, and the use of *nijiło'í* in New Mexico for sweet blue corn tamales.

Another aspect of this project that is worthy of future investigation, now that Tall Woman's recipes are available, would be a comparison of her recipes with others published in the literature for the same foods. Although this would definitely be interesting, and many of the resources required for such a comparison are included in the reference list herein, such a comparison was not within the scope of the present work. The same is true for the question of relationships between recipes. The fact that tortillas and frybread are made from the same dough but cooked differently has already been mentioned. Other examples are the several foods that derive from the *'alkaan* recipe and the several ways to make Navajo ice cream, or *dahaastiin.*

For this work I was able to track developments in the Navajo Nation and elsewhere through much of 2016. It is obvious that the interest in earlier subsistence practices, healthy foods, and the establishment of food sovereignty continues to grow among the Navajos and others around the world. One area where this is evident but easily overlooked is the increasing number of Navajo students interested in studying the culinary arts, first at schools on the reservation, such as Chinle High School (Yurth 2016b) and Navajo Technical University, and then elsewhere. Many people say that the time is ripe for Native American foods to move to the forefront, given the nationwide interest in organic foods; the farm-to-table, farm-to-fork, farm-to-market, and farm-to-folk movements; indigenous foods; local foods; and special diets such as vegetarian, vegan, gluten-free, low-fat, and paleo. Even though a restaurant like the Pueblo Harvest Café has been part of the Indian Pueblo Cultural Center in Albuquerque since the 1970s, indigenous foods are still not familiar to many Americans. Native chefs have already discovered that to be successful, their own foods must be introduced slowly and accompanied with patient teaching about the culture and its traditions. Thus, gradually, new restaurants, food trucks, food halls, catering businesses, menu choices, and cooking classes are being started and offered by Native chefs around the country, on the Northwest coast and in New York City, Washington, DC, Chicago, Minneapolis, Albuquerque, Santa Fe, and other cities. Food trucks are an increasingly familiar sight in St. Louis, Madison, and other cities, and the excitement about learning about others' foods and food cultures is now growing rapidly.

Some established Native chefs are publishing, traveling internationally to prepare meals, appearing as guest or keynote speakers, and the like. The multitalented Lois Ellen Frank (Kiowa and Sephardic Jew) is one example. She published an award-winning book in 2002, earned a PhD in culinary anthropology in 2011, and became an established photographer; now this Native American foods historian is based in Santa Fe, teaches at the Institute for American Indian Art and the Santa Fe School of Cooking, does guest-chef appearances with Navajo chef Walter Whitewater, and with him runs Red Mesa Cuisine, a Native American catering and food company.

A Google search leads to other Native chefs, such as Loretta Barrett Oden (Potawotami), who for more than ten years ran the Corn Dance Café in Santa Fe, starting in the early 1990s, but who now travels to teach classically trained chefs about indigenous ingredients and menus. Another is Sean Sherman (Oglala Lakota), a Sioux chef with a food truck called Tatanka and a restaurant in the Twin Cities that focuses solely on "precolonization Sioux and Ojibwe cuisine." Sioux Chef, the Minneapolis consulting and catering company that he founded in 2014 and runs with Dana Thompson, is already expanding the demand for Native-owned food businesses.

Many Native American chefs are interested in introducing the foods of their great-grandparents, those called precolonization foods, what was being eaten before European settlers came to the Americas. These foods are made with no deep frying; no factory-produced or modern processed ingredients such as white flour, processed sugar, and dairy products; and no farmed meats like beef, pork, and chicken. Instead of soda, a standard drink is maple water and infusions of cedar, spruce, cranberry, and sage. The emphasis is on local foods, those indigenous to one's area, and simple cooking techniques such as drying, stewing, smoking, and cooking foods on or in a fire.

Recent articles about these developments are finally available to a wider audience, such as Rao (2016a, 2016b) and the coverage given to Navajo Chef Freddie Bitsoie when he was selected in August 2016 as the executive chef at the Mitsitam Café at the Smithsonian National Museum of the American Indian (NMAI) in Washington, DC (L. Allen 2016; Bowman 2016a; Weiland 2016). A Utah Navajo who originally planned on becoming a cultural anthropologist, Bitsoie moved into culinary endeavors after taking a course on food history. A graduate of the Scottsdale Culinary Institute (now Le Cordon Bleu College of Culinary Arts), Bitsoie brings to the NMAI job his experience at the Heard Museum in Phoenix and other venues in Arizona and New Mexico. He is at the center of NMAI conversations about defining Native American cuisine and serves as the museum's bridge from ancestral foods and Native cooking techniques to contemporary cuisine.

Elsewhere other things are happening. For example, the St. Louis Science Center (2016) opened the exhibit "GROW: The Journey of Food." The center's largest expansion project in more than thirty years, it is based on years of research and discussion and on the realization that it's time to educate people on where their food comes from, how to grow their own, and how to be effective stewards of the world's food supply. In Illinois's Crystal Lake community, the town's food coordinator has decided it is essential that food pantry clients learn to grow their own food. The plan is to expand this already successful project across the state in the future (Mordi 2016). Colleagues have also alerted me to the fact that literary criticism scholars are studying the indigenous food sovereignty movement in Native North American and other Native literary studies (see, e.g., Adamson 2011).

To return to Navajoland: Reactions to the Navajo Nation Council's approval of the tax on junk food came from a wide range of places around the United States. Although some newscasters and late-night talk-show hosts chose to poke fun at the move, the comments were usually very positive, praising Navajos for being the first Native Americans to take action against the well-known unhealthy characteristics of junk food and encouraging other Native American nations to follow suit (see, e.g., Halbritter 2015; *Indian Country Today* 2015). The *Navajo Times* continues to cover food sovereignty events at schools, workshops, and community centers. Health organizations, hospitals, and governmental agencies are now involved in supporting studies on a variety of health problems on the reservation and are implementing suggestions for addressing them.

I certainly don't hear about everything going on, but friends try to keep me updated when I am not in the Southwest. For example, on December 28, 2015, my colleague Klara Kelley sent me a two-page flyer from NAPI that was available in the lobby of the Navajo Nation Museum. On the left side it listed pinto beans, russet potatoes, all-purpose flour (in both paper and cloth bags, bleached and unbleached), frybread mix, and whole wheat flour. On the right side was the heading PRESERVING TRADITIONAL NAVAJO FOODS, sponsored by www.navajopride.com, over three sections: blue corn products, including pancake mix and roasted cornmeal; white corn products, including unroasted cornmeal and roasted cornmeal; and a miscellaneous assortment of Navajo foods that included coffee creamer, Navajo corn nuts, cedar ash, and smoked corn.

A brief review of some of the 2015–2016 coverage that the *Navajo Times* gave to food sovereignty must include Black (2015). Mallory Black, a freelance Navajo reporter and a founding journalist of the Native Health News Alliance, summarized some of the findings of *Feeding Ourselves* (Echo Hawk Consulting 2015), a major study commissioned by the American Heart Association on an indigenous food and agricultural initiative at the University of Arkansas School of Law. Like some other studies, this one concluded that most tribal lands are food deserts and that "the ability of Indian Country to feed itself with *healthy, local, and traditional foods* is not only a critical part of a strong tribal community, it's vital to tribal sovereignty."

Like the 2014 DPI study mentioned earlier, the Echo Hawk Consulting (2015) study, which is ninety-nine pages long, is available online. Even if readers are already familiar with the history and continuing challenges facing Native Americans in food, food access, food systems, and health issues, especially diabetes and obesity, described in the case studies in this report, they may learn new information about funding sources, community-based solutions, networks, and food sovereignty assessment. The report's last two chapters are full of excellent suggestions about what tribal governments and concerned groups, grassroots and others, need to do. Chapter 6 is entitled, "We Stand on the Solution: Recommendations to Empower Indian Country Food Systems and Health," and chapter 7 is "Steps toward Increased and Strategic Partnership with Indian Country: Recommendations for Funders, Stakeholders, and Policymakers."

Pineo (2015) covered a conference for the Tsehootsooi Medical Center staff that explored integrating culture, traditional ways, and sustainable food sources into healthy living and establishing partnerships to improve community health. As the accompanying illustrations showed, the medical center was already building earth ovens and teaching others to do so, as well as establishing community gardens at schools, cafés, playgrounds, and senior centers to encourage people to practice food sovereignty. It was also teaching about traditional Navajo seeds, composting, dealing with sparse precious water resources, and encouraging learning from one's neighbors. The *Navajo Times*'s traditional annual review included "Junk Food Tax Takes Effect," a summary of the history of the Healthy Diné Act of November 21, 2014, which took effect in 2015 (Pineo and Donovan 2015). Another report (Allen 2015) highlighted "Reclaiming the Traditional Food," which reviewed the paper's coverage of the grassroots food movement through articles, sometimes illustrated, on traditional food; the environment and communities; the interest in learning about farming, sustainable agriculture, and long-term land management; the latest trends in gardening, landscaping, and edibles; growing native plants, shrubs, and trees with drip systems, sculpted land, and other permaculture techniques; making and using earth ovens; developing school outdoor kitchens; gardening and sharing foods grown with the community; and celebrating successes with harvest festivals.

That the interest in the food sovereignty movement is not just a fad is clear in Bitsoi (2016a), which describes a work session held at the Navajo Nation Museum for members of the Navajo Nation Council's Health, Education, and Human Services (HEHS) Committee, chaired by Jonathon L. Hale. The event introduced HEHS members to the Navajo food policy tool kit developed to help communities navigate the food system, gain access to healthy foods, and increase healthy food production along with information about traditional Navajo foods, associated cultural practices, and Diné foodways. The tool kit was developed between May 2012 and May 2015 in partnership with the Harvard Law School Food Law and Policy Clinic, Community Outreach and Patient Empowerment (an important nonprofit organization with Sonlatsa Jim-Martin as the program coordinator and Sonya Shin as the executive director), and the Nation. Amber Crotty, the Navajo Nation Council delegate and a former DPI director, led much of the discussion, bringing in data from the Diné food sovereignty report (DPI 2014) on how Navajos need to revive their traditional farms, reclaim their food system, and revive their traditional foods to achieve health and healing.

Other examples continue to emerge. For example, Tafoya (2016) reminded readers that Navajos *are* in control of most aspects of their lives but just lack the will and action to take control. Control comes from the Diyin Diné'é (Holy People) as Fundamental Law and the federal self-determination laws and policies. The start of any fight against diabetes, obesity, junk food habits, or anything else always has to be at home, because basically, in Navajo culture, "it's up to you." Among the needs are comprehensive food and health laws and policy reform, a Navajo Nation wellness department or a department of food security. Schools should be serving Navajo beef, mutton, and NAPI products; stores should be stocked with traditional healthy Navajo foods.

Franklin (2016) focuses on the nonprofit organization Native Seeds/ SEARCH, explaining how on-reservation Native Americans in the Greater Southwest can get ten free packets of heirloom seeds. The Shiprock chapter of the Navajo Nation, under its president, Duane "Chili" Yazzie, and some other members, has already secured a community seed grant from this organization. It plans to pair youth with elderly farmers to pass on traditional techniques and knowledge while working to achieve food security for the community after the tragic Gold King Mine spill that affected hundreds of Navajo farmers along the San Juan River in August 2015. The goal is to revitalize Navajo culture, start a seed bank, share crops at seed fairs, and "become an agricultural hub and the bread basket of the Navajo Nation."

Bitsoi (2016b) reported on a workshop in Naschitti (New Mexico) that focused on agricultural planning and marketing led by the Native American Producer Success III project, which aims to improve agriculture with farmers and ranchers, especially in areas with clusters of land-use plots. The topics included composting, permaculture, companion planting, and other techniques to help farmers relearn their craft and thus help make fresh food available. As with many other places on the reservation, for the residents of Naschitti and Sheepsprings (New Mexico), the nearest grocery store is at least forty-five miles away.

Food sovereignty, or independence from external food sources, and all Navajos having access to fresh nourishing food produced on the Navajo Nation, continues to be covered. Yurth (2016b) announced the free Fourth Annual Indigenous Food Sovereignty Conference to be held at Chinle High School. Started by Dana Eldridge, this year's conference was being sponsored by Diné College, the Tsehootsooi Medical Center, New Mexico State University, Native American Producer Success, and Aramark. Topics to be covered included food sovereignty; learning how to gather, plant, grow, market, and preserve food; food safety; and, of course, food and health, with an emphasis on diabetes prevention. A follow-up of the conference revealed that in her keynote, Eldridge blasted NAPI for growing GMO crops (Yurth 2016a), as did Begay (2016).[1]

Allen (2016a) reported the demonstration of a solar-powered water pump at a garden expo in Tuba City. The *Gallup Independent* (2016) publicized Navajo Nation Vice President Jonathan Nez's announcement of his "gardening challenge." Nez reiterated the current administration's belief that the Navajos must return to the basic tenets of helping one another and becoming self-sufficient; leaders are pushing to strengthen families while teaching the importance of language, culture, and tradition. "True sovereignty is the ability of a nation to feed its people," Nez declared.

Discussing the garden being planted at the vice president's residence, the article included information about techniques (such as double dug, lasagna technique, and drip irrigation), the assistance available from Tolani Lake Enterprises, and the fact that the office of the president and vice president were distributing non-GMO seeds on a first-come, first-served basis, as well as information on tribal gardening and farming programs in the five agencies. This was soon followed by an announcement of "paths across Navajoland " (Pineo 2016b), detailing expansions of the trail system across the reservation with information about newly built and newly opened trails, thanks to help mainly from volunteers drawn from local people, Navajo Nation chapters, the Department of Natural Resources, and Youth Empowerment Services.

In June 2016 DPI Director Moroni Benally and Deputy Director Andrew Curley announced the institute's new challenge: producing recommendations for the Healthy Office Workers Initiative (Pineo 2016a). Given the amount of sitting that Navajos do at work and also while driving long distances, the DPI has been asked by the Navajo Nation Council to develop and implement techniques to challenge or mitigate sedentary lifestyles. The council announced the approval of a distribution policy for the money raised by the junk food tax (Becenti 2016b). Some members of the Budget and Finance Committee still opposed the tax, and there was more heated discussion. Its approval was followed by training workshops for chapter officers on how the funds may be used; when that is completed, the funds will be distributed.[2] The possibilities are almost endless: wellness centers, playgrounds, picnic areas, community gardens, farmers' markets, sports fields, trails and tracks (biking, walking, running), skating parks, fitness programs, trainers, and equipment (Becenti 2016a).

During July it was common to see roadside stands where tamales and frybread were being sold and to hear radio announcements of grants available for wellness projects, nutrition educators conferences, and soil testing and drip irrigation demonstrations open to the public. One program even presented a summary of a recent NPR program from the University of Maryland on the value of eating insects. Cicadas have more protein than soy and take much less water to harvest the same amount of protein. Thus, eat insects! Many of the daily KTNN radio reports included announcements of community running plans, in conjunction with "Running for a Stronger and Healthier Navajo Nation," a program started in 2012 by former Navajo Nation Vice President Rex Lee Jim. Some races, such as the Thirty-Seventh Annual Narbona Pass Classic 5K and 10K had longer histories, but numerous walking and running clubs, some with names like Classic Fitness Walk and Fun Walks, were becoming common. Ground was also broken for Fort Defiance's Navajo wellness center; when it is completed in the fall of 2017, it will support basketball, volleyball, badminton, and running indoors.

August brought news of a major two-day forum hosted by the Shiprock chapter entitled "Food Sovereignty Is a Human Right" (from the UN Declaration of Human Rights) (Shebala 2016). Cohosted by the International Indian Treaty Council, with the theme "Our Earth Mother Is Our Life and Our Hope," the event included the preparation of traditional Navajo foods: steamed corn, blue cornmeal mush, Navajo tea, corn cakes, and kneel-down bread. Bowman (2016b) also reported the completion of the Klagetoh Veteran's Courtyard community garden at the Klagetoh Chapter House, thanks to the Little Colorado River Watershed Chapters Association founded in 2012 to help chapters monitor natural resources in the Colorado River Basin.

These reports were followed by those on the Miss Navajo competition at the Navajo Nation Fair, which continued to include the traditional activities of butchering a sheep and, through 2016, making frybread. In 2017, making frybread was replaced by preparing part of the newly butchered meat as well as one traditional food. Other reports highlighted baby parades and competitions in various communities during which some little girls explained the grinding stones, hairbrushes, and stirring sticks as traditional tools. The reports of the Navajo Nation Fair included the foods associated with the fair (such as turkey legs, curly fries, and the Texas Twister, a nonalcoholic fruit drink) as well as traditional foods, including kneel-down bread, steamed corn, mutton, and 'ach'íí' (Allen 2016c).

Other items of note are the announcements in each issue of the *Navajo Times* of the Diné bi Da'ak'eh working garden sessions held each month (at least May through October 2016, except during the fair) at the Navajo Nation Demonstration Garden at the Window Rock fairgrounds. Youth representatives reported excitedly on a three-day seminar in Española, New Mexico, the Native Youth in Food Agriculture Regional Summit, hosted by the University of Arkansas School of Law's Food and Agriculture Initiative and the Intertribal Agriculture Council (Keane 2016). Equally exciting was the report (Largo 2016) on the very first Tesla battery installation in Arizona at the Forest Lake chapter, which will now be able to use solar power for 90 percent of its electricity needs. The Navajo Tribal Utility Authority is among those studying the system, the first of its kind of technology on the Navajo Nation or in the state of Arizona, and the future appears to be bright.

These consistent, continuing developments suggest that the commitment to addressing food sovereignty and all its components is strong and ever growing. It is my hope that by sharing Tall Woman's recipes, as well as what is known from earlier years of professional work by both Navajos and outside others—be they journalists, nutritionists, anthropologists, dietitians, missionaries, teachers, social workers, clinicians, or medical workers—this work can contribute to this movement, which has now developed well beyond the initial grassroots stage. That said, perhaps it's appropriate to close with a few more possible new directions.

As indicated earlier in this text, during our work together Tall Woman occasionally made comments about certain foods that would be interesting to learn more about, if possible. For example, and now undoubtedly past the point of anyone's recall, in early times when the Navajos were starving, there were certain foods that she called "desperate hunger food" or "a *starvation food*," something the People did not eat unless they absolutely *had* to—that is, they were literally starving to death.

There were also two wild plants that she called *foundational plants, those of central importance to Navajos in earlier times, before corn* but also during her own childhood and young adult years. She said that "if you had access to these two, there was no way you'd ever go hungry." They were *tł'oh deesk'idí* (pigweed or amaranth) and *tł'ohdeeí* (goosefoot).

Then there were the *strong foods*; one example of these is Indian corn, which she saw as much stronger than Anglo sweet corn. There were also the favorite foods and favorite parts of edible things—for example, the chest meat of sheep, the four organs considered delicacies (lung, heart, kidney, and liver), and the whole head of a sheep or goat. Others have different lists and ideas.

There were certain foods that Tall Woman said were *old-time foods*, or *old-time plants* that went *way back* in history, such as *k'íneeshbízhii* and *naaltsoii*. Our discussions of ancient foods led further, and as I was working on this book I was fortunate enough to be able to continue these discussions with several colleagues and a few ceremonialists. Tall Woman had mentioned this ancient foods category when telling me about Frank's pride in her extensive knowledge of foods from earlier times. This was very important to her, and she told me about it repeatedly.

As I was thinking about it, I started worrying about the connection between ancient and sacred and whether I was crossing a line meant to protect intellectual property if I discussed ancient foods in this work. Thus I asked a ceremonialist and colleague, Steven Begay (personal communication, 2015), for his opinion, and he replied, "Ancient foods are *not* sacred foods and thus should not be considered inappropriate to include in this work." They do not cross any lines established by the Historic Preservation Department to protect sacred knowledge. "The ancient foods are those which we know were made and eaten in the early days, even before Fort Sumner, for some of them," he explained. "These are old-time foods, foods that have a long history of use for the Navajos. Just because they have a long history does not mean they are considered sacred. Old does not mean sacred." He added, "People need to be aware of these ancient foods because this knowledge is becoming lost. Keep the ancient foods in your book."

Further discussions taught me that it's the context in which the food is made rather than the type of food itself that determines whether it is sacred or not. There are many foods that have to be prepared for individual ceremonies and for specific uses within the ceremonies, either by themselves or in combination with other foods. And just because a food is associated with a particular ceremony doesn't mean it can't be made for a different ceremony as well. Begay used the corn cake for the Girls' Puberty Ceremony as an example, saying, "There are certain ceremonies when it [the *'alkaan*] is expected to be made and given as a kind of payment." If the food is connected with any of the curing ceremonials—the Diyin K'é, or Holy Ways— then it is sacred, highly guarded and protected, and not open to public discussion in casual conversations or in print.

Thus the few new things I learned about sacred foods during this project have been assembled into a confidential appendix and filed with the Navajo Nation Historic Preservation Department in Window Rock, as I have done on earlier occasions. Tall Woman did tell me a few general things about ceremonial foods that she thought I could and should include. One was that food to be used in curing ceremonies had to be prepared in Navajo pottery— a Navajo pot of whatever size and shape was appropriate.

Another point illustrated something she did not elaborate on: the question of what kinds of foods *should not* be served during ceremonies. For example, during our conversations about dumplings and marbles, *k'íneeshbízhii*, she told me to be *very* careful when serving these foods, which were enjoyed by the family. They should *never* be brought into a ceremony, because many people equate them with hail, so if you bring them in, a severe hailstorm will ensue.

In terms of what *should* be served, and when, during ceremonies, she noted that when everything has been finished in the Kinaaldá, the last meal served in the hogan should be hominy with mutton. Even these brief glimpses made it clear that there is a rich, complex world surrounding the ceremonial use of foods, of which she was highly knowledgeable but which was beyond the parameters of our work together.

The 'alkaan is one of the foods that Tall Woman identified as an ancient traditional food. According to her it was made in a ceremonial context, and *only* then—even though today people make it whenever they are hungry for it. Again worried, I asked Steven Begay to help me understand why it was all right to talk about this sacred food. Tall Woman clearly had no problem telling me about this food and including it in her recipes; she actually taught me how to make it, which I have now done a number of times, and she wanted it included in my earlier study of the Kinaaldá (Frisbie [1967] 1993). She never told me that it could also be prepared as a payment during a curing ceremony. Although we had never discussed it, her own ceremonial knowledge made it clear to her that as sacred information, this aspect was not open to sharing or any kind of discussion.

Begay explained that the difference is the fact that the Kinaaldá is part of the Hózhǫ́ǫ́jí, or Blessingway ceremony. As Mitchell ([1978] 2003) discussed, the Blessingway, "the backbone of Navajo religion," emphasizes and reinforces the ideal, desired state known as *hózhǫ́*, which signifies harmony, peace, balance, good fortune, good health, and happiness. The Hózhǫ́ǫ́jí ceremony prevents misfortune before it occurs and restores a person's mind and body to *hózhǫ́*. It sustains a good life and stabilizes well-being.

There is a lot of literature on the 'alkaan, and its recipe is no secret. Begay (personal communication, 2016) said, "It is food for the People" and as he reminded me, "the Creation narrative tells us that this food is so ancient that it existed *before* Changing Woman came into being; she was instructed on how to make the cake. The whole reason for the *kinaaldá* making the cake," Begay explained, "is to feed everyone—people, livestock, the earth, the sun, and so forth. It is her gift, and now it becomes her responsibility, her lifelong task, to provide as a new nurturer."

I did ask four other Blessingway singers, each taught by a different person, if there were any prescribed foods associated with the Blessingway, either when it is performed for common reasons or for more special occasions such as renewing a Mountain Earth medicine bundle, or *jish*. Salaybe and

Manolescu (2016, 8) include information from one practitioner who says there *are* traditional foods that have to be prepared for the bundle and who identifies them as *waa'* (wild spinach), *haashch'éédą́ą́* (wolfberry), and *neesdoo'* (yucca fruit roll). But the four other singers I asked all disagreed, saying it is up to the practitioner in charge of the Blessingway what ancient foods should be prepared, if any. None of these individuals had been taught that there were any sacred foods associated with the Blessingway except for the Girls' Puberty Ceremony corn cake, and although that is made in the Kinaaldá context, it is well-known, documented, and, most important, made for the benefit of all.

Thus, it seems that there is at least one exception to the rule; this cake is food that is *both* ancient *and* sacred, by definition, but, as Begay said, "It is important to and all right to keep it in this book where it now is." However, people should remember that no ceremonial practitioner divulges all that he or she knows when transmitting sacred knowledge, even to an apprentice. This deliberate withholding of knowledge, which is prescribed, is what protects the person who possesses and holds the knowledge. Another way to say this is "Do nothing in excess." Thus any definitive statements about anything should be avoided.

During further discussions about corn foods, Begay (personal communication, 2016) mentioned another mush, clearly another ancient food, called *gad 'ádin*. When I heard its name, I did not think that Tall Woman had ever told me about it. But when I went back to check on the mushes we had talked about, I discovered that she *had* done so but had not given me any name for it. The name refers to the absence of juniper, *gad*, implying that culinary ash, often made from juniper, is not used when making this mush. *Gad 'ádin*, according to what Begay was taught, was first prepared by Salt Woman for the Twins. It is made from raw, unroasted cornmeal. In time it became associated with traditional weddings. When prepared for that context, both white (for the man) and yellow (for the woman) cornmeal are combined to symbolize the couple coming together.

But in addition to its use in traditional weddings, a ceremony that *is* included in the Blessingway, this mush is used at specific times during some of the Diyin K'é (Holy Ways). On those occasions, if the patient is male, then white cornmeal must be used; for a female patient, yellow cornmeal must be used when the *gad 'ádin* is prepared. But Begay also said that *gad 'ádin* can serve as a first meal on other occasions. Sometimes its "use is more like grits. People get hungry for it and thus just boil some raw unroasted cornmeal and this way make something to eat." At such times the color of the cornmeal does not matter; instead the crucial factor is the absence of juniper ash. The *gad 'ádin* mush can also be used to alleviate medical problems; for example, it is often served to restore a person who is sick, has no appetite, and is unable to keep any other food down. Thus, as a food it can be used in ceremonial contexts, in both Blessingway and curing ceremonies, but also in daily life. As is true with the Kinaaldá's *'alkaan*, people get hungry for *gad 'ádin*, and now they just make it at any time to satisfy that hunger, without the requirement of a ceremonial context.

In closing, given the growing concerns among Navajos about obesity, diabetes, and other health issues and the continuing international expansion of interest in returning to the original ways of raising and growing one's own food, being self-sufficient, and thus expressing sovereignty, Tall Woman's knowledge of food takes on new importance, and it should affect a broader audience than one limited to the reservation. May her knowledge contribute to the current movements toward maintaining a healthy lifestyle, reactivating older subsistence practices, again valuing elders and learning from them about environmental resources and the practices necessary to benefit from them, and reinstituting food sovereignty.

The Commodity Food Program

According to Young (1961, 341–43), the Commodity Food Program, which began distributing commodity foods and augmenting Navajo diets in February 1959, was based on the 1933 federal Commodity Credit Corporation Charter Act, P.L. 108-358.[1] Designed to stabilize farm prices and help farmers suffering from the Great Depression by making loans to them, the act enabled farmers to store nonperishable commodities until prices were better. The 1935 Agricultural Act, specifically section 32 of P.L. 74-320, provided funds for the secretary of agriculture to buy surplus commodities from farmers, thus creating a pool from which such products could be donated to "eligible recipients," who were defined in the act.

But farmers' forfeiting crops to the federal government as payment for the loans led to the government being forced to sell or distribute the crops to domestic programs to avoid spoilage and waste. In 1943 state agencies assumed the administration and financial responsibilities of the donated food program. Other legislation, such as the National School Lunch Act of 1946 and the Agricultural Act of 1949—which added the Bureau of Indian Affairs (BIA) and federal, state, and local public welfare organizations serving needy Indians and other needy persons to other welfare organizations eligible for donated commodities—expanded the scope.

It was up to the states to distribute the commodity foods. According to Young (1961), Navajo Tribal Council resolutions (CJ-10-57) on January 31 and June 20, 1957, approved surplus commodities as part of the Tribal Welfare

Program established on January 31. However, funding for the tribe to be a subdistributing agent for the Arizona State Department of Public Welfare was not passed by the council until 1958 (CA-55-58 and ACA-88-58). Eligibility standards were determined by the state; a person was to be receiving state public assistance or general assistance from the BIA or to have a low income.

The tribe was accountable to the state through monthly reports; commodities were shipped to the nearest railhead, where tribal welfare trucks transferred them to warehouses. In Arizona these were in Tuba City and Window Rock. Distribution schedules were announced on Navajo radio programs broadcasting from Farmington and Gallup, New Mexico, and Flagstaff, Arizona. The Tribe's Public Services Division—the new name, in 1960, for the unit previously called the Community Services Department—assumed the cost of storage, transportation, distribution, and certification of recipients. Despite the spring 1958 planning for distribution and other aspects of the program, as well as the claims by McDonald (1965) and others that the first program for the regular distribution of federally donated surplus commodities began on the Navajo reservation in 1958, there was no actual distribution until February 1959.[2]

At the beginning only four items were available: flour, cornmeal, rice, and dry milk. It is important to remember that each state had its own program, and memories differ about what was actually available in the early days.[3] Three states—New Mexico, Arizona, and Utah—had counties that included some reservation lands. Each of these states handled distribution differently. In New Mexico, for example, the welfare departments in McKinley, San Juan, and Bernalillo Counties were in charge, with state standards determining how much food would be available per person. The county welfare workers certified eligibility and established schedules for monthly distributions. In Arizona and Utah, the Navajo Tribe was the subdistributor for the Arizona State Department of Public Welfare (with warehouses, as noted, at Window Rock and Tuba City). Navajo tribal trucks would haul commodities once a month to each of the fifty-two distribution points, with state standards again determining eligibility and the tribe's welfare department handling distribution. The schedules were known a month in advance, and one could apply at the distribution place on the day of the distribution.

Young (1961) said that by 1960 a fifth item, lard, had been added to the four items listed above. Two Navajo friends said that the 1960 list also included brown sugar, peanut butter, butter, and a bag of raisins. By 1961 the choices had improved, and the list had been expanded to definitely include lard and peanut butter, as well as dry beans and chopped meat, and New Mexico's recipients also definitely got butter as well as cheese. In 1965 all three states were distributing dry milk, flour, cornmeal, rice, lard, peanut butter, dried beans, rolled wheat, and chopped meat, and New Mexico also gave out butter and cheese. Or, as some say, by 1965 between nine and twelve different foods were available, depending on where you lived.[4]

Numerous researchers have pointed out that none of these foods were a source of vitamin C. McDonald (1965, 29–30) also noted that dried eggs were not issued because they could not be kept safely and because of limited cooking equipment and unsafe drinking water. Several groups of nutritionists from the Public Health Service and BIA home demonstration agents gave programs at chapter houses, county buildings, clinics, and elsewhere trying to teach the preparation and use of these foods. Other specialists, such as dietitians, social workers, and nurses, became involved for people with special needs, such as diabetics and pregnant and lactating mothers.

As of the mid-1960s, 60–70 percent of Navajos were receiving surplus commodities, making these supplies extremely important to the population's health and nutrition (McDonald 1965, 28). People were eligible because of low incomes, employment that was only seasonal, and limited numbers of livestock animals. Nevertheless, some refused participation because they did not want to be seen as poor, they had no transportation to get to the distribution sites, and/or they saw commodity food as inferior to other types of food.

Part of the problem one faces when trying to understand the food programs available to the Navajos stems from the confusing name changes some of the programs went through.[5] The program of most importance nationwide as of December 2016 was the Food Distribution Program on Indian Reservations (FDPIR). Established by the Food Stamp Act of 1977 (P.L. 95-113), which also redesigned the Food Stamp Program, the FDPIR "technically came into existence on June 19, 1979, with the publication of a final rule that implemented the program based on the mandate established by the Food Stamp Act of 1977" (Nancy Theodore, personal communication, 2008). All tribes participating in the Needy Family Program before 1979 were transferred to FDPIR in June 1979. The Needy Family Program was not originally administered by the United States Department of Agriculture (USDA) because under the original 1949 legislation, price-support commodities were donated by the USDA to the BIA for distribution to needy families on reservations. The US Food and Nutrition Service (FNS) was formed on May 27, 1969, to coordinate all assistance programs, and that was probably when responsibility for the reservations was transferred from the BIA to the USDA.

In the 1960s, the era of President Lyndon Johnson's War on Poverty, the establishment of the national Office of Economic Opportunity (OEO), and other legislation, commodity distributions were being phased out by the federal government. The August 31, 1964, Food Stamp Act, P.L. 88-525, made the Food Stamp Program permanent and prohibited commodity distribution to households where this program operated, except in disasters. In 1969 another program started: the USDA's Supplemental Food Program for Infants, Preschool Children, and Pregnant and Lactating Mothers, better known as Women, Infants, and Children (WIC). By 1972 both WIC and the Commodity Food Program were being run by the Navajo Tribe, not the individual states. This improved the delivery system and increased participation.

This was also a time of many new service programs, some of which provided jobs and housing development and were sponsored by the OEO. Because of a 1973 court case known as *Andrews v. Butz*, for a while tribes were able to choose to have both the Commodity Food Program and the Food Stamp Programs on their reservations. On August 10, 1973, the Agriculture and Consumer Protection Act, P.L. 93-86, required the national expansion of the Food Stamp Program. In 1974 and with more legislation in 1975, the Commodity Food Program, which provided donated foods to low-income households, officially ended and was replaced by the Food Stamp Program. At first, the reactions to this forced the extension of the Commodity Food Program on Indian reservations until 1977. The tribes had the option of continuing the Commodity Food Program during the phase-in of the Food Stamp Program, and the Navajo Tribe opted to do so during the transition. The Food Stamp Act of 1977 (P.L. 95-113) allowed the tribes to continue the Commodity Food Program along with the Food Stamp Program or to separate from it. The FDPIR was then established in June 1979, as noted above, and the change reportedly improved the variety and quantity of available foods.[6]

At the time of Wolfe's thesis research in 1982 the Navajos were using both programs, with the tribe running the Commodity Food Program and the states running the Food Stamp Program (Wolfe 1984). There were pros and cons for each program; the Commodity Food Program, also known as the Donated Food Program, provided monthly food packages, consisting mainly of dried and canned foods, to eligible families. The Food Stamp Program provided vouchers to those who were eligible, and individuals could not participate in both programs. Wolfe found an increase in enrollment in the Food Stamp Program and a decrease in the number of Commodity Food Program recipients in 1979–1980. People said that the latter program had limited choices and quantities, but it appears that each program was used for different things, with Food Stamps mainly being converted to candy, soda pop, snack foods, and gasoline. Attitudes varied widely; some viewed food stamps as too much hassle, too much red tape, and said that the program's food was not good, that there was not enough of it, and that it was really difficult to re-enroll in the program.

Comments about the Commodity Food Program stressed that it was hard to participate in the program if you did not live near a distribution site. Wolfe's (1984) observations led to her conclusion that the Food Stamp Program at least allowed people to buy fresh fruits and vegetables, to have more choice and variety in their diets, and, as a result, to have better nutrition—yet not everyone used it that way. Seeing that the Commodity Food Program contributed greatly to the intake of most nutrients—especially calcium, less so for fat and vitamin C, and at the 40–50 percent level of all nutrients—Wolfe concluded that it really would be better to offer the Navajos the Food Stamp Program and the Commodity Food Program simultaneously.

Later, Wolfe and Sanjur (1988, 822) noted that for 72 percent of the sample participating in the program, the Commodity Food Program provided 43 percent of caloric intake and 37–57 percent of intake of all other nutrients except fat and vitamin C; this confirmed that the Commodity Food Program was providing an important nutritional contribution to the contemporary Navajo diet. The major source of calcium was the bread group, through the addition of commodity dry milk to tortillas and frybread. Formerly, the major sources of calcium had been milk from sheep and goats along with culinary ash.[7]

Just how much the commodity foods affected meals in a Navajo household depended on many factors, such as who was cooking, how many people needed to be fed, what time of day it was, and what season it was. Individuals developed preferences for certain items over others, and within a family people would often trade foods after returning home from the distribution points. They also shared the foods with family members who were not eligible for the program because of employment or assets. I never recorded the specific commodity items that Tall Woman's family and I picked up on a regular basis in the early 1960s by going to the chapter house in the wagon, but Wolfe (1984) documented commodity food packages for one month in June 1982.[8] As my experiences over the years indicate (confirmed by Wolfe), all six of the Commodity Food Program warehouses did not get the same foods.

People interested in this important aspect of the Navajo diet should continue to follow the developments by visiting the FNS (2015) website (given in note 1), which includes links to SNAP, the Commodities Supplemental Food Program, the FDPIR, and WIC. It also lists various memos released after the passage of the 2014 Farm Bill to explain current changes in all of these programs. For more on the Farm Bill, see USDA (2014; 2015), Nixon (2014), and Wikipedia's five-page article, "The Agricultural Act of 2014."[9]

Farm bills began in 1933 during the Great Depression as part of the New Deal. In 1973 the bills started to include titles on commodity programs, rural development, food and nutrition programs, and other related issues. The agricultural subsidy programs mandated by these bills are always heatedly debated. The current bill, signed into law on February 7, 2014, was two years late, since farm bills are usually passed every five years; the previous one, the Food, Conservation, and Energy Act of 2008, had expired in 2012. The 2014 Farm Bill authorized $956 billion in spending over the next ten years, $756 billion of which was earmarked for food stamps and nutrition.

However, it also included $8 billion worth of cuts to SNAP. According to Feeding America, these cuts "would result in 34 lost meals per month for the affected households" (Nixon 2014). According to USDA (2014), it maintained SNAP eligibility for millions of low-income families, provided $200 million for job training (for those on food stamps), provided $100 million to increase fruit and vegetable purchases, provided $250 million additional funding for the Emergency Food Assistance Program, which supports food banks and food pantries, and authorized $125 million for the Healthy Food Financing Initiative to make nutritious food more accessible. It did, however, put some limits on and also remove some deductions formerly allowed for those on food stamps, and it also ruled that lottery winners and people convicted of certain crimes (murder, aggravated sexual abuse, sexual assault, sexual exploitation, and child abuse) were no longer eligible for food stamps.

As of September 2016, how the changes brought about by the 2014 Farm Bill have affected the Navajos is not yet very apparent. I do know, however, that women depending on WIC programs *are* getting more whole grains, fruits, and vegetables; also, thanks to the USDA's support of the Healthy, Hunger-Free Kids Act, school meals, both at breakfast and lunch, have been reformed for the first time in thirty years to meet the new science-based school meal standards in the National School Lunch Program. Besides getting more exercise in school, children now have meals based on an increase of fruits, vegetables, whole grains, and low-fat dairy and on a reduction of sodium, fat, and sugar. Combining these federal mandates and changes with the Navajo Nation's push to reduce the epidemics of both obesity and diabetes on the reservation, it is hoped that healthier lives will become a reality.

A History of Restaurants in Chinle, Arizona

If you are not particularly interested in the history of the development of fast-food places and other restaurants, or places to eat outside the home in this specific community on the reservation, feel free to skip this appendix. It is presented to document one such history because to the best of my knowledge as of September 30, 2016, we have none. Since the 1960s the residents of Chinle have had access to an ever increasing selection of places to eat as well as places to shop for prepared foods. But just as the 2014 DPI study showed, these foods are almost always those of mainstream America, and thus anything but healthy and nutritious.

I have been able to develop this history only because of much continuing assistance; thus, at the outset, I want to express much gratitude to the following individuals: Jon Colvin, Father Blane Grein, Glenn Stoner, Augusta Sandoval, Mary Jones, Sybil Baldwin, Klara Kelley, and Harris Francis. Colvin came to Chinle in 1969, and in 1971 he started Dineh Cooperatives Inc. As its president, his efforts are supported by his staff, Arthur Newman Jr. and Linda Kee-Rockbridge. Father Blane arrived in 1978 and served as pastor of Our Lady of Fatima Church from 1978 until October 2012. Glenn Stoner came to Chinle in 1966 and lived there serving in numerous capacities for more than four decades before retiring to Flagstaff.

Colvin, Father Blane, and Stoner served on the Chinle Planning Board at various times; Colvin became the secretary in October 1977, Father Blane became a voting member in March 1984, and Stoner joined the board in January 1986 as the Apache County representative. When their terms ended is unknown, but Colvin's office has documents showing that they were all still serving on February 1, 1990. Sometime thereafter the Chinle Planning Board was replaced by the Chinle Land Use Planning Committee, but neither Colvin nor the Chinle chapter has records documenting when this occurred. Augusta Sandoval also provided some information about public eating places before 1970. Other residents, including Harris Francis, Sybil Baldwin, and Jasper Tso, helped by critiquing earlier drafts. Having worked in the community from 1963 to the present, I also drew on my own knowledge in constructing this appendix.

I do not claim that what follows is the last word on the subject or that it wouldn't benefit from input from others familiar with the community through residence, employment, research, or regular visits. Corrections are always welcome. As this account demonstrates, franchises come and go, ownership changes frequently, and sometimes what is transpiring is not clear even to the local people.

According to Colvin and his staff, sometime between 1970 and 1978 Chinle got its *first national fast-food chain*, Kentucky Fried Chicken, run by Mason Burbank in a stand-alone building. Now it is Church's Chicken, run by Michael Nelson. The place was so popular when it first opened that it reportedly won a national award for the greatest sales volume in the state or the region.[1] The Chinle mall, Tséyi' Shopping Center, opened in 1981, with Bashas' supermarket as the anchor store. Bashas' has a deli counter where you can get prepared hot and cold foods, mostly takeout, although there is a small eating place on the second floor.

As of September 16, 2016, the mall also included the following stores and offices: the post office, a long-awaited Ace Hardware, Wells Fargo Bank, H&R Block, the Social Security Administration, the shopping center's management office, Arizona Long Term Care Services, the USDA Natural Resources Conservation Service, and a laundromat. In addition, the following fast-food places could be found in the shopping center: King Dragon (run by Mike Hsu); Burger King (run by Richard Mike), which opened in the winter of 1992 in a stand-alone building next door to the mall; and Pizza Edge, which opened on February 11, 1994, and was formerly Val's Pizza (which had opened on June 21, 1987, and closed on June 20, 1992).[2]

Tenants came and went, as the above illustrates. At one point there was an ice cream store just north of Bashas', Rainbow Ice Cream, which opened in September 1981. For a while its focus was on numerous flavors of ice cream, but after several years it added hamburgers and other sandwiches. The original owners, Gayle and Lorenzo Chacon, closed the store in August 1986, selling it to her parents, Frank and Galena Dineyazhe. They (and for a while another daughter, Cynthia) operated the new store as Sunrise Ice Cream from October 17, 1986, until November 14, 1992, when it closed.

For twenty years there was a Taco Bell in the Tséyi' Shopping Center, east of the post office. The franchise, owned by George and Wilma Tiara of Gallup, opened on March 9, 1987, and was managed from the beginning by Julia Claw. She obtained an ownership interest and ultimately a controlling interest, but when the corporate office required a new building to extend the franchise, Julia Claw opted to retire instead. For a while she investigated the possibility of leasing land across from the junior high school, with the idea that her daughter and son-in-law, Colleen and Daniel Yazzie, would run a new restaurant, but that never materialized. The Tiaras closed the Chinle Taco Bell on March 8, 2007. By May 15, 2008, its place had been taken by King Dragon.

There was also an A&W restaurant in a stand-alone building on land leased by Fleming D. Begaye Sr. and subleased from him. After suffering two fires, the place closed, and it was boarded up in the fall of 2013. Its future continues to remain unknown at present.

When I came to Chinle in June 1963, the northeast corner (where US Route 191 and Navajo Route 7 intersect) was known as Begaye's Corner. Here Fleming Begaye Sr., one of the original Navajo Code Talkers, had a lease and had developed a business that included a Shell gas station, an automobile repair shop, a convenience store, and a small restaurant or café. Begaye told Augusta Sandoval that he opened his café and store on April 25, 1960. She worked for him as his cook during the summers when she was not working for the Chinle school system, from around 1962 until 1975. She started working at Fleming's Café the same year that her family moved back to its home next to her parents, from its earlier location up by the Catholic mission. Augusta said that Fleming brought in bottled gas and hooked it up so that they had hot water to wash dishes. The café's kitchen, where Augusta worked, was in the back, where there was also a large porch for deliveries. She said that the south and east walls of the café were painted with scenes of Canyon de Chelly by either Robert or Teddy Draper, known artists in Chinle.[3]

Augusta also reported that the garage and auto repair shop were on the bottom floor of a separate two-story building behind Begaye's main building; the second floor of this building had office space that Begaye rented out.The Begayes lived behind this building (which was eventually torn down) in a big pinkish-red house set back slightly to the north and east; it's still there. Fleming and his wife, Helen Tso Begaye, raised three children there; Helen and the two sons are now dead, and the daughter, Veronica was living with her dad in 2015. Nearby, Helen's sister's former home has become a church. When Helen got sick, the Giant company moved in and opened a small grocery store and a laundromat in the space that had been Begaye's convenience store. According to Colvin, Begaye received an award for his business because of its location, size, and rarity in the 1960s as a Navajo-owned business. At present, the Shell gas station (subleased by Giant), laundromat, and convenience store are still operating.

East of Begaye's Corner was a business site leased by Paul Tso (Helen's brother), who was a judge in Chinle at one time. Stoner remarked that Paul was a retired judge, not a businessman; others said that he had a farm in Many Farms and lived in Valley Store at one point. He had at least two sisters (as well as other siblings): besides Helen, there was Martha, who married Teddy Draper Sr. Their father was Zhealy Tso, who played a role in Frank Mitchell's earlier days in Chinle (Mitchell [1978] 2003). In September 2016 this site included a large area of empty land, east of which was a walkway from three public housing areas to the high school, the Silver Coin Car Wash, and the Silver Coin Laundry and Video.

According to Stoner, back in 1966 this area, now empty, included a service station, a convenience store that also housed the Arizona DMV office, and Tso's Drive-In restaurant. Paul Tso finally built a home when Stoner took over the drive-in; until then, he and his family had lived in each building he added for his business. Later he added a feed store, too. Tso's businesses were in competition with Begaye's; even though they were brothers-in-law, "they were not close friends in the business sense," Stoner explained. Stoner subleased the area from Tso and went into business in 1966, beginning with the service station and adding an auto parts store with mechanics who could fix cars.

Stoner took over the restaurant in 1967 or 1968, at first continuing its earlier name, Tso's Drive-In. Stoner said he had made it a good restaurant, in contrast to Tso: "Paul was not set up for lots of people, and if there were too many standing around waiting, he'd just shut the door and close up, lock up. . . . Tso changed its name to Tso's Café when he finally added a dining room with three or four booths so it could be a sit-down place, not just a drive-in with drive-through windows." Stoner "hired a cook and drink servers." His most popular menu items were the Wildcat Burger (Wildcats are the Chinle High School mascot) with greasy fries invented by his cook, and there was also a once-a-week Mexican food night. Some local people started calling the restaurant Stoner's Café. Augusta said the restaurant was "more like a sandwich shop, really small, with only two or three tables where you could sit and eat." In the summer Nancy Preston, who cooked for the school, cooked for the restaurant. The back room, where the Tsos had lived earlier, was cleaned out so that special events could be accommodated. Stoner also located his justice of the peace office in that area.

Next Stoner wanted to lease the convenience store from Tso, and because his wife at that time wanted him to add a beauty shop and a barber shop, he added an old trailer behind the restaurant in which to house those services; he also added several other trailers for employee housing. He said that the beauty and barber shops were a disaster.

Stoner thinks that he took over Tso's whole lease (which extended all the way east to the Silver Coin Laundry) in 1969. At that point he had a Texaco service station, an auto parts store, a wrecker service, a restaurant (Stoner's Café), a convenience store, and the barber and beauty shops. Stoner's businesses thrived until 1973–1974, when "a bitter, hard-fought divorce made everything fall apart." He restored his businesses by working long hours, and in 1977 he became more involved in the community, successfully running for the school board and serving for two years. He was chosen to serve as the justice of the peace and eventually as a member of the Chinle Planning Board.

A few years later Stoner decided he wanted out of his businesses; planning to get married again, he reportedly offered businessman George Hartsock Sr. "a great deal he couldn't refuse."[4] In either late 1979 or early 1980, Stoner sold his sublease to Evangeline (Vangie) Hartsock and George Hartsock Sr.; at that time all the businesses mentioned above were open and running. The Hartsocks planned to remodel. Eventually George reopened the Texaco gas station, behind which was a fenced area and a towing place run by their son George Jr.

To the east, on the other side of Silver Coin, George Sr. erected two metal buildings joined together, which housed a hardware store and a variety store. He also added a lumberyard. Their son Joey ran the hardware store, Vangie ran the variety store, and their daughter, Patricia (Trish), ran the restaurant (earlier Tso's Café and Stoner's Café, but eventually renamed SCooters after Trish's first child). Various members of the Hartsock family lived in a two-story house right behind the hardware and variety stores.

After Joey left, Vangie took over the hardware store. When neither the gas station nor the hardware store worked out, Vangie worked in the restaurant with Trish; that did well, unlike other parts of the business. Stoner said that the Hartsocks had "real bad luck running things," and in a short amount of time things fell apart. The Texaco station caught on fire and George Sr. boarded it up. Pretty soon everything else was shut down except the restaurant. Later there was a big fire that damaged part of the Hartsock home but not the trailer. Although the burned-out house and the trailer remained on the site for several decades (during which time the Hartsocks eventually lost their lease), they were demolished in December 2015, leaving the land empty.

East of the Hartsocks' lease area on the north side of Route 7 was Sybil Baldwin's land. As of September 2016, the structures there were a blue trailer, a blue metal storage building with the sign HAY FOR SALE, and a feed store. Further east was the road into three of the public housing areas in Chinle and the Chinle Wash. The major Baldwin business, a service station and convenience store, was on the south side of Route 7. After Sybil's death in November 2002, Conoco moved in and took over.

Augusta noted that while she was working as a cook for Fleming Begaye Sr., Ben Hess had a big doughnut shop where the Silver Coin Laundry is today. At that time, to the east, there was an empty space where the car wash is now, then the doughnut shop, then the Silver Coin Laundry, and then Hartsock's metal buildings and lumberyard. The first person hired to work in the doughnut shop was Mary Tayah. Stoner described Hess as "a heavyset Mormon from Monticello, Utah" and said that his shop, Spudnitt (possibly a takeoff on Spudnuts, then a well-known brand of potato-flour doughnuts) served coffee and doughnuts. When Hess closed that place, he started the Silver Coin Laundry and also built a hay barn out back. His plans to sell hay from there didn't work out, but the building was still there in September 2016, apparently being used for storage. East of the barn is a white residential trailer, and adjoined to the back of Silver Coin is a two-story building that also appears to be a residence. Stoner also said that Hess built the space where a video store is now, but he doesn't remember what Hess had in there—"maybe knickknacks." (Colvin knows nothing about this doughnut shop and says that it clearly had to be earlier than 1969, when he arrived in Chinle.)

Elsewhere in the community, a Subway sandwich shop (inside the former Baldwin's Mini Mart) opened in either 2005 or 2006 (the current management doesn't remember). Baldwin's Mini Mart and gas station, run by Sybil Baldwin and some of her sons, was on the south side of Route 7. It sold a limited number of basic groceries, but until Subway replaced it (after it was no longer Baldwin's), you couldn't get meals there. Other places to eat included Church's Chicken, Burger King, and a restaurant named La Casa Blanca, possibly built by Robert Martinez (called "Kiddy" or even "Felix Jr." by some).[5] Martinez, a contractor, also built the Imperial Mart building on the north side of Route 7.

The restaurant, on the south side of the highway (where Cellular One is now) was run first by Robert Martinez and then by his brother Stanley, as was the Imperial Mart. Other members of the Martinez family—including the parents, Felix Sr. and Rosita; two other brothers of Stanley's, Hank (Henry, called Jughead by some) and Ray; and maybe one of his sisters, Ruthie—helped out in the restaurant for a while. Stoner said that when La Casa Blanca opened, he feared it would drive him out of business by the end of the summer, "but it didn't hurt my business one bit." Later Ray took over running La Casa Blanca. Ray was married to Roberta Nez from Chinle; he ran Ray's Western Wear, next to the Imperial Mart, along with the restaurant. Eventually, he and his wife went to Albuquerque and other places for contracting work. La Casa Blanca was taken over by Dale Nelson but eventually went out of business.

Stanley Martinez told Father Blane that everything on both sides of the road was under one corporation; Stanley and his wife, Rose Wallace Martinez, owned everything, and ran the Imperial Mart. They had three children: David, Debbie, and Stanley Jr. Stanley Sr.'s brother Hank was married to Lorraine Sanchez; they had three children, and Hank ran the Malco gas station, auto repair shop, and service garage next to the Imperial Mart. He also sometimes worked at Big O Tires. After Hank retired and went to either Maricopa or Phoenix, Stanley Sr. and his son David remodeled the gas station by making bays where the gas pumps had been, to work on tires; they also fixed up the entrance and the old office, put in racks in the back to hold all the tires, and created a waiting room where people could sit and watch television while their cars were being serviced. When this was completed, Debbie, who was very artistic, got a Big O franchise and ran the business for at least a decade. She did not renew the franchise, however, and moved to Sedona; then Stanley Sr. shut down Big O.

More than a year after the Tséyi' Shopping Center opened (and Bashas' arrived), Stanley also closed the Imperial Mart and converted it into office spaces.[6] David now runs the Navajo Glass Art Studio and Gallery in the basement of the former La Casa Blanca restaurant. After a while Robert, the contractor, went into education and eventually moved to either Show Low or Phoenix. Other siblings also moved away; Ruthie went to Texas with her daughter, and the other sister, Isabelle, went to Albuquerque. Both Stanley Sr. and his wife, Rose, served on the Chinle School Board for a while. Even after Stanley's term was up, Rose remained on the board for many years. She eventually retired, became ill, and passed away in June 2014.

On November 29, 2015, Denny's, the community's *first sit-down chain restaurant,* opened in Chinle. Located east of the office building on the north side of Route 7 and owned by Romero Brown (who also owns the Denny's franchise in St. Michaels), the restaurant reportedly brought eighty additional jobs to the community. Brown stated that he hopes to open a motel behind the Chinle Denny's similar to the Navajoland Inn and Suites behind his franchise in St. Michaels (Yurth 2015). While working in Chinle during the summer of 2016, I heard many comments about the new Denny's. A number of people had tried it once and had already decided that they were not going to return unless they heard from others that things had improved. The taking of orders and the delivery of the food were said to be unacceptably slow. Allegedly, despite a number of complaints about this, there had been no improvements. The other problem, voiced mainly by older residents, was that there had been no cleansing ceremony done on the site, where the original owner, Tom Cullison, had been murdered. Until that happened, the elders said, it was just too dangerous to go there.

For a short time travelers and others could get something to eat in the dining room at the "Big House." This was a two-story trading post and hotel originally built in the spring of 1916 by Hubbell, sold to C. N. Cotton probably in

1918, and then managed, after others, by Camillo Garcia from 1920 until it closed in 1923 (Frisbie 1998).

As of September 2016, besides the places mentioned above, there were three other places to "eat out" in Chinle: the Junction Restaurant, the Holiday Inn, and the cafeteria associated with the Thunderbird Lodge.

The Junction Restaurant became part of the Best Western Canyon de Chelly Motel. Owned originally by Roland and Rosita LaFont, Roland added a second floor to one section of the motel and added the Junction Restaurant in the middle. Because he didn't want to compete with Stoner's Café across the road, LaFont waited to add his restaurant until Stoner sold his sublease to the Hartsocks. The same year (around 1986), he also bought the motel outside Monument Valley. The LaFonts sold the Canyon de Chelly Motel to a party in Phoenix years ago.

The Holiday Inn is where Garcia's Trading Post used to be. The post, purchased by Camillo and Pauline Garcia in either 1920 or 1923 from an unidentified individual (Frisbie 1998, 81n2), closed in either December 1985 or early 1986, evidently then becoming a tribal property. Despite an initial interest in seeking national historic site status for the post since it was about a mile west of the Canyon de Chelly National Monument Visitor's Center, the 6.4-acre property was eventually sold to Ocean Properties Ltd. for economic development purposes. The Holiday Inn construction began on June 7, 1992, and the grand opening was October 15 of that year.

The Thunderbird Lodge was owned by Mary and Chet Jones from Gallup, who purchased it on February 15, 1984, from the LaFont family. The property was operated under a concession agreement with the National Park Service (NPS) because of its location near the Canyon de Chelly National Monument. The Joneses signed a twenty-year contract with the NPS to operate the Thunderbird for a monthly franchise fee. The contract required them to build additional motel rooms and provide additional landscaping. The NPS set the hours of operation, motel room rates, cafeteria food, gift shop items, truck tours, and practically everything else.

Mary originally negotiated the purchase with Roland LaFont; he and his brother, Gerald, were then in charge of daily operations after their parents retired. The Joneses' corporation, White Dove, Inc., was the NPS concessionaire; Mary was the corporation president and owner of the Thunderbird Lodge. Mary was well-loved in the Navajo community even though she was

Anglo. Her twenty-year contract was extended one year at a time from 2004 to 2012 and then again briefly until midnight on February 11, 2013.

As of February 12, 2013, the day after Mary Jones's contract ended, ownership changed to the Shadi Company, headed by Armanda Ortega-Gordon and Rebecca Ortega, who were reportedly half-Navajo. According to Yurth (2013), after the NPS began strenuous, serious, grant-supported work to eradicate a dense forest of invasive tamarisk and Russian olive trees in the canyon, the Ortegas got several Navajos to plant twenty peach trees on farms in the canyon as part of a project to "reclaim the lost heritage and heal the land." The Ortegas were "first-time Native American full-service concessionaires in NPS." They changed the name to the Sacred Canyon Lodge and did not want to do canyon tours.

When the Ortegas' contract expired on December 20, 2015, the Navajo Nation Hospitality Enterprise purchased the property, changed the signage to HISTORIC TRADING POST, and changed its name back to the Thunderbird Lodge, much to the happiness of the local residents and others aware of the Thunderbird's long history and historical significance.

You can also buy some fast food at three gas stations, mainly from machines. The former Thriftway near the Mormon church as well as the Shell station at the junction of US 191 and Route 7 are now both Shell stations and convenience stores run by the Giant Corporation. The third place is a Chevron station and store owned first by Eddie Arthur and then bought by the Navajo Nation Oil and Gas Company. The leaseholder of Giant's Shell station at the junction, which may have been the first gas station in Chinle, was Fleming D. Begaye Sr.[7]

As the information in this appendix makes clear, at least in Chinle some of the fast-food places have changed hands over time, and some of the physical locations have changed from one franchise to another. Besides tracking the franchises—where they have been, how long they have existed in various communities, and under whose management they have been operated—researchers would like to know which people eat fast food, how often, and why. Are the customers mainly schoolchildren hungry for snacks at the end of the day, workers needing a snack on the way to or from work, or an unemployed family member who is running errands stopping to get takeout for the family's dinner because everybody will be too tired to cook when they get home? Are they local families having lunch or dinner either by eating inside the restaurant or picking up food through the drive-through lane? Or are they mainly tourists, who make up a good part of the restaurant business at certain times of year in Chinle? What about food sales at flea markets or by vendors who circulate through offices and laundromats and who set up stands outside various stores and along the roadsides? Are they selling Spam burritos and banana bread or more traditional foods like kneel-down bread and tamales? Could anyone involved with the DPI (2014) study and healthy diet programs now work with the vendors to encourage a shift to healthy traditional foods? And given the ongoing changes in the fast-food industry to offer healthier choices because of the widespread problems of obesity and diabetes, are any of these changes noticeable in these industries on the reservation?[8]

NOTES

Introduction

1. This work is another piece of my earlier work with Tall Woman. Even though the Navajo Nation Historic Preservation Department (NNHPD) and its procedures for requesting research permits for ethnographic and archaeological work was not established until 1990, I obtained a permit for ongoing work with the information that Tall Woman had given me. Her story (Mitchell 2001) went through the required manuscript review by the department's Cultural Resources Compliance Section before publication, and some materials that were withheld from publication were filed in a confidential appendix in that department's office in Window Rock, Arizona. Since the information Tall Woman gave me on plants and their medical and ceremonial uses has already been filed, only a few additions to that appendix have been generated by the current work. They concern some of the things I learned about the ceremonial uses of specific foods during my discussions with both Tall Woman and ceremonial practitioners. The present work was shared with the NNHPD in April 2016, when the University of New Mexico Press sent it out for external review. On July 12, 2016, I met with Tamara Billie, the senior archaeologist at the Cultural Resources Compliance Section, and Timothy C. Begay, a Navajo cultural specialist at the Traditional Culture Program, to discuss the project in detail, answer questions, and share the external reviewers' reports. At the end of this meeting the NNHPD staff approved the work for publication; a record of this approval is now on file with the NNHPD.

2. My first work was followed by studies of the House Blessing Ceremony (Frisbie 1970), Navajo medicine bundles, or *jish* (Frisbie 1987), and temporal change in Navajo religion (Frisbie 1992) and recording the life stories of Frank Mitchell (Mitchell [1978] 2003) and his wife, Tall Woman (Mitchell 2001). I also pursued

work on gender issues in Navajo music, boarding school experiences, Chinle history (Frisbie 1998), and a variety of other topics.

3. Kelley and Francis (2006–2015; forthcoming) compiled information on all the trading posts and continually updated it. The original work, unrevised and unfinished, was online, and that was the version I used. The trading posts listed are retail stores that offer general merchandise in exchange for commodities or money, at least partly through secured or unsecured credit. The list includes stores in and around Navajoland with significant Navajo clientele. It excludes stores in major border towns and those established after 1980. The authors incorporate Navajo historical perspectives on individual trading posts, since non-Navajo perspectives dominate the literature. They emphasize Navajo store owners and managers in the entries and in the biographical sketches of the traders who are or were Navajos. By January 1, 2016, the work was no longer online. I regret now that I did not keep track of my own trading post trips and what transpired during them more closely. For an important work see Russell (1991).

4. Since 2001 my own research endeavors have mainly remained focused on Navajo topics, but they have not necessarily involved the Mitchells, except for writing Howard Mitchell's obituary for the *Navajo Times* and drafting an obituary for his brother Seya. From 2002 to 2007, my major efforts went into preparing the application necessary to get the Franciscan Mission Historic District in Chinle recognized and accepted by both the Arizona State Historic Preservation Office (AZSHPO) and the National Register of Historic Places. That was successful in June 2007; in the interim I coauthored the centennial book for Our Lady of Fatima Parish with Father Blane Grein (Grein and Frisbie 2005), and we began restoration work on the Annunciation Mission at the request of the parish. Thus far, while I was writing other articles and reviews (e.g., Frisbie 2012, 2015, 2016), we have saved the 1909 building, replaced the roof, and repaired the outside, and now we are working on the inside, all in consultation with the NNHPD and AZSHPO. I continue to make regular reports to the parish and the diocese and to spearhead fund-raising in the hope of completing the project in the foreseeable future.

As I shifted gears to refocus on Tall Woman's recipes, I started researching relevant literature on Navajo diets through time, the Commodity Food Program, the Navajo Nation food distribution programs, food and health, food sovereignty, and the rapidly expanding global concerns about the relationships among foods, eating habits, obesity, diabetes, the environment, history, sovereignty, drought, farmers' markets, the Supplemental Nutrition Assistance Program, and the US Farm Bill.

I returned to Tall Woman's data on foods in 2010 after completing some other projects. Researching and trying to understand the federal, state, and Navajo Nation food programs consumed almost a year; multiple drafts of appendix A were generated until those who read it believed I had developed a clear description of how these programs worked, or were supposed to work. As time became available, I also started computerizing all the information Tall Woman had ever given me about foods and all the discussions we had had about food resources and how they were utilized.

A certain degree of familiarity with the Navajos (the largest Indian nation in the United States) and the American Southwest is assumed in this work. Thus, readers should be comfortable with the *j* spelling of Navajo, settled by tribal resolution in April 1969, and be familiar with the traditional Navajo home known in English as a *hogan*. The hogan can be of several different styles, building materials, and shapes, although circular or polygonal (with six or eight sides) are perhaps the most common shapes. A hogan usually consists of a single room and has one doorway, which faces east. Although many Navajos today live in other kinds of dwellings, such as public housing, trailers, or rectangular-frame houses, the multisided hogan is still considered to be the only appropriate place to hold a ceremony (Jett and Spencer 1981). Readers should know that the Navajo reservation includes land in three states—Arizona, New Mexico, and Utah, totaling more than 27,400 square miles—and should be aware that Navajos refer to themselves as the Diné, which means "the People."

In addition to this background, which is readily supported by extensive research and publications, some editorial matters concerned with this work must be discussed. In the matters of orthography, I decided to follow the standard practice of using the Navajo orthography developed by Young and Morgan (1980, 1987), except in a few cases where family linguistic practices differed. In those cases, the term or phrase is given in Navajo in italics, transliterated as pronounced by Tall Woman or members of her family, and followed by an interpreter's English translation. In some areas, such as wild food resources, there seemed to be frequent instances in which the Navajo terms she gave me did not match those given in any published dictionaries or other resources concerned with the Navajo language. For the current work, these instances led to interesting discussions about linguistic particulars with colleagues on the phone, face-to-face, and by e-mail. The glossary was developed to provide a list of the Navajo terms used herein; variants, sometimes caused by regional differences in speech practices, are included when they were apparent. The Latin names of plants (genus and species), when known, may also be found in the glossary.

As the food data were entered into my computer, questions and the need for clarification became obvious. I began setting aside time when I was in Arizona working on the restoration of the Annunciation Mission to start addressing these issues. Several employees of the Navajo Nation in Window Rock were involved in helping with appendix A; a number of members of the community of Chinle were involved in the construction of appendix B. And, of course, members of Tall Woman's family were involved in answering questions that had arisen while I was processing data. Thus I did additional fieldwork in 2010–2016, with at least two trips a year to Arizona to address the questions that emerged. Sometimes a trip might be focused mainly on working with the DPI at Diné College in Tsaile, Arizona, and the food sovereignty project there. Sometimes traveling was done mainly to find elders in other communities, all in their nineties or older, to seek clarification about certain food resources, their preparation, and other related matters.

During the additional fieldwork I also searched for tools comparable to those used by Tall Woman (none of which were extant within the family), for one kind of oven she built and used as well as for illustrations for this work. Once her daughters started to see the data I had from their mother, we had a number of discussions about organizational details. Augusta Sandoval ended up being my major helper on cooking details after her mother passed away. She had a major role in reviewing possible organizational schemes, considering common organizations of cookbooks, and comparing and reviewing others in existence that focused on a specific Native American tribe or on Native American foods in general. Although I remain indebted to all who helped, I increasingly realized that it was more than appropriate to include some information about Augusta's life to illustrate how she became a professional cook. In May 2015, with her help, I developed the description that follows, and after several revisions I present it here with her approval. For other details, see both of her parents' life stories, Mitchell ([1978] 2003) and Mitchell (2001).

The eleventh of Tall Woman and Frank Mitchell's twelve children, Augusta was born on August 14, 1928, and (as of June 2017) has one remaining sibling, Isabelle Deschine. Augusta attended the government boarding school in Chinle, Arizona, for grades one through six (1935–1943), with one school year at the Fort Defiance boarding school (1936–37). From there she went to St. Michaels boarding school for junior high, and then, in 1945, to St. Catherine's in Santa Fe for high school. After two years there, she went to Riverside Indian School in Anadarko, Oklahoma, and graduated in 1949.

As is well-known, the boarding schools were organized on a military model, with boys and girls separated and assigned to numerous kinds of jobs that rotated every two weeks—including cleaning the schools, since there were no janitors (Frisbie 1996). The children had to be up before dawn, which was not a new experience for Augusta, since Frank and Tall Woman had raised her that way. In fourth grade, Augusta was assigned with other girls to help with kitchen work: peeling potatoes and carrots and washing fruits and vegetables. Both boys and girls had other kitchen or dining room jobs, including cleaning off tables, sweeping and mopping floors, and scrubbing pots and pans. The cooks handled the food.

At Chinle and St. Michaels, students also took care of cows, pigs, and chickens, with the boys milking the dairy cows and the girls feeding the chickens and being responsible for the successful raising of the baby chicks. Girls also learned how to sew by hand and on machines, do embroidery, make clothing, cook, clean the dorms, and wash and iron laundry. Different skills were taught each year. At St. Michaels a teacher named Sister Victoria took a special interest in Augusta and taught her how to construct "a log cake that had to be rolled up"; this resulted in Augusta's very first cooking prize. Also at St. Michaels, kitchen duty included getting the coal and wood from outside and building the fires in the two big kitchen stoves every morning before going to Mass at six o'clock. On weekends the children were also expected to make sack lunches.

At Riverside Augusta was again assigned to the kitchen but detailed to different jobs. For the first time, the girls had to wear aprons and were allowed to help with the actual food preparation and with serving the students. Riverside had an automatic dishwasher, but all other jobs continued as before.

When Augusta graduated from Riverside she returned to Chinle and worked as a switchboard operator at the boarding school for several months. When dial technology came in, she was asked to move to Window Rock, where the main switchboard would be located, but she declined. Instead she started working as a substitute matron in the boarding school dorms. For about six months she lived upstairs in the Employees Club with other staff members, and she got to know a Mrs. Pucha, a Hopi woman who was the cook there. One day Augusta asked her if she needed any help, and Mrs. Pucha said yes. The employees were served three meals a day, and others stopped to eat there, too, sometimes bringing visitors. In the summer it was common for movie crews staying at the Thunderbird Lodge to have sack lunches prepared in the kitchen at the Employees Club. Augusta's memories included the automatic dishwasher there and learning recipes from Mrs. Pucha, including how to make lemon meringue pie, which was made every Sunday.

Augusta says she got into cooking when she started working at the public schools. But first she filled in as a boarding school matron for Ruth Winney, who was on sick leave. Augusta had been collecting recipes the whole time, and after helping Mrs. Pucha, she told me, she "went over to the Thunderbird with other ladies to watch how they did things in the kitchen over there." Eventually she applied for a job there as a dishwasher. The LaFonts, who owned the Thunderbird, hired her, and when their cook didn't show up one day, Augusta asked to be a waitress. One of the bosses wasn't pleased with how she worked, because she stopped to talk with the customers and be friendly. But the two LaFont boys, Roland and Gerald, who gave jeep tours in the canyon while they were home from college for the summer, stood up for her.

After another discussion with Mrs. LaFont, Augusta was moved to the snack bar, where she worked all by herself. The snack bar offered hamburgers and sandwiches of cold roast beef, cold cuts, and tuna salad, as well as canned soup, chips, and french fries. In time, and for about a month, Augusta was also making breakfast and dinner. The Anglo cook for the restaurant prepared the meats and stews used in the snack bar, but Augusta made the hamburgers, sandwiches, soups, and tuna salad. The LaFont boys helped her as time permitted. Augusta recalls that she worked there for two summers and then had a summer job taking care of a nurse's two children in Winslow; her brother, Seya, took her home on weekends or back to Flagstaff, where he and his family lived at that time.

For a while thereafter, Augusta cooked and cleaned for the Franciscan Fathers at the mission in Chinle; she and her family moved up there in October 1959 from the new home they had built during the summer of 1958 near her parents. Chinle built a public elementary school in the late 1950s, and Augusta applied for a job there as a dishwasher in 1959. However, she was hired as a cook instead and gradually worked her way up to become the head cook. In the summer of 1962 she and her family moved back to their own home. When the new Chinle High School opened in December 1963, she was hired as the head cook there. That, as she said, is when she really got into cooking. Personnel changes were frequent in the food service departments at different schools, so Augusta expanded her skills at running a kitchen, planning and creating meals, evaluating employees, and hiring and firing them.

Since the school jobs were on nine-month contracts, Augusta also started working for Fleming Begaye Sr. a year or two after he opened his café in 1960 (see appendix B). The salary there was much better than what the schools paid her. However, she had to work many late hours because the café offered breakfast, lunch, and dinner. She kept working for Begaye during the summers until 1975, when the school district started the Summer Food Service Program (SFSP), which offered free lunches for eligible schoolchildren in the summer. This gave her a twelve-month contract, which was what she wanted.

While serving as the head cook at the Chinle High School, Augusta began to think about retirement. But in 1974 she was chosen to attend a one-week government-sponsored class on traditional foods held at the University of Arizona; she contributed a number of Navajo recipes (Sandoval 1974), as did participants from the San Carlos Apache and Hualapai Nations. In 1976 Augusta was named the food service superintendent on a ten-month contract; that meant supervising nine kitchens and driving around to all of them in an older-model green jeep: Chinle's four kitchens (at the kindergarten and the elementary, junior high, and high schools) and five others (at Many Farms, Tsaile, Red Mesa, Round Rock, and Sweetwater). Eventually the organizational structure was changed so that Round Rock, Red Mesa, and Sweetwater were put under Shiprock's supervision rather than Chinle's.

Augusta filled in the other two months working with the SFSP, which had been fully implemented in 1975. When her food service superintendent contract ended, instead of returning to Chinle High School as she had been promised, a bureaucratic snafu sent her to Tsaile Elementary School in the fall of 1977. She had to commute daily from Chinle until housing became available in Tsaile in January 1978. Augusta was the head cook at Tsaile until she officially retired in October 1992. However, those who retired at that point were brought back to work through May 1993, so it wasn't until June 11, 1993, that she officially moved back to Chinle for good. By that time, both of her parents had passed away, and four of her own six children had made her a grandmother.

Augusta's love of cooking continues to be expressed in her interest in trying new recipes; being supportive of the discussions and other work entailed in finalizing her mother's recipes for this volume; making her famous bread, rolls, banana bread, and other dishes for people, sometimes upon request for certain functions; and being interested in international foods and the issues being highlighted in the food sovereignty movement, which has become global. She and I are "sisters" and have been for years, and I can't thank her enough for her help with finalizing this project.

5. Among the many parts of this project that I found interesting were the conversations about the final organization of the recipes. I had a number of discussions with Tall Woman's daughters about how this should be done. In August 2012, after going through stacks of standard Anglo cookbooks as well as some of the Southwestern ones I brought with me, we first identified what would *not* be included: there were to be no sections for appetizers, snacks, salads, poultry, fish, dairy dishes, eggs, pastries, desserts, and cocktails. Then we hammered out a plan that essentially consisted of identifying what *should* be included and, in some cases, what should be grouped together: soups, stews, and mush; sweeteners; cheese; salt; gravy; shortening; juniper ash; sausage; jerky; meat from both wild and domesticated animals; beverages; breads; and fruits and vegetables, each divided into wild ones gathered versus cultivated crops. These ideas were further refined during discussions in May and August 2014. When I returned to Chinle in May, I had finally entered all of Tall Woman's food data into my computer and was just starting to do the same for the recipes she had given me years earlier. Once the family was able to visualize different topics and the kinds of data we had, it became possible to sort the printed pages into piles and to try different arrangements of both sections and groupings. We then let these rest overnight and returned the next day for more discussions. On August 21, 2014, the final organization that you see in this book was agreed upon. We also identified possible illustrations at this time. The inclusion in the glossary of the scientific names of plants, when known, was suggested by Wendy Wolfe.

In 2015, while sharing our decisions about organizing the recipes, I was immediately reminded that people have different mental or cognitive maps and organizational schemes, even in the same family. When I made it clear I was going to respect Tall Woman's family's scheme for the recipes, I was given different points of view by other Navajos on how we should be organizing things.

Clearly, the scheme used herein is just one possible map of a cognitive domain that ethnoscientists or cognitive anthropologists might call "traditional foods." It would undoubtedly prove interesting to discover the different taxonomies that other Navajos use.

6. The sources most helpful on Navajo food habits are Wolfe (1981, 1984, 11–35), Steggerda and Eckhardt (1940), Bailey (1940), Elmore (1943), McDonald (1965), Darby, Salsbury, and McGariety (1956), Johnson (1973), Bailey and Bailey (1986), Kopp (1986), Iverson (2002), and Eldridge (2012). Among the very best readily available resource now is *Leading the Way: The Wisdom of the Navajo People.* "A teaching publication that seeks to give youth and families the foundation of what it means to be Navajo," this colorful monthly magazine is edited and produced by Kathleen Manolescu, at Kmanolescu@gmail.com. "*Leading the Way* features the voices of elders and medicine people from all over the reservation; it recognizes the importance of the Navajo language and publishes articles in and about the language regularly, as well as special articles for and about youth. It also frequently includes articles about food and nutrition, and step-by-step instructions for making traditional recipes, with those featuring corn being especially valued" (Manolescu, personal communication, 2013).

Chapter 1

1. As of 2016, discussions of Navajo ancestry include many voices with diverse opinions. Rather than get involved in these issues in this work, I have opted for a balanced view that includes reference to both the indigenous points of view, or the traditional Navajo explanations, and those belonging to outsider anthropologists. Instead of perpetuating the old scholarly dichotomy between Navajos and Pueblos, I have touched on various viewpoints about Navajo ancestry. I realize that this does not satisfy those who now support ethnogenesis explanations, or just presenting the indigenous viewpoint. To do so would require delving into and discussing the spiritual and philosophical beliefs and practices of the Navajos, and many of these are not to be shared with outsiders.

2. When asked about what he had been taught about the creation of wild and domesticated animals, Steven Begay (personal communication, 2016, 2017) said that a collaboration of several Holy People were responsible, including Talking God, Begochidí, Dibé Dooltsoodí, Coyote, and even Changing Woman. Horse and sheep were created under the cover of plants. Cattle were considered to be the jealous relatives of the buffalo. The donkey is a combination of all the left-overs of all the domestic animals that were thrown out to the ash pile. This is why donkeys roll in ashes.

3. Dry farming uses no irrigation but instead depends on rain. The places chosen tend to stay wet by themselves. Although some such farms are in high

mountainous areas, most are in valleys and canyons (Bingham and Bingham 1979; Jett n.d.).

4. Other sources suggest adding wild celery, cattail, wild buckwheat roots, different cacti, pigweed, and milkweed to this list, along with various greens, roots, berries, and other food sources. Clearly location affected resources.

5. Those interested in the earliest food resources used by the Navajos are encouraged to see a variety of life histories of people born in the nineteenth century and the extensive lists of plants, seeds, fruits, berries, animals, birds, insects, and ways of preparing food in both the Franciscan Fathers (1910) and Matthews ([1902] 1995). Even Yazzie's (2014, 2016) two novels provide information. Bailey (1940) also includes comments about foods that had already become obsolete by 1940, such as acorns, wild cherries, blister beetles, squirrel, juniper tea, bear and jackrabbit meat, ponderosa pine bark, locusts, native salt, and numerous seeds. She as well as Carpenter and Steggerda (1939) demonstrate how the use and knowledge of traditional foods continued even as Navajos adapted to new food resources from the outside. As quoted earlier in the text, Kelley (personal communication, 2013) has demonstrated that the interviews done for the Navajo Land Claims Collection in the 1960s are full of information on early sources of food. Underhill (1953) also identifies some of the early foods.

6. Kelley and Francis (2006–2015; forthcoming); see also note 3 in the introduction. Trading posts and their histories continue to fascinate scholars from many disciplines as well as the general public. Among the latest studies is Cottam (2015) on the Hubbell Trading Post in Ganado, Arizona, from its beginning until 1967, when it was designated a National Historic Site.

7. Those who went to Fort Sumner had already become familiar with white flour, coffee, and other "foods" introduced by the US Army; others had been introduced to them earlier by the Spanish. Young and Morgan (1980, 20) include a list of loanwords that entered the Navajo language from Spanish in earlier times, before many speakers became bilingual. Among the words of importance on their list are the Navajo words for Anglo or white person, bread, cheese, apple, coffee, tea, and rice.

8. Wendy Wolfe grew up in Michigan and had an early interest in different peoples and cultures, which was enriched by her experiences in Micronesia and Germany. She earned her bachelor's degree in anthropology in 1981 from Northwestern University, graduating Phi Beta Kappa with honors. Her senior honors thesis was "Navajo Foods and Foodways: Cultural and Nutritional Changes with Acculturation." During her undergraduate years she did anthropological fieldwork on the reservation on Navajo foods and foodways and volunteered in a nutrition education program. This led to her multidisciplinary interest in nutrition and anthropology. The research for her bachelor's degree was supported by the National Endowment for the Humanities and led to additional fieldwork and the collection of food samples for a tribally sponsored

Navajo traditional foods nutritional analysis project (Wolfe, Weber, and Arviso 1985). Her interest in nutritional anthropology, supported by a National Science Foundation graduate fellowship, led her to Cornell University in 1981 to study nutrition. She returned to the Navajo reservation to research the current diet of Navajo women receiving commodity foods (Wolfe and Sanjur 1988). After earning a master's degree in international nutrition in 1983, Wolfe worked as a public health nutritionist and a coordinator of the Women, Infants, and Children nutrition program for the St. Regis Mohawk Tribe in upstate New York. In 1991 Wolfe earned a PhD in community nutrition from Cornell, where she continues to work as a research associate in the Division of Nutritional Sciences. Her specialties are youth nutrition, childhood obesity prevention, and food insecurity. Dr. Oswald Werner at Northwestern University introduced Wolfe to the Navajos through his field school and was her senior honors advisor. In her Navajo work, especially for her master's thesis, she was assisted by Katherine D. Arviso, the director of Navajo Nation Food and Nutrition Services, five Navajo nutrition educators, Sadie Yazzie, and others knowledgeable about traditional foods and their preparation. Thanks to Ossy and the late June Werner, I was able to locate Wolfe in 2012 and secure a copy of her senior honors thesis; since then I have benefited from numerous helpful discussions with her.

9. Bailey (1940) found that multiple kinds of bread were being made solely from wheat or corn or from a combination of both and that whole wheat flour was still used more than white flour.

10. Wolfe (1984) says that some alcohol was also apparent during this period, and Kelley (personal communication, 2015) reminded me that the historical record shows that alcohol was being sold to the Navajos at least by 1880, if not earlier.

11. Dana Bah'łgai Eldridge is a Navajo woman who worked from 2011 until the fall of 2013 as a policy analyst at DPI, where she directed the Diné Food Sovereignty Initiative. This will be discussed more later.

12. Young and Morgan (1980) do not include a term for poured bread. Wolfe (1981, 71) calls it *ńdinoolyíshí* and *nanoyezhi*; Morgan (2011, 6) calls it *náhinooyęshí* and *nánooyęshí*.

13. Eventually, through Women, Infants, and Children and other assistance programs, milk became available in both canned and powdered forms. Today powdered milk is added by some women to frybread, tortillas, and pancakes, and reportedly you can even make cheese with it.

14. When I first met Tall Woman, the family's farming efforts were focused on corn and alfalfa.

15. Kelley (personal communication, 2013) noted that a few traders grew produce to sell, such as at Borrego Pass, and some bought produce from Navajo clients to sell. There was also an active intertribal trade between the Navajos and the Pueblos: the Jemez, Acoma, and other Rio Grande groups with the Eastern Navajos, and the Hopis with the Western Navajos, with meat exchanged for

corn. The Hopis used to travel around the surrounding Navajo communities with burros, as did the Acoma people in their area. The Mitchell (2001, [1978] 2003) life stories, among others, give examples of such trading.

16. District 1 was one of eighteen land management districts established in 1936 to facilitate stock reduction and land management; located in the far northwestern part of the reservation, it includes Kaibeto and Red Lake.

17. The ovens studied by Reh were preheated for a day with wood, then the ashes were removed through a small door on the side, and the oven was sealed with a stone slab and wet mud. A wagonload of green corn was put in at the top, and a basin of water was thrown on it to make steam. Then the top opening was sealed with a stone and mud, and the corn was left in there for a day. Other discussions of this kind of oven will follow in chapter 2.

18. The 1928 Meriam Report described the conditions in the eight extant boarding schools and the nine day schools then available on the reservation as deplorable and providing mainly vocational training. In the mid-1930s, fifty new day schools were built, and after World War II the Navajo Nation identified formal education as a primary need and increased its demands for schools. A survey by Dr. George Sanchez found that 66 percent of the Navajo people had no schooling whatsoever as of the 1946–47 school year (Young 1961, 10–15).

19. Darby et al. (1956) found that native plants had essentially been abandoned; domesticated animals had replaced wild ones; wheat flour had replaced cornmeal; and coffee, commercial tea, and soda pop were widely substituted for native teas.

20. Tall Woman was still making this cheese in 1963 and 1964, and I was able to taste it and try to make it; it was very tasty. It is included in the recipes in this book.

21. Augusta Sandoval said that one of her mother's favorite items from the trading post was canned tomatoes; "she used to love them served with sugar and hot tortillas." Augusta noted that canned tomatoes were well liked in her own boarding school, too, because they were sweet. The boarding school students were also given cans of milk that was cream mixed with water. They used tin or aluminum plates, saucers, cups, and silverware and brown paper napkins. Later the napkins used were white. While Augusta was in school, she never used plastic utensils. St. Michaels used china bowls and plates, and St. Catherine's used tin ones.

22. Studies of the Navajo diet such as the 1955 survey by Darby et al. (1956) found no nutritional deficiencies in the study populations in either the 1940s or the 1950s but did suggest a possible inadequate vitamin C intake. French (1967) later found high morbidity and mortality rates in Navajo children from birth to two years old. Also interested in studying nutrition and health issues at this time, including their relation to government food programs, were McDonald (1965) and Alford and Nance (1976).

23. Eldridge noted that the insistence on dairy products at boarding schools was negative because 75 percent of Native Americans are lactose intolerant. I have not been able to confirm this statistic, but I know that some dietary studies of the Navajos do note lactose intolerance among some of the population.

24. I disagree that there were no changes during this period. Given the increased access to mobility through cars and pickup trucks, there were many more opportunities to leave the reservation to shop in border towns for food and to participate in the various supplemental food programs detailed in appendix A.

25. Russell (1991) notes that trading posts dominated the grocery market on the reservation until the 1960s; as they declined in importance, convenience stores increased, offering the same services, extended hours, general merchandise, and small selection of grocery items. Trading posts had the advantage for a long time of providing personal care to customers, offering credit, playing a middleman role in buying arts and crafts items from the Navajos, and being conveniently located. Convenience stores such as 7-Eleven, Circle K, and Thriftway are now thriving. Supermarkets suddenly entered the Navajo marketplace, signifying a rapid change in the food marketing system on the reservation. Russell attributes the changes to the self-determination policy of the 1960s, studies in the 1970s that pinpointed the amount of expenditure leakage suffered by the Navajo Nation because of little on-reservation economic development, the shift from wagons to automobiles in the mid-1960s, road improvements, the growth of population and urban centers, and consumer awareness.

The Navajo Nation adopted a planned development policy in the mid-1970s that included the expansion of on-reservation supermarkets and shopping centers. Bashas' Market Inc., a privately held, family-owned company headquartered in Chandler, Arizona, is one of the major grocery chains in Arizona. When Russell did his work, Bashas' had fifty-five stores in its chain, including five stores on the reservation and another about to open; it also had stores on the Tohono O'odham reservation in Arizona and in border towns adjacent to the Navajo reservation; and it was planning stores to serve Hopis and others. Bashas' stresses quality, service, and commitment to the community and its employees. The family had warm relations with the Pimas in the 1930s and has felt a strong bond to Native Americans since the beginning of the company's history. Dineh Cooperatives Inc. (DCI), a community development corporation in Chinle, started in 1971, and by 1976 it had decided to build a shopping center there. DCI approached supermarket chains about operating stores in the center, and only Bashas' showed interest. With financing by DCI, the supermarket opened in March 1981. Other stores, built by the Navajo Nation, opened in Tuba City in 1983, Kayenta, Arizona, in 1985, Shiprock (known as City Market) in 1986, Crownpoint in 1989, and Window Rock in 1989. The history of another store, Fed Mart, the anchor store in the Window Rock Fed Mart Shopping Center that opened in the early 1960s, was recently told by Donovan (2014). Fed Mart closed all its Arizona stores except the one at Window Rock in the late 1980s. The Window Rock Bashas' is the largest supermarket on the reservation. Unlike the other stores, it is built on land withdrawn from the Navajo Nation, and Bashas' real estate company financed the building (Russell 1991, 49). As in Crownpoint, the Navajo Nation requested a Bashas' at Pinon, which opened as the most remote of Bashas' stores in 1992 (74). At that time the company was also planning to open a store on the San Carlos reservation and at Polacca on the Hopi reservation. The Bashas' in Tuba City had its thirtieth anniversary in 2014.

Bashas' reservation stores are known for the use of Navajo designs, its wide parking places for pickups, signage with pictures, and its attention to Navajo food preferences. Russell (1991, 50–51) identified Navajo traditional foods as roast mutton, mutton stew, potatoes, frybread, homemade tortillas, corn, squash, sheep organs such as brains and intestines, blue cornmeal, and posole (a stew made from backbone and dried corn). He also noted that the stores were heavily stocked in the ingredients needed for making frybread: flour (preferably Blue Bird), baking powder, and lard or shortening. Other frequently requested items were Cracker Jacks, canned milk (to feed newborn lambs), regular cola drinks, Folger's or Hills Brothers coffee, Spam, red Jell-O, and Skoal chewing tobacco. Baby products also sold well, especially disposable diapers; the deli department was popular, as was the part of the bakery that sells pastries and cakes. Navajos could also find tools such as axes, shovels, and stovepipes at Bashas'. Stovepipes provided roof vents for the small cast-iron stoves that burned wood or coal. The stores also sold porcelain tableware, washbasins, and coffeepots; livestock supplies could also be found there, including salt licks. No liquor was sold, and fresh flowers, greeting cards, stationery, and frozen foods did not do well on the reservation.

Russell (1991, 75–76) includes information about the Basha family through the generations. He also documents the contributions to economic development made by the store, which is one of the largest nongovernment employers on the reservation. Competing stores use pricing strategies and extended business hours to try to attract customers, but Bashas' has been able to maintain a price advantage over them.

Eddie Basha, the chairman and chief executive officer of Bashas', passed away on March 26, 2013, at age seventy-five (Donovan 2013; Begaye 2013). The articles written in tribute to him documented Bashas' annual contributions from store profits to the Navajo scholarship program and other community-oriented charities. Eddie was called a great person with a big heart who was able to survive bankruptcy and the closing of some nonreservation stores and make a successful comeback. Bashas' supermarkets were definitely a cornerstone in lending stability to the Navajo economy by providing jobs, services, goods, revenues, and scholarships, being the mainstay in shopping centers, and encouraging other Navajo businesses.

26. Kelley stated that a large number of store owners had twenty-five-year leases, dating from 1955. When the Navajo Nation trading regulations took hold, they could not get long-term renewals in 1980; instead they got renewals only for one or two years at a time and only if they invested in substantial and necessary improvements. Thus, by the late 1980s a lot of traders had sold their businesses to convenience-store chains or just closed down and retired.

27. In December 2015 NAPI printed flyers advertising products it had for sale at NAPI Region Farm Scales in two locations near Farmington. The products included different kinds of flour, blue and white corn products, and a variety of traditional foods.

28. For a summary of the life history genre, see Mitchell (2001, xviii-xxi) and more recent works, such as Nez (2011), McPherson, Dandy, and Burak (2012), and Holiday and McPherson (2013).

29. Food assistance is clearly a political football in Washington, DC. Recall, for example, the arguments in the late fall and winter of 2013–2014 around the farm subsidy program, the continuation of food assistance, and the Supplemental Nutrition Assistance Program (SNAP). The US Farm Bill that was passed in February 2014 cut $8 billion from SNAP. How the large numbers of individuals, including Navajos, who depend on SNAP and other programs for actual survival will now adjust to this devastation remains to be seen.

   Some of the trends unfolding on the Navajo reservation that make it easier for people to have access to fresh fruit and vegetables were mirrored in Illinois. The US Department of Agriculture funded the Illinois Electronic Benefits Transfer (EBT) Wireless Project grant, which was announced in relation to the Goshen Market, a farmers' market, in Edwardsville on June 13, 2013. The grant made possible the purchase of an EBT card-processing machine so that people can access their SNAP benefits electronically while shopping for locally grown fresh fruits and vegetables.

   Unrest continued in New Mexico when the proposed cuts to SNAP were announced. The All Pueblo Council of Governors, the Southwest Organizing Project, the New Mexico Conference of Catholic Bishops, the Native American Voters Alliance, and a number of other groups and individuals protested in Santa Fe when they learned about the proposed rule changes, since there had been no consultation with the tribes as expected. Among the newly proposed changes were that able-bodied adults ages eighteen to fifty-nine without children would be required to work twenty hours a week, parents with children over six years old would be required to do job searches, and others would have to attend education and training programs.

30. It has been hard learning about Mormon tea. Wolfe (1984) reported that she was not able to get the Latin name for the plant, and Kathleen Manolescu (personal communication, 2013) said there had been no discussion of it in *Leading the Way* despite the opposite being true about Navajo tea. Wolfe et al. (1985, 331)

give the genus name as *Ephedra*. Yetman (2009, 29) also lists the genus as *Ephedra* and says that the three species in the Southwest have stems that can be chewed, sucked, or brewed into a tea. The plant contains ephedrine, a stimulant. Navajos also use the twigs to dye wool, he added.

31. Culinary ash, which is discussed in chapter 3, was usually made by burning green juniper or cedar branches. Wolfe's (1984) sources said that people also used *'iiłtsoii* ash but did not identify the plant. Kelley (personal communication, 2015) told me this is the same as *k'iiłtsoii* (big rabbit bush), a three- to four-foot-tall round plant with small yellow flowers that bloom in late September or in October. Some also used tumbleweed ash or dried cantaloupe leaves, or they burned any of the following to make ash: dried bean leaves, peach tree branches, squash blossoms, cottonwood bark, or greasewood branches. People also had different opinions about what culinary ash should be used for. Some said to use it only for blue cornmeal dishes, a practice that was followed in Tall Woman's family. Others said to use it for all cornmeal dishes. Some said to use it in all blue cornmeal dishes unless you were making these for babies or someone who was ill. Some also added it to hominy, and some put it in mutton stew. When people were asked why they followed the practices they identified, their answers varied. Some said that's what they learned to do while growing up—it gives a blue color, it adds flavor, and it enhances the taste. Wolfe (1984) noted that it is true that it adds a blue color. Dry blue cornmeal without ash is grayblue, but in boiling water it becomes pink, which is believed to cause heartburn or a sore throat. Blue corn contains an anthocyanin pigment that turns the corn blue when it is put in an alkaline medium such as that created by ash. Many say it works like baking powder and prevents heartburn. Wolfe did not do research on these reasons, but she demonstrated that ash does increase calcium, potassium, and magnesium, and also iron and zinc in cornbreads and cornmeal mush, even if only a small amount is used. The ash is usually sifted, mixed with boiling water, and strained into the cornmeal to create the dish. Many of Wolfe's sources wondered if certain traditional foods and dishes were declining in frequency of preparation and use today because it is more difficult to get the ash and because of a change in the beliefs about the need for it. Clearly the decline has had detrimental nutritional consequences for the Navajos. Ash really does increase the nutrient value of corn foods, not only by adding its own nutrients, such as calcium, but also by freeing otherwise unavailable nutrients, such as niacin, in the corn.

32. I do not mean to imply that nobody was farming. Shiprock, Fruitland, Leupp, and Many Farms, for example, are areas formerly known for successful farming, but given the current drought conditions and the 2015 Gold King Mine disaster, farming efforts in many places are minimal at present.

33. Kopp (1986, 14) also notes that to call mutton, white flour, and the limited use of cornmeal and native plants "traditional Navajo foods" is actually referring to

late nineteenth-century practices. Special functions, most often ceremonies, continue to be occasions for mutton stew, roasted mutton, blood sausage, sheep's head, blue corn cake baked in the ground, melon, frybread, blue corn-meal mush, and other well-loved foods. Organ meats are also traditional; these include all parts of goats and sheep except the digestive tract contents, gall-bladder, bladder, hair, horns, and third lobe of the liver (20).

34. The clay actually appears to bind the poison so that it does not get absorbed in the gut; this was established by the work of Tim Johns (Wolfe 1984).

35. One source said that *dit'oodí w*as the word her family used for apricots; others said the word should be *dzidzétsoh yázhí.*

36. Wolfe's (1984, 218) sources also mentioned several other items that she did not learn about; for example, *chaat'íní* (dock) and other wild plants viewed as possible types of wild spinach.

37. All studies have to end sometime; in this case, December 31, 2014 was originally chosen as the date on which I would stop tracking most of the continuing developments and discussions. But then I made a few exceptions in order to include the implementation of two 2014 actions of the Navajo Nation Council. Later, in 2015–2016, while writing chapter 4, I decided to update the coverage of the trends and add a discussion of another major and important study that had just become available (Echo Hawk Consulting 2015). From then on, I kept track of developments until the manuscript went through its final revisions for publication (September 2016). I also decided in December 2015 that the latest additions, essentially reflecting 2016 activities and developments, would be part of the final chapter.

The council's action to remove the 5 percent sales tax on fresh vegetables and fruit was passed in October 2014. The companion bill, the Healthy Diné Act (Navajo Nation Council CN-54-14) was signed into law on November 21, with the agreed-upon implementation date of April 1, 2015, for the new taxes on everything defined as junk food. Included under this label were chips, pastries, fried foods, sodas, sweetened beverages, and "prepackaged and non-prepackaged snacks stripped of essential nutrients and high in salt, saturated fats, and sugar" (Navajo Nation Council 2014, 7–15). It has been satisfying to see these actions as well as the extensive media compliments given to the Navajo Nation for being the *first* to take action against junk food. The ensuing discussions have been equally encouraging: the problem of food deserts; the need to return to traditional diets and growing one's own food, not just by the Navajo Nation but in many other places; the increased media attention given to Navajo chefs who are introducing traditional food choices in their workplaces; the continuing focus on world food issues, the importance of environmental issues in Navajoland, from soil erosion to recycling and trash; teaching communities about traditional farming; heirloom seed repositories; and even the evolution of the human diet. A discussion also continues about food stamp recipients now looking for jobs and US Department of Agriculture grants aimed at identifying what is effective in getting people to work. Although the federal government provides the money for food stamps, the states administer the program, and these grants will help ten states test new programs for training, career counseling, and mental health assistance. Reportedly about one-fifth of the 46 million people who receive food stamps are eligible for training. The rest are elderly, disabled, children, or already working (*Edwardsville Intelligencer* 2015).

38. Fast-food consumption is a topic in need of study. One of the few publications that mentions it is Wolfe and Sanjur (1988, 824). While discussing Navajo contemporary diets based on data gathered in 1979–1980 and 1982, the authors say, "Several meals were eaten at fast-food restaurants, which have reached some reservation towns." See appendix B for the timeline I have been able to construct for the arrival of such places in Chinle, Arizona.

39. At the Navajo Studies Conference in Flagstaff, Arizona, in May 2015, I met Bernhard Michaelis, who founded and directs Native Child, a resource for Navajo schoolchildren. Among his interests are traditional Navajo foods, and he told me that he had already established a website that he will use to share recipes, Navajorecipes.com. When I accessed it on January 1, 2016, it included entries from 2013 and 2014 for the following items: blue cornmeal mush, blue cornmeal mush fried, kneel-down bread, juniper ash, juniper ash water, roasting corn, and purslane (with no content). The recipe given for kneel-down bread was credited to Hensperger (1997).

40. Navajos, as well as many other humans, view the Earth as "our mother" (Mother Nature, Mother Earth). In the Navajo language, the term for one's birth mother, *shimá* (my mother), is also applied to the Earth, thus recognizing her as the mother of all living beings. Navajos view the Earth as female and the Sky as male and see them as existing in a complementary relationship: Mother Earth provides the nutrients, and Father Sky provides the water; together they make life possible.

41. Whereas Young and Morgan (1980) and others give *'alką̄ąd* as the term for the corn cake made for the Kinaaldá, the Girls' Puberty Ceremony, my collaborators in Chinle, Arizona, have always used *'alkaan*, and this is the term I have used throughout my own work. Some others prefer *'alkaad*.

42. Dana Bah'łgai Eldridge worked as a policy analyst at DPI from 2011 through the fall of 2013, where she was the major person spearheading the Diné Food Sovereignty Initiative. Originally from Fort Defiance, Dana got a scholarship to go to Choate, a prep school in Wallingford, Connecticut, with long-standing connections to the Navajo Nation. From there Dana went to Brown University. After graduating with a bachelor's degree in ethnic studies, she wanted to return to Navajoland but had trouble finding a job until the staff position at DPI became available. The report that her work, and that of her staff and interns, produced is of major importance (DPI 2014). When Dana left DPI, it

was to pursue local agricultural projects by returning to her family land and learning more about agriculture and sheepherding. Amber Kanazbah Crotty from Sheepsprings, New Mexico, became the executive director of DPI in January 2014. Both she and Eldridge were interviewed in Curley (2014) when the report was completed and available. Of the four women who ran in the most recent election for seats on the Navajo Nation Council, Crotty was the only one to be successful, becoming a member of the twenty-third council. She represents the districts of Toadelena/Two Gray Hills, Beclabito, Gadii'ahi/To'koi (Cudei/Rattlesnake), Cove, Sheepsprings, Red Valley, and Tsé 'alnaozt'i'í' (Sanostee). Her main goals are to strengthen her community's agricultural practices and to facilitate access to clean water, which would propel economic development and community health. Crotty's policy analyst at DPI, Crystalyne Curley, a former Miss Navajo, also ran, to represent the districts of Low Mountain, Tachee/Blue Gap, Nazlini, Tséláni/Cottonwood, and Many Farms. Her interests were to bring water and electricity to her community and to address the needs of the home and children. Curley, however, lost to Kee Allen Begay by a vote of 897–519. Moroni Benally replaced Crotty as the DPI director, and Andrew Curley is the deputy director. Crotty continues to be actively involved on the council in all activities related to food sovereignty and wellness.

43. This list is available from me upon request.

44. Dana became aware of my own interests and the Tall Woman traditional foods project when I met her in 2011, and from then on I willingly shared literature references and findings with her as well as updates on my own work.

45. This assessment tool was recently rereleased and is available for free to Native Americans and their nonprofit organizations from the Indigenous Food Systems Network (2016), http://www.indigenousfoodsystems.org/sites/default/files/tools/FNDIFSATFinal.pdf.

46. While the project was ongoing you could follow it on Facebook through the DPI website. The site, through the link "Travels with Erik," showed the beginning of the project when a person named Erik, on a spring 2012 visit to Diné College, visited DPI and had discussions with Director Robert Yazzie and Dana Eldridge. The site also detailed Eldridge's activities, including her participation in the Food and Wellness Policy Summit at the Navajo Nation Museum in Window Rock on June 13, 2013; the Sheep Is Life Conference at Diné College on June 21–22, 2013; and the Corn Is Life Conference at the college on September 18, 2013. The January 15, 2014, post concerned a fall 2013 Humanities Institute presentation at Scripps College focused on Re-visioning Food Sovereignty. There, on November 20, 2013, Dana spoke on, "Indigenous Perspectives on Food Sovereignty: Efforts of the Navajo Nation to Rebuild a Self-Sufficient Food System." Another PowerPoint presentation, "Food Sovereignty Assessment," updated the project results as of January 16, 2014 (http://www.swmarketingnetwork.org.). With time and support, Eldridge's work, because it was a DPI initiative, will

hopefully initiate some positive changes. The focus on this project here, however, is not meant to detract from the work that many others are doing on food insecurity and related issues for the Navajos (e.g., Pardilla et al. 2013).

Some of the many envisioned developments include community-based wellness projects such as walking, running, and biking trails; farming and vegetable gardens; food co-ops; greenhouses; farmers' markets; swimming pools; community gardens; wellness exercise equipment and supplies; basketball courts; skate parks; picnic grounds; health classes (Bitsoi 2014a, 2014e, 2014f; Navajo Nation Council 2014, 7–8). Coverage of relevant issues continued through 2014 in the *Navajo Times*—not just the annual Sheep Is Life celebrations and conferences but also the ongoing fight over the proposal to tax junk food (Bitsoi 2014a–f), the need for education about food (Becenti 2013), the far-ranging rangeland improvement proposal (Yurth 2014a, 2014c), and the feral horse issue. For example, Bitsoi (2014d) documents how nonprofits are helping to bring farming to the communities of Ojo Encino, Counselor, and Torreon, with both dry farming and drip irrigation farming, solar hoop houses, mobile farmers' market, and raised beds. These efforts are meeting local demands for fresh food. The paper also provided an interesting discussion (Landry 2014) with Amber Crotty of DPI of Godfrey's (2014) book on poverty, which is based on eight years of fieldwork in Ghana, Paraguay, and the Navajo Nation, where he was studying both national and individual poverty. Crotty pointed out that poverty is often invisible in Navajoland because in Navajo Fundamental Law, poverty means no family, livestock, or ties to the land rather than a lack of material possessions and money.

47. K'é is a code of behavior based on traditional kinship and reciprocity. Navajos have an all-encompassing idea of kinship, extending it to other Navajos and even non-Navajos as well as to other beings with whom they share the universe: nature, the earth, the sky, the moon, the stars, animals, plants, homes, a fire poker, stirring sticks, minerals, and so forth—animate and inanimate entities alike.

Chapter 2

1. According to one of Tall Woman's children, "We ate flying bugs or locusts; we removed their heads and wings and then roasted them. They brought good health. There were also several kinds of little yellow birds; one of them, *tsídiiłtsooí* (goldfinches), the boys would often kill with their slingshots. They would break off the birds' heads, peel off the skin, open the bodies up and flatten them out, and then put them on small grills to roast. Our brother Seya usually had a small grill with him when we were herding, and he'd fix four or five of these birds at a time; he always told us that according to our parents, if we ate these we'd have nice-looking children."

2. Some of Tall Woman's other nephews continue to hunt, but mainly small game such as rabbits and prairie dogs with slingshots. Big game hunting is still popular on at least some areas of the reservation. The Navajo Nation Fish and Wildlife Department offers free courses on big game hunting, noting that Arizona offers bighorn sheep, bears, buffalo, javelinas, mountain lions, mule deer, pronghorn deer, turkeys, and white-tailed deer—all of which it classifies as big game. For a classic study of Navajo Hunting, see Hill (1938, 96–194).

3. Augusta laughed while reviewing this, saying that the Gormans' farm always reminded her of the "Jane and Mary on the farm" books they read in school.

4. As both Tall Woman's (Mitchell 2001) and Frank Mitchell's (Mitchell [1978] 2003) life stories indicate, in the early days in Chinle there was blatant hostility between Catholics and Protestants, mainly Presbyterians, the first non-Catholic group to establish itself in the community more than a decade after the Franciscans arrived.

5. We went to the home of Chester Begay, one of Myrtle Begay's sons, in 2013 to photograph a *bááh bighan*, a small outdoor earth or mud oven like the kind that Tall Woman used. Leo R. Begay, another of her sons, had served earlier as the Chinle Chapter president and then become active as a preacher. Both he and his wife conducted his sister Mary Alice's funeral in June 2013, to which we went.

6. Today, given drought and climate change, Navajo ranchers are struggling just like others who say the ranching industry is in transition, with many selling their livestock for very low prices. Navajos face the same problems as farmers elsewhere, including shortages of land, feed, and water and hay prices that are prohibitive. During the summer of 2016 in Chinle, hay trucked in from Colorado was selling at the flea market for twelve to twenty dollars a bale. People were starting to attend conferences to discuss how to return to traditional knowledge, which used to be successful in times when they had personal relationships with their animals and no pressures from big organizations or corporate peers. Bitsoi (2013b) and other articles in the *Navajo Times* from May through September 2013 consisted of heated discussions about the pros and cons of rounding up stray feral horses to improve the condition of the range. Letters to the editor during this period revealed the politics involved as well as a variety of attitudes toward horses in both past and present Navajo culture.

7. For example, there are several articles in a 2009 issue of *Leading the Way* (7 [9]: 2–3, 5–7, 12–15). Navajo friends of mine added comments from their own family practices. Steven Begay (personal communication, 2015), for example, said that after the sheep to be butchered is chosen, you should pull out a tuft of wool from its forehead, pass the tuft through the sheep's mouth, and leave the tuft in the sheep corral. This ensures the flock will not be depleted and that you will always have plenty of sheep. The sheep should be put on the ground for butchering, with the head toward the north and its tied legs toward the east. No one

who has been bitten by a dog or anything else should be around during the butchering because such a person brings bad luck and causes the fat on the carcass to "bubble up and melt away," making meat dry and tough. Begay was told never to eat the small lobe that juts out from the liver because doing so will make your relatives hate you. Just cut that off and throw it to the north, he said, which is where you also should throw the gallbladder.

A number of people have expressed concerns about present-day Navajos not valuing sheep as they should but instead wasting lots of the animal and being disrespectful. There was also continuing dismay over the fact that butchering knowledge and skills were not being taught to the younger generation.

8. Augusta, when reviewing the manuscript, added, "Nowadays, if you have diabetes, you have to be careful about controlling your fat intake, among other things."

9. Tall Woman never wanted to use any commercially ground corn; she believed that if you wanted corn, you should plant it, harvest it, and grind it yourself. Although the stores sometimes had corn, everybody said that was just feed corn for the animals. Some people tried grinding that but found that even though it could be ground really fine, it crumbled when you tried to prepare food with it, because that corn was just too hard.

10. Navajos and many other Southwesterners use the English words *cedar* and *juniper* interchangeably, so this is a moot point. One person from a different family, however, described their storage pit as a "big round hole in the ground that was lined with shredded juniper bark."

11. Using Google, Klara Kelley (personal communication, 2015) found this very same sack listed on eBay on September 12, 2015 as "VTG Heavy Duty Feed Sack FULTON A SEAMLESS with Eagle Logo" for $18.25.

12. I never saw Tall Woman's grill stone. Although she was still making paperbread when I first met her, we didn't discuss this stone when she was sharing her recipes. However, when she was telling me her life story, she did talk about this grill stone (Mitchell 2001, 55–57, 406–7, 441n5) needed for making paperbread, or *tsé'ást'éí*. First one must find a flat rock that was smooth all over to use for that; her mother used to go by herself, way out into the Black Mountain area, and would come home with usually two slabs of that special kind of stone; she was the only one who did that and who knew where to find those stones. Tall Woman said she never knew what kind of stone it was. Her mother showed her in her late girlhood how to fix the stone: she would fix the surface by chipping a piece of it and grinding it down until it was nice and round on the top. Then she'd take some stones made smooth in the water and rub the top over and over. That sanded it and polished it until it was smooth. The surface had to be perfect, as smooth as glass. Then she would treat it with pitch by heating some on the surface and letting it cook into the stone. When it cooled off, it was ready to use. She also talked about trying to teach her daughters to make

paperbread, but some of them were afraid to try doing it. Everybody, however, loved to eat it, but its preparation took so much wood that she didn't make it very often.

As two of her daughters, Mary Davis and Augusta Sandoval, noted in their dad's story (Mitchell [1978] 2003, 158–59), it was their maternal grandparents who knew how to make paperbread and who taught both of them how to do that. Hastiin Delawoshí, Tall Woman's father, used to haul in white rocks of all different sizes to use in making the grill. "He showed us how to grind the rock down so that it was smooth on the surface." He always started with stones that had been smoothed down from being in the water for a long time. After the stone was ground down, he put pitch on the top of it. During this time the stone was sitting in a burning fire; he and their grandmother would heat that rock to burn off the pitch, and then he would get a pine brush and brush the stone to clean it up. Then he put sheep fat on it and let the heat melt it into the stone. When that was finished, he removed the stone from the fire and put it aside to cool. By then, Mary and Augusta said, it was as smooth as ice.

Other people, when describing similar stones owned by other Navajo women, would say they were large, flat, and dark gray and measured about four inches thick, twenty-eight inches long, and eighteen inches wide. The grill stone reportedly had four stone legs, one in each corner. Women at the Hopi village of Moenkopi reportedly started doing the gathering and preparing of these grill stones for others by 1974 and then sold them to other women for about twenty-five dollars (Niethammer 1999, 143). Bailey (1940, 275) described the griddle as being made from a sheet of metal about twenty inches square that was put over the fire by resting on stones or on empty evaporated milk cans. The Franciscan Fathers (1910, 207, 219), using a different orthography, gave the words for stone griddle as *tsét'ēs* and *tsĕ ăst'é'* and said that these meant baked on the stone, designating the well-known paperbread. The batter was spread over a heated stone griddle with the hand and baked. They also gave *tsĕ ăst'é' łagaí* and three other terms to cover the colors of corn used in making this bread: first white, then blue mixed with cedar ashes, yellow containing saliva glucose, and red made of blue corn without cedar ashes.

13. The owners of the objects shown in figures 11–15 are as follows: The set of grinding stones (fig. 11) belongs to Isabelle Deschine. The stirring sticks, gourd dippers, and grass hairbrush (figs. 12–14) originally belonged to Ruth (Mitchell) Shirley Yazzie and were passed to her daughter, Evonne Shirley, who died unexpectedly on June 20, 2016. The transmission of these tools, which Evonne had kept in a locked, glass-front cabinet, had not been clarified as of September 2016. The brush for the grinding stones (fig. 15), also called a strainer, belongs to Augusta Sandoval.

14. Many issues of *Leading the Way* (e.g., 9 [11]: 9, 11) contain relevant discussions about the origins of these sticks and other information. Some people had

definite ideas about the numbers of sticks needed and what constituted appropriate preparation. Some prefer to separate the stirring sticks used in ceremonial cooking from those used on a more regular basis. And some prefer to have longer sticks to use when making 'alkaan, the corn cake for the Girls' Puberty Ceremony, since a lot of batter was poured into washtubs for further processing.

15. With weaving tools it was different. Tall Woman wanted to show her daughters directly how to make those and have them practice in front of her. Her father, Hastiin Delawhoshí, was the best weaver in the family; Mary Davis, Tall Woman's oldest daughter, always had to herd sheep with him; he made her a small loom to take with them and taught her how to weave on that. Finally she learned how to set up a big loom.

16. Steven Begay disagreed, saying that in ceremonies a singer will instruct a woman to take out two sticks or a single one to use in stirring whatever she has been instructed to make. He also noted that he has seen women who specialize in making 'alkaan have many sets of huge stirring sticks that they take with them when they are hired to make the ceremonial cake.

17. Steven Begay (personal communication, 2016) shared some other uses of the hairbrush. When a pregnant woman is experiencing a tough labor and delivery, the hairbrush is used like a bundle of eagle wing feathers to sweep away the evil that is causing the delayed delivery. It is used to "chase out" the baby. Also, because an infant is never left alone, the hairbrush may be put beside the baby as its protector, just like a fire poker or a perfect ear of corn; they all can serve as babysitters.

18. The other times I saw Tall Woman and her husband praying and making offerings were at dawn with white cornmeal facing east. In earlier times some people also reportedly prayed at noon and at twilight, using corn pollen and yellow cornmeal, respectively. Prayers to the Holy People were also said when Tall Woman finished using the stirring sticks, and later, after she finished cooking over the grill or whatever she was cooking on; at the latter time she had the fire poker in her hand rather than the stirring sticks. These prayers gave thanks to the Holy People for the wood, the fire, the food for the family, and continued well-being.

19. One woman told me about a friend who now supplements her income by grinding corn for medicine men and women who buy it (especially white corn) from her.

20. In the past corn grinding was accompanied by songs. Today some of these songs are still known and sung during competitions involving corn grinding and other demonstrations of cultural knowledge. One person mentioned that twenty to twenty-five years ago his grandfather liked to sing these songs and eventually found himself a stick longer than a stirring stick with a ball-like bottom on it that he started using to keep time or beat out the rhythm on the

ground while singing them. When some were sung for me in the 1960s and 1970s, the rhythm was tapped out on an inverted Navajo basket with a variety of objects, including a moccasin, a folded belt, and a padded stick. These songs are also available on some commercial recordings (Johnson 1964).

21. I was never able to find out what kind of stone Tall Woman preferred for making the grinding stones, or even what kinds might be considered. The manos and metates (the archaeological names for the top stones and bottom stones, respectively) that my husband, Ted, was given by Zuni women, who said they were "retiring them," have been fashioned either from vesicular basalt or from sandstone. Ted noted that volcanic rock is preferred, at least by the Zunis, for making the coarse grinding stones.

22. Others say that before the Navajos learned about raising corn, beans, and squash, "way back, in the early, early days," they used small, circular grinding stones for processing seeds, nuts, and some berries, among other things they gathered for food. With the advent of corn, they started using the big, oblong grinding stones also being used by the Pueblos. The motion with the big ones was pushing and pulling: moving the smaller, top stone back and forth with both hands in the long direction on the bottom stone. The smaller, circular stones required one hand to move in a circle, around and around, to do the grinding of seeds and the like.

23. Young and Morgan (1980) give the terms as *náníshne*—to hit repeatedly with a rock, to pound on—or *bídíshniih*. After saying she didn't know the Navajo terms for the grinding stones (*tsédaashch'íní* and *tsédaashjéé'*), a woman I will simply call MC, who frequently joked with us during our visit, said she called them *chatchizigi*, perhaps giving us an example of onomatopoeia with her answer. She and her late husband, Seya, used to go to a small canyon near the Greasewood Trading Post. "There the rocks were really good, very hard stone." That's where MC's grandmother went to get the rocks for her grinding stones, so MC went to the same place. "You have to shape them, of course, after you find them, and you use the same stone to pound on them"; according to her, *tsébinteeł* is the name for the rock that is used to shape the stones. The same rock used for the top and bottom grinding stones is also used to shape them, and also to sharpen them when they need to be sharpened. In 2013 MC had her grandmother's grinding stones, which had been passed on to MC by her mother. Both her grandmother and her mother used Navajo pottery for cooking, making cornmeal mush, and mixing ingredients up with stirring sticks. In 2013 her set of grinding stones was at her winter camp in the Greasewood Mountains, where her younger sister stays with the sheep.

24. While I was having this discussion in 2013, a water pitcher that used a charcoal filter was sitting on the kitchen counter. It's the same principle.

25. This is not the same as the pond next to the Chinle Wash, where people brought livestock to drink and Seya taught Howard and others to swim.

26. The first propane supplier I remember seeing in Chinle in the early 1960s was Ferrellgas. However, Augusta said there were earlier suppliers, one of which she thought was Doxol.

27. The men in the family—Frank and their sons Seya and Howard when they were at home—would take the wagon and go into the mountains to cut wood and bring it home. Tall Woman said they always preferred juniper (or cedar), which was usually plentiful. If you burned pinyon, it made a really smoky fire.

28. Seya worked at various jobs in Chinle from late 1934 to 1939 after finishing Leader School and then teaching in Lukachukai, Arizona, until October 1934 (Mitchell 2001, 449–50). Tall Woman said that when Seya had the job at the Chinle Dairy she was often able to go there and procure "pigmeat," as she called it. She was especially interested in getting the intestines, various cuts of meat, and the rind of the skin when they butchered at the dairy. This was the first time the family had a stove made from a drum or a barrel.

29. Pueblo people often had more than one large outdoor oven, and it was a man's job to put cedar and pinyon wood in it and get the fire going. Dough for the oven bread was made by the women the night before and then kneaded again in the morning while the fire burned down to the coals. After the coals were removed, the oven's temperature was tested by throwing a corn husk in it; if the husk shriveled, the oven was ready to use. A long-handled wooden paddle-type board was used to slide multiple loaves of bread into the oven (or other baked goods, or even green chilis or pinyons), and then the doorway was closed with a piece of tin, another type of metal, or a large flat stone.

    Archaeological reports of these beehive ovens, or hornos, are available from the Santa Fe and Cochiti Reservoir area as well as from San Gabriel and the Chaco area (all in New Mexico) (Brugge 1986). Interesting references sent to me by Brugge and by David Snow (personal communications, 2011) include Simmons (2005), who attributes the beehive ovens to the Spanish entrada but notes that underground cooking pits in Pueblo and Hispanic villages predate the Spanish. Dickey (1949) and Montaño (2001) explain the use of these ovens and attribute their origin to the Middle East and Arabian Peninsula. Montaño also notes that when these ovens are not in use for cooking in the Southwest, in some places they are used as doghouses.

30. Tall Woman and Frank each independently told me of incidents of hay being stolen, either after it was cut and drying in the field or after it was baled and waiting on the wagon to be taken home or to the trading post to sell. They said that once they started processing the hay, Howard always spent the night in the hay field to protect the crop until they were finished.

31. After numerous unsuccessful inquiries, I was able to learn the Navajo word for mole by asking Martha Austin-Garrison (personal communication, 2016), who answered with information from Wikipedia's Navajo page, which was new to me.

32. At this point in the manuscript review, Augusta added, "The Mormons made a film when they first came to Salt Lake; in it the dark cloud was actually grasshoppers moving along. The birds came, covered the sky, and then ate them up. That's why the Mormons settled in Utah. That happened during the time people were moving west in covered wagons." I have not been able to track down this film; Augusta saw it when she was in high school at St. Catherine's. From my own experiences, I know that for the last ten years, at least, the grasshoppers have become thick in the Chinle Valley by the middle of August.

33. Nobody seemed sure what kind of snake this was. Perhaps it was Tall Woman's name for bullsnakes, *diyóósh*.

34. How many different kinds of noxious weeds have ruined farming, I do not know, but I certainly saw at least two kinds of thistles, and others. According to MC (personal communication, 2013), a weed that grew in Lukachukai, Chinle, and Shiprock was called "*clauscheebitsi*" (from Tł'ááshchí'í *bitsilí*, a younger brother of a member of the Red Bottom People clan). It was known for spreading rapidly, killing every plant in its way (including alfalfa), and tasting very bitter. Both sheep and horses love to eat it. It is a small vine with white blossoms that look like tiny morning glories. Even if it is dug out every year, it comes back. A bitter powder ends up on people's clothes and skin if they walk through it. MC said she heard that Carl Gorman took some home when he was trying to recover from an accident. He boiled it, poured the boiled mixture in a tub, and then sat in the tub for a long time while the water was warm. He told people that he did that many times and that the weed helped his hip and removed the pain. From then on he believed in this weed as a medicine and thought doctors should analyze it and see if it might help those with diabetes, too. Some people reported harvesting it to feed to sheep and horses. Klara Kelley (personal communication, 2014) suggested that this might be bindweed, which at least some people call *ch'il na'átł'óíí*, a term some use for wild grapes. We both knew that the name MC had given me was a family joke. I had asked MC about that when I heard the name, but she said, "No, that's not a joke. That's what everybody calls it around here." According to Kelley, *ch'il ntł'íní* is the name for bindweed, and it infests nitrogen-depleted cornfields and other disturbed areas.

   There was another weed that showed up reportedly in the late 1950s in areas farmed earlier by the Mitchells; it was a vine with an orange flower, and it crawled under anything in its way. Nobody seemed to have a name for it, and Kelley wasn't familiar with it, either. She reminded me, however, that among the samples I had brought to her in June 2013 to research in her library's botanical resources, there was one we had identified as Russian knapweed. This too was problematic for farmers in Chinle because it crept and spread all over the fields and ruined them; when it blooms, it has a purplish flower. Probably the one causing the most trouble as of 2015–2016, at least for many people in the Chinle Valley, is tumbleweed, which comes in a number of varieties, spreads quickly, and

must be hand-dug repeatedly. Among the multiple Navajo names for tumbleweed are *ch'il 'awoshí, ch'il deeníní,* and *tł'ohdeeí naayizí.*

35. Steven Begay, a good friend and colleague, was a major help during the preparation of this book—of the glossary in particular, but also frequently during the
final preparation of the manuscript, when I was checking details and needed
another Navajo voice, especially a professional one with e-mail, to answer questions I could no longer ask Tall Woman. Steven hails from Naschitti, New Mexico, where he and his wife, Carlene, reside with their two children. His clans
are Tł'ááshchí'í (Red Bottom People; maternal), born for Áshįįhí (Salt People;
paternal); he comes from a traditional Navajo family of ranchers, farmers, and
hataałii, or singers. He and his family live on their family ranch north of
Naschitti with their livestock.

After graduating from Tohatchi High School, Steven earned his bachelor's
degree in anthropology with a minor in southwest studies at Colorado College,
Colorado Springs, in 1997. After working for the Navajo Nation Office of Legisla-
tive Services, he spent eleven years at the Navajo Nation Historic Preservation
Department. He was first employed as a cultural specialist, became the program
manager for the Traditional Culture Program after two years, and later headed
the Glen Canyon Dam Adaptive Management Program. After training in cultural resource management, the Native American Graves Protection and Repatriation Act, and other relevant federal and Navajo Nation laws, he became the
NNHPD deputy director in 2003 and served as one of the leaders for the Navajo
Nation in this area. In 2008 Steven resigned from the NNHPD and started to
work with the Navajo Area Indian Health Service (IHS); that same year he established the Office of Native Medicine at the Gallup Indian Medical Center, where
he and other Native American healers provided direct patient care. After resign-
ing from IHS on July 8, 2016, Steven was elected to the Twenty-Third Navajo
Nation Council, representing District 14, which included Naschitti, Tohatchi,
Mexican Springs, Coyote Canyon, and Bahastł'ah (formerly Twin Lakes). He also
continues to be a full-time practitioner of Navajo medicine.

Chapter 3

1. I was not able to learn more about this practice from anybody I asked, despite
my curiosity. Everybody confirmed liking both honey and honeycombs, and
many still consider honey in any form as a delicacy. One elderly man said that
although he had never heard of doing this to bees, he had been told that when
the Navajos were starving in the early days, they often ate the middle section of
various spiders and certain insects, the types of which he did not identify.

2. Allen (2014) gives much information on the insects: their appearance; their different sounds, calls, and cries; and the fifteen groups that return after a cycle of
disappearance, which varies in length each time. Others appear annually in

July and August and are larger. The Paiutes also eat them. These insects crawl and fly but do not jump. Some said they tasted like tree sap and are delicious.

3. Mitchell (2001) shows that it's hard work to gather pinyons, and there are many well-known family stories in the Mitchell oral histories connected with various pinyon-picking expeditions. Although Tall Woman sometimes sold some of the nuts they gathered at the trading post "if the price was good," more often she would exchange them for groceries, apples or oranges, shoes, and other necessities. The *Navajo Times* annually includes pictures of people picking pinyons and reminds its readers to get permission first if they are picking on someone else's land and say thank you by leaving a sack of nuts for the owner. In one case I know of, a diagnostician blamed a person's loss of voice on eating pinyons; once the individual stopped eating them, that person never again suffered from a lost voice.

4. According to traditional practices, people are not supposed to shake the trees, since "only bears act like that," said Tall Woman. In her family, however, people sometimes did that to make their harvesting of the pinyons easier; she laughed while sharing this information with me.

5. Tall Woman sometimes also sprinkled pinyons with water, but this is not traditional because to do so is seen as bringing cold weather.

6. Among those I asked in 2011 were two women both in their nineties; they too made this treat for their families the same way that Tall Woman was described as doing it, and they had also grown up eating it because their mothers had made it the same way.

7. The wild plants known as Navajo tea and Mormon tea can be found in section 7. Some plants that other studies have identified as being used for food were not mentioned by Tall Woman, and when I started asking elderly women in the Lukachukai, Wheatfields, and Chinle areas, they had never heard of them. These included *'iłtł'ihii*, a gummy, sticky plant that grew in sandy places; *tsiighájiłchi* (dodder), reportedly used like dried cornmeal; and *ch'iłt'óó'íí* (curly dock). Wolfe's (1984) sources said that the latter had dark roots used for dyeing wool or tanning leather. People gathered the stems or shoots and would suck on them to get the juice out. If the young stems in the spring were boiled, they reportedly tasted like applesauce. Depending on the size of the stems, they might have to be cut in half before being boiled. Some people liked to bake the stems on hot stones and eat them. I also heard nicknames for some plants, such as "the plant that cools" and "velvet weed," that I could not learn more about. As noted in chapter 2, there are also plenty of weeds today that are ruining some of the fields or have already done so, causing people who used to be successful farmers to give up because they lack any way to eradicate them. One of these is an orange vine that crawls underneath lots of plants. There's a small vine with white blossoms that look like miniature morning glories. Sheep and horses love to eat this vine, but like the

orange one, it ruins the fields by spreading all over and making it impossible for anything else to grow.

The plants that Tall Woman said were used ceremonially or as home remedies for various ailments have not been included because of restrictions on sharing sacred knowledge.

8. Steven Begay (personal communication, 2016) and his family told me that boiled and/or fried oak leaves were also considered starvation foods, available in cases of desperate hunger.

9. One woman remarked that the old people had told her that you could pound this root on a stone and then use it to make suds when washing your hair, and it would make your hair grow long. Others thought someone had confused this root with yucca root.

10. Tall Woman's daughters insisted that this term only means "tumbleweed," which clearly was not what their mother was talking about here. One of them said that she couldn't talk about wild asparagus because it was used in ceremonies. Others confirmed that *ch'il deenini* is tumbleweed, but tumbleweed is also called *ch'il 'awoshí*.

11. Several people I talked with considered *haza'aleeh* to be either wild parsley or wild celery, but Tall Woman insisted that wild parsley and wild celery are two different plants. Some who included both wild celery and wild parsley in the name agreed that there is yet another kind of wild parsley on the reservation that is also called *haza'aleeh* but that has reddish-purple stems and flowers and a stronger taste. It seems possible that this latter plant may be biscuit root, the other plant that Tall Woman talks about here.

12. Some other uses of this plant were mentioned by others, including soaking its leaves in hot water to create a deodorant; mixing them with water to pour onto anthills to kill red ants; using them to cool burns and inflammations but I am not sure if it was really *waa'* being discussed in each case.

13. Young and Morgan (1980) give *hooch'a'* as the term for seepweed. A fluent Navajo speaker told me that both *hooch'a'* and *łichí'íí* are names for this food source, which was most common in very low desert areas in the northern and western parts of the reservation.

14. Wendy Wolfe (personal communication, 2015) said that her brief online searching made her wonder if this was a variety of the yellow nightshade ground-cherry (*Physalis crassifolia*), which grows wild in Arizona at elevations of 4,000 feet and has yellow berries that grow inside husks and are edible when ripe.

15. Many of the other types of cactus are small and are used in ceremonies.

16. Among these were *hosh bei déé'éh, hosh bedeełhí, hoshdęę,* and *hosh belde'íí*. One woman told me she used snake bush for that purpose, but she didn't know its Navajo name.

17. Two Navajo women reported being allergic to soap made from narrow-leaf yucca roots. I don't know how common this is.

18. Whether the ranges of the narrow- and wide-leaf yucca are specific throughout the reservation, I do not know. There are many varieties of each kind, and specific varieties probably have specific preferred elevations. When I am looking for yucca I often find both kinds at the same elevation. I regret that I did not ask Tall Woman what her understanding of the distribution was.

19. In the mid- to late 1960s and the early 1970s, Tall Woman used to travel with me in my car to show me where various wild food resources had been available to her and her family in earlier times. She was frequently disappointed to learn that foods such as certain berries, plants, and grasses that were once commonly seen and used had disappeared from the landscape. The trips often led her to verbalize her belief that the resources had disappeared because the People had stopped depending on them, using them, and passing on the knowledge about them to future generations. From her perspective, the plants, shrubs, and trees knew that they were no longer valued by the Navajos.

20. Several of Tall Woman's daughters believed she must have added either cornmeal or flour to make this stick together, but they were not sure.

21. Augusta, who worked as a cook in schools, reported that when she took juniper ash to a workshop in Phoenix in the summer of 1974 and produced blue cornbread with and without this ash, the analysis of both showed that the one with the juniper ash had more iron, and it also had more iron than a loaf of white bread from the store (Sandoval 1974).

22. Two Navajos told me that you could also burn wild spinach or wild mustard to make culinary ash. Some Navajos use the English terms *juniper* and *cedar* as synonyms and interchange them frequently. What is meant here, though, is juniper, or *gad*.

23. An elderly Navajo woman we visited in 2013 used to be a source of juniper ash for the family, after Tall Woman's death. However, since she has stopped riding horses, she now has to find people who are willing to take her way up in the mountains in a pickup truck to find the right kind of juniper. Before 2013 she would sell a big coffee can full of ash to friends for fifteen dollars. She described her "new way of making it" by using the woodstove in her trailer. First she cleans the stove out, then she roasts the juniper slowly in it all night. In the morning she removes the ash and puts everything through a sifter. She said that given where she now lives, "it's impossible to make it outside most of the time because the winds are too strong. I was losing most of it really quickly; the winds come up and just blow it away when you try to make it outside over an open fire. So I had to come up with a new way to do it, since a lot of the People still need it and use it, as I still do."

24. One ceremonialist told me that he had been taught there were three kinds of juniper, one of which was used for making culinary ash and the other two for creating ceremonial medicines.

25. Adding boiling water to blue cornmeal without ash reportedly turns it pink.

26. Tall Woman told me that her great-grandparents had brown sugar ('áshįįh łikan yishtłizhígíí). Initially I didn't think that could have been possible, but Dave Snow (personal communication, 2015) reminded me that the sugar industry was alive and well in Central and South America very early. Snow remarked that brown sugar was introduced by the Spanish perhaps as early as the seventeenth century, given the fact that the sugar cane industry was in full swing east of the Valley of Mexico (Puebla and Vera Cruz). The twenty-five pounds of sugar that priests received every three or so years for mission use in the seventeenth century was undoubtedly not refined. Sugar cones, called *piloncillo* in Mexico, were among the Spanish trade goods that passed through Santa Fe to Plains Indians and others, probably including the Navajos, by the end of the eighteenth century. So Navajo access to brown sugar way before the Long Walk does not seem farfetched.

    There is no way to date when white sugar became known to the Navajos, since, as Snow reminded me, the early documents don't specify the color of sugar except for the brown piloncillo from Mexico. Sometimes territorial documents include brand names but not color. Perhaps it accompanied the army rations that came into the Southwest in 1848. But invoices reviewed by Snow for supplies from Mexico to the presidio at Santa Barbara, California, list forty pounds of mixed white sugar in 1810; twenty-five loads of white-sugar cake, well packaged, in 1808; and thirty pounds of sugar, half white and half mixed, also in 1808. The earliest invoice, 1782, refers to six loads of brown-sugar cakes (piloncillo?) and ten pounds of "sugar." Thanks to Dave Snow for sending me the above information, which he contributed from a variety of references: Viola and Margolis (1991), MacLachlan and Rodriguez O. (1980), Ahlborn (1983), Perissinotto (1998), Weber (1996), and Elder and Weber (1996).

27. I have not been able to identify this plant. Klara Kelley (personal communication, 2015) pointed out that *k'aabizhii* is a cactus that grows around Cove, Arizona; it too has not been identified with an English name.

28. Although Tall Woman mentioned *ts'áátbái* only as a coffee creamer, Steven Begay (personal communication, 2016) said that this was a real misnomer. "In prehistoric oral history times," he said, "pre–Fort Sumner and precontact times, *ts'áátbái* was a thick gravy or mush. Only with time did it morph into a beverage additive."

29. Although *naaltsoii* was mentioned in section 1, it was decided, after much discussion with her daughters and others, to keep Tall Woman's cheese-making information together and include it all here.

30. I am indebted to David Snow for expanding my understanding of some of the details of earlier centuries of New Mexican history.

31. As stories from the Long Walk reveal, flour was sometimes moldy; full of smut, grit, manure, and other foreign substances; in the process of deteriorating; or already bad. Food was often at a minimum, and those contracting with the

military to provide cattle, sheep, flour, corn, wheat, salt, and other things also suffered from drought, crops damaged by worms and grasshoppers, flooding, competition, and rivalries. Some of the tests for "good flour" are particularly interesting, especially as the military tried to get local farmers to grow more wheat and corn and to modernize the methods used to dry, clean, and thresh wheat. I am indebted to Klara Kelley for telling me about Miller's (1989) very informative study.

Snow (personal communication, 2014) indicated that earlier ethnic and class issues remain today: wheat tortillas are an ethnic symbol in New Mexico for Hispanics, yet white bread remains a staple, and the texture of bread reflects social standing (i.e., the softer the bread, the higher the social status). Yellow corn is fed to chickens and cows and is used only for making tortillas, enchiladas, and posole (a stew made from backbone and dried corn). Native Americans continue to prefer corn tortillas, and earlier they ground the corn on the grinding stones until traders introduced corn grinders. Now blue corn tortillas and *'adola* (hot cereal) are readily found, as are tamales made with corn flour or white corn. Yellow corn produces yellow tortillas; white tortillas are now scarce because the commercial yellow hybrid corn varieties have taken over. Indians use wheat flour for making frybread, oven bread, sopapillas (fried dough fritters), *buñuelos* (fried dough balls), and fruit pies.

32. In 1965 Halworth Tanner, the grandfather of the current owners, Trent and Gary Tanner, started running the Cortez Milling Company, where Blue Bird Flour is made. It has always been packaged in cloth bags rather than paper, even though doing so is more expensive. Around 2008 a very popular change was made when five- and ten-pound bags were added as an option to the larger, twenty-five- and fifty-pound bags. The largest size has now been discontinued. The flour is based on local red winter wheat grown by dryland farmers. It is run through separators and then sprayed on a conveyor belt to wash and soften the bran coat on each kernel. Then it rests for twelve to fourteen hours. The mill has four old grinders, and the wheat passes through all of them, becoming increasingly smoother with each one. Then it goes through a series of sifters with a unique design. Thereafter the nutrients are put back into the flour, and bleach is added to speed up the whitening process. Then the flour is ready to go to market at T & R Grocery, Lowe's, Bashas', Kroger, Albertsons, and Safeway. The flour is not sold by Walmart because the mill can't produce enough to stock that chain. The flour is also shipped to customers outside the Southwest. The demand is especially high during the summer, during fair season, and when children are home from school. Cortez Milling Company produces other kinds of flour, too (Calvin 2010).

Personal communications in 2014 with Colin, Gary, and Tony Tanner added the following information to the history of Blue Bird Flour. The first mill was opened by Donald Tanner, Halworth's father, in Allison, Colorado, in 1934. He actually took an old water mill and converted it to a flour mill by adding a diesel engine. Donald had worked in Kirtland, New Mexico, driving a truck and hauling goods from Gallup to Farmington for a year or two before opening the first mill. That was during the Depression. In time, this mill, which was a Midget Marvel Roller Mill, was transferred into a long system so that the wheat could be ground up and various parts of it separated out. Donald Tanner ran that mill until around 1944.

In 1938 the Tanners moved to Bayfield, Colorado, and Donald's son, Halworth, bought another mill there. They spent time renovating and remodeling this second mill, which was not used until World War II was over. When the Bayfield Mill started up, the mill in Allison was closed. The Bayfield Mill, however, burned down in 1963 or 1964. Shortly thereafter the family moved to Cortez, where they "really got the business of Blue Bird Flour going." Halworth opened the Cortez Milling Company, and today the company is still in the same facility. Colin, Halworth's son, said he went into business for himself in 1972 and focused on producing Blue Bird Flour for the Navajo people.

33. People have different ways of talking about flour and different understandings of what is meant. Flour ground from white corn was very popular in the Southwest. Most people said this was coarse because it was first ground directly from corn kernels. Some people say that cornmeal, which is coarse, is corn flour or flour ground from dried maize. The British reportedly call cornstarch, a white powdered starch of maize grain, "corn flour." Masa is the flour of hominy. When masa is finely ground and treated with finely ground lime, it becomes masa harina. That is the base for tortillas and tamales for many groups of people.

34. Mayes and Lacy (1989, 108) say that a layer of spiny salt bush was used to cover the corn before hot dirt was added, since it added a salty taste to the corn while it cooked all night.

35. Some people, if they were freezing blue cornmeal mush on the roof to make *dahaastiin*, believed that you had to put a few hot coals in the center of it to protect everybody in the family from bad spirits and to ward off predators.

36. Since pigmeat was not readily available because the family didn't raise pigs, Frank frequently bought the salt pork Tall Woman needed from the store.

37. This discussion triggered a memory from Augusta, who noted that although she and the family grew white potatoes, they never grew sweet potatoes, and she had never even seen one of those until she went to the Chinle Boarding School. After she learned about sweet potatoes at school and discovered she liked them, she came home and told her parents about this new food.

38. Family members who did grow orange field pumpkins usually cut them into pieces and then boiled or baked them on the coals or in a big outdoor beehive-shaped oven. The pieces were also dried for later use, and for this the pumpkin was peeled and sliced into rings or cut into a continuing spiral. The dried

bundles were tied and hung up in storerooms. When it was time to use them, the pieces were soaked first and then boiled until they became soft. These could be added to meat that had been fried in fat, stirred, and mashed. Family members did not carve pumpkins as part of Halloween, but there was some dressing up in costumes and trick-or-treating that involved calling on extended-family members. For people who now live in town, the trick-or-treating is focused in the neighborhood.

39. The idea was that if you picked the older blossoms, the plant would produce more new, small, tender ones.

40. One of Frank's clan relatives, William Wilson, asked the Mitchells to take over his peach trees in the canyon, which they did until they could no longer do the work involved. David Mitchell, one of the sons of Frank and Tall Woman, worked for the Soil Conservation Service and planted peach trees in the Island Place, Tóta, in the Chinle Wash, as well as in the jetties created in the Nazlini Wash. David cared for all the trees he planted, and they had just begun producing fruit when he died from what was thought to be spinal meningitis.

41. Kaibetoney (2009) mentions that the children who are asked to chew cornmeal and then spit into the batter, 'ii'nídít'aał, must be healthy. Doing this task "helps children grow up to be good listeners, respectful, hardworking, and industrious." According to Kaibetoney, anyone who has had a Fire Dance done for them and any hunters should stay away from the fire while the cake is baking.

Kaibetoney's recipe for 'alkaan, which comes from years of "playing around" with the ingredients, is included here with her permission. She combines twelve to fifteen pounds of ground white cornmeal with boiling water—adding five pounds at a time while constantly stirring and thereafter by the handful. When the batter has some body, she returns it to the fire and brings it back to a boil, stirring constantly for about ten minutes. (She considers this step to be her secret to a good cake.) Then she puts the mixture back into a mixing bowl and adds three cups of whole wheat flour, four to five pounds of brown sugar, and two cups of Blue Bird Flour, stirring all the time. She tastes it after adding the Blue Bird Flour and adds more handfuls of cornmeal if necessary. When she is satisfied with the texture, she adds two cups of oatmeal (and raisins, if desired). The mixture is too thick if it can't be cut; it will be as hard as a rock.

Kaibetoney lets the batter cool for thirty to forty-five minutes, and during that time it liquefies, so she adds more cornmeal as necessary. The batter should keep its shape when dripping off the stirring sticks. Then she lines a pan with corn husks doing the sides first, with the inside of the husks against the pan. She puts in the center corn husk and then pours the batter into the center first. She fills the pan to the top and covers it first with husks, then with foil to seal the pan. The pit should be totally free of hot coals and ashes. She covers the pan with metal plates and covers those with hot ashes. Then she adds burning coals and dried wood on the top. After letting the cake cook for twelve hours or overnight, she removes the pan and turns the cake upside down to cool for two to three hours. "Then," Kaibetoney concluded, "slice and enjoy."

One of the many other practices I learned about over the years came from a family that made a very huge cake; the women used ten pounds of white sugar to make it. In this case all the husks for the pit were woven together, and the pit was first lined with damp brown paper bags before the woven corn husks were put in, followed by the batter. That family reportedly had no dirt or dust on the girl's six-inch thick 'alkaan because they let the edges of the damp paper bags stick up around the edge of the pit.

42. Steven Begay (personal communication, 2015) said that the older women in his family told him that in earlier times when sugar was scarce, they would soak wheat or corn and have the children chew the raw seeds and then spit into the batter. The chewed seeds were also used in making a smaller version of 'alkaan called łééyilzhóózh.

43. The recipe Overstreet (2014, 14) gives is for one cake baked ten minutes per side on a greased griddle. It uses two cups of finely ground blue (or yellow or white) cornmeal, two tablespoons of juniper ash, one cup of boiling water, and a pinch of salt. The ashes are mixed in the boiling water and then strained; the water is added to the cornmeal, made into dough, flattened into a cake, and baked.

44. If you use a recipe for tortillas, it will include baking powder as well as white flour. Baking powder will make the dumplings expand; they will be thicker and will cook faster.

45. Young and Morgan (1987, 855) also refer to a corn cake, a type of native griddle cake, called tsé bąąh naalzhóó'. I was not able to learn anything about this corn cake except that it was clearly baked on a stone griddle.

46. Luci Tapahonso's (2008, 69–70) fans might enjoy her poem "Náneeskadí," in which she gives her tortilla recipe. The ingredients are a few handfuls of flour (either Blue Bird or Navajo Pride), a bit of salt, a palmful of baking powder, two fingertips of lard, one and a half cups of very hot water, and olive oil with which to grease the griddle.

47. People in different areas have different names for tortillas cooked over charcoal. Steven Begay said that in the Naschitti area they are called tsíídkáá shích'íłí and that shích'íł is an old word that means dried and roasted.

48. Unfortunately, I did not get proportions from Tall Woman for making nanoyeeshi. For four summers (2010 through 2013) Augusta and I did try to find elderly women who knew about this kind of bread, but without success. The important points that Tall Woman stressed were that the batter had to be thin but firm and not too runny when it was poured into the hot ashes. It expands slowly as it cooks; when it has stopped expanding, cover it and then build the cooking fire on top of the cover. When the bread is finished, it should be round.

49. For example, in 2011 at the Chinle parade during the Central Fair, kneel-down bread was sold for $1.50 a piece from kids' wagons. In 2013 at another parade, small pieces were $5, a big one was $20, and a loaf, about six inches long and one and a half inches wide, was $2. In May 2015 in Window Rock, a teenage girl standing outside Lowe's was selling "Navajo bread," wrapped in corn husks and tied in three places, for $2, and a boy was selling Rice Krispie treats, about three inches square, for $1 each. People were readily sharing information about what they were adding to make kneel-down bread sweeter: brown sugar, honey, syrup, yucca fruit juice, or cactus fruit juice. Some now make kneel-down bread with fresh milk and wheat. Some women depend on selling it all summer and at any other times they can to support their families and pay the bills. They transport the bread in children's wagons and put up handmade signs. The latter often advertise that their bread is moist and sweet, not dry and hard. The *Navajo Times* has described women who bake all day on Friday to make 600 loaves and sell all of them on Saturday at the Gallup flea market or elsewhere, such as in Tuba City, Kayenta, Leupp, and Window Rock. Some women are now paying family members to cut kernels off cobs and grind the corn so it's ready to be made into kneel-down bread, and then they share the profits. Some are branching out by selling bowls of mush for $4 or by developing networks so they have regular customers who want to buy in quantity. In such cases women may buy boxes of fresh corn from private distributors in Phoenix or Tucson, from NAPI, or even from local Navajos with large farms (Shebala 2007b).

50. Some people say that now most women are not making real kneel-down bread, but instead things that are more like Mexican burritos. They are using store-bought tortillas, the really thin kind, for the wrapping, and adding "all kinds of junk like rice and beans. That's Mexican, not Navajo."

Augusta asked me to include her recipe for Mexican tamales, which are *not* Navajo kneel-down bread. She learned to make them from her sister Agnes and also by seeing how they were made in Mexican and Spanish restaurants. By 2014 some people she knew were using a wok instead of a steamer or a slow cooker, which is what she uses when making tamales; they said the tamales cook faster in a wok.

Augusta makes tamales using chicken, pork, beef, mutton, or venison, but she prefers pork unless venison is available. She buys masa harina (finely ground hominy flour with lime) and packaged corn husks at Bashas' or Lowe's. Before she fixes her meat, she prepares the corn husks, since they have to soak overnight, if not longer. After they have soaked, she spreads them out flat, pats them dry, and wraps them in a wet cloth. They have to be moist on both sides and flat.

After preparing the corn husks, she makes the dough, following the directions on the masa harina package. She described it as follows. Using a separate bowl, take three to four cups of masa, add two teaspoons of baking powder, a little salt, and one-half to three-fourths cup of lard. In a small saucepan, and using two to three tablespoons of lard and half a cup of white flour, brown the flour, stirring constantly until it turns tan. Then mix one tablespoon of chili powder with cold water and pour that into the browned flour, stirring so it remains smooth while it thickens.

Once the meat is cooked, it has to be chopped very fine, almost shredded. Augusta puts it in a skillet; adds garlic powder, salt, the chili mixture she has just made, and pepper; and stirs while it cooks on low heat. She also adds a little warm water to a bit of the meat broth from the slow cooker and combines that with the meat mixture, too, so it's not too dry or watery. It should be thin when it spreads out.

When the dough and meat mixture are ready, open four of the husks at a time. Put the masa mixture on the smooth side of the husk, not the rough one, making it as thick as you want. On top of that, put about two tablespoons of the meat mixture. Then fold both sides of the husk and one end down. Prepare all the husks that way and then put them in the cooker or steamer in a single layer, for forty-five to fifty-five minutes. She does not tie her tamales. When they are done, remove them and let them cool; the husks will come off easily when peeled from the unfolded end.

51. Some friends from Naschitti, New Mexico, said they were not familiar with the term *taajilééhíí* but presumed it must mean a form of *ntsidigo'í* as a tamale-like bread tied off with corn husks. They had also heard their sweetened cornmeal tamale, *nijiło'í*, called *jool'óhí* and *be'estł'óní*. *Nijiło'í*, they said, can be made with or without juniper ash. Mix dry roasted blue cornmeal with sugar or wheat germ for sweetness and add enough hot water to get a sturdy dough. Clean and soak some corn husks. Take about one tablespoon of dough and roll it into a one-and-a-half- to two-inch tube. Wrap that in the corn husk and tie it in tamale fashion, at opposite ends, or "make them like a tea bag and tie them at the top," according to Steven Begay's family (personal communication, 2016). When you have tied all of them, boil them in a large stew pot for two hours or more.

52. For some, the difference between kneel-down bread and tamales may be whether they are tied. Augusta said that some Navajos she knows say that if they are tied they are called tamales. She doesn't tie her tamales, but she does add chili and possibly bay leaves. Now people also add other things, like rice. Some people say that if the bread is to be steamed, it doesn't need to be tied, but if it will be boiled, then it needs to be tied. Some tie both the small and large kneel-down bread packets.

53. For some people, the addition of meat may be the difference between kneel-down bread and tamales. Others say that tamales are boiled and that kneel-down bread is baked. Some say only tamales, the boiled ones, are tied with corn husk ties. And for some, the major difference is that kneel-down bread is made from fresh corn rather than raw cornmeal.

The term *taa be'estł'óní* was given to me to refer to very stiff mush placed on corn husks that are folded, tied in the center and at the ends, and then boiled in this shape. Whether these are related to *łeehilzhoozh*, which reportedly have a stiffer, heavier batter than *taajilééhíí*, is unclear. Given the above descriptions of the preparation and tying of various kinds of tamales, *taa be'éstł'óní* seem to be a combination of the two.

54. A few people told me that *tsé'ást'éí* is the word for the griddle and *nóogazi* is the name of the paperbread made on it.

55. Roasting was done very slowly over live coals on the end of a stick, right on the coals, in the ground, or under live coals with another fire built on top. Broiling consisted of slowly turning the meat over, most often above live coals. Baking, which was frequently used, was done in several ways, such as turning the meat over occasionally on live coals or putting it in a pan in some kind of oven. If the meat was an organ, such as a liver (*'azid*), it might be spread open and greased with mutton fat before baking, or it might be boiled for several hours.

56. Even though some of these organs were not eaten, this does not mean they were not used. For example, the sheep's gallbladder was used as medicine, to treat sores and colds. Both Tall Woman and John Gorman kept gallbladders on hand for this purpose. John also kept skunk gallbladders. During the flu epidemic of 1918–1920, the Navajos reportedly used gallbladders and one-fourth teaspoon of kerosene to cure people. (For more recent research on this pandemic, see Brady and Bahr 2014; they show that Navajo mortality was undercounted and that the pandemic lasted into 1920.)

57. Although each organ has a separate term, the lungs, heart, and liver are the thoracic organs, *'ajéí*.

58. The small intestine is *'ach'íí' dootł'izhí*. Augusta added more information about blood sausage, saying that there were three ways to make it, all of which were used by her mother. *'Ach'íídííl* refers to blood sausage made from the large intestine—as well as to the large intestine itself, which is the first choice when making blood sausage. You can also use the stomach and divide that into two parts, or you can use the small part that's attached to the end of the small intestine, known as the grinder (*'abidíyázhí*), the part of the stomach that grinds the food as it goes from the stomach into the intestine. Which one of the three you use depends on how much blood you have and what else you have to use when stuffing the sausage. In any case, you always turn whatever part of the animal you are using inside out after washing it out and cleaning it thoroughly. Some people use vinegar to do the cleaning. Then you put the fat on the inside. You can also cut up the small intestine into pieces to add to the stuffing if you want.

If you use the second choice, the stomach, use a full-grown sheep for this. That will give you a medium-size stomach. Divide it into two sections and put only a little of the mixture into each part before you tie it off with a thread or string; if you overfill it, it will burst, so fill it only a little over halfway. Boil it for about an hour, then poke it with a stick or a fork in one or two places to let air out, because steam will be building up. Keep stirring it so it doesn't stick to the pot.

To make blood sausage the third way, fill what's called the grinder: the sheep's rennet stomach, small stomach, or small place at the end of the small stomach where food goes after it's digested. This part is folded up on the inside like an accordion.

59. Evidently the proper term for this food is *'ach'íí' bik'ídeesdizí*, tallow twisted with entrails and fried or roasted. According to Young and Morgan (1980), *'ach'íí'* means intestine. However, I have only ever heard this specialty food referred to as *'ach'íí'*.

60. See Shebala (2007a) for an excellent discussion of the more than fifty-year-old family business in Waterflow, New Mexico, that caters to Navajos' love of sweetmeat. The store constantly battles with the US Department of Agriculture and New Mexico's Livestock Inspection Board over the production and sale of sheep heads, blood, stomachs, hearts, and intestines wrapped with fatty sections of organ meats. The article says that the store uses about 1,000 sheep a month and has five people employed to butcher three times a week, whereas other employees make the fresh and roast mutton cuts for Navajo customers. One sheep, according to the article, yields about twenty-five rolls of *'ach'íí'*.

61. Although Tall Woman had a variety of Navajo pots around her home in the 1960s, none of them were the big one referred to here. None of her children knew what happened to this pot. Augusta told me that her mother only ever had one big pot, and it seemed to have disappeared, maybe even in the 1940s, a long time before her mother "got into old age." Needless to say, I never saw this pot. She said Tall Woman never used that pot while cooking their meals, but she did cook foods for ceremonial occasions in it, when Navajo pottery was required. The pot was tall and had very thick sides and a rounded bottom, and she put it right down in the ashes or charcoal. Reportedly, she also had a cast-iron skillet that she used for making *'akágí*.

62. Today, given the increased awareness of and concern about health problems such as diabetes and obesity, people are warned to limit their salt intake and also how much jerky they eat because it is very high in calories. Now people say not to use more than 300 milligrams of salt in making jerky.

63. Augusta noted that today some people use a blender to shred or cut up the meat. However, many traditional women say that if you make it this way, it isn't real jerky.

64. Meat reportedly dries very fast in the wintertime. Augusta said that some people now prefer to store the jerky in vacuum-sealed plastic bags. A few people told me that they now prefer to dry their jerky in an oven at 140°–160°F for four to six hours with the oven door open "just a crack"; many others said

that jerky tastes better if you make it "the old way" or "naturally, drying the meat outside." (These comments do not, of course, represent a reservation-wide sample.)

65. Although everybody in the family used this term, no such term is included in Young and Morgan (1980), who call beef jerky *béégashii bitsį' 'ałk'ídaniilgizhígíí*. Family members did frequently express meat hunger with the term *'ach'ą́* .

66. I don't know whether this is also true of antelope jerky.

67. After the return from the Long Walk, government rations included plates, cups, and the like until 1878.

68. Three ceremonialists told me that *neeshjį́zhii* is *more important or "more profound" than other foods*, such as hominy, made from regular dried corn.

69. Steven Begay's aunt told him that the difference is in the cornmeal used for *'adola*. That is raw unroasted cornmeal, and it has to boil longer (Begay, personal communication, 2016).

70. Young and Morgan (1987, 702) say that *tanáá'niil* is a remixed mush used in ceremonies, where it is remixed again for subsequent use.

71. Tall Woman said that some people add juniper ash to this mush, but others say no, not unless you are using blue cornmeal to make it. Other people disagree but say that if you use white cornmeal to make it and add juniper ash, you will need much less of the ash than would be required for blue cornmeal.

72. Begay (personal communication, 2016) said that this mush, *gad 'ádin*, rather than blue cornmeal mush, should be made for a traditional wedding. *Gad 'ádin* is comparable to the vows recited in public by the couple in a Bilagáana (Anglo) wedding. It's the focal point, the thing that binds the ceremony together. You eat this mush with your spouse only once in your lifetime. When it is prepared for a wedding, white (for the male) and yellow (for the female) cornmeal are combined to symbolize the couple.

73. This section does not include medicinal broths, although Tall Woman knew how to make many and understood all the diseases and medical problems for which they were remedies. Despite her vast knowledge of medicinal plants, herbs, and various preparations and the great respect shown to her because of this knowledge (which she sometimes employed in her work as a midwife), such knowledge has not been included in this work because it is protected intellectual property. Also, we did not discuss intoxicating drinks even though her husband mentioned some when telling me about his life (Mitchell [1978] 2003). During Prohibition, wine, beer, whiskey, and other intoxicating drinks became illegal throughout the country. When soda pop, cider, and canned juices became available from stores, many shifted their preferences to these sugary drinks. Peterson and Webster (2013, 102) note that the Navajo terms for soda can also refer to juice, wine, Kool-Aid, champagne, or other drinks, depending on the context.

74. One of the favorite memories in the family was of Dick Dunaway going by on the dirt road while doing his job for the US Bureau of Reclamation of checking the wells and windmills from Chinle to Kayenta (Mitchell 2001, 444–45).

75. See Young (1961, 174–76) for a discussion of the federal Long Range Act and what it accomplished for water development on the reservation. During the 1950s, when the tribe and the Bureau of Indian Affairs actually cooperated on water development projects, 490 new wells were drilled in Navajo country.

76. The popularity of Arbuckle's coffee showed up again during research on the Annunciation Mission in Chinle, Arizona. Brother Gervase Thuemmel, OFM, who went to Chinle in August 1906 to help Father Leopold Ostermann, OFM, finish building the friary, was next responsible for helping to build the Annunciation Mission (1909–1910). During a later interview with Father Mark Sandford, OFM, Brother Gervase said he had carved the altars and built the vestment case "mostly out of Starbuckel [sic] coffee cases" (Grein and Frisbie 2005, 18).

77. Some people told Tall Woman that they made coffee from plants, such as mistletoe, marigold, and beggar-ticks. All these were boiled to make plant coffee, or *ch'il gohwéhé*. However, she herself never tried doing that and had never tasted any of those things. The only information I could gather was confirmation of a drink made in earlier times from juniper mistletoe, called *dahts'aa'* (or sometimes *gad bidahts'aa'*).

78. She also mentioned teas from juniper, sagebrush, copper mallow, and other plants used for medical purposes.

79. Tall Woman mentioned Lipton and said there were several jokes in the family about the Lipton man on the box.

80. Seya, one of Tall Woman's sons, called the small tea plant owl's foot tea because, he said, the plant reminded him of an owl's foot.

81. For some native Navajo-speakers, *ts'áálbái* is a generic label for several kinds of corn creamers and even *tóshchíín* (blue cornmeal mush). Some claim that *łee'shibéézh* is the same thing as *ts'áálbái*. But according to Steven Begay (personal communication, 2016), to call *ts'áálbái* a powdered steamed corn creamer or a coffee creamer is a misnomer and should not be done. In prehistoric oral history times, pre–Fort Sumner and precontact times, *ts'áálbái* was a thick gravy or mush.

Chapter 4

1. It will be important to track Navajo discussions of multinational events already causing grave concerns in many parts of the world. At the end of September 2016, the most serious threats to the world's food supplies are the proposed mergers in the international agribusiness community of more giant corporations, such as Dow-Dupont (with or without BASF) and Monsanto-Bayer. Unless these mergers are blocked by the US Justice Department, control of the

world's food supply could soon be in the hands of only four multinational agrochemical corporations, a move that could easily have dire consequences for all humans. Concerned citizens involved in the global food sovereignty movement are closely monitoring and actively protesting these potential developments.

2. At the end of September 2016, individuals from the Navajo Nation Tax Office and Community Development Office were involved in holding training sesions for chapter officers throughout the reservation. These continued through the fall. Actual disbursements, at least for some chapters, started at the end of March or in early April 2017. At present, the disbursements do not appear to be on a reservation-wide schedule.

Appendix A

1. Thanks to Joanne McCloskey for her e-mail of February 22, 2008, as well as numerous discussions earlier and later. Her suggestions for relevant reports, publications, and websites were invaluable. Thanks also to Victor Oliveira, Alex Majchrowicz, and Nancy Theodore of the Food Distribution Program, Food and Nutrition Service, US Department of Agriculture (USDA), especially for communications in February and March 2008. For the history of the Food Distribution Program, see https://www.fns.usda.gov/fdd/aboutfd/history.htm. I am grateful to the late David M. Brugge for an interview in November 2008 and discussing it on November 4, 2011, and to Martha Blue for including my questions for Bill Beaver during her own interviews with him on August 11, 2007. Also thanks to Sister Adelaide Link, Aline Davis, Irving Nelson, and Klara Kelley. The website for the Food Distribution Program on Indian Reservations, https://www.fns.usda.gov/fdpir/food-distribution-program-indian-reservations-fdpir, provides a list of currently available USDA products; information about packaging, storage, and nutrition; and suggested recipes. See also Young (1961, 341–43), McDonald (1965), and Wolfe (1984). For an ironic reference, see Vizenor's (2008, 56–57) account of "exotic commodity rations": Father Meme's delivery of several boxes of canned food, beans, peanut butter, and hard blocks of cheese-commodity bounty provided by corrupt federal agents to priests, who then made gifts of it to mothers whose sons were altar boys. See also Vizenor (2014, 224–25) for Father Aloysius's critiques, which include declaring that "commodity food was an exterminator cuisine," that "more natives had vanished on a commodity diet of federal fat, salt, and sugar than by love, politics, war, weather, or any other cause," and that "fry bread was the most pernicious eradication fare on the reservation." For some other humor, see Peterson and Webster's (2013, 108–9) discussion of federally subsidized cell phones for reservation residents. As they report, these phones are being called "ná áá jáah [na'ajaah] phones," commodity phones. People told them that "it's like the cheese . . . when you go to the Chapter house every

month to get your free government food," which is parceled out piece by piece. The term for cell phones is a playful use of grammar, a critique of governmental policies of doling out items to Navajos (or "handing out small bits of commodity food to needy recipients"), and also an index of socioeconomic disparities and shared experiences.

2. Some of Tall Woman's daughters say they received commodity foods in the 1920s; they were probably remembering foods available through the state welfare program, before the tribal program started in 1959. They remember the commodities program being expanded to include soap and powdered milk.

3. In the course of my research on commodity programs, I discovered that two colleagues, David M. Brugge and Bill Beaver, had firsthand experience with the programs in New Mexico and Arizona, respectively. I proceeded to ask each about his memories of those days. Brugge, who worked for the New Mexico Welfare Assistance Program from March through September 1952, before the tribe got involved, said that at that time the items included powdered eggs, honey (in five-pound cans), and powdered milk. Both the eggs and the milk came in large containers, similar to fifty-pound drums. New Mexico used three sizes of bags: one-, two-, and five-pound bags tied at the end. In the mid-1950s, according to Brugge, cheese, canned meat, and pinto beans were added. He also said that the Navajos used the powdered milk to feed orphaned lambs as well as for cooking.

While Alexander Jack was head of the New Mexico commodities program in Santa Fe during Brugge's tenure, Robert J. Drake, known as Jake Drake, was in charge of the Navajo end of it. He was stationed in Gallup as the field supervisor at the warehouse on old Zuni Road. There was also a foreman at the warehouse, who initially may have been Zane Towne, a Navajo; then Raymond Garcia; and then, temporarily in 1952, Brugge. The state's commodities program also employed an elderly Navajo man who ran the machine that put food into bags at the warehouse, a young Navajo assistant, two truck drivers (Edward Ortiz and Zane Towne), and two drivers' helpers (Dave Brugge, who also drove sometimes, and James Bonham). Before their employment, both Bonham and Brugge had been anthropology students at the University of New Mexico. Once a month, using two state trucks, the teams went to their distribution sites to issue food; most often the sites were trading posts, but occasionally, a chapter house or a school was used. Brugge did not recall his team ever visiting the New Mexican towns of Canoncito, Alamo, or Ramah. He said they made weekly trips in a big circuit out from the Gallup warehouse, with announcements about both the site and their expected arrival time being carried on Gallup's KGAK radio during the Navajo Hour.

Bill Beaver said (according to Martha Blue, personal communication, 2007) that he was asked by Alexander Jack in the early 1950s if he would be willing to head up the commodity program distribution in Arizona. He declined, not wanting to move, and said that initially Arizona had turned down the program, but later the state changed its mind. Thus Arizona also had a program running in the early 1950s that included Navajos among the "needy people" to be served; the tribe agreed to get involved in 1957, developed its plan of operation in March 1958, and actually started distributing food in February 1959.

4. Kopp (1986, 12) said that the 1965 additions also included sugar, syrup, fruit juices, macaroni, cereals, and dehydrated products. She also noted that the Donated Food Program replaced the Commodity Food Program in 1971. Both my research and that of Wendy Wolfe show that the Donated Food Program was just *another name* for the Commodities Food Program. I do agree with Kopp, however, that the assistance program missed an incredibly important opportunity by not including, supporting, stressing, and building on the traditional foods that were a nutritious and an established part of the Navajo subsistence diet. Although the program did make more food available in the 1960s and 1970s, the foods it included were certainly less nutritious, focusing on refined cereals, fat, and commercial products and leaving a shortage of minerals, meat sources, and plant foods. However, the lack of useful records before the beginning of the Indian Health Service in 1955 makes it impossible to draw conclusions about many changes that occurred as the Navajos transitioned from a subsistence existence into a wage-based economy and began to buy more and more food instead of growing and raising it, trading for it, and sharing it within extended families.

5. The same thing is true on the federal level; in the 2008 Farm Bill, the federal Food Stamp Program was renamed the Supplemental Nutrition Assistance Program, or SNAP.

6. Theodore (personal communication, 2008) indicated that she had little information on what was happening before 1979, and nothing before 1977, and that the published data from the National Data Bank go back only to 1982, when an earlier data system was replaced. She also noted that the paper reports show only what types of food were *available*, not what each tribe actually *selected*, which is an important point. Also significant is that the data for the Navajo Tribe are not broken down further, such as by geographic region or chapter; instead they just show total numbers by years. For example, for the federal fiscal year 1978 in the Needy Family Program, the average monthly participation was 28,522 Navajos, whereas it was 23,363 in 1979, the first federal fiscal year of the FDPIR. In 2008, the most recent data, which were for 2007, showed 9,460.

In 2015–2016 I was able, with the help of Suzanne Callor (Arizona Department of Education, Health and Nutrition Programs), to track down the history of the Special Food Service Program for Children (SFSPC), P.L. 90-302, which was enacted on May 8, 1968, to ensure that schoolchildren had food to eat during the summer. The SFSPC was a three-year pilot program that was the forerunner of both the Child Care Food Program and the Summer Food Service Program (SFSP). With additional legislation, the SFSPC was extended until September 30, 1975, and on October 7, 1975, the SFSP was enacted into law as P.L. 94-105. This is when individuals working on nine-month contracts in public school kitchens were able to start working twelve months a year, because the eligible schoolchildren would be fed during the summer.

7. As expected, traditional food use was infrequent (Wolfe and Sanjur 1988, 824). The only foods mentioned in this category (with varying frequency) were mutton, tortillas, frybread, wild Navajo tea, blue cornmeal mush with ash, yellow cornmeal mush, hominy corn, Navajo pancakes, wild sumac berry pudding, and goat's milk. The most commonly mentioned items in the diet were coffee, Navajo tortillas and frybread (defined as homemade bread made from white wheat flour, baking powder, salt, water, and—since the 1950s, in some cases—commodity instant nonfat dry milk), potatoes, eggs, and sugar (usually in coffee or tea). Other items commonly consumed and recalled included sweetened drink mixes, soda pop, store-bought bread, fresh mutton, beef, and canned or fresh milk (mostly in coffee). Three cooked meals were usually eaten a day. Bread was always part of a meal; in the morning the meal reportedly included fried eggs, fried potatoes, and sometimes bacon or other meat. The rest of the meals usually included one boiled stew or bean dish and one fried or roasted meat each day. "Several meals were eaten at fast-food restaurants," noted Wolfe and Sanjur, which had now reached some reservation towns. Fruits and vegetables, major sources of vitamins A and C, were infrequently consumed. The Commodity Food Program was found to be making important nutritional contributions to the contemporary Navajo diet. "But that diet was below the RDA in Vitamin A and C, and it was recommended that the program provide more sources of these vitamins, more fiber, and less saturated fat" (826–27).

8. The items Wolfe (1984) listed were as follows:

Meat and other protein. Canned pork, chicken, meatball stew, tuna fish, dry beans, canned vegetables, canned beans, roasted peanuts, dehydrated egg mix.

Dairy products. Evaporated milk, instant milk (nonfat dried), processed cheese.

Grains. Milled rice, rolled oats, cornmeal, macaroni, spaghetti, farina, bread flour.

Vegetables. Canned green beans, creamed corn, whole corn, green peas, spinach, whole potatoes, sweet potatoes, dehydrated potatoes.

Fruits. Canned applesauce, apricots, peaches, fruit cocktail, pears, pineapple, plums.

Juices. Apple, orange, pineapple, tomato.

Fats and sweets. Vegetable shortening, corn syrup.

Other foods distributed. Peanut butter, canned butter, rice cereal for babies, raisins, canned carrots.

The 1982 monthly food package documented by Wolfe and Sanjur (1988, 823) included canned meats, canned and dry beans, dehydrated eggs and potatoes, peanut butter, evaporated and nonfat dry milk, cheese, pasta, rice, oats, corn-meal, flour, canned vegetables, canned fruits and fruit juices, butter and short-ening, corn syrup, and raisins.

9. Thanks are due to Samuel Pearson, a friend and colleague, for accessing cover-age of the bill and post-passage discussions from the *New York Times.*

Appendix B

1. Kentucky Fried Chicken was operating in 1978 when Father Blane came to Chinle. He said that the franchise later claimed that Burbank had not followed through on meeting some standards and that thereafter, because of a divorce, Burbank had to sell business assets. He allegedly reopened it as a chicken and shrimp place about four to six weeks later, but that didn't take off, and after only a few months he had to close. Mike Nelson, a Navajo businessman from Window Rock, then stepped in. Father Blane thinks that this was in the late 1980s, and people at Church's Chicken say they don't know. In December 2014 Nelson announced plans to build another Church's Chicken in Kayenta, Ari-zona; it was to be the fourth one on the reservation. It opened on April 17, 2016 (K. Allen 2016b).

2. Colvin reported that Burger King's lease with the tribe is dated October 18, 1990, but the DCI Shopping Center Inc. had no reciprocal access agreement with Richard Mike until November 3, 1997. When Burger King actually opened appears unclear, but Nina Heflin, the franchise owner along with Richard Mike, confirms that it was in the winter of 1992. Colvin's notes say it may have been February.

3. According to Father Blane, Teddy created the paintings that hung in the north and south of Our Lady of Fatima Church, and Robert did the painting dis-played in the east. Justin Tso did the painting hanging in the west.

4. Stoner said that businessman and good friend George Hartsock had the mis-fortune of dying from a blood clot the night after a simple surgery. His wife, Vangie Attson Hartsock, did not have the business sense her husband did. Stoner reported that when he wanted to sell to George, he asked a price that "only covered the equipment and the inventory." The Hartsocks had two sons, George Jr. and Joey; a daughter, Patricia; and a nephew, Craig, among other rel-atives. East of Begaye's Corner, before the road into the public housing area and the Chinle Wash, the leaseholders at various times were Fleming Begaye Sr., Paul Tso, Glenn Stoner, George Hartsock, the Silver Coin Laundry, and Sybil

Baldwin. On the other side of the road, again starting at the corner and going east, was the public school, LaFont's motel and restaurant (eventually known as the Best Western Canyon de Chelly Motel and the Junction Restaurant), and Baldwin's Mini Mart.

5. My sources disagree on who built La Casa Blanca: Kiddy (Robert) or his brother Ray. As of September 2016 I had not had a chance to talk directly with Stanley Martinez about the rest of the family; thus this account is based on the memories of Father Blane, Augusta, and Stoner, which didn't always agree. There were even disagreements over the nickname Kiddy; maybe it was Giddy. And maybe Stan Jr. was the contractor.

6. Reportedly Chinle residents pleaded with Stanley to keep the Imperial Mart open after Bashas' came, saying that his meats were much fresher—not covered with cellophane and put into coolers until they were sold—and that his mutton was the best.

7. Reportedly, at some point another Thriftway was put in at Begaye's Corner, replacing what may have been a Shell station. Apparently Begaye closed (reasons and date still unknown to me), and for a short time there was nothing on that corner. Thriftway wanted to come in, and both Father Blane and Colvin, who were serving on the community's planning board at the time, said that the board was opposed because there was already a Thriftway store near the Mormon church. However, this Thriftway, with its sixteen pumps, convenience store, and laundromat section, went in over the opposition of the Chinle Planning Board. I have not been able to learn when this became a Shell station run by Giant.

8. During the Navajo Food and Wellness Policy Summit held on June 13, 2013, at the Navajo Nation Museum in Window Rock, some presenters suggested that Bashas' market was to blame for the diabetes, obesity, and other diseases and health problems now prevalent on the reservation. Johnny Basha (A. J. Basha Jr.), who was at the conference, was not happy about such unsubstantiated claims. Of course, one of the premises of the food sovereignty movement is that colonialism—which is identified as having started with the incarceration of the Navajos at Fort Sumner and then continuing through the trading posts, the railroad, boarding schools, and other events and influences that took control of Navajo diet and food consumption—was responsible for the loss of traditional food practices and the resulting health problems of today.

Plant names include the scientific name if known. Certain categories (such as foods made from wild plants and foods made from corn) are more extensive than others. As the text demonstrates, especially in the category of breads and other things, at times foods were made in the same way or the same shape, differing from each other by one ingredient or its amount, the method of cooking, or the occasion for which they were made. Besides Tall Woman, who was my major source, of course, others consulted include Young and Morgan (1980, 1987), Morgan (2011), Wolfe (1981, 1984), Austin and Lynch (1983), and native Navajo-speaking colleagues. When people had different ways of pronouncing things or used slightly different words, these are included in the entries below as variants or alternatives. Tall Woman's way of saying the term is always given first. It should be noted that the alphabetizing follows Young and Morgan's (1970, xvi; 1980, x) system. While it is letter by letter, certain additions or changes are incorporated to accommodate features of the Navajo language. Thus, nasals follow regular vowels (or orals); barred ł follows regular l; and ', the glottal stop phoneme, comes before regular l except when used initially. In definitions of words, Navajo nouns are translated in the singular since, unlike in English, in Navajo number is carried in verbs, not nouns. It would have been impossible for me to resolve many of the questions that arose while assembling this glossary without help from linguist friends and colleagues; special thanks go to one of my native speaker colleagues, Steven Begay, to whom I am deeply indebted. All errors, of course, are solely mine.

'abe': Milk.

'abe' bee neezmasí: Griddle cake or pancake made with milk.

'abe' neesk'ihi, 'abe' neesk'įh: Cottage cheese.

'abe' taa'niil: Milk mush.

'abid: Stomach.

'abidíyázhí: Grinder; stomach part that grinds the food as it goes from the stomach into the small intestine.

'ach'ą́: Meat hunger.

'ach'íí': Sheep intestine; some say it means sausage; a specialty food.

'ach'íí' bik'ídeesdizí: Tallow twisted with entrails and fried or roasted.

'ach'íídííl, 'ach'íídił: Large intestine; some say it means blood sausage made with the big intestine.

'ach'íí' dootł'izhí: Small intestine.

'ach'íí' łik'aaí: Colon; large intestine.

'ach'ííts'osi, 'ach'įįts'osí: Blood sausage made with the small intestine.

'achǫ: Beef jerky.

'adił: Blood sausage.

'ádístsiin: Stirring stick.

'adola: Navajo word for Spanish 'atole; hot cereal.

'ahwééh, gohwééh: Coffee.

'ajéí: The thoracic organs (lungs; liver; and heart).

'akágí: Skin; rind; bark; or sheepskin fixed as a food.

'ak'áán: Flour.

'ak'ah: Grease or fat.

'ak'ahłání: Adipose fat or chitin.

'alizh bizis: Bladder.

'alkaad, 'alkągd: Sweetened corn cake; in earlier times, it was just for the Girls' Puberty Ceremony.

'alkaan: Tall Woman's term for corn cake for the Girls' Puberty Ceremony.

'ałk'íniilgizh: Meat made into jerky.

'ásaa' neiyéhii: Blister beetle.

'Asdzáán Nééz: Tall Woman; Rose Mitchell.

'áshįįh: Salt.

'Áshįįhí: Salt People; a Navajo clan.

'áshįįh łikan: White sugar.

'áshįįh łikan yishtłizhígíí: Brown sugar.

'áshįįh ntl'izí: Rock salt.

'atłish: Pinyon nut butter.

'atł'izh: Bile.

'atoo': Stew; soup; or mush.

'atsá 'azee', 'atsá ch'il: Eagleway medicine; wild plant used for flavoring; maybe a kind of mint.

'atsį: Meat.

'atsį biskáni: Dried meat; generic term for jerky.

'ats'id: Ligament from a sheep's backbone.

'atsiighąą': Sheep's brain.

'atsi łeeshibeezh: Sheep's head wrapped in husks and baked in coals.

'ats'ǫ 'asis: Sheep's rennet stomach or small stomach.

'ayááshiłtsoii: Small yellow bird.

'ayaazh, 'ayáázh: Tiny corn kernel; corn barely ripening.

'ayid, 'ayidí: Breastbone.

'ayid 'atsį: Upper chest meat.

'ayidítsį': Chest flesh; stem meat; or upper chest meat.

'azee': Medicine.

'azid: Liver.

'azóól: Corn tassel.

bááh: Bread (Arizonan word).

bááh bighan: Small earth or mud oven; literally, "bread, its house."

bááh díík'ǫsh bił 'ál'íní: Yeast bread; bread made from something rotten or spoiled.

bááh ditódi: Soft bread or pancake.

bááh dootł'ízhi: Blue cornbread (baked in loaves).

bááh nímazí: Biscuit.

béégashii: Cow.

béégashii bitsį' 'ałk'ídaniilgizhígíí: Alternative term for beef jerky. See also *'achǫ*.

béégashii bitsį' shibézhígíí: Beef stew.

Begochidí: Sun's younger son; the invisible Moon Bearer.

bé'élts'éé': Wild vegetable soup; some call it gravy.

be'estł'óní, be'estł'óóní, be'ástł'óní: Hair bun shape; tied up in the shape of a hair bun; another name for a sweetened cornmeal tamale.

bé'ézhóó': Hairbrush; also a brush for grinding stones.

bichaan: Manure.

bidichíí: Red mark on Tall Woman's sack.

bídíshniih: To pound on.

bįįh: Deer.

bii'oo'éél, bii'ooléél: Gravy or gravy-like soup.

biínídoot'aal: Method of sweetening cornmeal in which one sucks on the cornmeal so that saliva enzymes convert starch to sugar.

bijį: Final night of a ceremony with all-night singing.

bíkáá'at'eesí: Stone grill for making paperbread; stone griddle.

Bilagáana: Anglo or white person.

Bilagáana binaadą́ą́': White people's corn; Anglo corn.

bilasáana: Apple.

bilasáana biskąą: Dried apple.

bił ha'nigáhí: Hominy or oven roasted corn.
bił 'ál'íní, bił 'é'él'íní: Baking powder.
bisóodi: Pig.

chąą': Feces.
chaasht'ézhíí: Carrot-like; a long white root eaten like a carrot.
chaat'íní: Dock.
chaat'ínii: Carrot.
chąąsht'ezhiitsoh: Wild carrot (*Daucus pusillus, Phellopterus montamus*); abundant
    leaves with a big orange root.
chatchizigi: Grinding stone [MC].
chéch'il bináá': Acorn.
cheii: Maternal grandfather.
chiiłchin: Sumac berry (*Rhus trilobata*).
ch'ééh jiyáán, ch'ééh jiyáání: Watermelon.
ch'ééh jiyáánłgai: White watermelon.
ch'il: Plant; shrub; weed; or bush.
ch'il 'ahwéhé, ch'il gohwéhé: Wild Navajo tea (*Thelesperma gracile, Bidens graciolis*);
    literally "plant coffee."
ch'il 'ahwéhé 'áłts'ísígíí: Small, short Navajo tea plant.
ch'il 'ahwéhé nineezígíí: Big, long Navajo tea plant.
ch'il 'awoshí, ch'il 'awóshí: Tumbleweed (according to some); see also *tł'ohdeeí naayízí*.
ch'il dabááhíí: Name for witchgrass in earlier times.
ch'il deeníní: Tumbleweed; wild asparagus.
ch'il na'atł'o'ii, ch'il na'átł'óíí: Wild grape (*Vitis*); bindweed.
ch'il na'atł'o'iitsoh: Cultivated grape or cultivated plum.
ch'il ntł'íní: Bindweed.
ch'ił bikétł'óól łitsxooígíí: Green gentian (yellow root plant).
ch'iłt'óó'íí: Wild rhubarb or curly dock (*Rumex hymenosepalus*).
ch'iyą, ch'iyáán: Food.
ch'osh: Worm; bug.
ch'osh ditł'ooí: Caterpillar.
ch'osh niłchxoní: Stinkbug.
Clauscheebitsi: Clauschee's younger brother.

daadlánigíí: Beverage.
dahaastiin, dahastin: Navajo ice cream.
dah díníilghaazh: Frybread.
dah díníilghaazh tł'oh naadą́ą́ bił 'ályaa: Frybread made from wheat flour.
dahts'aa', dáts'a: Mistletoe; some say the name of a drink made from mistletoe.
dajidlá: Drinkable substances.
dá'áchaan: Corn smut.

dá'ákaz: Cornstalk.

dá'azóól: When the corn tassels are growing.

dá'da'iisól: When the corn kernels fill up and ripen.

dééh: Tea.

deestálii: Split-open cantaloupe.

dibé: Sheep.

dibé bibe': Sheep's milk.

dibé bichaan: Sheep manure.

dibé bitsį bitoo': Mutton stew.

Dibé Dooltsoodi: Sheep Possessor.

dichin: Hunger.

Dichin Diné'é: Hunger People; Poverty People.

dich'íízh: Rough.

didzé: Wild plum; a native berry (many kinds recognized).

didzé dík'ǫzhí: Chokecherry (*Prunus melanocarpa*).

didzé dit'ódí: Serviceberry (*Amelanchier alnifolia*).

didzétsoh, dzidzétsoh: Peach.

didzétsoh bisgą': Dried peach.

didzétsoh dik'ǫzhí, dzidzétsoh dik'ǫzhí: Wild plum; sour berry.

díík'ǫsh: Yeast.

dík'ǫ́ǫzh: Sauce; salty.

diltáłii: Popcorn (one of several terms).

dił: Blood or blood sausage.

dił shibéézh: Blood sausage made by boiling.

Diné: The People; the Navajos.

Diné bi Da'ak'eh: Navajo cornfield.

dínéísá: Sprouted wheat for corn cake.

dit'oodí, didzétsoh yázhí, dzidzétsoh yázhi: Apricot.

ditłógí: Ground green corn.

dítł'ógí' alkaan, dítł'ógí' alkaad: Small individual corn cake.

díwózhii: Greasewood.

Diyin Diné'é: Holy People.

Diyin K'é: Holy Ways.

diyoołish: Snake (type not specified); see also *tł'iish*.

diyóósh: Bull snake.

dleesh: Light-colored clay.

dleesh łibáhí: Gray clay.

dleesh łigaaí: White clay.

dlǫ́ǫ': Prairie dog.

doola: Corn creamer.

gáagii: Crow.

gáagii bitł'ohchin: Crow's onion (*Allium cernuum*).

gad: Juniper or cedar (*Juniperus monosperma*).

gad 'ádin: Traditional cornmeal mush, without juniper ash.

gad bidahts'aa': Juniper mistletoe.

gah: Rabbit.

gah bich'iiyą': Rabbit food; carrot.

gahtsoh: Jackrabbit.

gałbáhí: Cottontail rabbit.

géeso: Cheese; from Spanish *queso*.

gish: Planting stick.

gohwééh, 'ahwééh: Coffee.

haashch'éédą́ą́: Wolfberry; tomatillo (*Lycium pallidum*); means "food of the Gods and their offerings."

Hajíínaí: The Emergence Place, where the Navajo ancestors emerged onto Earth's Surface.

ha'ałtsédii: Walnut.

haníígaii: Stew with backbone and dried corn; some say it is the same as posole.

hasbídí: Turtledove.

hashk'aan: Yucca fruit (*Yucca angustissima*; *Y. baccata*).

Hastiin Delawoshí: Man Who Shouts.

Hastiin Tsoh: Big Man.

hataałii: Ceremonial practitioner; singer.

haza'aleeh: Wild celery; wild parsley; biscuit root (*Cymopterus*).

hazéí: Squirrel.

honishgish: Fire poker.

hooch'a': Seepweed; see also *łichí'íí*.

hosh: Cactus; see also *wosh*.

hosh bee wóbéhé: Cactus fruit picker.

hosh bee yildéhé, hosh bedeełhí, hosh bei déé'éh, hosh belde'íí, hoshdęę: Cactus brush plant.

hosh beldei'hééh: Tall Woman's name for *naaltsoii* (*Solanum elaeagnifolium*); a very old plant.

hosh nteelí: Prickly pear cactus (*Opuntia*).

hózhǫ́: Harmony, peace, balance, happiness, good health, and good fortune.

Hózhǫ́ǫ́jí: Blessingway Ceremony.

'ii'nídít'aał: Chewing cornmeal and spitting into the batter.

'ii'ol'éél: Gravy.

'iiłtsínii, 'iiłts'ínii: Mariposa lily; Sego lily (*Calochortus aureus, C. nutallii*); edible tuber. Tall Woman's word for a wild potato–like vegetable in early days.

'iiłtsoii: Plant burned to make culinary ash; probably *k'iiłtsoii*, rabbit bush.

'iltł'ihii: Unidentified gummy, sticky plant.

Jaa'i: Name of Tall Woman's horse with big ears.
jiłhazhí: Hackberry (*Celtis pallida*).
jiłt'ooí: Another name for wild rhubarb.
jish: Medicine bundle.
jool'óhí: Sweetened cornmeal tamale (one of several terms); see also *nijiło'í*.

ka bizhi: Plant used as a sweetener. (I did not get an English name.)
kiis'áanii bibááh: Bread baked by Pueblo people.
Kinaaldá: Girls' Puberty Ceremony.
kinaaldá: The girl having the puberty ceremony.
Kiyaa'áanii: Towering House People, a Navajo clan.
k'aabizhii: Cactus that grows around Cove, Arizona. (I did not get an English name.)
k'aa': Women's arrows.
k'e: Central Navajo value; behavioral code stressing traditional kinship and
    reciprocity.
k'íiłtsoii: Big rabbit bush (*Chrysothamnus nauseosus*); may be burned for culinary
    ash.
k'íneeshbízhii, k'íneeshbizhii: Dumpling; blue corn marble.
k'íneeshbízhii ts'óózi: Long, skinny dumpling.
k'íneeshbízhii ts'ósí: Noodle.
k'íńjíł'ahí: Wild currant (*Ribes cereum*).

lók'aa': Cattail.
łeehilzhoozh, łeehilhóozh: Large kneel-down bread, baked; some say big tamale.
łee'shibéézh, łeeshibéézh: Green corn that is pit-roasted or steamed in its husk.
łeeshch'ih: Culinary ash.
łees'áán: New Mexican word for bread baked outside.
łees'áán dit'ódi: Pancake.
łeets'aa' bee yit'oodí: Dish towel.
łeets'aa' béjolí: Dishrag.
łeeyáán: White crusty alkali on surface of ground; native salt.
łééyilzhóózh: Smaller version of *'alkaan* (according to some).
łé'étsoh: Pack rat.
łichí'íí: Tall Woman's term for seepweed (*Suaeda torreyana*); see also *hooch'a*.
łį́į́: Horse.
łį́į́ łchí'í: Bay-colored horse.
łįį náshgǫzhi: Horsemeat sausage.
łikaan: Sweetmeat.

naadą́ą́': Corn (*Zea mays*).

naadą́ą́' bich'osh: Corn worm.

naadą́ą́' bitłééʼígíí tsit'eeʼ, naadą́ą́' neestʼą́ą́nígíí tsit'eeʼ: Ripe roasted corn.

naadą́ą́' biwooʼ: Corn kernel.

naadą́ą́' delchosi, naadą́ą́' dilchxoshí: Popcorn; see also *diltáłii*.

naadą́ą́' łeesʼáán: Blue cornbread baked in ashes.

naadą́ą́' neez: White people's corn; sweet corn.

naadą́ą́' shichiʼili: Fully ripe corn.

naadą́ą́' sitʼeeʼ: Parched corn.

naagáází: Short name for *ʼabeʼ bee neezmasí*; griddle cake made with milk.

naaltsoii, nááłtsoi, nááʼłitsooí, nááʼłitsoo: Silverleaf nightshade plant (*Solanum elaeagnifolium*), used in making cheese; a very old plant.

naaʼołí: Bean.

naaʼołíłbáhí: Beige bean; pinto bean.

naayízí: Squash.

naayízí bikʼǫ́ǫ́ sitʼé: Squash seed.

naayízíłbáhí: Gray squash.

naayízíłchííʼ: Red squash or pumpkin (according to some).

naayízíłtsooí: Pumpkin.

naayízí yázhí: Summer squash.

naazkaadii: Prostate pigweed; prostate amaranth (*Amaranthus blitoides*).

nabį́į́h, nábį́į́h: Plant used to ward off snakes.

nádleeh: Transvestite; hermaphrodite; Two-Spirit Person.

naemazi: Pancake made from green corn, shaped corn griddle cake.

nahachagii: Grasshopper.

nahashchʼidí: Badger.

náhinistʼas: Prepared for storage by being cut in spirals (e.g., melon or squash).

nahooyéí: Sweet potato.

naʼagédí bizaʼazis hólóní: Mole.

naʼajaah: Handing out, giving out (as in the Commodity Food Program).

naʼazísí: Gopher.

nanakʼad: To flatten; slap back and forth.

náneeskaadí: Griddle bread or tortilla.

náneeskaadí tłʼoh naadą́ą́' bił ʼályaa: Tortilla made from wheat flour.

naniseʼ: Plant.

náníshne: To hit repeatedly with a rock; pound on.

nanoyeeshi, ńdínoolyíshí, nanoyezhí, nánooyęshí, náhinooyęshí: Poured cornbread baked in ashes; hurry-up bread; quick bread.

náshgǫzh: Sausage.

ndetlidi: Sweetgrass; many kinds recognized.

ndidlidii: Scorched grass; rice grass; millet; bunch grass.

ndíshchíí yaa béʼézhóóʼ: Under the pine tree brush grass.

ndíyílii: Sunflower.

ndíyíliitsoh: Big sunflower.

neesdoo': Yucca fruit roll.

neeshch'íí': Pinyon nut; pinyon pine (*Pinus edulis, P. ponderosa*).

neeshch'íí' bik'ah: Pinyon nut oil.

neeshja: Tall Woman's term for corn whose kernels are all perfectly whole.

neeshjáhih: Creamer made from Anglo sweet corn.

neeshjízhii, neeshjízhíí, neshjizhi, neshjizhíí, naashjizhii: Dried steamed corn (shelled *łee'shibéézh*), which is boiled in a stew.

neshgizhi: Fresh corn.

nidídlídii: Scorched grass, burned to expose the seeds for harvest.

nijíló'í, nijiło'í: One of several names, at least in New Mexico, for sweetened cornmeal tamale; literally, it means "carried by its tie string."

nímasii: Wild potato; also domesticated potato (*Solanum jamesii*).

nímasii dleesh: Light-colored clay used as a sweetener.

nímasii łikaní: Wild sweet potato.

nímasii łikaní łichíí'í: Beet; red sweet potato.

nímasii yázhí: Gopher potato or globe-shaped potato.

nóogazí: Paperbread.

ntsidigo'í, nitsidigó'í: Kneel-down bread.

'ostse': Tumble mustard; tansy mustard; hedge mustard (*Descurainia, Sisymbrium altissimum, Norta altissima*).

shash: Bear.

shíchílí: Reportedly, an old word for dried and roasted.

shíínaaltsídí, shiyínaldzídí: Afraid of the sun.

shimá: Birth mother; Mother Earth; literally "my mother."

taa be'éstł'óní: Very stiff mush of ground cornmeal put on corn husk.

taajilééhíí, taajilehíí, taah jiileehi: Small kneel-down bread; some say small tamale.

táá'iitsóhii, tá'iitsóhii, naayízí tá'iitsóhii: Squash blossom.

táá'iitsohii 'atoo', naayízí bitá'iitsóhí bii'oo'éél: Squash blossom soup.

taa'niil: Thick cornmeal mush; a kind of cereal.

Tábąąhá: Water Edge People; a Navajo clan.

Tábąąhá Nééz: Tall Water Edge Man.

tádidíín: Corn pollen.

tadiłchoshi: Leaf pocket plant with yellow berries; maybe the yellow nightshade ground-cherry (*Physalis crassifolia*).

ta'neesk'ání: Cantaloupe; muskmelon.

ta'neesk'ání dích'ízhí: Rough-skinned cantaloupe.

ta'neesk'ání dik'ǫzhí: Cucumber; salty cantaloupe.

tanáá'niil: Sweetened white cornmeal mush.

tanaashgiizh, tánaashgiizh, taneeshgiizh, táneeshgiizh: Very thick blue cornmeal mush made with juniper ash.

t'áadoo le'é yidlánígíí: Beverage; see also *daadlánigíí*.

Tł'ááshchí'í: Red Bottom People; a Navajo clan.

Tł'ááshchí'í bitsilí: Red Bottom person's younger brother.

tł'iish: Snake (generic term).

tł'ízí: Goat.

tł'ízí bibe': Goat's milk.

tł'oh: Hay; grass.

tł'oh 'azihii: Mormon tea (*Ephedra*).

tł'ohchin: Onion (*Allium cernuum*).

tł'oh dahikaałi: Witchgrass; rustling grass (*Panicum capillare*).

tł'óh dééhí: Indian rice grass; bunchgrass; or millet.

tł'ohdeeí: Grass whose seeds fall; lamb's quarter; goosefoot; Freemont goosefoot; Freemont pigweed; or amaranth (*Chenopodium fremontii, Chenopodium*).

tł'ohdeeí hoshí: Pigweed or amaranth.

tł'ohdeeí łees'áán: Griddle cake or grill stone.

tł'ohdeeí naayizí: Tumbleweed (according to some); see also *ch'il 'awoshí*.

tł'oh deesk'idí, tł'oh deesk'ídíí: Green amaranth; pigweed; or amaranth (*Amaranthus retroflexus*).

tł'oh naadą́ą́', tł'óh naadą́ą́': Wheat.

tł'oh naadą́ą́' bááh: Wheat bread.

tł'oh naadą́ą́' díneesą: Wheat sprout.

tł'oh naadą́ą́' łees'áán: Wheat and green cornbread or wheat roll.

tł'óh niłchíín: Sweetgrass; see also *ndetlidi*.

tł'oh tsááhíí: Name for rustling grass in earlier times.

tł'oh ts'ózí: Narrow-leaf grass (*Sporobolus cryptandrus*).

tó: Water.

Tó'aheedlíinii: Water Flows Together People; a Navajo clan.

Tó dích'ii'nii: Bitter Water People; a Navajo clan.

Tó dích'ii'nii Dziłijini: Bitter Water Mountain Man.

tó dík'ǫ́ǫ́zh: Salty water.

tódilchxoshí: Soda pop; bubbly water.

to'iłchííhí: Strange-shaped green bug that eats squash.

tółichí'í: Soda or red water.

tółikáni: Soda or sweet water.

tóshchíín: Blue cornmeal mush; hot cereal made from ground blue corn.

tsą́ą́'bíí: Swiss chard.

tsá'ászi' nteelí: Wide-leaf or broad-leaf yucca, the mountain banana variety (*Yucca baccata*).

tsá'ászi' ts'óóz: Narrow-leaf yucca, the desert variety (*Yucca angustissima*).

tsé: Stone; rock.

tsé bąąh naalzhóó': Type of native griddle cake, according to Young and Morgan
(1970, 728); also one of the names for the grinding stone brush; see *bé'ézhóó'*.

tsébee' nálzhóól: Name given to a rejuvenated grinding stone brush after it has been
used to clean the stone; literally "swept off the stone."

tsé beenatséélí: Rock used to pound.

tsébinteel: Rock used to pound and shape bottom grinding stone.

tsédaashch'íní: Top grinding stone (*mano*).

tsédaashjéé': Bottom grinding stone (*metate*).

tseek'i nástánii: Gray ground squirrel.

tsék'i 'ast'ees: Making paperbread.

tsé'ást'éí, tsé'ást'é', tsé'ast'ééh: Paperbread; a very thin cornmeal bread.

tsĕ ăst'ē: Paperbread made on stone griddle.

tsĕ ăst'é' łagaí: Paperbread made from white corn.

tsełbahi: Oven-roasted or ground-roasted corn.

tsét'ees, tsét'ēs: Stone griddle; cooking stone; stone grill.

Tséyi': Canyon; specifically, Canyon de Chelly, Arizona.

tsídii: Bird.

tsídiiłtsooí: Goldfinch.

tsííd: Hot coals of a fire.

tsíídkáá: On top of charcoal; see also *tsííkáá'*.

tsíídkáá bááh, tsííkáá' bááh, tsíídkáá shíchílí: Bread made on top of charcoal.

tsiighájiłchi: Unidentified plant; possibly dodder.

tsííkáá': On or over coals.

tsííkáá' yideezí: Tortilla grilled over charcoal.

tsís'ná: Black and yellow bee.

ts'áałbáí, ts'áálbé: Powdered dried steamed corn creamer.

waa': Beeweed; Rocky Mountain beeweed; wild spinach (*Peritoma serulatum, Cleome
serulatum*).

wóóneeshch'įįdii: Locust; cicada.

wosh: Cactus; see also *hosh*.

yideez: Singed.

yilkąąd 'alkąąd: Corn cake that has been dried and stored to be eaten later.

REFERENCES

Aberle, David F. 1969. "A Plan for Navajo Economic Development." In *Toward Economic Development for Native American Communities*. Vol. 1, 223–76. Washington, DC: US Government Printing Office.

Adair, John, and Kurt W. Deuschle, eds. 1970. *The People's Health: Medicine and Anthropology in a Navajo Community*. New York: Appleton-Century-Crofts.

Adamson, Joni. 2011. "Medicine Food: Critical Environmental Justice Studies, Native North American Literature, and the Movement for Food Sovereignty." *Environmental Justice* 4 (4): 213–19.

Ahlborn, Richard E. 1983. "Frontier Possessions: The Evidence from Colonial Documents." In *Colonial Frontiers: Art and Life in Spanish New Mexico; The Fred Harvey Collection*, edited by Christine Mather, 35–69. Santa Fe, NM: Ancient City Press.

Alford, Betty B., and Emma B. Nance. 1976. "Customary Foods in the Navajo Diet." *Journal of the American Dietetic Association* 69 (5): 538–39.

Allen, Krista. 2012. "Making Kneel-Down Bread." *Navajo Times*, October 4.

———. 2013a. "Cameron Learns to Recycle for Earth Day." *Navajo Times*, May 2.

———. 2013b. "Experts: Gaining Support for Junk Food Tax Proving Tough." *Navajo Times*, June 6.

———. 2013c. "No Space? No Water? You Can Still Garden." *Navajo Times*, April 18.

———. 2014. "Dining on the Cicada and other Curious Facts." *Navajo Times*, May 22.

———. 2015. "From Fashion to Photography, Natives' Work to Preserve Diné Culture, Language." *Navajo Times*, December 30.

———. 2016a. "Garden Expo Offers Demo on Solar-Powered Water Pump." *Navajo Times*, April 7.

———. 2016b. "New Church's Chicken Opens Its Doors in Kayenta." *Navajo Times*, April 21.

———. 2016c. "Time for Mouth-Watering Fair Food." *Navajo Times*, September 8.

Allen, Lee. 2016. "Navajo Chef Turns Up the Heat on National Stage." *Native Peoples*, November/December.

Austin, Martha, and Regina Lynch, eds. 1983. *Saad Ahąąh Sinil: A Navajo-English Dictionary*. Rev. ed. Rough Rock, AZ: Rough Rock Demonstration School.

Austin, Raymond. 2009. *Navajo Courts and Navajo Common Law: A Tradition of Tribal Self-Governance*. Minneapolis: University of Minnesota Press.

Bailey, Flora L. 1940. "Navaho Foods and Cooking Methods." *American Anthropologist* 42 (2): 270–90.

Bailey, Garrick, and Roberta Glenn Bailey. 1986. *A History of the Navajos: The Reservation Years*. Santa Fe, NM: School of American Research.

Ballew, Carol, Linda L. White, Karen F. Strauss, Lois J. Benson, James M. Mendlein, and Ali H. Mokdad. 1997. "Intake of Nutrients and Food Sources of Nutrients among the Navajo: Findings from the Navajo Health and Nutrition Survey." *Journal of Nutrition* 127: 2085S–93S.

Becenti, Arlyssa. 2013. "You Are What You Eat: Food Education, from Eating Homegrown Foods to Hot Cheetos." *Gallup Independent*, May 31.

———. 2016a. "Chapters to Attend Work Sessions for Junk Food Tax Distribution." *Navajo Times*, August 11.

———. 2016b. "Committee Approves Distribution Policy for Junk Food Tax." *Navajo Times*, June 23.

Begay, Shirley M. 1983. *Kinaaldá: A Navajo Puberty Ceremony*. 2nd ed. Rough Rock, AZ: Rough Rock Demonstration School.

Begay, Teddy. 2016. "Natives Standing against Biotech Farming Industry." Letter to the Editor. *Navajo Times*, March 17.

Begaye, Nathaniel T. 2013. "A Tribute to Eddie Basha Jr." *Navajo Times*, April 4.

Beyal, Duane. 2013. "The Simple Lesson of Piñon Picking." *Navajo Times*, May 16.

Bingham, Sam, and Janet Bingham. 1979. *Navajo Farming*. Chinle, AZ: Rock Point Community School.

Bitsoi, Alastair Lee. 2013a. "Expert: GMOs Are Alive and Well on Navajo Land." *Navajo Times*, June 6.

———. 2013b. "Experts Say Navajos Must Confront Long-Term Drought." *Navajo Times*, May 9.

———. 2013c. "Frybread *Báahádzíd, Jíní*; Food Summit Aimed at Preventing Extinction of Tribe." *Navajo Times*, June 13.

———. 2013d. "'Hope' Central Theme of Israeli Conference." *Navajo Times*, April 11.

———. 2013e. "Shelly: Navajo Lands Can 'Bloom' Like Israeli Deserts." *Navajo Times*, April 11.

———. 2014a. "DCAA 'Shocked' with Shelly's Veto of Junk Food Tax Bill." *Navajo Times*, February 13.

———. 2014b. "For 3rd Time, Junk Food Tax on Its Way to Council." *Navajo Times*, July 31.

———. 2014c. "Group Hails Effort to Get Junk Food Tax Passed by Council." *Navajo Times*, November 20.

———. 2014d. "I'm Proud of What We Did." *Navajo Times*, June 12.

———. 2014e. "Junk Food Tax Now on Shelly's Table." *Navajo Times*, February 6.

———. 2014f. "Simpson Vows Override of Junk Food Tax Veto." *Navajo Times*, February 20.

———. 2016a. "'Good Laws, Good Food' Work Session Addresses Food Policy on Navajo." *Navajo Times*, January 7.

———. 2016b. "Workshop Teaches Farmers How to Market Crops." *Navajo Times*, January 21.

Black, Mallory. 2015. "Report Urges More Tribal Control over Food Systems." *Navajo Times*, December 3.

Bowman, Terry. 2013. "Harvard Offers Ideas on Curbing Diabetes on Navajo Nation." *Navajo Times*, June 13.

———. 2016a. "Diné Chef Presides at NMAI's Restaurant." *Navajo Times*, November 17.

———. 2016b. "Grassroots Group Brings Garden to Klagetoh." *Navajo Times*, August 25.

Brady, Benjamin R., and Howard Bahr. 2014. "The Influenza Epidemic of 1918–1920 among the Navajos: Marginality, Mortality, and the Implications of Some Neglected Eyewitness Accounts." *American Indian Quarterly* 38 (4): 459–91.

Browne, Vee F. 2008. *The Stone Cutter and the Navajo Maiden: Tsé Yitsidi dóó Ch'ikééh Bitsédaashjéé'*. Illustrated by Johnson Yazzie. Flagstaff, AZ: Salina Bookshelf.

Brugge, David M. 1986. *Tsegai: An Archaeological Ethnohistory of the Chaco Region*. Washington, DC: US National Park Service.

Brzezinski, Hilary, OFM, with Kay Benton, Willie Keeto Jr., Flossie B. Mitchell, Josphine Mogan, Genevieve M. Smith, and Hilda H. Smith. 1993. *Recipes from Navajoland*. Olathe, KS: Cookbook. (Spiral-bound copies available at St. Anthony's Parish, Many Farms, AZ.)

Butte, N. F., D. H. Calloway, and J. L. Van Duzen. 1981. "Nutritional Assessment of Pregnant and Lactating Navajo Women." *American Journal of Clinical Nutrition* 34: 2216–28.

Calloway, D. H., R. D. Giauque, and F. M. Costa. 1974. "The Superior Mineral Content of Some American Indian Foods in Comparison to Federally Donated Counterpart Commodities." *Ecology of Food and Nutrition* 3: 203–11.

Calvin, Carolyn. 2010. "The People's Flour: Cortez Company Produces 600,000 Bags of Blue Bird Flour Each Year." *Navajo Times*, September 30.

Carpenter, Thorne M., and Morris Steggerda. 1939. "The Food of the Present-Day Navajo Indians of New Mexico and Arizona." *Journal of Nutrition* 18: 297–306.

Castetter, Edward F., and Morris E. Opler. 1935. "Uncultivated Native Plants Used as Sources of Food." In *Ethnobiological Studies in the American Southwest*, 3–62. Albuquerque: University of New Mexico Press.

Coolidge, Dane, and Mary Roberts Coolidge. 1930. *The Navajo Indians*. Boston: Houghton Mifflin.

COPE (Community Outreach and Patient Empowerment Program). 2015. *Catalyst: COPE 2015 Annual Report*. http://parthealth.3cdn.net/240369816759992304_kxm6ylgsh.pdf.

Cottam, Erica. 2015. *Hubbell Trading Post: Trade, Tourism, and the Navajo Southwest*. Norman: University of Oklahoma Press.

Cox, Beverly, and Martin Jacobs. 1991. *Spirit of the Harvest: North American Indian Cooking*. New York: Stewart, Tabori, and Chang.

Curley, Andrew. 2014. "Nation Must Grow Own Food." *Navajo Times*, May 8.

Dahl, Kevin. 2006. *Native Harvest: Authentic Southwestern Gardening*. Tucson, AZ: Western National Parks Association.

Darby, William J., C. G. Salsbury, and W. J. McGariety. 1956. "A Study of the Dietary Background and Nutrition of the Navajo Indians." *Journal of Nutrition* 60 (Suppl. 2).

Davies, Wade. 2001. *Healing Ways: Navajo Health Care in the Twentieth Century*. Albuquerque: University of New Mexico Press.

d'Elgin, Tershia. 2016. *The Man Who Thought He Owned Water: On the Brink with American Farms, Cities, and Food*. Boulder: University Press of Colorado.

Dickey, Roland. 1949. *New Mexico Village Arts*. Albuquerque: University of New Mexico Press.

Diné Policy Institute (DPI). 2014. *Diné Food Sovereignty: A Report on the Navajo Nation Food System and the Case to Rebuild a Self-Sufficient Food System for the Diné People*. Tsaile, AZ: Diné College. http://www.dinecollege.edu/institutes/DPI/Docs/dpi-food-sovereignty-report.pdf.

Donovan, Bill. 2012. "A Milestone in Diné History: The Navajo Taco." *Navajo Times*, November 29.

———. 2013. "Navajos Mourn Passing of Eddie Basha." *Navajo Times*, March 28.

———. 2014. "Go-Ahead Given for Shopping Center Development." *Navajo Times*, January 16.

Downs, James F. 1972. *The Navajo*. New York: Holt, Rinehart & Winston.

Dunmire, William W., and Gail D. Tierney. 1997. *Wild Plants and Native Peoples of the Four Corners*. Santa Fe: Museum of New Mexico Press.

Echo Hawk Consulting. 2015. *Feeding Ourselves: Food Access, Health Disparities, and the Pathways to Healthy Native American Communities*. Longmont, CO: Echo Hawk Consulting. http://www.echohawkconsulting.com/feeding-ourselves.html.

Edaakie, Rita. 1999. *Idonapshe / Let's Eat: Traditional Zuni Foods*. Albuquerque: A:shiwi A:wan Museum and Heritage Center and University of New Mexico Press, 1999.

Edwardsville Intelligencer. 2015. "Food Stamp Users Looking for Jobs." March 31.

Elder, Jane Lenz, and David J. Weber. 1996. *Trading in Santa Fe: John M. Kingsbury's Correspondence with James Josiah Webb, 1853–1861.* Dallas, TX: Southern Methodist University Press.

Eldridge, Dana. 2012. "The Food We Eat." PowerPoint presentation at the nineteenth Navajo Studies Conference, Santa Fe, March 14–17.

———. 2013. "There's Plenty of Home-Grown Expertise." *Navajo Times,* April 18.

Elmore, Francis H. 1938. "Food Animals of the Navaho." *El Palacio* 44 (22–24): 149–54.

———. 1943. *Ethnobotany of the Navajo.* Albuquerque: University of New Mexico Press.

Fergusson, Erna. 1945. *Mexican Cookbook.* Albuquerque: University of New Mexico Press.

Fischer, Al, and Mildred Fischer. 1983. *Arizona Cook Book: Indian, Mexican, Western.* Phoenix, AZ: Gold West.

Fonseca, Felicia. 2011. "Hopi Hoping to Grow Tourism into Big Green." *Albuquerque Journal,* June 19.

Food Secure Canada. 2016. "What Is Food Sovereignty?" http://foodsecurecanada.org/who-we-are/what-food-sovereignty.

Franciscan Fathers. 1910. *Ethnologic Dictionary of the Navaho Language.* St. Michaels, AZ: Franciscan Fathers.

Franklin, Lane. 2016. "Nonprofit Group Preserves Indigenous Identity through Seeds." *Navajo Times,* January 21.

Franklin, Lois Ellen. 1995. *Native American Cooking.* New York: Random House.

———. 2002. *Foods of the Southwestern Indian Nations.* Berkeley, CA: Ten Speed Press.

French, J. G. 1967. "Relationship of Morbidity to the Feeding Patterns of Navajo Children from Birth through Twenty-Four Months." *American Journal of Clinical Nutrition* 20: 375–85.

Frisbie, Charlotte J. (1967) 1993. *Kinaaldá: A Study of the Navaho Girl's Puberty Ceremony.* Middletown, CT: Wesleyan University Press. Reprint with new preface, Salt Lake City: University of Utah Press.

———. 1970. "Navajo House Blessing Ceremonial: A Study of Cultural Change." PhD dissertation, University of New Mexico, Albuquerque. Ann Arbor, MI: University Microfilms.

———. 1987. *Navajo Medicine Bundles or Jish: Acquisition, Transmission, and Disposition in the Past and Present.* Albuquerque: University of New Mexico Press.

———. 1992. "Temporal Change in Navajo Religion: 1868–1990." *Journal of the Southwest* 34 (4): 457–514.

———. 1996. "Gender Issues in Navajo Boarding School Experiences." In *The Construction of Gender and the Experience of Women in American Indian Societies,* edited by Harvey Markowitz, 138–79. Chicago: Newberry Library.

———. 1998. "On the Trail of Chinle's 'Big House.'" In *Diné Bíkéyah: Papers in Honor of David M. Brugge*, edited by Meliha S. Duran and David T. Kirkpatrick, 69–85. Albuquerque: Archaeological Society of New Mexico 24. Post-publication errata sheet published in 1999 in *Archaeological Society of New Mexico* 25 (241).

———. 2012. "Researching a Chinle Church Bell." *New Mexico Historical Review* 87 (3): 299–328.

———. 2015. "'Clubbing the Boots': The Navajo Moccasin Game in Today's World." In *This Thing Called Music: Essays in Honor of Bruno Nettl*, edited by Victoria Lindsay Levine and Philip V. Bohlman, 406–18. Lanham, MD: Rowman & Littlefield.

———. 2016. "Canvas Ceiling Covers Discovered during Restoration Work at the Annunciation Mission in Chinle, Arizona." In *History and Archaeology: Connecting the Dots; Papers in Honor of David H. Snow*, edited by Emily J. Brown, Carol J. Condie, and Helen E. Crotty, 87–99. Albuquerque: Archaeological Society of New Mexico 43.

Gallup Independent. 2016. "Navajo Nation Gardening Challenge Aims to Unite and Empower Families." June 15.

Gittelsohn, Joel, Elizabeth M. Kim, Siran He, and Marla Pardilla. 2013. "A Food Store–Based Environmental Intervention Is Associated with Reduced BMI and Improved Psychosocial Factors and Food-Related Behaviors on the Navajo Nation." *Journal of Nutrition* 143 (9): 1494–1500.

Global Food Politics. 2016. "Food Security vs. Food Sovereignty." https://globalfoodpolitics.wordpress.com/2012/11/30/food-security-vs-food-sovereignty.

Goddard, Pliny Earle. 1933. "Navajo Texts." *Anthropological Papers of the American Museum of Natural History* 34, pt. 1. New York: American Museum of Natural History.

Godfrey, Paul. 2014. *More Than Money*. Stanford, CA: Stanford University Press.

Gorman, Faye. 2013. "A Tradition of Growing Corn." *Leading the Way* 11 (6): 6–9.

Grassroots International. 2016. "Food Sovereignty." http://www.grassrootsonline.org/issues/food-sovereignty.

Grein, Blane, OFM, and Charlotte J. Frisbie. 2005. *Blessings Brought, Blessings Found: Annunciation Mission, 1905–2005, Our Lady of Fatima Parish; Celebrating 100 Years of Franciscan and Church Presence in Chinle, Arizona*. Albuquerque, NM: Cottonwood.

Haile, Berard, OFM. 1981. *Upward Moving and Emergence Way: The Gishin Biye' Version*. Vol. 7 of *American Tribal Religions*, edited by Karl W. Luckert. Lincoln: University of Nebraska Press.

Halbritter, Ray. 2015. "Letter from the Publisher." *This Week from Indian Country Today* 2 (38):1, April 22. http://www.IndianCountryTodayMediaNetwork.com.

Hardwick, William. 1993. *Authentic Indian-Mexican Recipes*. Fort Stockton, TX: William Hardwick. First published in 1965.

Harrington, H. D. 1976. *Edible Native Plants of the Rocky Mountains*. Albuquerque: University of New Mexico Press.

Hensperger, Beth. 1997. *Breads of the Southwest: Recipes in the Native American, Spanish, and Mexican Traditions*. San Francisco: Chronicle Books.

Hesse, Zora. 1998. *Southwestern Indian Recipe Book: Apache, Pima, Papago, Pueblo, and Navajo*. Palmer Lake, CO: Filter Press.

Hill, Willard W. 1938. *Agriculture and Hunting Methods of the Navaho Indians*. New Haven, CT: Yale University Press.

Holiday, Samuel, and Robert S. McPherson. 2013. *Under the Eagle: Sam Holiday, Navajo Code Talker*. Norman: University of Oklahoma Press.

Indian Country Today. 2015. "Combating A Nutritional Desert." April 22. http://www.IndianCountryTodayMediaNetwork.com.

Indigenous Food Systems Network. 2016. "Indigenous Food Sovereignty." http://www.indigenousfoodsystems.org/food-sovereignty.

Iverson, Peter. 2002. *Diné: A History of the Navajos*. Photographs by Monty Roessel. Albuquerque: University of New Mexico Press.

Jett, Stephen C. 1974. "The Destruction of Navajo Orchards in 1864: Captain John Thompson's Report." *Arizona and the West* 16 (4): 365–78.

———. 1979. "Peach Cultivation and Use among the Canyon de Chelly Navajo." *Economic Botany* 33 (3): 298–310.

———. n.d. "The History and Geography of Navajo Farming." Unpublished manuscript.

Jett, Stephen C,. and Virginia E. Spencer. 1981. *Navajo Architecture: Forms, History, Distributions*. Tucson: University of Arizona Press.

Jimmy, Larissa. 2013. "Navajo Cake Takes Teamwork to Make and Eat." *Navajo Times*, July 25.

Johns, Tim A. 1985. "Chemical Ecology of the Aymara of Western Bolivia: Selection of Glycoalkaloids in the Solanum X Ajanhuiri Domestication Complex." PhD dissertation, University of Michigan, Ann Arbor.

Johnson, Broderick H., ed. 1973. *Navajo Stories of the Long Walk Period*. Tsaile, AZ: Navajo Community College Press.

Johnson, Charlotte I. 1964. "Navaho Corn Grinding Songs." *Ethnomusicology* 8: 101–20.

Johnson, Robert. 2011. "Explanation of Traditional Tools." Display above exhibit in Navajo Nation Museum, Window Rock, AZ.

Jordan, Jennifer A. 2015. *Edible Memory: The Lure of Heirloom Tomatoes and Other Forgotten Foods*. Chicago: University of Chicago Press.

Kaibetoney, Nora. 2009. "Making Navajo Cake." Translated by Lawrence Kaibetoney. *Leading the Way* 7 (8): 1, 12–15.

Kavena, Juanita Tiger. (1980) 2004. *Hopi Cookery*. 7th ed. Tucson: University of Arizona Press.

Keane, Colleen. 2013. "Experts: Tourists Want to Know the Real Story." *Navajo Times*, May 2.

———. 2016. "Young Dreamers Envision Sustainable Communities—Ag Experts Show the Way." *Navajo Times*, September 1.

Keegan, Marcia. 1987. *Southwest Indian Cookbook: Pueblo and Navajo Images, Quotes, and Recipes*. Santa Fe, NM: Clear Light.

Keith, Anne Brown. 1964. "The Navajo Girls' Puberty Ceremony: Function and Meaning for the Adolescent." *El Palacio* 71 (1): 27–36.

Kelley, Klara, and Harris Francis. 2006–2015. *Navajoland Trading Post Encyclopedia in Progress*. http://www.navajotradingposts.info.

———. Forthcoming. *Navajoland Trading Post Encyclopedia*. Window Rock, AZ: Navajo Nation Museum and Navajo Heritage and Historic Preservation Department.

Kelley, Klara B., and Peter M. Whiteley. 1989. *Navajoland: Family and Settlement and Land Use*. Tsaile, AZ: Navajo Community College Press.

Knuth, Lidija, and Margret Vidar. 2011. *Constitutional and Legal Protection of the Right to Food around the World*. Report for the United Nations Food and Agriculture Organization, Rome. http://www.fao.org/docrep/016/ap554e/ap554e.pdf.

Kopp, Judy. 1986. "Crosscultural Contacts: Changes in the Diet and Nutrition of the Navajo Indians." *American Indian Culture and Research Journal* 10 (4): 1–30.

Kuehlein, H., D. Calloway, and B. Harland. 1979. "Composition of Traditional Hopi Foods." *Journal of the American Dietetic Association* 75: 37–41.

Kunitz, Stephen J. 1983. *Disease Change and the Role of Medicine: The Navajo Experience*. Berkeley: University of California Press.

Lamphere, Louise, with Eva Price, Carole Cadman, and Valerie Darwin. 2007. *Weaving Women's Lives: Three Generations in a Navajo Family*. Albuquerque: University of New Mexico Press.

Landry, Alysa. 2013. "Farm Bills Would Cut Food Assistance Programs for Needy." *Navajo Times*, June 20.

———. 2014. "New Book on Poverty Offers Some Solutions." *Navajo Times*, June 26.

Largo, Chrissy. 2016. "First Tesla Battery Installed at Forest Lake Chapter." *Navajo Times*, September 1.

La Via Campesina. 2016. "Building an International Movement for Food and Seed Sovereignty." http://viacampesina.org/en/index.php/main-issues-mainmenu-27/food-sovereignty-and-trade-mainmenu-38/1963-la-via-campesina-building-an-international-movement.

Leading the Way: The Wisdom of the Navajo People. 2003 to present. Monthly publication edited and published by Kathleen Manolescu, P. O. Box 272, Gamerco, New Mexico 87317.

Loughlin, Bernice W. 1963. "Aide Training Reaches the Navajo Reservation." *American Journal of Nursing* 63 (7): 106–9.

Lynch, Regina, Roy Lynch, and T. L. McCarty. 1986. *Cookbook: Ch'iyáán 'ííł'íní binaaltsoos*. Chinle, AZ: Navajo Curriculum Center, Rough Rock Demonstration School.

MacLachlan, Colin M., and Jaime E. Rodriguez O. 1980. *The Forging of the Cosmic Race: A Reinterpretation of Colonial Mexico*. Berkeley: University of California Press.

Manolescu, Kathleen. 2010. "Traditional Corn Foods with Harry N. Begay." *Leading the Way* 8 (9): 18–21.

Matthews, Washington. 1886. "Navajo Names for Plants." *American Naturalist* 20 (9): 767–77.

———. 1897. *Navaho Legends*. Vol. 5 of *Memoirs of the American Folklore Society*. New York: G. E. Stechert.

———. (1902) 1995. *The Night Chant: A Navaho Ceremony*. Reprint with foreword by John Farella. Salt Lake City: University of Utah Press.

Mayes, Vernon O., and Barbara Bayless Lacy. (1989) 1994. *Nanise': A Navajo Herbal; One Hundred Plants from the Navajo Reservation*. Tsaile, AZ: Navajo Community College Press.

———. 2012. *Nanise': A Navajo Herbal; One Hundred Plants from the Navajo Reservation*. Chandler, AZ: Five Star.

Mayes, Vernon O., and James Rominger. 1994. *Navajoland Plant Catalog*. 2nd ed. Lake Ann, MI: National Woodsland.

McCloskey, Joanne. 2007. *Living through the Generations: Continuity and Change in Navajo Women's Lives*. Tucson: University of Arizona Press.

McCullough-Brabson, Ellen, and Marilyn Help. 2001. *We'll Be in Your Mountains, We'll Be in Your Songs: A Navajo Woman Sings*. Albuquerque: University of New Mexico Press.

McDonald, Barbara S. 1965 (Supplement 1967). *Nutrition on the Navajo*. 2nd ed. Window Rock, AZ: US Public Health Service.

McPherson, Robert S., Jim Dandy, and Sarah E. Burak. 2012. *Navajo Tradition, Mormon Life: The Autobiography and Teachings of Jim Dandy*. Salt Lake City: University of Utah Press.

Middleton, Beth Rose. 2016. *Trust in the Land: New Directions in Tribal Conservation*. Tucson: University of Arizona Press.

Milburn, Michael P. 2004. "Indigenous Nutrition: Using Traditional Food Knowledge to Solve Contemporary Health Problems." *American Indian Quarterly* 28 (3–4): 411–34.

Miller, Darlis A. 1989. *Soldiers and Settlers: Military Supply in the Southwest, 1861–1886*. Albuquerque: University of New Mexico Press.

Mitchell, Frank. (1978) 2003. *Navajo Blessingway Singer: The Autobiography of Frank Mitchell, 1881–1967.* Edited by Charlotte J. Frisbie and David P. McAllester. Albuquerque: University of New Mexico Press.

Mitchell, Rose. 2001. *Tall Woman: The Life Story of Rose Mitchell, A Navajo Woman, c. 1874–1977.* Edited by Charlotte J. Frisbie. Albuquerque: University of New Mexico Press.

Montaño, Mary. 2001. *Tradiciones Nuevomexicana: Hispano Arts and Culture of New Mexico.* Albuquerque: University of New Mexico Press.

Mordi, Chris. 2016. "Pantry Users Learn to Grown Own Vegetables." *Edwardsville Intelligencer,* July 1.

Morgan, Frank. 2011. *Navajo Terminology for Foods and Nutrients: Kindness, Caring, and Blessings through our Food.* Window Rock, AZ: Navajo Nation Special Diabetes Project.

Nabhan, Gary Paul. (1989) 2002. *Enduring Seeds: Native American Agriculture and Wild Plant Conservation.* Tucson: University of Arizona Press.

———. 2016. *Ethnobiology for the Future: Linking Cultural and Ecological Diversity.* Tucson: University of Arizona Press.

Native Food Systems Resource Center. 2012. "Formation of New 'Native American Food Sovereignty Alliance' Moving Ahead Following Introductory Webinar That Drew Nearly 200 National Participants." http://www.nativefoodsystems.org/about/news/fsa.

———. 2016. "About Food Sovereignty." http://www.nativefoodsystems.org/about/sovereignty.

Navajo Nation Council. 2014. The Healthy Diné Act (CN-54-14), signed into law November 21.

Navajo Tribe. (1960) 1963. *A Syllabus for Teachers in Navajo Health.* Navajo-Cornell Field Health Research Project. Window Rock, AZ: n.p. Available at the Navajo Tribal Offices Community Services Division.

———. 1974. *Navajo Nation: Overall Economic Development Program.* Window Rock, AZ: Office of Program Development.

Nazarea, Virginia D. (2005) 2014. *Heirloom Seeds and Their Keepers: Marginality and Memory in the Conservation of Biological Diversity.* Tucson: University of Arizona Press.

Newcomb, Franc Johnson. 1967. *Navaho Folk Tales.* Santa Fe, NM: Museum of Navaho Ceremonial Art.

Nez, Chester, with Judith Schiess Avila. 2011. *Code Talker.* New York: Berkley Caliber.

Niethammer, Carolyn. 1974. *American Indian Food and Lore.* New York: Collier Macmillan.

———. 1999. *American Indian Cooking: Recipes from the Southwest.* Lincoln: University of Nebraska Press.

———. 2011. *Cooking the Wild Southwest: Delicious Recipes for Desert Plants*. Tucson: University of Arizona Press.

Nixon, Ron. 2014. "House Approves Farm Bill, Ending 2-Year Impasse." *New York Times*, January 29.

Noble, Marilyn, Susan Lowell, and Caroline Cook. 2013. *The Essential Southwest Cookbook*. Tucson, AZ: Rio Nuevo.

Nusom, Lynn. 1999. *Authentic Southwestern Cooking*. Tucson, AZ: Western National Parks Association.

Office of Navajo Economic Opportunity (ONEO). n.d. [before 1963]. "Navajo Cook Book." Unpublished manuscript.

———. n.d. [before 1963]. "The Navajo Homemaker." Unpublished manuscript.

Overstreet, Daphne. (1975) 2014. *Arizona Territory Cookbook: Recipes from 1864 to 1912*. 2nd ed. Phoenix, AZ: Gold West.

Pardilla, Marla, Divya Prasad, Sonali Suratkar, and Joel Gittelsohn. 2013. "High Levels of Household Food Insecurity on the Navajo Nation." *Public Health Nutrition*, February 1.

Pedal and Plow. 2016. "Food Sovereignty vs. Food Security: Why It's Different and Why It Matters." http://www.pedalandplow.com/2014/02/16/what-is-real-food-security/.

Perissinotto, Giorgio, ed. 1998. *Documenting Everyday Life in Early Spanish California: The Santa Barbara Presidio Memorias y Factura, 1779–1810*. Santa Barbara, CA: Santa Barbara Trust for Historic Preservation.

Pesman, M. Walter. (1942) 1967. *Meet the Natives: An Easy Way to Recognize Wildflowers, Trees, and Shrubs of the Central Rocky Mountain Region*. 7th ed. Denver: Botanic Gardens.

Peterson, Leighton C., and Anthony K. Webster. 2013. "Speech Play and Language Ideologies in Navajo Terminology Development." *Pragmatics* 23 (1): 93–116.

Pineo, Christopher S. 2015. "TMC builds Ovens, Gardens to Allow Communities to Practice Food Sovereignty." *Navajo Times*, November 21.

———. 2016a. "Diné Policy Institute to Produce Recommendations for Healthy Office Workers." *Navajo Times*, June 30.

———. 2016b. "Window Rock Trail Kicks Off Paths across Navajoland." *Navajo Times*, July 21.

Pineo, Christopher, and Bill Donovan. 2015. "2015: One of the Most Chaotic." *Navajo Times*, December 30.

Powers, Willow Roberts. 2001. *Navajo Trading: The End of an Era*. Albuquerque: University of New Mexico Press.

Ramirez, Antonio. 2013a. "Council Votes Down Junk Food Tax." *Navajo Times*, July 18.

———. 2013b. "Health Group Hasn't Given Up Crusade against Junk Food." *Navajo Times*, July 25.

REFERENCES

Rao, Tejal. 2016a. "The Movement to Define Native American Cuisine." *New York Times*, August 18.

——. 2016b. "The Native American Cuisine." *New York Times*, August 17.

Reh, Emma. 1983. *Navajo Consumption Habits (for District 1), 1939*. Edited and annotated by Terry R. Reynolds. Las Cruces: New Mexico State University Museum.

Reichard, Gladys A. 1928. *Social Life of the Navajo Indians*. New York: Columbia University Press.

——. 1963. *Navaho Religion: A Study of Symbolism*. Rev. ed. New York: Bollingen Foundation. First published in 1950 as two volumes.

Roessel, Monty. 1991. "Navajo Puberty Rites." *New Mexico Magazine* 69 (8): 86–95.

Rogers, Kara. 2015. *The Quiet Extinction: Stories of North America's Rare and Threatened Plants*. Tucson: University of Arizona Press.

Russell, Scott. 1991. "From Trading Post to Supermarket: Changing Food Marketing Systems on the Navajo Indian Reservation." Master's thesis, Arizona State University, Tempe.

Salaybe, John Jr., and Kathleen Manolescu. 2016. "*Hózhǫ́ǫ́jí* and the Mountain Soil Bundle." *Leading the Way* 14 (2): 2–11.

Salmón, Enrique. 2012. *Eating the Landscape: American Indian Stories of Food, Identity, and Resilience*. Tucson: University of Arizona Press.

Sandoval, Augusta. 1974. "Navajo Recipes." Unpublished manuscript compiled for distribution at Office of Navajo Economic Opportunity workshop, Tucson, AZ, May.

Shebala, Marley. 2007a. "Dreaming of 'Ach'íí'." *Navajo Times*, September 6.

——. 2007b. "A Family Affair: Kneel-Down Bread a Special Treat at Navajo Mountain." *Navajo Times*, August 9.

——. 2016. "Group: Food Sovereignty Is a Human Right." *Gallup Independent*, August 16.

Simmons, Marc. 2005. "Baking the Old Way, New Mexico." *Prime Time*, June.

Steggerda, Morris, and Ruth B. Eckardt. 1940. "Navajo Foods and Their Preparation." *Journal of the American Dietetic Association* 17: 217–25.

St. Louis Science Center. 2016. "Explore GROW, the Journey of Food." *New Science*, June/July.

Swentzell, Roxanne, and Patricia M. Perea, eds. 2016. *The Pueblo Food Experience Cookbook: Whole Food of Our Ancestors*. Santa Fe: Museum of New Mexico Press.

Tafoya, Matthew. 2016. "We Have the Authority to Create a Healthy Environment." Letter to the Editor. *Navajo Times*, January 28.

Tapahonso, Luci. (1993) 1998. "In 1864." In *Sáanii Dahataał: The Women Are Singing*, 7–10. Tucson: University of Arizona Press.

——. 2008. *A Radiant Curve: Poems and Stories*. Tucson: University of Arizona Press.

Taylor, Janice E. 2007. *Healthy Southwest Table*. Tucson, AZ: Rio Nuevo.

Tilford, Gregory L. 1997. *Edible and Medicinal Plants of the West*. Missoula, MT: Mountain Press.

Turner, Jan Loechell, and Charles Turner. 2008. *Wildflowers of Canyon de Chelly.* Golden, CO: Rabbitbrush.

Underhill, Ruth. 1953. *Here Come the Navaho!* Washington, DC: US Bureau of Indian Affairs.

United States Department of Agriculture (USDA). 2003. *A River of Recipes: Native American Recipes Using Commodity Foods.* Washington, DC: USDA Food Distribution Program on Indian Reservations, Food and Nutrition Service.

———. 2014. "Farm Bill Highlights." http://www.usda.gov/documents/usda-2014-farm-bill-highlights.pdf.

———. 2015. "The [2014] Farm Bill." http://www.usda.gov/wps/portal/usda/usdahome?navid=farmbill.

United States Food and Nutritional Service (FNS). 2015. "Food and Nutrition: History and Background." http://www.fns.usda.gov/fdd/fdd-history-and-background.

United States Food Sovereignty Alliance. 2016. "Food Sovereignty." http://usfoodsovereigntyalliance.org/what-is-food-sovereignty/.

University of Pittsburgh. 1969. *Nutrition Survey of the Lower Greasewood Chapter Navajo Tribe, 1968–69.* University of Pittsburgh National Nutritional Survey. Pittsburgh: University of Pittsburgh.

Van Duzen, J., J. Carter, J. Secondi, and C. Federspiel. 1969. "Protein and Calorie Malnutrition among Preschool Navajo Indian Children." *American Journal of Clinical Nutrition* 22: 1362–70.

Van Duzen, J., J. P. Carter, and R. Vander Zwagg. 1976. "Protein and Calorie Malnutrition among Preschool Navajo Indian Children: A Follow-Up." *American Journal of Clinical Nutrition* 29: 657–62.

Viola, Herman J., and Carolyn Margolis, eds. 1991. *Seeds of Change: Five Hundred Years since Columbus; A Quincentennial Commemoration.* Washington, DC: Smithsonian Institution Press.

Vizenor, Gerald. 2008. *Father Meme.* Albuquerque: University of New Mexico Press.

———. 2014. *Blue Ravens.* Middletown, CT: Wesleyan University Press.

Weber, David. 1996. *On the Edge of Empire: The Taos Hacienda of Los Martinez.* Santa Fe: Museum of New Mexico Press.

Weiland, Noah. 2016. "A Navajo Chef Looks to History in His Homage to Native Cuisine." *New York Times,* November 25.

Wheelwright, Mary C. 1946. *Wind Chant and Feather Chant.* Santa Fe, NM: Museum of Navajo Ceremonial Art.

White, Richard. 1983. *Roots of Dependency: Subsistence, Environment, and Social Change among the Choctaws, Pawnees, and Navajos.* Lincoln: University of Nebraska Press.

Wolfe, Wendy Susan. 1981. "Navajo Foods and Foodways: Cultural and Nutritional Changes with Acculturation." Senior honors thesis, Northwestern University, Evanston, IL.

———. 1984. "An Ethnographic and Nutritional Investigation of Navajo Indian Foodways, Dietary Patterns, and Nutritional Status." Master's thesis, Cornell University, New York.

———. 1994. "Dietary Change among the Navajo: Implications for Diabetes." In *Diabetes as a Disease of Civilization: The Impact of Culture Change on Indigenous People*, edited by R. S. Young, and J. R. Joe, 435–49. Berlin: Mouton de Gruyter.

Wolfe, Wendy S., and Diva Sanjur. 1988. "Contemporary Diet and Body Weight of Navajo Women Receiving Food Assistance: An Ethnographic and Nutritional Investigation." *Journal of the American Dietetic Association* 88 (7): 22–27.

Wolfe, Wendy S., Charles W. Weber, and Katherine Dahozy Arviso. 1985. "Use and Nutrient Composition of Traditional Navajo Foods." *Ecology of Food and Nutrition* 17 (4): 323–44.

Wyman, Leland C. 1970. *Blessingway: Three Versions of the Myth*. Recorded and translated by Father Berard Haile, OFM. Tucson: University of Arizona Press.

Wyman, Leland C., and Stuart K. Harris. 1941. *Navajo Indian Medical Ethnobotany*. Albuquerque: University of New Mexico Press.

———. 1951. *The Ethnobotany of the Kayenta Navaho*. Albuquerque: University of New Mexico Publications in Biology 5.

Yazzie, Evangeline Parsons. 2014. *Her Land, Her Love*. Flagstaff, AZ: Salina Bookshelf.

———. 2016. *Her Enemy, Her Love*. Flagstaff, AZ: Salina Bookshelf.

Yetman, David. 2009. *50 Common Edible and Useful Plants of the Southwest*. Tucson, AZ: Western National Parks Association.

Young, Robert W. 1961. *The Navajo Yearbook 8. 1951–1961: A Decade of Progress*. Window Rock, AZ: Navajo Agency.

Young, Robert W., and William Morgan Sr. 1980. *The Navajo Language: A Grammar and Colloquial Dictionary*. Albuquerque: University of New Mexico Press.

———. 1987. *The Navajo Language: A Grammar and Colloquial Dictionary*. Rev. ed. Albuquerque: University of New Mexico Press.

Yurth, Cindy. 2012. "Pinon Pickers Harvesting a Bumper Crop." *Navajo Times*, September 27.

———. 2013. "Ortegas Buy the Thunderbird, Plant Fruit Trees in Canyon." *Navajo Times*, April 25.

———. 2014a. "Ag Department Floats a Far-Ranging Proposal." *Navajo Times*, January 23.

———. 2014b. "Corn, Craps, and Cryptids." *Navajo Times*, September 18.

———. 2014c. "Support for Grazing Act Is as Scarce as Rainfall." *Navajo Times*, July 3.

———. 2015. "Chinle Water Delays Denny's Grand Opening." *Navajo Times*, December 3.

———. 2016a. "Conference Speaker Blasts NAPI for growing GMOs." *Navajo Times*, March 10.

———. 2016b. "Indigenous Food Sovereignty Conference to Be Served Up Next Month." *Navajo Times*, February 11.

INDEX

Page numbers in italic text indicate illustrations.

www.ingramcontent.com/pod-product-compliance
Lightning Source LLC
Chambersburg PA
CBHW020331270326
41926CB00007B/142